POWER AND DECISION

The Social Control of Reproduction

Gita Sen
Rachel C. Snow

HSPH

Harvard Series on Population and International Health

Harvard Center for Population and Development Studies

Department of Population and International Health
Harvard School of Public Health
Boston, Massachusetts

March 1994

Distributed by Harvard University Press

ISBN 0-674-69533-X

Library of Congress 93-075000

Books in the Harvard Series on Population and International Health

Population Policies Reconsidered: Health, Empowerment and Rights
Edited by Gita Sen, Adrienne Germain and Lincoln C. Chen

Power & Decision: The Social Control of Reproduction
Edited by Gita Sen and Rachel Snow

Health and Social Change in International Perspective
Edited by Lincoln C. Chen, Arthur Kleinman and Norma C. Ware

Assessing Child Survival Programs in Developing Countries
By Joseph J. Valadez

for Suhasini and Julian

Table of Contents

Section II: The Technologies: For Whom, and to What End?

Preface

As the 20th century draws to a close, it is timely to take stock of the progress made by the disparate feminist struggles for reproductive rights and choice that have characterized the latter half of this century. There have been notable achievements in many spheres: abortion rights have increased in many countries, family planning is directly supported by the majority of United Nations member states, and the scientific establishment has provided more effective contraceptives and infertility treatments than were probably imaginable in 1900. But the progress in selected arenas underscores the overwhelming gaps and disparities yet to be reckoned with.

There are two types of disparity that we need to address: the disparities between women of different nations, races and economic classes; and the lingering disparity within nations between what has been achieved and what full societal support for healthy childbearing and childrearing might really look like. Even in countries where considerable advances have been in social welfare, in child support, and in the provision of health and reproductive technologies, there are deeply rooted political and cultural legacies that leave much of what we call *reproductive rights and choice* shackled by profound gender inequality throughout society.

This book is a collective effort to provide, in one publication, an overview of the disparate social forces that circumscribe reproduction within specific social parameters, with a complementary examination of how biomedical research and the new reproductive technologies reflect and sustain those parameters. Including case studies from a range of countries, this book offers a collection of Southern and Northern feminist perspectives on which social controls offer protective support for parenting, and suggestions on how to redress those which do not. The chapters in this volume illustrate both the commonalities and disparities between first and third world settings.

Initial plans for this volume grew out of a Working Group at the Center for Population and Development Studies (CPDS) at Harvard University that included several of the authors, as well as Mercy Bercerra-Valdivia,

Gabriella Canepa and Jennifer Zeitlin. A Workshop in May 1993, also at CPDS, provided a forum for the chapters collected here, and we gratefully acknowledge the participation of several individuals who fostered debate and offered expert comment: these include Nirmala Bannerjee, David Bell, Mallavarapu Prakasamma, Michael Reich, Cheywa Spindel, Grace Wyshak and George Zeidenstein. We are particularly grateful to Diana Harris for her assistance in organizing both the Working Group meetings and the Workshop at CPDS.

In large part, the inter-disciplinary nature of this book reflects the unique, inter-disciplinary climate at the Center for Population and Development Studies. Rarely do biologists and economists sit down routinely, over several months, to grapple with problems of social policy. The Center, under the leadership of Lincoln Chen, provided us with the benefits of lively collegial exchange with persons outside the conventional range of our respective disciplines; the experience has been intellectually and personally enriching. For this opportunity, we are both grateful.

Of course, no such initiative can function without the hard work of an editorial and administrative staff. For the sustained good cheer and expert support of Chris Cahill, Winifred Fitzgerald, Sarah Hemphill, Jennifer Meyers, Charlie Mitchell, Colleen Murphy, Liz Pelcyger and Jennifer Poulos, we owe much more than can be adequately expressed here. We also benefitted greatly from the seamless professional support of Marc Kaufman and his staff at Desktop Publishing & Design Co.

Finally, we wish to thank the MacArthur Foundation in Chicago and the Swedish International Development Agency (SIDA) in Stockholm, for their generous support of the time and research required to bring this book to publication. Their continuing commitment to the advancement of women's health and human welfare gives us cause for optimism and hope for the coming decades. Of course, the opinions expressed in this volume are the sole responsibility of the authors themselves, and in no way reflect the opinions of the MacArthur Foundation, SIDA or the Center for Population and Development Studies at Harvard. And we, the editors, assume responsibility for the shortcomings.

Rachel Snow and Gita Sen
March 1994

Section I

Reproduction: Policies and Politics

by Gita Sen

What is reproduction? In our daily, common-sense understandings, human reproduction refers to the process of child-bearing. Social science has long recognized this to be more than a biological phenomenon; child-bearing everywhere has always been surrounded by ritual proscriptions and prescriptions, by myth and symbol. But, for feminists, human reproduction has meant even more than this. Feminist theory has postulated a connection from child-bearing forward to child-rearing and the care of adults, and backward to human sexuality and its social mediations.

Broadening the meaning of reproduction in this way allows us to see the continuum between different aspects of human care needs over the average person's life-cycle. While infancy and old age represent the extremes, humans are remarkably dependent beings at all ages, requiring the involvement and assistance of others for the fulfillment of very basic needs. The difference between adults and children in their need for someone to provide food, to wash, to clean, to nurse during illness, and to provide comfort and solace during times of distress, is a difference in degree not in kind. Growing social complexity and technological sophistication do not reduce or simplify this dependence, they deepen it.

The primary providers of this care in all known societies are women, designated as such not solely by the exigencies of biology but by the weight of gender relations and the related division of social labor. Broadening the concept of reproduction renders the connections among different parts of women's work-day and working life more obvious. An incidental, but not unimportant, effect is that it weakens the hold of biology over the analytical imagination, and makes the effect of social forces more transparent or at least translucent. That women in their daily lives juggle the needs of income-earning, the requirements of jobs, the pressures of domestic work, and the demands of family members for support and assistance is now well recognized by the general public. But the policy world has remained remarkably turgid in its inability or unwillingness to acknowledge the policy implications of this recognition.

The reasons for policy inflexibility and fragmentation are not far to seek. Reproduction is governed by the interplay by biology and the social relations of gender, class, caste, and race. While it has elements that are universal, it is, in fact, shaped by forces that are highly contextual and strongly politicized. Neither the role of economic factors nor the importance of gender ideology, and in particular, notions of what is or ought to be in the realms of sexuality and family, can be overstated. They drive the politics that push the deeply personal realms of sex, birth, and family relationships into the public arena. That these politics can be highly conflictive, and that policies can therefore be shifting and internally inconsistent, is a major theme of this section of the volume.

Carla Obermeyer, in *Religious Doctrine, State Ideology, and Reproductive Options in Islam,* uses the multiple reversals in Iran's population policies in the recent past to argue that economic pressures and political expediency played a considerable role. In each case, the reversal was justified using religious ideology and selective references to Islamic tradition. She argues that Islam (like many other religions) in itself is relatively open, containing the seeds of both liberal and conservative approaches to reproduction. But the actual attitudes taken, and the resultant policies espoused by the state are the result of historical struggles within religion, between religious and secular forces, and between states and societies. Women and their sexuality become through such processes major foci of political concern and control, but the state can also act as in Iran to shape the underlying political forces.

The complexity of the contemporary politics of reproduction is the focus of the chapters by Jacqueline Pitanguy and Janine Brodie. In *Feminist Politics and Reproductive Rights: The Case of Brazil,* Pitanguy traces the fascinating connections between Brazilian feminists struggling for reproductive justice and other actors such as the progressive wing of the church, the trade unions, and political parties, in the evolution of the struggle against dictatorship. Her chapter contributes much to our understanding of how the demand of genuine citizenship has become so central to the struggle of the feminist health movement in the country.

Janine Brodie's chapter, *Health versus Rights: Comparative Perspectives on Abortion Policy in Canada and the United States,* compares the politics of abortion in Canada and the United States to show how feminist political strategies were influenced by very different health care systems, and hence very different public perceptions of social entitlements. In the United States, where health care was not acknowledged to be a social entitlement, abortion came to be legally justified as part of a Constitutional right to privacy; in Canada, on the other hand, with its more socialized health-care system, abortion came to be justified as part of an entitlement to health. These differences in countries, otherwise similar in culture and ideology, underline the importance of the social and economic context of reproductive struggles.

Such a dialectic between states and societal politics in the sphere of reproduction is by no means new. In my chapter, *Reproduction: The Feminist Challenge to Social Policy*, I argue that state welfare policies in parts of Europe and North America in the nineteenth and early twentieth centuries, were driven by conflicting pressures to expand the economic entitlements of male workers and of women, and were profoundly influenced by the race and class divisions within societies. The relative political weight of social actors speaking from a vantage point of gender, of class, or of race had a profound impact on the kinds of social welfare policies that emerged in different countries. The complexity of these historical struggles and their sometimes paradoxical outcomes can help shed light on contemporary policy dilemmas in both Third World and advanced capitalist countries. In a time of global economic crisis and restructuring, states have used the fragmented struggle over entitlements among different social groups to ignore and increase women's reproductive burdens.

The extent to which states use women's reproductive responsibilities and the power of gender subordination to further economic or social goals is a second important theme of this section. In *Reproductive Experiences and Needs of Thai Women: Where has Development Taken Us?* Hnin Hnin Pyne examines the uses that the modern Thai state has made of both women's labor and their sexuality for economic ends. The irony is that state policies have built upon the fact that in many parts of Northern Thailand, traditional societies have been matrilineal and matrilocal, with less gender subordination and greater openness about female sexuality than in other parts of Asia. The greater physical mobility, control over economic resources, and freer sexual lives of Thai women have been used by the state to generate export earnings, but without providing an adequate base of public health infrastructure to deal with women's reproductive health problems or their growing economic burdens.

Jody Heymann's chapter, *Labor Policy: Its Influence on Women's Reproductive Lives*, draws on North American experience to show the extent to which, even in a high income economy with a high rate of female participation in the formal labor force, policies and practices affecting working conditions and the terms of employment conflict with schooling and parenting needs. Policies have been remarkably insensitive to the conditions under which large numbers of women struggle to balance the demands of jobs and parenting. The consequences are felt not only in women's physical and psychological stress, but in the health of children. This chapter shows that we need, in all countries and globally, a broader look at policy and at the links among different policies such as those affecting working conditions, health, amd child-bearing, to name a few. A more integrated policy focus on reproduction understood in its broader sense will not only reduce the pressures on women who are the human links among these different policies, but can make policies more effective in achieving their goals.

Arline Geronimus' chapter, *The Weathering Hypothesis and the Health of African-American Women and Infants: Implications for Reproductive Strategies and Policy Analysis*, ties together the two major themes of politics and policy failures by asking whether the concern over teenage pregnancies among Black women in the United States is legitimate. Marshalling an impressive array of statistical evidence, she shows that there is strong reason to believe that, given their health trajectories over the life-cycle, the teen years may be the best years for Black women to bear children. Black women's health risks increase progressively after the teen years as a consequence of racism and social policies that do not support the reproduction of Black communities, a pattern markedly different from that among Whites. Her argument is that policy concern has been wrongly directed at the age of Black motherhood rather than at the economic and social conditions under which it occurs and to which it is forced to adapt.

An implicit theme in all the chapters in this section is the importance of women organizing in their own right. Where women do not (or cannot) organize in their own interest, politics and policies work to marginalize or ignore women's needs and concerns (Heymann); instrumentalize and use women's work, child-bearing, or sexuality for other interests often defined as "national" (Obermeyer, Pyne); or blame women for reproduction failures or problems that are, in fact, the result of social inequalities or poor policies (Geronimus). Yet even when women do organize, the battle is not over; it has only begun. The ideology and the practical politics of alliances are critically important. Even when organized and highly vocal in the public sphere, the "maternalists" of an earlier era in the United States were unable to bring about lasting policy support for reproduction because they were unable to ally with male workers to broaden the base of general entitlements (Sen). Nor is it always possible for women to organize in their own full interests. Feminists know only too well how often nationalist or other struggles are played out culturally using the language and symbols of corruption and moral decay which are centered around female bodies and control over women's participation in the public sphere (Obermeyer).

Even when women do organize, the political struggles can be fierce (Pitanguy, Brodie). But these chapters also show how much is learned by women in the process of struggle. The importance of an ideology that recognizes the cross cutting of gender subordination by class, race or other hierarchies, and the necessity of strategic alliances to broaden the scope of reproductive entitlements point to the need for both principle and practical engagement. Although the chapters in this section cannot point to dramatic successes, they bear witness to the painful but productive process of collective learning in which we as feminists are constantly engaged.

1

Reproduction: The Feminist Challenge to Social Policy

by Gita Sen

Introduction

In all societies, the reproduction of human beings stands at the intersection of two sets of basic social relationships. On one hand are the relations that determine different claims on subsistence or entitlements; what and how much different members of society consume. On the other hand are the relations that govern who does the work of reproduction and under what conditions; not only who bears children but who does the daily and generational tasks involved in feeding, cleaning, and caring for both children and adults. How societies handle human reproduction depends on the interplay between these two sets of relationships, which also shapes hierarchy and subordination on the basis of class, gender, age, race and a host of other social orderings, and is a core concern of the social policies of states.

Each of these relationships is subject to historical changes resulting from varying economic conditions, changes in technology, shifting perceptions of the proper division between public and private spheres of action, and changes in the political strength of different advocacy groups in national and international arenas. This paper will argue that, state welfare policies, both historically and contemporaneously, are themselves a resultant of political forces, and have often reinforced the gender, class and race/ethnic disparities in societies through the ways in which they have addressed or not addressed reproduction. This happens in three different ways:

i) by *shrinking* entitlements to the poor; this has not only class or race implications, but imbues policies with gender bias insofar as the costs of reproduction are shifted from the paid economy onto the unpaid labor of women;

ii) even if entitlements are expanding, their *distribution* may be seriously biased by gender, class or race; and

iii) through inattention to how the *work* of reproduction gets done. How much labor is involved? Who does it? Under what sets of social relations? With what kinds of technology? Even though reproduction is largely women's work, not all women may be engaged in doing it in quite the same way, due to class, race or other differences among them.[1]

By reinforcing gender-, class- and race-based divisions of labor, policies impose significant costs on many women, and constrain their options. Ironically, but perhaps not surprisingly, these constraints operate even in cases where the general entitlements of the poor have expanded. The paper draws selectively from the history of Western Europe and North America, and from state policies in the contemporary Third World, to illustrate these points. Its focus is on the child- and adult-care aspects of human reproduction, rather than on the bearing of children *per se.*

Shifting Basis of Entitlements/Reproduction

In most societies, prior to the historical emergence of the capitalist world system, claims to subsistence were based on one's membership in a tribe, caste, lineage, parish, village, or other social group. With the emergence of capitalism, these ascriptive claims tended to break down. Instead, one's relationship to the production, accumulation, and distribution of economic goods, either as an owner of productive resources or as a wage worker, became the key to one's entitlement. Older forms of entitlement, by and large, gave way as economic relations were reorganized wholesale.

For those who did not own or have access to productive resources, access to waged employment became the key to entitlement. And since the demand for labor was itself increasingly subject to a complex of shifting variables — economic trends, business cycle relationships between rates of economic growth, technological change, and profitability, as well as the natural increase of populations — the ability of people to meet their subsistence needs became contingent and unreliable. The great social debate about the Poor Laws in eighteenth and nineteenth century England is a celebrated example of the dilemmas for social policy occasioned by this shift in the entitlement basis of human reproduction.

Not that entitlements completely lost an ascriptive basis. Labor policies at the periphery of the colonial system were often overtly based on race, ethnicity, birth or gender.[2] Race constituted a central basis for differential entitlement in the major capitalist countries until earlier in this century. And even as some forms of ascriptive entitlement were challenged and began to lose legitimacy in the liberal welfare states of post-World War II Europe and the United States, another ascriptive category, citizenship, became the largely unchallenged basis for claims on subsistence, excluding non-citizens and those regarded as illegal aliens.

Thus newer forms of ascriptive entitlement have gained ground even as the state has increasingly been called upon to remedy the inability of the economic system to guarantee reproduction. Gender constitutes a unique category of such ascription because it combines dual features. The first is that the shift towards wage-labor based systems of production typically leaves women economically more vulnerable because they are disabled by traditional constraints on mobility and participation. Even when they have been the workers of choice, as in the early British or American textile mills, or in the export processing zones of the contemporary Third World, employers have taken advantage of gendered patterns of subordination to prevent women workers from improving their entitlements through collective action. The second feature is that the central burden of reproductive tasks generally falls on women. How states treat the work involved in reproduction, together with who they entitle and to what, is therefore crucially important to women's well-being.

The uniqueness of gender stems from the fact that it defines not only entitlements but also work and responsibility. This has four implications. It means first of all that in most societies women do most of the work and bear most of the costs/burdens of reproduction. Second, social and political forces aiming to affect any aspect of reproduction often work through women, i.e., by controlling or constraining women's behavior or options. Third, gender power itself is often cemented through control over reproduction. And, central to the purpose of this paper, state policies can often transfer previously socialized costs of reproduction back onto women, or keep such costs private (and borne by women) if they have not already been socialized.

Contested Terrain: The Boundaries between Public and Private

The role of the state in the sphere of reproduction has been a terrain of intense struggle in many countries. In the late nineteenth and early twentieth centuries, capitalists in Europe and North America disagreed among themselves and with workers and socialists over the extent to which the state ought to take responsibility for the nutrition, health and welfare of the working classes. Male workers often sought to have the best of both worlds — a family wage from their employers and a wife at home to undertake the labor of reproduction. Social reformers attempted to harmonize the inherent conflicts among different groups; women's organizations acted in different ways to legitimize their perceptions of women's needs.

The views of these different social actors often conflicted, although coalitions of interest also formed to address specific situations. These struggles to define the proper role of states in managing the reproduction of persons were, at the same time, struggles to delimit the boundaries of public and private spheres. What got accepted as the legitimate sphere of the state on one hand, or of individuals or families on the other, defined which aspects of whose reproduction would be guaranteed in the public domain.

Social historians disagree in their interpretations of the dominant forces affecting state welfare policies in different countries. Society-centered theorists tend to explain them through either the power of working-class organizations or of capitalists attempting to co-opt or subvert radical change (Shalev 1983; Berkowitz and McQuaid 1988). State-centered theorists, on the other hand, focus on the role of bureaucracies and the functioning of the machinery of the state (Evans, Rueschemeyer and Skocpol 1985). In the last decade or so, feminist and other historians have begun to examine the contributions of women's organizations and their ideologies to the shaping of social welfare policies in different countries.[3]

It is this last group of writings that points to the complexity of the negotiations and struggles in which women's organizations were engaged. Operating at a time when women did not have the right to vote in either Europe or the United States, these organizations attempted to redefine the social meaning of the public/private distinction in a variety of ways. Redefining the public sphere and the role of the state was not, obviously, the exclusive preserve of women. Indeed, the outcomes of women's attempts often depended on the attitudes and strengths of other actors, such as male-dominated unions and bureaucracies who were themselves engaged in the task of expanding the scope of entitlements guaranteed by the state. These actors did not always see eye to eye with women. Nor were women themselves of one voice in the articulation of their demands for expanded entitlements and political participation.

Struggles over the adequacy of wages, the quality of working conditions, and the responsibility of the state both to provide for the needy and to expand the entitlements of the "working poor" were particularly intense during the eighteenth and nineteenth centuries in both Western Europe and North America. It was not, however, until late in the nineteenth and early in the twentieth centuries that legislative and policy changes were effected in most countries. The public debates about social policy covered three broad areas. The first was limiting legislation that largely related to workplace conditions, and included limits on the employment of children and women in occupations considered "hazardous." The second was programs whose aim was to create a healthier, more disciplined and productive workforce; these included compulsory education, expanded public health facilities as well as defrayed health care costs, and maternal and child welfare, including nutrition support. The third was redistributive legislation, which included unemployment insurance, workers' pensions, old age pensions, widows' and mothers' allowances, and general family allowances.[4] Of these, only the third group and some of the second clearly altered entitlements; however, the climate of public debate was shaped by the fact that all these issues were linked in the public mind by underlying ideological positions regarding not only the role of the state but also the role of the family.

Parallel debates and major changes in family law highlight these links. Laws regarding child support, married women's rights to property, women's rights to work and to control the income from work (*vis à vis* the prerogatives of husbands), and marriage and divorce all underwent major changes during and after this period. Not all of these changes favored women. For instance, until early in the eighteenth century the word of the mother was generally sufficient to hold accountable the father of a child born out of wedlock; by the end of the century it became legally almost impossible to hold fathers accountable for child support in either England or France (Folbre 1993). This increased women's difficulties in achieving financial autonomy outside the boundaries of patriarchally dominated family life, a pattern reinforced by male workers through their later attempts to obtain a family wage paid to the male worker.

Two additional subjects of public controversy at the time are relevant to our understanding of the links between the entitlements debate and ideologies of family life. They are contraception/abortion and suffrage. Both aroused passionate and well-known opposition on the grounds that they would destroy the moral basis of family and society. Interestingly, not all politically active women supported female suffrage. For instance, the women who in 1889 signed the "Appeal against Female Suffrage" included Beatrice Webb, who argued that winning the franchise would implicate women in the business of wars and empire (Koven and Michel 1990). Multiple and competing views of family morality were at work. While some viewed the patriarchally dominated family as inherently moral, others viewed women's nurturing role within families as the basis of family morality, while still others saw women's distance from the public (and immoral) world of economics and statecraft as giving them a special moral sensibility.

Considerable historical research now exists that uses a gender lens to filter and interpret differences across countries in the timing, extent, and character of social policies (Koven and Michel 1990; Skocpol 1992; Folbre 1993). Earlier analysis largely attributed this variability to the class character of regimes; social democracy in Scandinavia stressed the rights of workers, corporatism in Germany expanded those programs and policies that would consolidate the long term interests of both capitalists and the state itself, and in England and the United States, the weakness of worker organizations and the power of liberal ideology put forth largely limiting legislation and relatively little by way of redistributive entitlements. The newer, more gendered analyses not only highlight the role of women's organizations in these processes, but also show how gender, age and race relations biased policy outcomes (Folbre 1993).

Focusing on the differences between countries helps direct attention to differences in the attitudes of key groups of actors. Two, in particular, that interest us are male wage earners whose concerns were articulated through workingmen's associations and trade unions, and "maternalists", those women who were extremely active in initiating social welfare activities and catalyzing policy in a number of countries. In some respects, the ideologies and concerns of these two groups appeared diametrically opposed despite their common belief in the need to reform and expand the role of the state.

Organized male workers were animated by an ideology of working class solidarity and opposition to capitalist exploitation, as well as firmly patriarchal views on gender and age relations within families.[5] Their beliefs were evident in the kinds of entitlements they supported and the legislative changes they supported or opposed. The former typically included a family wage to be paid to the male worker, workers' pensions, protective legislation that would exclude women from occupations and industries where men dominated, health-care support, and old age pensions. They typically opposed family laws that required or increased male obligations for child support, expanded property rights for married women, and greater control by women over family allowances or their own incomes, on the grounds that they would destabilize the family.

Maternalists, on the other hand, were motivated by "domestic ideologies that stressed women's differences from men, humanitarian concerns for the conditions of child life and labor, and the emergence of activist interpretations of the gospel...Women's moral vision, compassion and capacity to nurture came increasingly to be linked to motherliness" (Koven and Michel 1990). These largely middle-class women believed that the nurturance, altruistic sense of responsibility and collectivity that they identified as the feminine animus of family life ought to become the ethos of public life as well.

Motivated by this belief, they threw their energies into, among other things, setting up creches and kindergartens in France and Germany, supporting mothers' and widows' pensions in the United States, helping set up the Children's Bureau in 1912, and backing the Sheppard-Towner Act to provide perinatal care in the United States. Between 1911 and the late 1930s, 46 American states passed laws enabling localities to pension needy widowed mothers so that they could care for children at home (Skocpol 1992). American maternalists also supported protective legislation limiting the hours of women workers and raising their minimum wage,[6] and fought for concomittant changes in family laws, including increased male responsibility for child support. Many of them were also deeply involved in the struggle to make contraception and abortion legally available, and in the battle for female suffrage.

Maternalists and male workers clearly had radically different attitudes towards both the family and public life, and focused on different entitlements. Referring to the three sources of gender, class and/or race biases defined in the introduction — the total extent of entitlements, their distribution, and the division of reproductive work — one can speculate about the likely effects of these differences. Male workers devoted most of their energies to expanding entitlements generally,[7] and ensuring that these were channelled through the male "breadwinner" as much as possible. Their lack of support for entitlements that would have specifically benefitted women, and their belief in domestic work being work only fit for women meant that their actions strengthened gender biases (and race bias where domestic work was the realm of distinct racial or ethnic groups).

Maternalists, on the other hand, spent relatively little energy on expanding general entitlements such as unemployment insurance, old age pensions, or general health care. By focusing on the needs of working and poor women, their efforts, where successful, functioned to redress gender bias. Rarely was their goal stated as explicitly as in a speech by Mrs. G. Harris Robertson, President of the Tennessee Congress of Mothers in 1911:

> We cannot afford to let a mother, one who has divided her body by creating other lives for the good of the state, one who has contributed to citizenship, be classed as a pauper, a dependent. She must be given value received by her nation, and stand as one honored... If our public mind is maternal, loving and generous, wanting to save and develop all, our Government will express this sentiment (cited in Skocpol 1992).

Ironically, such a statement tells us as much about Mrs. Robertson's support of women as mothers as it does about her antipathy to paupers and dependents. Class bias was not, unfortunately, the only problem of the American women's movement in this period. Thus, in the struggle for women's suffrage, Elizabeth Cady Stanton stated:

> If you do not wish the lower orders of Chinese, Africans, Germans, and Irish, with their low ideas of womanhood, to make laws for you and your daughters...demand that women, too, shall be repre-sented in the government (cited in Folbre 1993).

Viewed from the vantage point of reproduction, race and class biases prevented maternalists from fully understanding the needs of working poor women, even though their welfare was the stated aim. It hampered their recognition of the importance of expanding general entitlements even when they did not directly target women. Furthermore, the fact that many maternalists themselves depended on other and poorer women to take care of their children and domestic tasks may well have desensitized them to the often deplorable conditions under which that work was done. Their concern for the gendered character of domestic work did not extend to a recognition of its equally pervasive class and race features.

Such biases among male activists and maternalists were not equally present in all countries. Perhaps the differences can help to partially explain the country variations in policies and their outcomes. In the United States many of the gains made by the maternalists were swept away by the time of the Great Depression. The Social Security Act of 1935 turned a new and more conservative page on all entitlements, including female ones: a modest amount of contributory retirement insurance was the single federal program, and Aid to Families with Dependent Children (AFDC) with its meagre resources and onerous eligibility requirements was a pale shadow of the maternalist ethos. Gender, class and race disparities became the hallmark of human reproduction in the United States. On the other hand, Sweden with its ethnically more homogeneous population and its attention to all three aspects (total entitlements, their distribution, and the distribution of work) developed one of the most comprehensive and least biased sets of social policies and programs.[8] In between these two lay the corporatist German state, which provided an extensive system of social welfare partially in response to male-dominated socialist pressure; its maternalists, however made little impact in imbueing these entitlements with a lasting ethos. Indeed, the state converted the schools started by the maternalists into breeding grounds for young national socialists in the 1930s (Koven and Michel 1990). The British system of social provisioning was more expansive than the American system, perhaps because organizations representing the interests of male workers were stronger. Nonetheless, it suffered from similar gender biases because the liberal ideology central to its women organizers hampered effective coalitions with poorer working women.

Contemporary Dilemmas for Social Policy

The complexity of these historical struggles and their sometimes paradoxical outcomes sheds some light on debates in contemporary social policy in both the advanced capitalist countries and in the Third World. In both regions, perceptions of unresolved fiscal crisis coupled with changing patterns of economic growth have had, in the present time, considerable influence in shaping the contested public terrain. In the post-colonial Third World, nationalist governments initially saw their mandate as combining economic development with social welfare, driven by the engine of state activism. At different points, social policy has therefore included the provision of a broad range of so-called basic needs, and anti-poverty programs. Here, social actors other than the ones that were historically influential in Europe — that is, international development organizations and foreign assistance donors, private and public — have often played key roles in defining the legitimate functions of the state.

With the current slowdown in the world and national economies, early optimism about the state's role and capacity has given way to a strong pessimism on the part of policy makers, and a concomitant shrinking in the public sphere. During the 1980s similar sentiments dominated public discourse in both South and North. The Reagan-Thatcher revolution of shrinking entitlements turned back the clock on activist social welfare policy in a fundamental way through its critique of "big government." In the Third World, the counterpart ideology was that of structural adjustment espoused by the Bretton Woods institutions. In both regions, balancing the government budget became the rallying cry of fiscal conservatives, and cuts in social expenditures became the easiest mechanism (if costly in political and social terms) for doing so.[9]

The consequences for the general level of entitlements, for the poor and for women, have been pointed out by a number of critics.[10] Feminists, in particular, have pointed out that gender biases have been reinforced during this period. There has been extensive discussion and documentation of the "feminization" of poverty in the United States. For the Third World, it has been argued that structural adjustment programs are not simply gender-blind, but gender biased by virtue of that very blindness. Elson has argued that, by failing to take into account the asymmetry of gender relations and women's subordination in economy and society, neoliberal policies are guilty of three types of bias. First, they ignore the implications of the gender division of labor. Second, they ignore women's unpaid work in reproduction, and fail to acknowledge that human beings have intrinsic value and not only instrumental worth as potential labor resources. Third, they ignore intra-household gender relations by focusing on the household as the micro unit of economic decision-making. The result of these three types of bias is that policies shift the costs of adjustment from the paid to the unpaid economy. The costs thus fall disproportionately onto women, who are the primary workers in the unpaid economy and subordinated by gender relations within the household (Elson 1992).

Palmer calls the shifting of the costs of human reproduction from the public to the private domain a "reproduction tax" on women. It occurs whenever such costs remain unacknowledged in the domestic realm and are mainly borne by women (Palmer 1991). Examples of such shifts in costs, consequent on structural adjustment programs, are the substitution of home-produced goods for goods previously bought on the market or provided socially. The additional unpaid labor might include, for example, foraging for fuel as a substitute for purchased cooking fuel whose price has been raised, cooking and cleaning at home rather than purchasing the same on the market, and taking care of family health through home remedies and nursing when health center hours are reduced. The increased costs in each of these examples are in terms of increased female labor, while the state reduces the costs to the public exchequer. Each of these can add significantly to the burdens on women who are already overburdened by poverty and shrinking real incomes (Afshar and Dennis 1992; Beneria and Feldman 1992).

Conclusion

Current social policies in many parts of the world clearly suffer from all three sources of gender, class, and race disparities. Overall entitlements have shrunk, and the costs of reproduction have been shifted onto the unpaid labor of women. The distribution of entitlements has also become more biased since better paid (and often male) workers in the public sector have often been able to protect their turf better than the poor and women who do not have jobs in the formal sector (Jolly et al. 1991). And there is very little acknowledgement or appreciation at the level of social policy of the conditions under which poor women perform the work of human reproduction.

What broad lessons does the foray into history provide for a feminist understanding of social policy needs at the present time? First, that the interweaving of gender with class and race in human reproduction means that equal attention must be given to all three, and to the interplay among them. Thus, protecting and expanding general entitlements even if they are not directly targeted at women is critical to reducing the burdens on women. Focusing on women as the maternalists did, while necessary, will not be sufficient. Second, expanding male entitlements alone often reinforces gender biases in the division of labor within and between private and public domains. Careful attention to the possibility of bias and the hidden costs of policies is essential. Third, parallel strategies to change family and property law are necessary as well if the longer-term entrenchment of bias is to be redressed.

Notes

1 Colen discusses what she aptly calls "stratified reproduction" in the context of domestic work (Colen 1990).

2 The South African apartheid system is only an extreme case of exclusionary entitlement policies that were common during the colonial period in many countries.

3 A recent example of this is Skocpol (1992). For a very useful review of this literature, see Koven and Michel (1990).

4 The terms limiting and redistributive have been used by Koven and Michel to describe respectively protective legislation and social welfare transfers (Koven and Michel 1990).

5 Obviously not all worker organizations held extreme views in this regard; for example, socialist writers such as August Bebel and Engels were critical of traditional family relations and called for overturning them along with capitalist domination.

6 Both male dominated unions and maternalists supported protective legislation though possibly for different reasons. Breen offers an interesting argument using historical data from San Francisco to show that male trade unionists wanted to keep women workers out of higher paying industries and occupations *in which women were in any case very poorly represented,* while women were concerned about improving the wages and working conditions of women workers in occupations where they already dominated (1988).

7 Some of these efforts undoubtedly benefitted women members of working class households, even if indirectly.

8 Unfortunately the literature on the historical contributions of the Swedish women's movement currently available in English seems to be rather thin.

9 For an interesting comparison of "Reaganomics" with structural adjustment see ALT-WID (1992).

10 For a careful review of both the policies and the evidence on their outcomes see Jolly et al. (1991).

References

Afshar, H., and C. Dennis, eds. 1992. *Women and adjustment policies in the Third World.* New York: St. Martin's Press.

ALT-WID. 1992. *Reagonomics and women: Structural adjustment U.S. style — 1980–1992.* Washington, D.C.

Beneria, L., and S. Feldman. 1992. *Unequal burden: Economic crises, persistent poverty and women's work.* Boulder, Colo.: Westview Press.

Berkowitz, E., and K. McQuaid. 1988. *Creating the welfare state: The political economy of twentieth-century reform.* New York: Praeger.

Breen, N. 1988. *Shedding light on women's work and wages: Consequences of protective legislation.* Ph.D. dissertation. New School for Social Research, New York.

Colen, S. 1990. Housekeeping for the green card: West Indian household workers, the state, and stratified reproduction in New York. In *At work in homes: Household workers in world perspective,* ed. R. Sanjek and S. Colen. American Ethnological Society Monograph no. 3. Washington D.C.: American Anthropological Association.

Elson, D. 1992. Male bias in structural adjustment. In *Women and adjustment policies in the third world,* ed. H. Afshar and C. Dennis. New York: St. Martin's Press.

Evans, P., D. Rueschemeyer, and T. Skocpol, eds. 1985. *Bringing the state back in.* New York: Cambridge University Press.

Folbre, N. 1993. *Who pays for the kids? Gender and the structures of constraint.* London and New York: Routledge.

Jolly, R., R. van der Hoeven, G.K. Helleiner, G. Cornia, and F. Stewart. 1991. Adjustment Revisited. *World Development* 19(12):1801–1864.

Koven, S., and S. Michel. 1990. Womanly duties: Maternalist politics and the origins of welfare states in France, Germany, Great Britain, and the United States, 1880–1920. *American Historical Review* 95:1076–1108.

Palmer, I. 1991. *Gender and population in the adjustment of African economies: Planning for change.* Geneva: International Labour Office.

Shalev, M. 1983. The social democratic model and beyond: Two generations of comparative research on the welfare state. *Comparative Social Research* 6:315–51.

Skocpol, T. 1992. *Protecting soldiers and mothers: The political origins of social policy in the United States.* Cambridge: Harvard University Press.

2

Reproductive Experiences and Needs of Thai Women: Where Has Development Taken Us?

by Hnin Hnin Pyne

Over the past two decades, Thailand's economy and society have experienced tremendous changes. In 1988, the country had the fastest-growing economy in the world with a growth rate of 13.2 percent (The Economist Intelligence Unit 1992), and appeared to be well on the way to becoming another newly industrialized country (NIC). International organizations and donor agencies applauded Thailand's success in promoting economic development and in controlling population growth. As one of the "Little Dragons," Thailand is now seen by many as a model of development for impoverished nations in the region. Rapid economic growth has touched every level of Thai society, and processes of industrialization and urbanization have transformed cities, villages and households.

In the course of this development, the productive and reproductive responsibilities of Thai women have extended beyond the sustenance of families and communities to the economic advancement of the entire country. Indeed one might argue that Thailand's economy has prospered on the backs of women, and their lives, in turn, have been transformed. This paper will focus on the many rural Thai women who migrate to urban areas to work in the manufacturing and service industries. These women represent a vital link between urban and rural communities, driving the progress of the cities while providing for the survival of the villages. In the last two decades, powerful forces of change have not only altered economic relationships in both rural and urban areas, but also affected the gender relations that shape women's reproductive needs and options. Unraveling some of these changes is critical to understanding those needs and the impact of different state policies on them.

The first section of this paper will analyze gender relations that permeate all levels of Thai society — the household, the workplace, the community, and the state — and will describe the implications for reproduction and sexuality. The second section will explore how Thailand's export-led growth process has relied upon traditional gender relations and power structures, and has, in turn, reshaped women's reproductive experiences and women's sexuality. This section will also examine reproductive needs that have emerged from the women's realities in the new political economy. The final portion of the paper will assess how some state policies and programs designed to promote health and family planning are addressing these needs.

Traditional Gender Relations and Roles

Although characterized by ethnic diversity, Thailand is relatively homogeneous with respect to religion; 95 percent of the population are Buddhists. The North and Northwest regions, which share mountains with Burma and Laos, are home to numerous ethnic groups — often referred to as hill tribes which are largely ignored by the national census and demographic surveys. The Northeast is home to a large Lao-Thai population, whereas the South, where 80 percent of Thai Muslims live, is influenced by neighboring Malaysia. Ethnic Chinese, estimated at 7 to 12 percent of the national population, are concentrated in the cities. Historically, the Central Plain, where Bangkok is located, has been economically and politically the dominant region of the country. It is "a demographically fluid area," shaped by forces seeking to capitalize on the agricultural richness of the Chao Phraya River basin (Pongpaichit 1982).

The twentieth century brought major changes to local cultures, including the surge in Chinese influence and the emergence of new social classes, which formed the basis for an urban culture. At the turn of the century, the commercialization of the rice trade attracted a large influx of migrants from China. Though professed Buddhists, they continue to practice ancestral worship and rituals. The migrants brought values and practices different from those of the local Thais, especially with respect to gender roles and marriage systems. Rigid control over women's lives, a preference for sons, worship of male ancestors, and dowry were introduced into Thailand (Pongpaichit 1982). Prostitution also flourished, as the migrants were mostly men.

By contrast, Thai women traditionally enjoyed a relatively high degree of autonomy in the social systems and local cultures. This independence could be seen in the sexual division of labor, patterns of inheritance, postnuptial residence, marriage customs, and sexuality. As is true in many societies, the traditional sexual division of labor was fairly well-defined. Throughout her life a Thai woman contributed to the welfare and sustenance of her family. From an early age, she was expected to help with domestic chores and to attend to younger siblings. As she grew older, she engaged in production either for home consumption or for the market. Once married, a Thai woman continued her active role in supporting the household — this time, her own. Even after marriage she maintained close ties with her parents, providing care and financial assistance. Parents relied on a daughter to be their caretaker in their old age.

Women in rural Thailand have been active participants in agricultural work. Although men and women were both involved in rice cultivation — the main source of income for most rural households — tasks were usually divided along gender lines. Men tended cattle, prepared land, and sowed rice seedlings. Women reared small animals, and transplanted and husked rice. This clearly-defined sexual division of labor was breached when necessary for household survival (e.g., when a household lacked the presence of an adult male, due to migration or death, a woman would plow the rice fields herself) (Pongpaichit 1982; Heyzer 1986).

Historically, women engaged in marketing as small-business owners, traders, market vendors and hawkers, and were perceived to handle money well. In Thai households, women managed the finances, though the power to allocate family resources remained in the hands of the men (Pongpaichit 1982; Heyzer 1986). Extra-household decisions were under men's control, whereas women carried the responsibility for fulfilling intra-household needs, in particular the requirements of children (food, health care and clothing). When the latter needs went unmet, a woman was obliged to seek alternate sources of income, such as vegetable gardening, cloth weaving, or petty trading. Clearly, while the sexual division of labor was well-defined, women traditionally had some control over resources, the handling of money, the ability to earn and control incomes, and to make important economic decisions in the household.

These elements of autonomy were supported by favorable patterns of inheritance and postnuptial residence. Women in Thailand traditionally owned and controlled land. Thais practiced bilateral inheritance, through which land and other properties were divided equally among children regardless of sex. In fact, a male child normally gave up his portion when he married, since he then acquired access to his wife's property. The process of inheritance was often articulated in the father's will, since he controlled the division of property (Yoddumnern-Attig et al. 1992). When one parent passed away, the land was shared by the surviving spouse and the children. When the other died, the daughter who stayed in the home to care for the elderly parent secured the remaining land and the house.

A Thai woman's autonomy was bolstered by a matrilocal pattern of residence after marriage. Although prevalent throughout Thailand, the pattern is most dominant among rural Thais (Potter 1977; Yoddumnern-Attig et al. 1992). After marriage, a couple traditionally resided with the wife's family until the first child was old enough to help on the farm. Only then did the couple establish an independent household, usually in the family compound, where they continued to work on the wife's parents' land. In one household, there might be several married daughters with their husbands, constituting a large extended family. A son-in-law was obligated to labor for the wife's family, which was often construed as a form of bride price. In the process, he also gained the right to cultivate the land of his parents-in-law in the future. Although families were organized around women, authority was passed down through men in the family, usually from the father to his son-in-law, who eventually became the head of the household (Potter 1976; Pongpaichit 1982).

Traditional Thai marriage patterns also gave greater decision-making power to women than is the case in patrilineal and patrilocal societies. In villages, marriage in the Buddhist tradition traditionally took the form of cohabitation after brideprice was paid; in some instances, payment was accompanied by a rite of "tying the bride and groom's wrists with holy string" (Yoddumnern-Attig et al. 1992). This informal ceremony, which symbolizes approval of the union from family and community, is enough to establish conjugal relationship between a man and a woman. A Thai woman generally chose her own partner, and then sought parental consent. For a man, marriage ideally took place after he became a novice in the monkshood, a rite of passage indicating adulthood; for a woman, marriage itself raised her status.

The birth of the first child was a critical event for a Thai couple, as it confirmed the union and symbolized a stable relationship. A woman entered adulthood when she became a mother. There was no strong gender preference for the child. Both sons and daughters were valued, for different reasons. While a son endowed the parents with merit when he became a novice (the child enters into Buddhist religious order, the *Sangha*, for a short period of time), a daughter was viewed as being more reliable and dependable (Knodel et al. 1987; Muecke 1989). Daughters were in fact responsible for the care of parents in old age. Parents, however, also regarded their girl-child as needing careful attention, to prevent her from falling into temptation. This view is manifested in a traditional characterization of boys as *rice with the husk* and girls as *rice without the husk* (Hantrakul 1988).

In discussing marriage in Thai society, it is crucial to consider class structures, and to distinguish the norms and practices of the aristocracy from those of lay people. Historically, intimate relationships between men and women in the royal courts differed greatly from those in the village. Polygamy and concubinage were common practices among royalty and courtiers; wives were classified as principal, secondary and slave. In the mid-1900s, Thailand experienced the rise of a bureaucratic and military class — which eventually gained political power — along with a growing commercial class (Pongpaichit 1982; Troung 1990). These new urban elites adopted the aristocratic values of polygamy. In the North, polygamy was associated with the new wealthy and the very poor (Muecke, in Yoddumnern-Attig et al. 1992); the minor wife contributed labor and financial support. Today, polygamy is perceived to be a status symbol, and remains largely a practice of the wealthy.

In order fully to understand gender relations, gender roles, and sexuality in Thailand, it is crucial to consider the often contradictory role Buddhism plays in promoting greater freedom for women and, at the same time, legitimizing unequal power relations and subordination of women. Buddhism has been viewed both as a religion which opens a path to enlightenment for all — regardless of race, sex, class or caste — and as one which fosters gender inequalities. Religious texts from certain time periods exhibit a misogynous tone, while at other times women are included and regarded with reverence and fairness (Cabezon 1992).

Despite her relative autonomy, a Thai woman is often not in a position of power or authority within either the public or private spheres, according to Thitsa (1980):

A clear reservation of ecclesiastical position, spiritual wisdom, learning and authority as masculine domains by traditional Buddhism, and the secular specialization of women in trading and marketing activities, have led directly to the anomalous position of the Thai woman today, who is debarred from real authority while exercising considerable economic influence.

The basic tenet of Buddhism is *karma,* the law of cause and effect, the force propelling the cycle of rebirths. Enlightenment signifies extinction of the karmic fire, the cessation of rebirths. The law of karma does not allow one to escape the consequences of one's own actions, speech or thoughts. One's life is shaped by immediate actions as well as by the effects of past conduct. The Thai culture, like that of other Theravada Buddhist countries, believes the individual is born a female because of one's inferior karma, since only a man can enter monkhood and potentially become a Buddha. Although a female can attain nirvana, she is incapable of revealing the Path of Enlightenment to others. For a woman, the separation between the ability to participate in and achieve her life's goals, and the inability to lead and manifest authority, is reflected in the freedoms and the constraints imposed in all spheres of her life — household, workplace, and community.

A Thai woman elevates her status and improves her inferior karma by being a responsible daughter, a reliable and supportive wife, and, most of all, a nurturing mother. The greatest act of merit she can perform as a woman is to physically, emotionally and financially care for the family and the *Sangha.* These expectations are imposed both by herself and by society. As she assumes these responsibilities, she accepts difficulties and inconveniences, and anticipates more hardships and injustices than would be confronted by a man.

The contradictory treatment of gender in Thai Buddhism is evident in the fact that mothers are considered deserving of utmost reverence and respect, even more so than fathers, as the base and strength of the family. But while "motherhood" raises the status of a young woman, the female body itself is regarded as filthy and polluting through its association with reproductive cycles. Exclusion of women from many religious rituals and sacred places is founded on the belief that menstrual blood would introduce a disruptive force (Thitsa 1980). The process of procreation (sexual intercourse, conception, and birth) is often disconnected from the virtues of motherhood (Truong 1990). Although not a "sin" in Buddhism, sex is perceived as a form of attachment, and therefore, as an inextricable causal component of *dukkha,* or suffering. Sexual relations are not compatible with a religious/spiritual life, in which only men can fully partake. For lay people, however, there are few restrictions inscribed in the Buddhist code of conduct with regard to sexual relations. One of the main precepts simply dictates abstention from sexual misconduct, often interpreted as adultery or violation of someone's daughter or son.

Men do have more sexual freedom than women. They are not only permitted, but are expected, to express their sexuality; their sexual needs are considered "natural," and therefore immutable. Maintaining polygamous relationships and frequenting prostitutes, therefore, have been sanctioned. Polygamy and prostitution "provide a man with access to the services of more than one woman" (Hantrakul 1988). On the contrary, it is not considered easy for a woman to become involved in an extramarital affair; this perception is rooted in the biological and social reproductive roles of a woman as a mother, who is presumed to possess stronger physiological bonds with her children. Parents teach daughters to take care of their families, to respect their elders, and to serve their husbands. A woman must always keep her sexuality in check. Hantrakul asserts, however, that the sexuality of women of the middle and upper classes is more rigidly controlled than among lower and working class women. Although the concept of a "good woman" is pervasive, the behavior of wealthy and educated women receives greater scrutiny.

In sum, a Thai woman traditionally possessed substantial but contradictory freedoms; she traditionally participated in agriculture and in trade, oversaw household finances, selected her own spouse and brought him into her family, and inherited property equally with her brothers. Economic value was attached to the birth of a daughter, as it implied brideprice (rather than dowry) and old-age security. Although the degree of control over female sexuality varied according to class, Buddhism left considerable room for interpretation regarding what is proper sexual behavior. But the Buddhist ideology of karma restricts a woman's autonomy; it does not extend to positions of leadership and power. She is simultaneously valued for and burdened by her obligations to parents, husband, and children. Furthermore, the economic transformation of Thai society over the last two to three decades has built on women's traditional mobility, greater economic responsibility for family care and maintenance, and less stringent social attitudes towards sexuality. In examining that process, we can argue that the very fact of women's greater traditional autonomy has become the source of their increasing burdens.

Rapid Economic Growth: the Role of Women

Two features of Thailand's economic growth are important for the purposes of this paper. The first is the extent of inequality and continuing poverty in certain regions of the country; the second is the way in which the growth process itself has relied on women's traditional freedoms, constraints and responsibilities. Over the two decades, the country averaged a real GDP growth rate of about 7 percent per annum (Yongkittikul and Sopchokchai 1990). During this period, the agricultural sector of the Thai economy has declined its share of GDP dropped from 33 percent in the early 1970s to 16 percent in 1989 — while the manufacturing and service sectors have correspondingly risen in importance. The state has made the promotion of the export industry and securing of foreign exchange its economic priority. Tourism constitutes the largest single source of foreign exchange (EIU 1992), with textiles and garments following second.

High economic growth rates often obscure the country's stark urban-rural and regional disparities. Wealth is concentrated in the cities. Bangkok, with 10 percent of the country's population, accounts for 30 percent of GDP, whereas the Northeast region, which has 35 percent of the population and the largest number of poor households, claims only 15 percent of GDP. Development strategies have been biased toward urban centers. Bangkok has gained from public utility subsidies, such as those for the transportation system, and from infrastructure development, such as telecommunications, entertainment, and medical and educational institutions. The city has also reaped the benefits of the tourist industry.

Over the last two to three decades, income inequalities have widened and poverty persists. In 1975, the top one-fifth of the population accounted for 49.3 percent of total income; in 1985, they accounted for 55.6 percent. All other groups experienced a decrease in their share (Yongkittikul and Sopchokchai 1990). The incidence of poverty declined during late 1970s, but this trend reversed in the early 1980s due to the fall of world prices for agricultural goods. Though there have been improvements since 1986, many rural areas continue to experience high percentages of people living below the poverty line, relative to the municipal areas. While Bangkok has 2.4 percent of the population living in poverty, the villages in the Northeast have 44.5 percent, in the North 23.6 percent, and in the South 27.5 percent (Thailand Development

Research Institute quoted in Yongkittikul and Sopchokchai 1990). Landlessness in the North and Northeast has exacerbated the disparity.

Thailand's population remains predominantly rural despite growing rates of urbanization which increased from 12.5 percent in 1960 (Tonguthai 1984) to 19 percent in 1990 (Robinson et al. 1991). These percentages disguise the importance and prevalence of rural-urban migration, which is often temporary (less than several months, such as during the agricultural slack season) or short term (one to five years), and which is critical for the economic survival of impoverished rural households. Tirasawat (1985) describes migration in Thailand as a two-way process: although Bangkok receives many people from provinces, nearly half of this movement is canceled out by migrants returning from the city to their homes. Rural-urban migration, a growing phenomenon since the 1960s, is propelled by depressed rural incomes, economic opportunities in the urban areas, a hierarchical education system, and a modernized urban life style (Adulavadhaya and Onchan 1985; Knodel et al. 1986; Tonguthai 1987; Mills 1991).[1] Although males exceed females with respect to the total number of migrants, close review of migration streams and age of migrants reveals that women comprise the majority of rural-urban streams, and the majority of the 15 to 24 age group. On the other hand, intra-regional, as well as rural-rural, migration streams are mainly composed of men. In recent years, women and girls have represented the majority of in-migrants to Bangkok. In 1986, 75 percent of the female migrants were single, and arrived unaccompanied (Yongkittikul and Sopchokchai 1990).

The sharp rural-urban income disparities have interacted with traditional gender roles to produce the current patterns of rural-urban migration for Thai women. Expected from an early age to sustain their families financially, Thai women now seek employment in urban areas to supplement the declining income available from agricultural pursuits. Their traditional role makes them available, amenable and exploitable in Thailand's efforts to develop economically.

The primary goal for a single woman in the workforce is to assist her parents and younger siblings, while a married woman strives for the economic survival of her household. A 1979 survey of 646 rural women who migrated to Bangkok for five years or less indicated that most of the migrants returned home once they had achieved their target income, but not before: "To return home empty-handed would be shameful"

(Tonguthai 1984). Pongpaichit (1982) also reported her interviews with masseuses indicated that the women have a long-term financial goal, such as building a house for their parents and establishing a small business for themselves. In a study of women in manufacturing, 143 out of 183 single women sent money to their parents regularly, and 23 intermittently; 17.4 percent were primary income earners, while one-half of the women stated that their parents still bore the economic burden for the family. Married female workers, on the other hand, spent all of their income on food, household items, and children's expenses (Charoenloet and Soonthorndhada 1988).

Young women are the target of recruitment into the urban sectors, particularly to work in manufacturing and services. They migrate to cities because of opportunities in domestic service, factories, and the tourist industry (including prostitution). A report from the Thailand Development Research Institute indicated that 90 percent of all female migrants into Bangkok entered the urban workforce as house maids (Bell 1991). Domestic service is generally the lowest-paying work. The Female Migration Survey of 1980 (Tonguthai 1984) reported the mean monthly income for housemaids as Baht 805 ($32). Beauticians and dressmakers earned Baht 1,459 ($58) and professional, administrative and clerical workers made Baht 1,480 ($59). Thailand's export industry, in particular textiles and garments, also relies heavily on female workers, who will work for lower wages than men. Women account for 80 percent of total employment in the ten largest export industries (canned seafood, textiles, jewelry, frozen seafood, cotton fabric, footwear, electrical parts, leather goods, and frozen foods), and 45.4 percent of manufacturing workforce (Jones 1984; Bell 1991). According to the 1983 National Statistical Office survey, women's earnings in the manufacturing sector were only 70.1 percent that of men's. Employers' preference for women workers is based not only on cost, but also on perceptions of women as hard-working, enthusiastic, loyal, patient, and attentive to detail.

Tourism, an extremely profitably industry which relies primarily on the labor of women, most clearly illustrates how Thailand has used, and at the same time undermined, traditional gender roles to fuel economic growth. In its initial phase, tourism was driven by the "Rest and Recreation" market during the Vietnam war, and was characterized by extensive investment in and supply of accommodation and entertainment facilities. When the United States military presence departed, this enormous service sector was maintained by the Thai ruling class and foreign investors, and became an integral part of the country's economic development strategy (Truong 1990). By 1986, gross revenues from tourism surpassed major export items, such as rice and textiles. Tourism is one of the driving forces behind the Thai sex industry, which encompasses various forms of prostitution, establishments, and services (Sittitrai and Brown 1991; Pyne 1992). Women in sex tourism primarily work in establishments such as bars, nightclubs, and massage parlors, and they can earn up to 25 times the median income earned by women in factories or clerical positions (Pongpaichit 1982).[2]

Tourism thrives on an image of Thai women as submissive, exotic, and sexually attainable, an image promoted not only by the private sector, but by the public sector as well. The Tourist Authority of Thailand (TAT), a government office, boasts of Bangkok's nightlife of go-go bars and nightclubs, and publicizes Thai women's "friendly" nature. Truong (1990) cites an advertisement from the government-owned Thai International Airlines which illustrates this strategy:

> Smooth as silk is a beautifully-prepared meal served by a delicious hostess. Some say it's our beautiful wide-bodied DC-10's that cause so many heads to turn at airports throughout the world. We think our beautiful slim-bodied hostesses have a lot to do with it.

Truong further explains that international campaigns to promote tourism focus on the open sexuality of Thai women as shaped by local norms and the market; the submissive nature of Thai women as satisfying the need for a man to dominate; and poverty as a justification (the clients are helping these prostitutes support themselves and their families). Local campaigns, on the other hand, stress that female sexuality plays a critical role in the country's economic development and growth.

Changing Reproductive Options: The Increasing Burden on Women

The process by which women are recruited into the urban workforce must be viewed in relation to changes in the formation and maintenance of Thai households. Emerging trends in marriage, family formation, postnuptial residence and inheritance point to important changes as well as elements of continuity which affect women's reproductive experiences and needs. The issues can be grouped into three areas: biological (pregnancy and childbearing), social (childrearing and taking care of elders), and sexual relations and sexuality.[3]

A Thai woman continues to play a significant role in selecting her own spouse, and brideprice is still a common practice among villagers. In rural areas, 69 percent of the women choose their own husbands, while the 79 percent do so in the urban context. Chinese-Thais, on the other hand, indicate a lower degree of choice in mate selection, only 41 percent (Hogan et al. 1987). Because age at marriage has always been relatively high in Thailand, it has only increased slightly in recent years. In 1970, the mean age of marriage for rural and urban women was 21.4 and 24.7 years old, respectively; in 1980 this figure rose to 22.0 and 25.0 years old.

While the above customs have not changed much, a woman's decision to marry, or have children, is now more severely constrained than before by her social and economic obligations to her parents and younger siblings, if she is single, and to her own family, if she is married. Employers openly favor single women, and deny financial support for maternal and child health care. Many employers view these services as a strain on their profits. The majority of female migrants into the urban workforce, therefore, are girls and single women between the ages of 11 and 24, although married women still comprise a substantial portion of the workforce. If pregnancy occurs, most companies request a voluntary leave of absence, endangering the financial security of the women. In addition, pregnancy for an unmarried woman brings shame not only to herself, but also to her family. Abortion is often the chosen solution, either in an urban clinic or through traditional methods of ingesting "hot" medicine or forceful massage (Yoddumnern-Attig et al. 1992).[4] These methods are often extremely painful and detrimental to the woman's health.

Pregnancy for a married working woman results in limited options: relying on the husband's income (which is often insufficient), acquiring a daytime child care provider, sending children back to her village, or obtaining an abortion. These options compel many female migrant laborers to leave their children in the village with grandparents. Child care is extremely costly in the urban environment, and is often not an option for poor women. With no extended family to provide assistance, the involvement of fathers is becoming a necessity in urban areas. There has been a noticeable decline in breastfeeding and an increase both in reliance on alternative milk products and in child malnutrition (Heyzer 1986; Yoddumnern-Attig et al. 1992). Charoenlet and Soonthorndhada (1988) also revealed that married women with young children tend to have higher rates of absenteeism from work, which could result in job loss. A female worker, single or married, prostitute or domestic servant, recognizes that starting a family could jeopardize the only source of income, for herself, her parents and younger siblings.

Like marriage, postnuptial residential patterns have undergone major changes. Analysis of the 1987 Demographic and Health Survey (DHS) indicates urban-rural and ethnic differences in postnuptial residence. The South and Central Regions (excluding Bangkok) manifest high percentages of patrilocal residence, reflecting a large population of Chinese-Thais (Limonanda 1989; Hogan et al. 1987), while Bangkok and other major urban areas are comprised mainly of couples who reside independently from original families. Although matrilocal residence is still the most prevalent pattern, particularly in the Northeast (70 percent) and North (57 percent), the duration and form of the pattern has altered. Recent changes include a shorter period of co-residence with parents as the economic burden on the couple increases and there is not enough money or time to devote to one's own family. The DHS (Limonanda 1989) indicates that coresidence only lasts about three years. Establishing a new household also entails receiving a portion of land and becoming free from economic responsibility to the wife's parents and other family members.

Caring for elders has also become a growing problem. Traditionally, daughters cared for their parents in old age. Today, as a result of increasing rural-urban migration, older women who have remained in the villages have emerging concerns about security. Although children provide assistance for the farm through remittances, actual physical care is absent. This problem is greater among the rural poor, since they lack land or resources to hire help on the farm or at home. Moreover, elderly women are increasingly required to assume sole responsibility for their grandchildren.

Care of the parents and the home has now been placed on the youngest daughter and her husband, who remain in the original household and inherit the home after the death of both parents (Pongpaichit 1982; Knodel et al. 1987). Today, the parental household usually includes only one married child. In an increasing number of cases, all the children have moved away, although they have continued to provide economic assistance. As mentioned earlier, many female migrants leave their young children with grandparents in their rural communities. In the North and Northeast regions, for example, the majority of households consist of elderly Thais with preschool or school-age children (Yoddumnern-Attig et al. 1992). The survival of these households depends upon remittances and profits from land with hired labor. For the landless, economic assistance from migrants has become even more significant.

Thailand's inheritance pattern remains predominantly bilateral, although some changes have taken place. A son generally no longer relinquishes his property, as landlessness is an increasing problem in the rural areas; his wife, through whom he traditionally gained access to land, may herself not own enough property, or any at all. Education for a daughter is now considered a form of inheritance, especially if the parents own little land; higher education provides a daughter with economic opportunities other than agriculture (Yoddumnern-Attig et al. 1992).

Fertility patterns in Thailand have also undergone dramatic changes. Knodel et al (1986) noted that the "reproductive revolution" has resulted in nearly every Thai perceiving the number of his or her children as an outcome of personal decision and choice. The total fertility rate for the nation dropped from 6.3 in 1965 to 2.4 in 1989, and more than 96 percent of ever-married women knew of at least one modern method of contraception by 1975 (Snow and Chen 1992).

Data from the DHS showed a shift from women initiating contraception for the purpose of limiting births, to initiating it for the purpose of spacing. Efforts to delay the start of childbearing are absent in the oldest married groups (1 percent), but are quite common in recently married couples (42 percent) and in urban areas. Half of all married women between ages 15 to 49 intend to have two children, and 80 percent want two or three. It is rare to desire only one child. An attitudinal survey revealed that, although there is an overall preference for boys, very few wanted only sons (Knodel et al. 1987; Hogan et al. 1987).

Issues related to sexuality and sexual relations are of greater concern today, as Thailand confronts the AIDS pandemic. Sexually transmitted diseases (STDs) pose a grave threat not only for commercial sex workers, but for all women, both in urban and rural areas. Thai male partners regularly frequent brothels and other sex establishments while maintaining steady relationships. Young migrant women, often lacking parental guidance in their new environments, find support among peers through sharing a living space. Removed from close scrutiny, they are more likely to become involved in sexual relations before marriage; unwanted pregnancies, abuse, and STDs are likely possibilities. Adoption of a modern lifestyle and the low wages paid by factories sometimes force a young woman to engage in prostitution on the side to support herself and her family. A young woman may also enter polygamous relationships, by becoming a *mia noi* (minor wife or mistress) of a wealthier man, who provides gifts and financial assistance. Thailand's population is highly mobile, as migration is a crucial component of economic survival, and this phenomenon has contributed to the rapid spread of human immunodeficiency virus (HIV) infection.

The emergent concerns of women spelled out above are often ignored. Thus, because of their productive and reproductive roles, women have borne the brunt of Thailand's structural changes, not only in the economy but also in the household. Their autonomy and relative sexual freedom have been exploited without a corresponding effort to help them meet their traditional responsibilities to the family in alternative ways. Their needs include adequate child care, social security for the aging, improved sexual and reproductive health including greater control over sexual relations, protection from unwanted pregnancies and STDs, and occupational and personal security.

Women's Reproductive Needs: The Challenge to Social Programs

Thailand has already established a foundation from which policies and programs to ensure healthy and fulfilling reproductive lives of its women and girls could be pursued. The country is home to innovative local and international nongovernmental organizations (NGOs); supports an extensive health infrastructure, mass media and communication systems; and boasts prominent research and academic institutions. The state has implemented policies and programs in the areas of basic needs, family planning, and AIDS prevention. I will focus on these three areas as they relate directly to reproduction.

Sharp and continuing regional and urban-rural disparities compelled the state to adopt a basic minimum needs (BMN) approach in 1982, which was later incorporated into the National Rural Development Program (NRDP) (MOPH 1991; Yongkittikul and Sopchokchai 1990). NRDP aimed to decentralize the delivery of services and goods, to encourage participation of villagers in identifying needs and problems, and to involve all administrative levels (province, district, *tambon*, and village). The goal was to meet the basic needs of nutrition, shelter, security, family planning, community, and spirituality. Health needs, from sanitation to maternal and child health, were a primary focus. The summary report of BMN indicators in 1988 revealed that although overall rural conditions in

Thailand had improved, and in many cases — such as access to safe water and sanitation — are better than other developing countries in Asia, the Central region fared better than other, poorer areas (Yongkittikul and Sopchokchai 1990). For example, 74.9 percent of the population in the Central region had access to sufficient safe drinking water, while only 53.8 percent of the Northeast, 54.8 percent of the North and 50.1 percent of the South enjoyed such access. With respect to owning a latrine meeting sanitary standards, 72.8 percent of the Central region, 51.5 percent of Northeast, 64.1 percent of the North, and 38.5 percent of South had such facilities.

The basic minimum needs approach, as applied in Thailand, explicitly embraces a gender-neutral stance, assuming that women and men share the same basic needs. Although similar concerns are faced by both sexes, women bear specific productive and reproductive responsibilities, obligations, and roles — and struggle under unequal power relations — because of their gender. Therefore, women have specific needs and require interventions that encompass gender. BMN indicators include the well-being of pregnant women, such as adequate food intake, vaccination against tetanus, and provision of prenatal and postnatal care (MOPH 1991; Yongkittikul and Sopchokchai 1990); however, only pregnant women are subjects of concern, and individual well-being is considered only to the extent that it benefits children and other family members.

It is crucial that the basic minimum needs program continues to address issues of environmental health, adequate housing and maternal and child health; however, it must also recognize that women have reproductive needs beyond pregnancy and childbirth. Reproduction cannot be viewed in isolation, or placed exclusively in the sphere of the household as this paper has demonstrated by exposing the links between a woman's work and her reproductive options and constraints. As Thailand undergoes vast social and economic changes, women's reproductive and productive lives are inseparable. Therefore, policies and programs must address a larger context of job security and occupational health. The state must also begin to take responsibility for the changes it has wrought in traditional familial relations and share the cost of child care and care for the elderly rather than relying on women in their traditional guise as caretakers.

Family planning, which is included as a basic need, has been a concern of the Thai government since the late 1960s. The view that rapid population growth had a negative impact on economic development spurred the government to embrace a firm anti-natalist stance, and to initiate the National Family Planning Program (NFPP) in 1970. Since then, each of the country's five-year development plans has included a specific target for population growth rates (United Nations 1991). Because NFPP, initiated under the authority of the Ministry of Public Health, was integrated into maternal and child health services, it benefited from the existing infrastructure for service delivery (Knodel et al. 1987). The facets of Thailand's success in controlling population growth include integration of development projects with family planning activities; innovative methods for outreach, in particular those of NGOs such as Population and Community Development Association (PDA); use of non-medical personnel, such as auxiliary midwives, in service delivery (distributing oral contraceptives, administering injectables, inserting IUDs, and even performing tubal ligation); involvement of the private sector; and early availability of multiple contraceptive methods (United Nations 1991; Knodel et al. 1987; Snow and Chen 1992). Thailand has achieved a reduction in fertility, from six births per woman in 1960s to two births per woman in the late 1980s and a decline in the population growth rate, from 3.5 percent in 1966 to 1.7 percent in 1985. There has also been an increase in the contraceptive prevalence rate, from 15 percent to 68 percent of married women over the last two decades (Knodel and Chayovan 1989). The most prevalent method in Thailand today is female sterilization, followed by the Pill, while the least popular method is condom (Snow and Chen 1992).

Unlike the BMN program, the National Family Planning Program has specifically focused on women for the purpose of fertility control. The emphasis on fertility is reflected in the indicators used to measure the program's effectiveness: fertility rates, number of new acceptors of contraceptive methods, and contraceptive prevalence rates. These indicators take into account only married women between the ages of 15 and 49. It is evident that the NFPP's mandate is to control population growth, not to attain reproductive health and well- being for all women and girls. It is also evident that NFPP's understanding of the locus of sexual activity — confined to married couples — does not comprehend the changing needs of urban dwellers, both those women who work in sex tourism, and others who do not.

Recently, the attention of Thailand's population activities have shifted somewhat to accommodate the more pressing problem of AIDS epidemic. Although the country's first case of AIDS was diagnosed in 1984, response from the Thai government was slow, since HIV and AIDS were viewed as a disease of *farangs* (Westerners) and gays. Another motivation for the government's reluctance to respond was a fear of hurting the extremely profitable tourist industry. In 1989, faced with relentless lobbying by NGOs and recognition that HIV infection was beginning to soar in certain population groups, such as heroin addicts, the Thai government secured the blood supply and launched a sentinel surveillance system to monitor the spread of the infection. The groups selected for the surveillance were intravenous drug users (IVDUs), prostitutes, clients at STD clinics, blood donors, and women attending antenatal clinics. Recent interventions have concentrated on deterring the transmission of the virus from "high risk" groups to the general population. Despite ongoing prevention and education campaigns by the state and non-governmental organizations, the epidemic continues to spread rapidly.

AIDS work has focused on groups with high risk behaviors, in particular female commercial sex workers. The heightened concern for controlling HIV infection among prostitutes is grounded in the belief that such women are the vectors by which the AIDS virus is transmitted to the "mainstream" population. What may happen to these women with respect to their health and lives after contracting the virus is often disregarded. The state's concern also falls on pregnant women, who may pass on the HIV infection to children. In both cases, women are viewed as instruments for preventing the transmission of the AIDS virus (Pyne 1992).

Family planning and AIDS prevention in Thailand today are important aspects of women's reproductive health. Women must have access to safe and effective contraceptive methods, and access to information about HIV and AIDS. But, these are just two components of a larger body of reproductive health needs. Family planning and AIDS prevention have not considered women of all ages, and they must be developed in a context of reproductive and sexual health services sensitive to the changing needs of women as they move through their life cycle. As of today, adolescents and single women have needs — which may be shared by married women — that are not being addressed. As they increasingly migrate into urban areas for educational and economic opportunities, and away from parental control and scrutiny, they are more likely to engage in premarital sexual relations. Therefore, providing options for unwanted pregnancies and promoting safe sex must become priorities. Although the government has turned a blind eye to the abortion services provided to urban and wealthy classes, harmful, life threatening techniques persist, particularly in rural areas and for the poor. Safe abortion services must be made available to all women, regardless of marital status, class, and age. Protection from STDs, including HIV, is another crucial dimension of Thai women's reproductive needs. Women in the sex industry are at great risk, but so are others. For most women, whether single or married, visiting STD clinics and seeking care can bring shame and fear of being perceived as promiscuous and defiled. This stigma would be eliminated if women of all ages had access to comprehensive reproductive and sexual health care that met needs ranging from maternal and child health, family planning, ob-gyn, and reproductive tract infections, to counseling, education, and referral services.

Gender relations and sexuality, the central forces underlying repro-duction, are barely touched upon by any of the programs described above. The AIDS crisis has revealed the chasm between knowledge and action, and opened a window of opportunity for addressing these politically and culturally sensitive issues. Male sexuality in Thailand is sanctioned, rather than questioned. The accepted behavior of men frequenting brothels and engaging in polygynous affairs must be "denaturalized," and, therefore, perceived as subject to change. Female sexuality in Thailand, on the other hand, is invoked to promote tourism and meet men's needs, while maintaining the notions of appropriate behavior for women. (In many cases, women themselves participate in perpetuating the patriarchal constructs of male-female sexuality, and of the division between "good" and "bad" girls.) Social and gender inequalities erect barriers for women seeking to act upon and respond to their needs. Although Thai women have enjoyed relative freedom to make decisions regarding their own fertility, contributing to the "success-ful reproductive revolution," they are unable to prevent men from engaging in risky behaviors, or to persuade their partners (or clients) to wear condoms and share the responsibility for reproduction. They are, therefore, unable to protect themselves.

Efforts by the Thai government to promote basic minimum needs, family planning and AIDS prevention and education have received international attention and praise. These attempts are, indeed, commend-able; however, they have not fully incorporated women's realities or addressed the implications of gender hierarchy. The policies and programs have been narrowly defined and implemented. They must begin to focus on women *and men* at different stages of life; to treat women's well-being as an end rather than as a means; to link productive and reproductive roles and responsibilities of women; to move beyond pregnancy and childbearing to include child care, elderly care, and safe sexual relations and sexuality; and to place gender at the center of analysis of problems and interventions.

Gendered analysis of emerging reproductive conditions in Thailand reveals a close linkage between the micro level of women's experiences (family formation, mothering and sexuality), and the macro level of developmental policies. The driving force behind Thailand's "success" is rooted in the pre-existing gender structures, which have allowed women a relatively high degree of autonomy, but have also restricted them from attaining positions of power and leadership. The export-led growth of the economy has relied heavily on women's labor in the manufacturing and service industries in the urban areas, affecting ways in which households are formed and maintained. Thai women's changing reproductive experiences and needs in the areas of biological and social reproduction, sexual relations and sexuality are largely ignored by existing policies and programs. The state has benefited, while women continue to bear the brunt of structural changes.

Policy makers must recognize the crucial role that women have played and will continue to play in the country's development. It is essential to consider policies and programs that acknowledge these emerging reproductive experiences and needs, and that will root out the country's deeply entrenched and unequal gender relations. The new approach must look to local level experiences and incorporate them as part of larger development directions. These interventions must aim to meet a variety of goals, through actions at the international and policy levels and at the grassroots.

The Thai government must assume greater responsibility for reproductive burdens that have, until now, rested largely on the backs of women. It must not only move to provide job security, health benefits, and child care, but also foster an environment where women have opportunities to organize and mobilize to articulate their own needs. Women working in the services, such as domestic service and the sex industry, are often isolated and in need of support networks and assistance, particularly when abuse occurs. Efforts to improve rural conditions must continue, to address the increasing problem of landlessness and basic needs of sanitation, environmental health, and housing. At the same time, women must be involved in the identification of problems, and design of projects. Reproductive and sexual health care must address not only maladies and illnesses but also the strategic goal of creating equal and healthy sexual relations. Such care should include means of empowering women and involving men to become responsible for the consequences of their behaviors and practices, harmful not only to their partners and families, but also to themselves.

Notes

1 I will not be discussing international migration in this paper.

2 Brothel prostitutes, who are primarily procured by Thai men, on the other hand, are paid little or nothing at all.

3 I have separated sexual relations from biological reproduction because relations that develop outside of marriage and childbearing are often ignored.

4 Abortion is technically illegal except in cases of rape or threat to the woman's health.

References

Adulavidhaya, K., and T. Onchan. 1985. Migration and agricultural development of Thailand: Past and future. In *Urbanization in ASEAN development*, ed. P.M. Hauser, D.B. Suits, and N. Ogawa. Tokyo: National Institute for Research Advancement.

Bell, P. 1991. Gender and economic development in Thailand. In *Gender and development in Southeast Asia: Proceedings of the twentieth meeting of the Canadian Council for Southeast Asian Studies*, ed. P. and J. Van Esterik. Montreal: Canadian Asian Studies Association.

Cabezon, J.I., ed. 1992. *Buddhism, sexuality and gender.* Albany, N.Y.: State University of New York Press.

Charoenloet, V., and A. Soonthorndhada. 1988. Factory management, skill formation and attitudes of women workers in Thailand: A comparison between an American and a Japanese factory. In *Daughters in industry: Work, skills and consciousness of women workers in Asia.* Kuala Lumpur: Asian and Pacific Development Centre.

The Economist Intelligence Unit. 1992. *Country report: Thailand, Burma.* London.

Hantrankul, S. 1988. Prostitution in Thailand. In *Development and displacement: Women in Southeast Asia*, ed. G. Chendler, N. Sullivan, and J. Branson. Monash, Australia: Centre of Southeast Asian Studies.

Heyzer, N. 1986. *Working women in South-east Asia: Development, subordination and emancipation.* Philadelphia, Pa.: Open University Press.

Hogan, D.P., A. Chamratrithirong, and P. Xenos. 1987. *Cultural and economic factors in the fertility of Thai women.* Honolulu, Hawaii: East-West Center.

Jones, G. W., ed. 1984. *Women in the urban and industrial workforce: Southeast and East Asia.* Development Studies Centre, Monograph no. 33. Canberra: The Australian National University.

Knodel, J., A. Chamratrithirong, and N. Debavalya. 1987. *Thailand's reproductive revolution: Rapid fertility decline in a Third-World setting.* Madison, Wis.: The University of Wisconsin Press.

Knodel, J., and N. Chayovan. 1989. Contraceptive initiation patterns in Thailand. *Health and population studies based on the 1987 Thailand Demographic and Health Survey.* Bangkok: Institute of Population Studies, Chulalongkorn University.

Limonanda, B. 1989. Analysis of postnuptial residence pattern of Thai women. *Health and population studies based on the 1987 Thailand Demographic and Health Survey.* Bangkok: Institute of Population Studies, Chulalongkorn University.

Mills, M.B. 1991. Modernity and gender vulnerability: Rural women working in Bangkok. In *Gender and development in Southeast Asia: Proceedings of the twentieth meeting of the Canadian Council for Southeast Asian Studies,* ed. P. and J. Van Esterik. Montreal: Canadian Asian Studies Association.

Ministry of Public Health. 1991. *Thailand health profile 1990.* Bangkok.

Mueke, M.A. 1989. Mother sells food: Daughter sells her body. Prostitution and cultual continuity in the social function in Thai women. Unpublished manuscript.

Phongpaichit, P. 1982. *From peasant girls to Bangkok masseuses.* Geneva: International Labor Office.

Potter, S.H. 1977. *Family life in a northern Thai village: A study in the structural significance of women.* Berkeley, Calif.: University of California Press.

Pyne, H.H. 1992. AIDS and prostitution in Thailand: The Burmese prostitutes in Ranong. Master's thesis. Department of Urban Studies and Planning, Massachusetts Institute of Technology.

Robinson, D., Y. Byeon, and R. Teja. 1991. *Thailand: Adjusting to success, current policy issues.* Occasional Paper no. 85. Washington, D.C.: International Monetary Fund.

Sittitrai, W., and T. Brown. 1991. *Female commercial sex workers in Thailand, a preliminary report.* Bangkok.

Snow, R., and L. Chen. 1992. Benefits and risks of the Pill: Perception and reality. *Advances in Contraception* 7(2):19–34.

———. 1991. Towards an appropriate contraceptive mix: Policy analyses of three Asian countries. Working Paper no. 5. Cambridge: Harvard Center for Population and Development Studies.

Thitsa, K. 1980. *Providence and prostitution: Image and reality for women in Buddhist Thailand.* London: Change International Reports.

Tirasawat, P. 1985. Migration in Thailand: Past and future. In *Urbanization in ASEAN development,* ed. P.M. Hauser, D.B. Suits, and N. Ogawa. Tokyo: National Institute for Research Advancement.

Tonguthai, P. 1984. Women migrants in Bangkok: An economic analysis of their employment and earnings. In *Women in the urban and industrial workforce: Southeast and East Asia,* ed. G.W. Jones. Canberra: The Australian National University.

———. 1987. Implicit policies and the urban bias as factors affecting urbanization. In *Urbanization and urban policies in Pacific Asia,* ed. R.J. Fuchs, G.W. Jones and E.M. Pernia. Boulder, Colo.: Westview Press.

Truong, T. 1990. *Sex, money, and morality: Prostitution and tourism in Southeast Asia.* Atlantic Highlands, N.J.: Zed Books.

United Nations. 1991. *Integrating development and population planning in Thailand.* New York.

Yoddumnern-Attig, B., M. Mahidon, and S.W. Prachakon la Sangkhom, eds. 1992. *Changing roles and statuses of women in Thailand: A documentary assessment.* Bangkok: Institute for Population and Social Research, Mahidol University.

Yongkittkul, T., and O. Sopchokchai. 1990. The impact of the basic minimum needs approach on alleviation of poverty and the status of women. Paper submitted to the Asian and Pacific Development Centre.

3

Labor Policy: Its Influence on Women's Reproductive Lives

by Jody Heymann

Unspoken Constraints

During this century, the context of reproductive choice has changed dramatically. Technology has made it possible for women to carry out a decision not to conceive or bear children, although social barriers prevent many women from doing so.

At the same time, social policy has limited the choice of women to bear and rear children in a variety of settings. These policies have ranged from governmental programs which use strong economic incentives at one end of the spectrum to surreptitious sterilization programs at the other. Programs to limit childbearing have been targeted at women living in poverty in the United States and in developing countries.

Social constraints which prevent women from being able to bear and rear children, and degrade the quality of women's lives if they do, need to be examined as carefully as those which prevent women from limiting their own childbearing. While some government programs were debated publicly prior to enactment, in many instances, the choice to bear and rear children has been limited inadvertently or in the absence of public consensus. This is the case for conditions under which women are employed. These conditions will be explored in detail in this chapter; the United States will be used as a case study.

Working in the Paid Labor Force and Mothering

Only toward the end of the nineteenth century were the locations in which women would work for pay and rear children separated in the United States (Kanter 1989). During the twentieth century, one of the most significant demographic shifts in the United States has been the movement of women in general — and mothers of preschool and school-age children in particular — into this separated labor space. In the last three decades alone, the labor force participation rate of married women with preschool children has almost tripled, rising from 18.6 percent in 1960 to 58.4 percent in 1989 (U.S. Bureau of the Census 1991). The labor force participation rate of married women with school-age children has risen over the same period from 39 percent to 73.2 percent. Among separated and divorced mothers of preschool-age children, 57.4 percent and 70.5 percent participate in the labor force respectively. Among mothers of school-age children, 73.5 percent of separated mothers and 85 percent of divorced mothers are in the labor force (U.S. Bureau of the Census 1991). Almost all never-married mothers either work in the paid labor force, live in poverty, or both.

During this century, demographic shifts in many developing countries have led to a similar rise in the number of mothers working in the formal labor sector. These shifts include in many countries a dramatic move from a primarily rural to a principally urban population (United Nations 1991) and accompanying that a move from primarily agricultural and informal sector labor to increasingly formal sector labor in which parenting and work lives are separated (United Nations 1991; Leslie and Paolisso 1989).

Previous studies have examined the interaction between whether or not women work in the formal sector in the United States, their well-being and that of any children they have. As others have noted, while contributing a great deal to our present understanding, existing research has been limited by insufficient detail about employment characteristics (Rogers, Parcel and Menaghan 1991), and in the women's and children's outcomes which have been examined (Wilson and Ellwood 1989; Parcel and Menaghan 1990; Earls and Carlson 1993). This chapter seeks to demonstrate why future studies need to focus further on the effects of specific working conditions on women's and children's health and welfare, and on parenting.

Changes in labor and family policy have not kept pace with the movement of mothers into the paid labor force. Labor policy discussions at times continue to focus solely on wages.[1] While wage policy is critically important, confining discussion of labor policy to wages leads to the omission of many issues central to women's ability to work and the quality of their working lives. This chapter will consider in greater depth two such issues: meeting a wide range of child care, and child health needs.

This chapter focuses on the barriers faced by women because in the overwhelming majority of cases they take more responsibility than men for child rearing[2] in the United States (Hochschild and Machung 1989). Men who take equal or more responsibility for rearing their children also face major hurdles in combining parenting and paid employment. These hurdles, some common, and some different from the ones women face, critically need to be addressed. They are large and deserve another paper.

Table 3-1 highlights examples of barriers faced by women parenting and working for pay. The table demonstrates the use of a conceptual framework which takes into account how dependent needs vary in character and with the dependent's age.

The Problem of Day Care, Preschool and After-school Care

One Case Example

In the United States, only a minority of preschool and school-age children (ages 5 to 14) are cared for by relatives (U.S. Bureau of the Census 1991). Thus, the availability of child care is critical to the lives of both mothers working in the paid labor force and their children.

Women's ability to bear and rear children while working at paid jobs depends on their being able to find child care. The availability of care for children is also a crucial foundation on which unemployed women must stand to find and keep jobs. For infants, toddlers and preschool children, this means finding full-day care. For school-age children, this means finding care during the before- and after-school hours, and on the non-school days during which the caretaking parent(s) work. While some middle- and all upper-class women have the resources to hire other women to provide one-on-one substitute care for their children, poor and most middle-class women do not.

Only 5 percent of women in medium and large firms worked for employers who provided child care benefits and only 9 percent received flexible benefits plans (U.S. Bureau of the Census 1991) in which they could put aside money for child care. The child care benefits provided by smaller firms, which have a disproportionate fraction of the lowest wage earners (Lichtenstein 1993), were far less than those provided by medium and large firms.

Poor women spend a disproportionately high fraction of their earnings on child care. Among those who had a family income of less

Table 3-1 Examples of Social Constraints on Women's Abilities to Both Work and Parent in the United States

Children's age	Predictable daily care needs	Unpredictable daily care needs	Predictable short term, episodic needs
0 to 5 year olds	Insufficient availability of day-care. Often unaffordable for the poor. Transportation to and from particularly problem for carless. Day-care hours not matching work hours particularly for entry level shift work of working poor. Particularly problematic for those with limited job choices.	No coverage for unexpected day-care closings or loss of day-care provider. For poor, no coverage for changes in eligibility for vouchers to assist in paying for care. No coverage for employer mandated overtime, work schedule or shift changes.	Difficulty in making preventive health care appointments, getting vaccinations, prenatal care, etc. Difficulty assisting in child's transition to day-care from the home which may include problems eating and sleeping, among others.
6 to 12 year olds	After-school care often unavailable. When available, often costly for poor. Often does not cover hours of shift work such as need for child care when regular work hours begin before school day.	No coverage for unexpected school or after-school care closings. No coverage for employer mandated overtime, work schedule or shift changes. Multiple absences from work may lead to job loss, particularly for low-skilled, or readily replaced workers.	Difficulty making preventive health care appointments, getting vaccinations, etc. Difficulty in meeting with teachers regarding child's progress and/or problems in school. (School problems serious for significant number of all children including one in seven children who do not complete high school.)
13 to 17 year olds	While adolescents can meet many of their own needs, the well being of adolescents may be significantly affected by extended unsupervised time, particularly if in high risk settings.	No coverage for unexpected school or after-school care closings. No coverage for employer mandated overtime, work schedule or shift changes. Multiple absences from work may lead to job loss, particularly for low-skilled, or readily replaced workers.	Difficulty making preventive health care appointments, getting vaccinations, reproductive health care, etc. Difficulty in meeting with teachers regarding child's progress and/or problems in school. (School problems serious for significant number of all children including one in seven children who do not complete high school.)

Table 3-1 Examples of Social Constraints on Women's Abilities to Both Work and Parent in the United States (cont.)

Children's age	Unpredictable short term, episodic needs	Predictable intermediate term, episodic needs	Unpredictable intermediate term, episodic needs
0 to 5 year olds	No provision for child care when child is ill. Difficulty in bringing child to health care provider in case of illness or injury.	Federal maternity leave passed only in 1993. Covers only half of working women. Leave is unpaid and thus will often be effectively inaccessible to poor. Restrictions on pregnant or reproductive age women holding certain jobs.	Federal legislation providing leave for major illness or injury of child passed only in 1993. Covers only half of working women. Leave is unpaid and thus inaccessible to most of poor.
6 to 12 year olds	No provision for school day or after-school care when child is ill. Difficulty in bringing child to health care provider in case of illness or injury.	Limited public activities, child care or supervision available for 25 percent of year when school is not in session.	See above.
13 to 17 year olds	No provision for care when child is ill. Difficulty in bringing child to health care provider in case of illness or injury.	Limited public activities, supervision or employment for adolescents for 25 percent of year when school is not in session.	See above.

than $15,000 per year, 20 percent of family income was spent on preschool child care alone. Women living below the poverty line spent 25 percent of their income on child care alone (U.S. Bureau of the Census 1991).

Millions of school-age children spend before- or after-school hours neither in an órganized program nor supervised by an adult at home. Seppanen et al. (1993) have examined before- and after-school programs in depth. Because of their low income, poor families have fewer choices in before- and after-school programs. In many areas, the demand for publicly-sponsored before- and after-school programs outstrips availability.

Finally, workers at or below the poverty line are far more likely than those in the middle- and upper-class to have to work on weekends when traditional day-care and after-school programs are unavailable, making child care harder to obtain (Hofferth 1992). Irregular work shifts make even informal, quality child care difficult to arrange.

The Problem of Children's Illnesses

A Second Case Example

A national survey estimated that, on average, each pre-school child has 11 days, and each school-age child has eight days, of restricted activity per year resulting from acute or chronic illness or injury. These figures average sick days for all children. The number of days of illness and injury associated with restricted activity is higher among poor children, whose parents often have less ability to take unpaid time from work and less flexible jobs. In families making less than $10,000 per year, each preschool child was estimated to have on average 14 days of illness and injury leading to restricted activity per year compared to 10 days for children in families whose income is over $20,000 (Adams and Benson 1991).

These figures may markedly under-represent the number of days of illness experienced by children because of the focus on "restricted" activity days. Families where all adults who care for the children work outside the home are frequently forced to send sick children to day-care, school, or before- and after-school care because of their inability to take time from work and lack of available sick child care. Such sick children may not have had their activity "restricted" despite the need. Furthermore, the averages cited probably underestimate the annual number of days of illness of children of working parents who are in day-care settings. Children in day-care have significantly higher rates of specific infectious diseases, though somewhat lower rates of injury (Thacker et al. 1992).

Employees' need for leave to care for sick children far outstrips available time. Among those working for small businesses (those with less than 100 employees), less than half receive any paid sick leave even for themselves. Among those who do receive sick leave, the average number of days received after one year's employment is 8.5 (Bureau of Labor Statistics 1992). Among those working for medium and large businesses, one-third of employees do not receive any paid sick leave. Among those who do receive paid sick leave, an average of 12.4 days of sick leave are available for the employee's own illness (Bureau of Labor Statistics 1993). In most workplaces, no sick days are given for care of a sick child. Only 5 percent of those working for the largest businesses receive any sick leave which is designed to be available for the illness of family members (Kane 1993).

Even if sick days meant for the employee's illnesses are used for the employee's children's illnesses, the 8.5 days available to those in small businesses who do receive paid sick leave would not cover the days needed on average for a single pre-school child, let alone the number of sick days predicted for a family of two or more children. The 12.4 days available on average to those in medium and large businesses who do receive sick leave would not cover the average number of days needed to care for even a single poor preschool child.

Not only do poor children have more days of illness but their families have fewer options for providing care. The working poor on average receive fewer days of paid sick leave. Those earning less than five dollars an hour are more likely to work in small firms with less sick leave (Lichtenstein 1993; Bureau of Labor Statistics 1992). Furthermore, within a given-size business, clerical, sales, production, and service employees receive fewer paid sick days than professional and technical employees (Bureau of Labor Statistics 1992; Bureau of Labor Statistics 1993). While high wage earners can pay for substitute care or afford to take unpaid leave when available, low wage earners can not. Furthermore, professionals can more often than factory workers make up hours by working evenings or on weekends, if alternate care can be arranged for their children at those times.

The Balance of the Burden

There is no doubt that the burden of social constraints on simultaneously rearing children and working for pay, borne by all women and their children, are borne disproportionately by the poor. Those parents in unskilled jobs are more readily replaced in an economy with high unemployment than those in skilled jobs and are thus in a more vulnerable position when work and family roles conflict. As discussed above, poor children have on average more days of restricted activity due to illness and injury, yet low wage workers have on average fewer paid sick days. The barriers to obtaining daily care for preschool and school-age children are also greater for the poor. As a consequence of the limited availability of publicly financed day care, before-school and after-school programs, those women who do not have family members who can provide care for their children while they work and who do not earn enough to afford private child care are left with few or no options.

The caretaking and illness barriers which are heightened by poverty are borne disproportionately by people of color. Significantly more black and Hispanic families than white families live in poverty. Fifteen percent of all white families earn less than $15,000 a year; 32 percent of Hispanic and 38 percent of black families do (U.S. Bureau of the Census 1991).

Furthermore, the problems associated with combining labor force participation and parenting are often greater for single-parent families, a disproportionate fraction of which are headed by women of color (U.S. Bureau of the Census 1991). In two-parent families, when mothers work outside the home, fathers partially compensate by spending more time with their children (Hofferth 1991; Nock and Kingston 1988). Single mothers often have little or no support from their children's father or the father's family. Fathers who live apart from their children usually do not help with child care; 56 percent of fathers who live apart from their children see their children less than once a month and 36 percent less than once a year (Goldstein 1993). In addition, the majority of single female headed families are poor; 56 percent have less than $15,000 a year in income (U.S. Bureau of the Census 1991).

Costs of the Conflict

The costs of these remediable conflicts between women's work and parenting roles are paid through threatened health, diminished welfare, and constrained reproductive and life options.

A few of these costs will be noted here. First, women who combine both employment and family responsibilities work more hours per year than either men who combine both or women who work solely in the labor force or in the home. As more women have entered the labor force over the past quarter-century, the total number of hours men spend working in the labor force and at home has declined and the number of hours women spend has risen (Fuchs 1988). As a result, women work the equivalent of at least two more full work weeks a year than men (Fuchs 1988; Hochschild and Machung 1989).

Second, a woman's wage decreases as the number of children she has increases, even when controlling for education and experience and looking at the wage changes as a woman goes from having zero to one and one to two children. Several researchers have argued that a causal relationship exists, with having children leading to lower wages (Fuchs 1988; Leslie and Paolisso 1989), and that the key variable responsible for the continued wage gap between men and women is women's greater responsibility for child care.

Among the unemployed, studies suggest that the inability to meet work and family obligations simultaneously has been an important barrier keeping single mothers from successfully finding and retaining permanent employment. The vast majority of families receiving Aid to Families with Dependent Children already leave welfare for work but most are unable to remain employed (Pavetti 1993). Welfare to work program evaluation studies have found that the difficulties single parents face in balancing multiple roles affect their ability to successfully keep a job (Hargreaves 1992; Cottingham and Ellwood 1989).

Third, women who combine work and family responsibilities have been found to be under greater stress than women who do not (Dowd 1989). Stress has been shown by previous research to be associated with higher rates of both physical and mental health problems.

Furthermore, as discussed in the previous sections, current barriers to women meeting dual paid work and parenting responsibilities may well lead to problems for the health and welfare of their children. These health problems are not inherent in maternal labor force participation, but are a consequence of current social constraints on carrying out multiple roles.

Different theories have been suggested to explain the variation in findings (Parcel and Menaghan 1990; Shreve 1987; Desai, Chase-Lansdale and Michael 1989; Hoffman 1989; Gottfried and Gottfried 1988; Galinsky 1986) measuring the overall impact of maternal labor force participation on children. These theories include, among others, that the direction of the effect depends on parental work hours and schedule, type of child care, level of support from family and friends, ages and gender of children, and maternal satisfaction with work (Goldstein 1993). These theories, if true, raise particular concern for poor families in which parents often work multiple jobs with extended hours, more frequently are required to work night shifts and weekend days, and have less choice about type of child care.

Barriers to women meeting dual employment and parenting responsibilities also contribute significantly to the perpetuation of poverty and gender inequality. In the United States, over one in five children live in poverty. Three out of five poor children live in single parent families, 85 percent of these in single mother households (U.S. Bureau of the Census 1991). As discussed earlier, barriers to entering the paid labor force and keeping jobs while caring for young children have contributed notably to families' inability to leave poverty.

Finally, studies have revealed how problems in the relationship between paid work and parenting perpetuate limited options for girls and women from one generation to the next. The options girls and women perceive as possible and the decisions they then go on to make are dramatically influenced by the decisions their mothers have made (Shreve 1987; Gerson 1985). Studies have shown that mothers' employment, type of work and attitude toward work significantly affect both their daughters' and sons' views of women's roles, reproductive and work choices (Shreve 1987). Job characteristics strongly influence whether women can choose to parent while working in the paid labor force and what decision they make if they have a choice (Gerson 1985).

The relationship between paid work and parenting and the results of that relationship vary significantly both between and among industrialized and developing countries. Still, in both settings, the need for quality affordable preschool, before- and after-school care and for time to meet children's health needs far outstrips their availability.

Joekes (1989) noted that, in many developing countries, barriers to fulfilling dual roles have led to women having fewer job opportunities and persistently lower wages just as they have in industrialized countries. As an example of the impact on children, she cited a Korean study which found that one in six mothers working in an urban area had to leave their preschool children alone while at work. In other settings, daughters in poor families were kept out of school by necessity to care for young children, effectively furthering gender and class inequality in the next generation.

In both industrialized and developing countries, the gap between what child care is needed and what is available has had a marked impact on the work and reproductive lives of women, the lives of children, and the perpetuation of poverty and gender inequality.

Vision for a Different Future

Much of previous reproductive research has focused on technological barriers to the prevention of pregnancy. While this research is important, we need to ensure that future research addresses: constraints on women's ability *to bear and rear* children as well as to prevent and terminate pregnancy, and social as well as technologic constraints. To break down current barriers to women combining employment, childbearing and child rearing, we need to accept as a society that the majority of mothers work in the labor force, to further men's equal responsibility as parents, to pay attention to the relationship between a parent's paid work and reproductive options, and to address in detail the obstacles that keep women and men from flourishing in these dual roles.

Some of the obstacles may be eradicated only through changes in the workplace or in the community, while others may be addressed in either location. Programs such as preschool child care can be provided either at the workplace or in the community at large. Examples of solutions which could be carried out in the community include the provision of health care, educational meetings and social services, at sites and hours that are accessible to working parents. Examples of the initiatives that workplaces could take are making all sick leave available for use when either an employee or the employee's dependents are ill, making the amount of sick leave reflect real individual and family needs, and making personal leave divisible for meeting needs that can only be addressed during work hours.

While at present the highest costs of the conflicts between paid employment and parenting are borne by women and children, society and employers also pay the price of not addressing the conflicts. Because of this, some programs that employers initiate may pay for themselves through increased employee productivity, decreased absences and turnover, and decreased recruitment and training costs. Where this is not the case, it is important that programs be socially financed, and not just nationally mandated, so that industries will not discriminate in hiring against those who will use the programs. Where programs can be offered on a community basis, the financing mechanisms may be straightforward. Government instead of employer provision of day care, before- and after-school programs is one example. Where the program needs to be administered at the workplace, mechanisms for cost-sharing, while somewhat more complex, are still available. Providing paid sick leave through a government or other insurance program, such as that used to finance national health insurance elsewhere, would be one potential example.

Policies should apply equally to female and male employees, whether they treat the availability of sick leave to care for ill dependents or parental leave. Policies that only enable employed women to care for children engender sex stereotyped roles outside the workplace. In addition, single gender policies such as maternity leave encourage discrimination in the workplace. Mexico passed progressive legislation which provides, in theory, for maternity leave for all jobs covered by social security. In practice, many women have been required to bring evidence of laboratory tests documenting that they are not pregnant before being hired (Miranda 1993). In the United States, where national maternity legislation has been far less progressive, companies with maternity leave policies have applied the policies unequally to different categories of employees and have often discouraged women from bearing and rearing children while holding certain positions.

The limited ways available for employed parents to meet well child care and sick child care needs are only two examples of the ways in which constraints borne by employed women affect their reproductive options. The effect of these constraints is worse for women living in poverty. Women living in poverty more frequently have to work on weekends, evenings and nights when less child care is available. Children living in poverty spend more days sick or injured, yet their parents have fewer days of paid leave from work and unpaid leave is less affordable to them. These problems need to be addressed in labor policy, but they also need to be addressed in reproductive health policy. We will only begin to truly address women's reproductive needs when we approach reproductive health as a life long process, one that not only begins before the pregnancy but that continues after.

Acknowledgements

I would like to thank Laura Miranda for bringing a wealth of knowledge about the comparative situation in Mexico, Meg Hargreaves for her ever-present help thinking about conditions in the United States, and Rachel Imes and Brian Egleston for their persistently patient help in preparing the manuscript. I am forever grateful for the help of Tim Brewer and many friends at the Longwood Medical Area Child Care Center in balancing my writing and mothering and the directness and laughter of Ben and Jeremy Heymann Brewer.

Notes

1 This paper will use and try to demonstrate the value of a broader definition of labor policy which includes work conditions which affect the lives of employees with caretaking responsibilities. These conditions include, among many others, work schedules, variability, reliability, paid leave and child care.

2 While they are not expressly the subject of this chapter, as this book focuses on reproductive options and constraints, it is crucial to recognize that many barriers similar to those discussed in this chapter are also faced by women who care for disabled or elderly relatives.

References

Adams, P.F., and V. Benson. 1991. Current estimates from the National Health Interview Survey. National Center for Health Statistics. *Vital Health Statistics* 10 (181).

Cottingham, P.H., and D.T. Ellwood, eds. 1989. *Welfare policy for the 1990s.* Cambridge: Harvard University Press.

Desai, S., P.L. Chase-Lansdale, and R.T. Michael. 1989. Mother or market? Effects of maternal employment on the intellectual ability of 4-year-old children. *Demography* 26(4):545–561.

Dowd, N.E. 1989. Work and family: The gender paradox and the limitations of discrimination analysis in restructuring the workplace. Voices of Experience: New Responses to Gender.

Discourse. *Harvard Civil Rights-Civil Liberties Law Review* 24(1):79–172.

Earls, F., and M. Carlson. 1993. Towards sustainable development for American families. *Daedalus* 122(1):93–122.

Fuchs, V.R. 1988. *Women's quest for economic equality.* Cambridge: Harvard University Press.

Galinsky, E. 1986. Family life and corporate policies. In *In support of families,* ed. M.W. Yogman and T.B. Brazelton. Cambridge: Harvard University Press.

Gerson, K. 1985. *Hard choices: How women decide about work, career, and motherhood.* Berkeley, Calif.: University of California Press.

Goldstein, N. 1993. Are changes in work and family harming children? Report to the Carnegie Corporation Task Force on Meeting the Needs of Young Children.

Gottfried, A.E., and A.W. Gottfried, eds. 1988. *Maternal employment and children's development: Longitudinal research.* New York: Plenum Press.

Hargreaves, M. 1992. *New York Child Assistance Program: Interim report on implementation.* Cambridge, Mass.: Abt Associates.

Hochschild, A., and A. Machung. 1990. *The second shift.* New York: Avon Books.

Hofferth, S.L. 1991. Making time for children: Family decisions about employment and child care. Paper presented at the Annual Meeting of the Population Association of America.

——. 1992. At the margin: Managing work and family life at the poverty line. Paper presented at the Annual Meeting of the American Sociological Association.

Hoffman, L.W. 1989. Effects of maternal employment in the two-parent family. *American Psychologist* 44(2):283–292.

Joekes, S. 1989. Women's work and social support for child care in the third world. In *Women, work, and child welfare in the Third World,* ed. J. Leslie and M. Paolisso. 1989. AAAS Selected Symposium no. 110. Boulder, Colo.: Westview Press.

Kane, L. 1993. Unpublished data. Families and Work Institute. New York.

Kanter, R.M. 1989. *When giants learn to dance.* New York: Simon and Schuster.

Leslie, J., and M. Paolisso, eds. 1989. *Women, work, and child welfare in the third world.* AAAS Selected Symposium no. 110. Boulder, Colo.: Westview Press.

Lichtenstein, J. 1993. Unpublished data. U.S. Small Business Administration. Washington, D.C.

Miranda, L. 1993. The reproductive choice of Mexican women. Presentation prepared for Reproductive Options and Constraints Authors' Workshop, Harvard Center for Population and Development Studies, Cambridge, Mass.

Nock, S.L., and A.W. Kingston. 1988. Time with children: The impact of couples' work-time commitments. *Social Forces* 67(1):59–85.

Parcel, T.L., and E.G. Menaghan. 1990. Maternal working conditions and children's verbal facility: Studying the intergenerational transmission of inequality from mothers to young children. *Social Psychology Quarterly* 53(2):132–147.

Pavetti, L.A. 1993. The dynamics of welfare and work: Exploring the process by which women work their way off welfare. Malcolm Wiener Center for Social Policy Working Papers, Dissertation Series #D-93-1.

Rogers, S.L., T.L. Parcel, and E.G. Menaghan. 1991. The effects of maternal working conditions and mastery on child behavior problems: Studying the intergenerational transmission of social control. *Journal of Health and Social Behavior* 32(2):145–164.

Seppanen, P.S., J.M. Love, D.K. deVries, and L. Berstein. 1993. *National study of before- and after-school programs.* Portsmouth: REC Research Corporation.

Shreve, A. 1987. *Remaking motherhood: How working mothers are shaping our children's future.* New York: Viking.

Thacker, S.B., D.G. Addiss, R.A. Goodman, B.R. Holloway, and H.C. Spencer. 1992. Infectious diseases and injuries in child day care: Opportunities for healthier children. *Journal of the American Medical Association* 268(13):1720–1726.

United Nations. 1991. *The world's women: Trends and statistics, 1970–1990.* New York.

U.S. Bureau of the Census. 1991. *Statistical abstract of the United States: 1991.* 111th ed. Washington, D.C: General Printing Office.

U.S. Department of Labor, Bureau of Labor Statistics. 1993. *Employee benefits in medium and large firms, 1991.* Bulletin 2422. Washington, D.C.

———. 1992. *Employee benefits in small private establishments, 1990.* Washington, D.C.

Wilson, J.B., and D.T. Ellwood. 1989. Welfare to work through the eyes of children: The impact on children of parental movement from AFDC to employment. Paper presented at the Forum on Children and the Family Support Act, National Academy of Sciences.

4

Religious Doctrine, State Ideology, and Reproductive Options in Islam

by Carla Makhlouf Obermeyer

This chapter assesses the compatibility of Islam with ideas of reproductive choice through an examination of Islam's doctrinal principles and their interpretations, and reviews available indicators of reproductive health in countries of the Middle East as a measure of reproductive choice. It argues that while the doctrine has a degree of flexibility on issues of reproduction, the political context is a key factor for understanding the way in which religious doctrine is interpreted. The role of the state in shaping women's options through interpretations of religious doctrine is illustrated through a discussion of the dramatic reversals in Iran's population policy.

Reproductive Choice in the Islamic Doctrine

From a feminist "human rights" perspective, the notion of reproductive choice implies two basic principles. The first is autonomy, which means that a woman can make decisions in matters of reproduction, and has access to the information and services that make her choice possible; this autonomy in turn implies a set of other rights for her as an adult individual and as a citizen. The second principle is the notion that reproductive health is an integral part of a woman's life, and hence is shaped not only by medical conditions, but also by social forces and power relationships that range from the level of the family to that of international institutions (Freedman and Isaacs 1993).

Before assessing the extent to which these preconditions can be fulfilled in the context of Islam, two points must be noted. First, there is a tension in Islamic doctrine between the egalitarian view that believers are judged solely according to merit, and the inegalitarian elements that define different roles for men and women. The second point that emerges from even a cursory examination of women's autonomy is the tremendous complexity and diversity that is found in the Muslim world. Given that in all Muslim countries different schools of jurisprudence coexist alongside civil codes derived from European legal systems, and even with customary laws that are often survivals of a pre-Islamic past, the legal dimension of women's status is shaped by elements that are sometimes contradictory. Moreover, the variability in levels of socio-economic development in Muslim countries generates great discrepancies in the social reality of women's autonomy, both between countries and, within the same country, between different sectors of the population. The tension in the doctrine and the variability in the social context are crucial for a balanced assessment of the situation, yet they are often ignored in discussions of women's status; the prevalent view is that Islam defines a subordinate role for women and hence is at the root of the unfavorable indicators of women's reproduction and health. It is argued here that the principles of Islam lend themselves to different interpretations and that the reality of reproductive choice in the region varies both between countries and over time.

Islamic law (*shari'a*) is based on the Qur'an, the *hadith* (the collected sayings of the Prophet Muhammad), and the *sunna* (the Prophet's biography). In deriving *shari'a*, the various schools of jurisprudence differ in two areas, the extent to which they allow *ijtihad* (the formulation of independent legal judgement) and the bases upon which such judgement can be developed. With respect to women's status, the ambiguity of the religious texts makes the process of interpretation crucial, but unlike Christianity, Islam does not have a hierarchically organized clergy. Thus, there is no central, authoritative interpretation of religious doctrine; instead, there are decentralized and sometimes dissimilar codes embodied in the various schools of law and religious sects. Islamic doctrine is ambivalent with regard to women's status because, while the sacred texts emphasize the equality of all believers before God, they also clearly differentiate between the rights and duties of men and women. As a result, the same texts can be used to legitimate divergent views. A literal interpretation could provide the basis for justifying women's subordinate position, while reformers have, at different periods in Islamic history, argued that the inegalitarian elements in Islam reflect the temporal context in which the religion emerged, were not intended to be immutable, and should be reinterpreted in light of contemporary conditions (Ahmed 1992).

Traditional interpretations emphasize those passages in the Qur'an and *hadith* that give women a lower valuation than men, and use them to define a distinctly subordinate social role for women. The statements in the religious texts that grant women the right to manage their own property and to conduct their business receive little attention, compared to those that value female testimony in court as worth half that of a man, and allot her a share of inheritance half the size of that of a man. In this tradition, women's options are limited to their domestic role and they have little freedom of choice in matters of marriage, divorce, and the custody of their children. Marriage is contracted by a woman's legal guardian, her consent being inferred rather than formally sought, and therefore early marriage and forced unions are not regarded as necessarily unethical, as they would be from a women's rights perspective. Husbands are entitled to four wives and can repudiate their wives by uttering the divorce formula, whereas women must go through an often difficult procedure if they wish to obtain a divorce. Fathers have custody of their children after infancy, while women have no grounds for claiming custody. And although the religious sources provide no clear rules on the degree to which women should have access to equal education and employment, conservatives have favored sexual segregation in schools and opposed women's work outside the home (Rahman 1980).

Reformists and feminists have contested this scriptural and "establishment" version of *shari'a*. Using the many instances in the Qur'an and *hadith* where no difference is made between believers, and the historical evidence on the status of women in the early decades of Islam, they argue that there is an egalitarian ethos in Islam that was historically distorted by patriarchal forces (Ahmed 1986, 1992). In their view, the religious texts can and should be interpreted in a more egalitarian manner. This perspective would be in harmony with the Western feminist notion of women's reproductive choice, and in fact, several aspects of Islamic doctrine are clearly compatible with such an interpretation.

A number of statements in the scriptures stress the idea that God does not wish to burden man, and suggest that "quality" is as important as "quantity" in children. In addition, there is a generally positive attitude in Islam towards sex in marriage, and a clear recognition of a woman's right to sexual enjoyment. With respect to family planning in particular, the texts do not present a major obstacle: little mention is made of contraception, except in the famous *hadith* where the Prophet condones the use of *coitus interruptus* (Omran 1992). By analogy, this permissive stance has been taken to apply to all non-terminal methods of contraception. The permissibility of abortion has been the subject of debate, because while most schools of law agree that abortion is acceptable before ensoulment and unacceptable afterwards, the question of when ensoulment takes place has been as difficult to resolve as it has in other theological traditions. With the exception of the Maliki school of jurisprudence, it is generally agreed that ensoulment, indicated by quickening, happens near the end of the first trimester, and consequently abortions are allowed until that point. Sterilization poses a greater difficulty, because the finality of the method is seen as interfering with divine will, and therefore Muslim authorities have not condoned its use (Omran 1992).

In sum, from the point of view of Islamic doctrine, it is possible to take two very different positions on reproductive choice: the more traditional one gives women very little freedom to make decisions that bear on reproduction; the second, increasingly espoused by Muslim reformists and feminists, argues that the constraints on reproductive choice that exist in Muslim countries are not inherently Islamic, and that the egalitarian elements in the sacred texts should be the guide to a reinterpretation of the doctrine that would be fully compatible with ideas of human rights and reproductive choice.

Reproductive Choice in Countries of the Middle East

To obtain a general view of reproductive choice in countries of the Middle East, I have summarized data on indicators of women's status and reproductive health in Table 4-1. These data are imperfect proxies for choice; women's status indicators are a crude measure of women's ability to make informed decisions, and indicators of reproductive health provide a rough idea of the outcomes of such decisions (or lack thereof). Taken together, they suggest that the constraints are considerable. Statistics showing a lower level of educational achievement for women compared to men, and figures showing low levels of labor force participation for women imply a low degree of autonomy. Indicators of reproductive behavior — the high total fertility rate, and the relatively low percentage of women using contraceptive methods — are consistent with available data on the high frequency of early marriage and the gap between stated fertility preferences and observed fertility levels (Farid 1987). They suggest that many women are not in a position to formulate and achieve clear reproductive goals. Measures of access to health care (percentage of the population with access to health care, percentage of births attended by trained personnel) show substantial gaps in coverage in some countries, and estimates of maternal mortality (Kane et al. 1991; Fortney et al. 1986) indicate that under conditions of difficult access, women are especially vulnerable.

These adverse outcomes have been attributed to the ideology of male dominance and son preference in the culture,[1] the limitations on the free mixing of the sexes,[2] the custom of arranged marriages, the male privileges of repudiation and multiple wives,[3] the pressures to bear children, and the low priority accorded to women's health and nutrition.[4] In seeking a general explanation for these patterns, it is often argued that the association between Islam, women's status, and demographic outcomes is inevitably unfavorable, and this notion seems to fit with popular images of the plight of women in the Middle East (and also with the anxieties generated in the West by militant Islam). One of the major obstacles to a balanced assessment of reproductive choice and its health consequences has been the paucity of data on reproductive health in the Middle East. As in other regions of the world, a great deal of attention has been devoted to contraceptive surveys of attitudes and practices, but when we try to consider reproductive health in a comprehensive manner, the evidence is very sketchy, and we often have to make do with imperfect proxies. Although there have been some studies focusing on indicators of women's status and health outcomes (Tekce and Shorter 1984; Doan and Bisharat 1990), most have been limited to the topic of child survival, and we know very little about the state of reproductive health in relation to women's status.[5] Statistics for the region as a whole are of limited use in linking women's health and fertility outcomes to the degree of reproductive choice in each country context. Because they measure outcomes, these statistics do not tell us whether the source of change is a result of improvements in the reproductive options that are open to women, such as increased autonomy, or improved access to health services and to health information. Because they are aggregates at the state level, these measures cannot capture important variations within countries between the elites and the less privileged segments of the population. It is possible, however, to develop a broad view of the extent to which the situation has changed over the last few decades, and some of these trends have been included in Table 4-1.

Table 4-1 Selected Indicators of Reproductive Choice in the Middle East

| | Education | | | | | | Employment | |
| | Primary School Enrollment | | | Secondary School Enrollment | | | | |
	percent of age group	Females per 100 males 1989	increase 1965-1989 (%)	percent of age group	Females per 100 males 1989	increase 1965-1989 (%)	Female labor force participation (%)	Change in preceding 25-30 years (%)
Column #	1	2	3	4	5	6	7	8
Algeria	94	81	31	61	77	71	4.3	87
Bahrain							10.8	300
Egypt	97	81	27	81	77	88	5.6	44
Iran	109	84	83	53	71	61	10.7	51
Iraq	96	79	88	47	63	117	11.8	337
Jordan	–	93	29	–	95	138	4.8	55
Kuwait	100	96	26	90	92	46	12.8	137
Lebanon	–	–	–	–	–	–	16.2	86
Libya	–	–	–	–	–	–	4.6	35
Mauritania	51	69	123	16	45	309	13.4	-12
Morocco	68	65	55	36	68	119	12.9	105
Oman	102	88	–	48	75	–	4.9	63
Quatar	–	–	–	–	–	–	8.8	138
Saudi Arabia	76	84	190	46	74	825	4.6	84
Somalia	–	–	–	–	–	–	32.1	-19
Sudan	–	–	–	–	–	–	14.1	-1
Syria	108	87	85	54	71	154	8.5	60
Tunisia	115	83	60	44	75	103	15.8	236
Turkey	112	89	35	51	62	68	30.1	-21
United Arab Emirates	111	93	–	64	102	–	9.7	137
Yemen, YAR (North)	–	–	–	–	–	–	–	–
Yemen, PDRY (South)	–	–	–	–	–	–	–	–

Sources: Columns 1, 2, 3, 4, 5, 6: World Bank, 1992. Columns 7 and 8, World Bank, 1991a.

Table 4-1 Selected Indicators of Reproductive Choice in the Middle East

Column #	Total Fertility Rate		Contraceptive Use (%)	Health Care		Mortality		
	1985-90	% Decline 1950-1990		Population with access to health care (%)	Births attended by medical personnel (%)	Female Life expectancy at birth*		Maternal mortality rate (estimates)
						1950-55	1985-90	
Column #	*9*	*10*	*11*	*12*	*13*	*14*	*15*	*16*
Algeria	5.4	26	36	88	85	44.2	65.0	140
Bahrain	4.1	41	–	100	98	52.5	72.9	8
Egypt	4.5	32	38	–	24	43.6	60.3	65
Iran	5.2	27	23	80	–	46.1	65.5	120
Iraq	6.4	11	14	93	50	44.9	64.8	120
Jordan	6.2	16	26	97	75	44.3	67.8	48
Kuwait	3.9	46	35	100	99	57.5	75.4	2
Lebanon	3.8	33	53	–	88	57.7	67.0	
Libya	6.9	0	<15	–	76	43.9	62.5	80
Mauritania	6.5	0	1	30	23	34.5	47.6	
Morocco	4.8	33	36	70	26	43.9	62.5	300
Oman	7.2	0	–	91	60	37.0	65.8	
Qatar	5.6	20	–	–	90	49.3	71.8	
Saudi Arabia	7.2	0	<15	97	78	40.7	65.2	
Somalia	6.6	0	2	27	2	34.5	46.6	1100
Sudan	6.4	4	5	51	20	38.3	51.0	550
Syria	6.8	4	20	76	37	47.2	66.9	140
Tunisia	4.1	41	50	90	60	45.1	66.4	50
Turkey	3.7	46	63	–	78	45.2	65.8	150
United Arab Emirates	4.8	31	31	90	96	49.3	72.9	
Yemen, YAR (North)	8.0	-8	1	35	12	32.5	50	
Yemen, PDRY (South)	6.7	4	<15	30	10	33.9	52.4	

*Percent of the population that can reach appropriate health services by local transportation in no more than one hour.

Sources: Columns 9 and 10, United Nations, 1991. Column 11: Figures for Bahrain, Egypt, Morocco, Oman, Qatar, Tunisia, and YAR are from World Bank, 1991b; figures for Algeria, Kuwait, Lybia, Saudia Arabia, UAE and PDYR are from Population Crisis Commitee, 1990; figures for Iraq, Jordan, Lebanon, Mauritania, Sudan and Syria are from United Nations, 1989; figure for Somalia is from World Bank 1989; figure for Turkey is from World Bank 1992; figure for Iran is from UNICEF, 1992. Column 12: UNICEF, 1990. Column 13: World Bank, 1991. Columns 14 and 15: United Nations 1991. Column 16, UNICEF, 1992; figures for Bahrain, Egypt and Kuwait are from United Nations, 1992.

It is clear from these data that there have been substantial changes over the last four decades. School enrollment in the region as a whole has increased very rapidly, and currently, more than four-fifths of all school-age girls are in primary school, up from an average of 55 percent just two decades ago. The ratio of females to males is around 90 percent for primary education, which represents a substantial increase in all countries. Secondary education lags behind, but the increase in the last 25 years has been very rapid. Employment statistics must be interpreted with caution because they exclude the informal sector, where women are especially active, but they also show very large increases in the last three decades. Fertility levels, which had remained high until recently, have begun to decrease in all countries, with declines of 25 percent or more in Algeria, Egypt, Iran, Jordan, Lebanon, Morocco, Turkey, and the Gulf countries corresponding to increases in contraceptive use. Women's life expectancies show major increases in all countries of the region, probably reflecting improved nutrition and better access to health care. In the region as a whole, females have on average a two-year advantage in life expectancy compared to males, a situation which represents a reversal of previous female disadvantage.[6] However, it is also clear that there are great disparities between countries with large populations of "rural poor" and the more affluent countries.

Both the rapid changes and the diversity of indicators are relevant to the question of the constraints imposed by Islam; the differences in the levels and trends cannot be accounted for with reference to Islamic doctrine. Rather than a simplistic model of the effect of religion on women's status and demographic outcomes — what I have elsewhere referred to as "fateful triangle thinking" — I argue here that the impact of Islam on women's options is a function of the political context in which the religious doctrine is interpreted (Obermeyer 1992). The relative flexibility of the texts means that they can be used by the groups in power, and those in the opposition, to legitimate different positions on women and population issues; indeed, Islamic doctrine has been used to justify contradictory policies.

The Reversals in Iran's Population Policies

Nowhere is the contrast between population policies adopted at different times in the same country more apparent than in Iran, where in the course of the 20th century, issues related to women have been affected by political struggles at the local, national and international levels. From the reign of the shahs to the post-Khomeini era, changing visions of the social order have been reflected in the conflicting views of women's roles.[7] The links between state goals, gender issues, and reproduction are dramatically illustrated in the reversals of policy that took place several times during a relatively short time period.

Early in this century, Reza Khan attempted unsuccessfully to redefine the role of women and initiate "modernizing" reforms by raising the minimum age at marriage to 14 years for girls, passing a compulsory education act, and forcing women to abandon the veil. These policies were not implemented, and 40 years later, another attempt at changing women's status was made by the last Shah. The Iranian Family Protection Act aimed at limiting the practice of polygyny; extending to women the right to file for divorce; entitling women to child support and custody rights in the event of a divorce; raising the minimum age at marriage to 18; and liberalizing abortion (Momeni 1981). Socioeconomic changes in Iran and the family planning program implemented during this period supported the onset of fertility decline, which was associated with a rise in the mean age at marriage, and modest rises in education and employment levels for women (Aghajanian 1991). Fertility decline, however, was limited to the urban centers and to the privileged segments of the society; most of the population considered the Shah's policies little more than the centralizing efforts of an autocratic ruler. A growing opposition rejected the Shah's reforms as un-Islamic, and advocated returning to a stricter interpretation of the scriptures concerning the status of women.

With the 1979 Revolution, a major reversal of policy occurred. The Islamic Republic did not formulate a population policy of its own, rejecting family planning programs as an imperialist mechanism, and considering increases in the population to be increases in the strength of the Muslim nation. Some of the policies of the Republic resulted in a curtailment of women's choices, but the redefinition of women's place in post-revolutionary Iran is fraught with contradictions, both because of the ambivalence of the leaders toward the issue of women, and because of the mixed results of the policies on the status of women and on reproductive choice. While the Shah was known to be personally anti-feminist, he embarked on a program of reforms to raise women's status. By contrast, Khomeini, who called for women's participation in politics and took pride in the "referendum of the streets" which led to the overthrow of the Shah's regime (Betteridge 1983), simultaneously reversed the reforms that gave women a greater say in matters of divorce and fertility control, and enacted legislation to promote women's domestic roles.

The policies of post-Revolutionary Iran were undoubtedly pro-natalist. The family planning program of the former regime was abandoned, abortion and sterilization were outlawed, the minimum legal age at marriage was reduced, and the labor force participation of women stagnated. The regime's pro-natalist orientation was strengthened by the war with Iraq, which started soon after the revolution, and resulted in heavy casualties. Women were exhorted to marry and bear children, the widowed and divorced were urged to remarry.[8] As a result of these forces, the fertility transition appeared to stall (Aghajanian 1991). Between 1976 and 1986 there was a reversal of the trend toward fertility decline and the total fertility rate increased from 6.3 to 7.0 children.[9] While contraceptives remained available in some health clinics and pharmacies, supplies were unreliable, and by 1986, the proportion of married women who were covered by the family planning services of the Ministry of Health had dropped to 6 percent, compared to 23 percent in 1977.[10] The population as a whole grew by 3.9 percent annually during this decade, and when the 1986 census revealed that the population of Iran had reached nearly 50 million, the leadership considered this growth to be a blessing for the *'umma* (community of believers), and a sign of the success of the Revolution. The regime justified its position on women with reference to the Koran and *hadith*, and as a return to the true Islam. The retrenchment of women's roles and the increase in the population were endowed with a special significance, linking political victory with religious fervor and the control over females. Through these transformations, the *chador* (veil) came to embody the paradoxes inherent in women's status: while it would, from a human rights perspective, be considered an impediment to liberty, it was in fact used as a symbol of the struggle for liberation against an oppressive regime. In the early months of the Revolution, the *chador* was one of the key symbols of the opposition. Later however, partly as a result of the zeal of the Revolutionary guards in enforcing modest clothing for women, the *chador* became again a sign of the pressures on women, and a constraint on their freedom.

In the late 1980s, the pro-natalism of the regime was tempered by the realities of war and deteriorating economic conditions. The damages resulting from the war with Iraq, the disastrous effects of the economic embargo, the falling price of oil, the flight of capital, and poor management (Amirahmadi 1988) created a major dilemma for the political leadership: how could they provide the basic necessities to citizens, as granted in the constitution of the Islamic Republic, when the rapidly increasing population and the stagnating economy were making this task impossible? Within three years, there was a radical reversal of the population policy. At the end of the war with Iraq in 1989, the Islamic Consultative Assembly re-evaluated its ideological stance with respect to population issues and issued a National Birth Control Policy to reduce population and increase contraceptive coverage. Parallel to changes in the population field, the new policy sought to promote women's education and participation in the socioeconomic management of family and society.

Strikingly, these liberal policies are justified with reference to the Islamic tradition, as were the constraints imposed on women in the early phases of the revolution. The religious leaders agree that limiting births is permissible, and that modern family planning methods are acceptable. The new population policy provides contraceptives and has abrogated the earlier pro-natalist legislation. The family planning program now provides a variety of means of contraception at no or very low cost; before the Revolution, by contrast, the Pill was virtually the only birth control method available. Since 1989, tubal ligations, which had been legalized in 1976, but were prohibited by the Revolution, are once again available, and abortions are no longer strictly forbidden as they were in the early years following the Revolution.

The media strategy adopted by the regime is a mixture of traditional and modern means of communication; radio and television spots, newspaper reports, and Friday prayer speeches given by religious leaders are now used to persuade the public of the need for family planning. The promotion of breastfeeding also uses traditional Qur'anic teachings as well as posters in health clinics, and the justifications for the recommended behaviors draw on both health reasons and quotations from the Qur'an, sometimes paraphrasing well-known citations. There are debates about overpopulation on national television, and research on population issues is encouraged. In other words, the government is now keenly aware of the economic consequences of population growth, and has apparently decided that focusing on overpopulation as the source of the country's problems may be politically useful to deflect some of the dissatisfaction with the economic situation.

The participation of women in the "management of the family and society" receives careful attention in government policies, although there are no clear strategies to improve women's education and "socioeconomic participation." Indicators of women's status reflect this ambivalence. Some indicators of women's status show little improvement, such as female employment, which had never exceeded 8 percent and dropped to 4 percent in 1986 (Mohajerani 1989). The enforcement of female veiling, which received extensive coverage in the western media, is also taken to indicate the repressiveness of the regime, especially in its "zealous" phase. Other indicators show clear improvements. There have been some legal reforms to protect women against the abuses of Islamic family law, largely as a result of the activities of women's groups working within the Islamic framework. There have also been increases in the education of girls. Primary school enrollment became universal in 1986; for secondary education, the proportion of girls increased to 38 percent in 1986. Female life expectancy, which in 1962 was at 52 years, the same level as male life expectancy, increased to 64 years in 1987, two years more than males (World Bank 1989). The mean age at marriage increased from 19.7 years in 1976 to 20.2 years in 1986 (Aghajanian 1991). The primary health care program has been successful in reducing both infant and maternal mortality, partially as a result of the expansion of the number of health personnel and facilities, the incorporation of family planning into health clinics, and the inclusion of female personnel among health workers. Overall, although they have been limited by the severe strain on the resources for health and education, there have been some improvements in women's reproductive choices, and paradoxically, these improvements have taken place under the "Islamist" revolution. It is somewhat ironic that the measures liberalizing women's reproductive options, which had been rejected because they were seen as part of the Shah's misguided modernization scheme, are now reinstated because they were necessary for the realization of the goals of the Islamic Republic.

State, Gender and Reproduction

The case of Iran clearly illustrates the many paradoxes that exist in the link between the status of women and the state policies that define it. The conditions that affect reproductive choice in the Middle East reflect fluctuations in the economic, political, and legal spheres. Perhaps to a greater extent than in other societies, issues related to women and reproduction are often the arena in which conflicting views of the social order are played out. This is especially striking when groups who oppose the state, colonial powers, or "the West" symbolize their opposition dramatically, through the veiling of Muslim women (Ahmed 1992).

Using gender roles as symbols for political positions, however, puts the topic of reproductive choice in the middle of local and international debates. The real difficulty of understanding women's status in its complexity is compounded by the confrontation between western feminists, who see Islam as incompatible with human rights, and conservative Muslims, who respond that Western notions of rights are inapplicable to their societies (Sha'rawi 1982; Stowasser 1987a and b; Tabandeh 1970). Thus, to make any headway, it is important that the various dimensions of reproductive choice — the doctrinal interpretation of Islam, the political struggles at the national and international levels, and the health outcomes — be conceptually separated. Historical studies indicate that the emergence and success of Islam were intricately linked to the kinship system of seventh century Arabia which, like all traditional systems, clearly differentiated the roles of men and women. An Islamic feminist perspective would argue that this inegalitarianism is not inherent to Islam but a function of temporal forces. That even an Islamic fundamentalist regime such as Iran's can come — however grudgingly — to support reforms that result in improvements of women's options, and can justify its position with reference to Islamic texts, clearly demonstrates the flexibility of the doctrine. And while it is true that a return to a literal interpretation of the scriptures is likely to have adverse implications for women's choices, it cannot be assumed that all the groups labeled "fundamentalist" advocate a curtailment of all freedoms for women. There may be greater variability than first appears, and even radical views can be tempered by practical realities.

What we do not clearly understand is how changes in ideology affect the choices that women make — or do not make — and how alternatives are translated into the behaviors of individual women. Even more relevant to our present discussion is the question of whether changes in gender roles are the pathway through which political values are translated into reproductive outcomes, and to what extent improvements in reproductive health can take place despite an inegalitarian ideology. From a policy point of view, there are few guidelines to help weigh the relative advantages of policies aimed at changing women's status as compared to those aimed at improving health and family planning services. Further research is needed to address the question of whether the obstacles to a better reproductive health are largely the outcomes of gender inequalities as such, or whether they are more general consequences of socioeconomic conditions.

Most generally, many of the changes now under way in the area of reproduction have to do with changing societal notions of relations between the sexes and redefinition of women's roles. Whether they are established by the Islamic tradition, shaped by the increasing levels of schooling, or influenced by the messages of the media, images of women and the roles that they define are powerful determinants of the policies of governments, the strategies of groups, and the attitudes and behaviors of individuals. Understanding the ideological dynamics that shape them could be key in understanding the improvements or setbacks in reproductive options for women.

Notes

1 For a good summary of recent data on sex differences of survival in the Arab world, see UNICEF (1990b).

2 Until the 1970s, most of the literature on modesty and veiling in Islamic culture was written from the "outsider" perspective of male travelers or researchers, and it emphasized the subordination of women. Studies in the last two decades, many of them carried out by women, have provided a more balanced view of patterns of seclusion (see reviews by Abu-Lughod 1989; Rassam 1984; Bates and Rassam 1983).

3 Much has been written on patterns of marriage in Islam, and the literature has emphasized repudiation and polygyny as practices that represent a constant threat to women, result in a complete loss of autonomy, and are at the root of high fertility and mortality. For a critique of some of the simplistic arguments on this subject, see Obermeyer 1992.

4 See, for example, Caldwell 1986. One of the women's health issues that has received the most attention is that of female circumcision because it seems to epitomize the subjugation of women's welfare to "cultural" constraints. Although much has been written on this topic, most of it is based on very little data and many misconceptions (see the recent debate in *Medical Anthropological Quarterly* 1991).

5 One exception is a project which carefully documents reproductive morbidity in Egypt, and attempts to put health outcomes in the context of women's lives (Zurayk et al. 1993; Khattab 1992).

6 In the 1950s, there were indications of higher female mortality in several countries of the Middle East, as well as some research documenting differential treatment of children by sex (Kimmance 1972; Cook and Hanslip

1964; UNICEF 1990b). Analyses of more recent data show that female disadvantage has all but disappeared (Al-Jem 1990).

7   The section that follows is based in part on Obermeyer and Mostashari 1991.

8   Khomeini even organized a *bunyadi izdivaj* ("foundation for marriage") which disbursed funds for needy men and women who wished to marry (Mossavar-Rahmani 1983).

9   The increase in marital fertility was most apparent in the urban population where the greatest fertility decline had occurred in the previous decade (Aghajanian 1991).

10 There is some evidence that women in higher age groups in particular experienced an increase in fertility (Aghajanian 1990).

References

Abu-Lughod, L. 1989. Zones of theory in the anthropology of the Arab world. *Annual Review of Anthropology* 18:267–306.

Aghajanian, A. 1990. Recent fertility trends in Iran. Paper presented at the Annual Meeting of the Population Association of America.

———. 1991. Population change in Iran 1966–86: A stalled demographic transition? *Population and Development Review* 17(4):703–715.

Ahmed, L. 1986. Women and the advent of Islam. *Signs: Journal of Women in Culture and Society* 11(4):665–691.

———. 1992. *Women and gender in Islam: Historical roots of a modern debate.* New Haven: Yale University Press.

Al-Jem, M., I. Timaeus, and S. Aoun. 1990. La mortalité au Maroc d'aprés les résultats de l'ENPS. In *Determinants of health and mortality in Africa*, ed. A. Hill. DHS Further Analysis Series no. 10. New York: The Population Council.

Amirahmadi, H. 1988. War damage and reconstruction in the Islamic Republic of Iran. In *Post-revolutionary Iran*, ed. H. Amirahmadi and M. Parvin. Boulder, Colo.: Westview Press.

Bates, D., and A. Rassam. 1983. *Peoples and cultures of the Middle East.* Englewood Cliffs, N.J.: Prentice-Hall.

Betteridge, A. 1983. To veil or not to veil: A matter of protest or policy. In *Women and revolution in Iran*, ed. G. Nashat. Boulder, Colo.: Westview Press.

Caldwell, J.C. 1986. Routes to low mortality in poor countries. *Population and Development Review* 12(2):171–220.

Cook, R., and A. Hanslip. 1964. Nutrition and mortality of females under five years of age compared with males in the Greater Syria region. *Journal of Tropical Pediatrics* 10:76–81.

Doan, R.M., and L. Bisharat. 1990. Female autonomy and child nutritional status: The extended family residential unit in Amman, Jordan. *Social Science and Medicine* 31(7):783–89.

Farid, S. 1987. A review of the fertility situation in the Arab countries of Western Asia and North Africa. In *Fertility behavior in the context of development: Evidence from the World Fertility Survey.* Department of International Economic and Social Affairs, Population Studies no. 100. New York: United Nations.

Fortney, J., I. Susanti, S. Gadalla, S. Saleh, S. Rogers, and M. Potts. 1986. Reproductive mortality in two developing countries. *American Journal of Public Health* 76(2):134–138.

Freedman, L.P., and S.L. Isaacs. 1993. Human rights and reproductive choice. *Studies in Family Planning* 24(1):18–30.

Kane, T., A.A. El-Kady, S. Saleh, M. Hage, J. Stanback, and L. Potter. 1991. Maternal mortality in Giza, Egypt: Magnitude, causes and prevention. *Studies in Family Planning* 23(1):45–57.

Khattab, H.A.S. 1992. *The silent endurance: Social conditions of women's reproductive health in rural Egypt,* ed. G. Potter. Cairo: UNICEF and the Population Council.

Kimmance, K. 1972. Failure to thrive and lactation failure in Jordanian villages. *Journal of Tropical Pediatrics* 18:313–316.

Mernissi, F. 1985. *Beyond the veil: Male-female dynamics in a modern Muslim society.* London: Al Saqi Books; Cambridge, Mass.: Schenkman, 1975.

——. 1992. *Islam and democracy: Fear of the modern world.* Reading, Mass.: Addison-Wesley Publishing Company.

Moghadam, V. 1988. Women, work, and ideology in the Islamic Republic. *International Journal of Middle East Studies* 20(2):221–243.

Mohajerani, A.A. 1989. An analysis of the labor force in Iran. *Social Science Letters of Teheran University* 1(3).

Momeni, J. 1981. The case of Iran: Women, population, and development in Islam. *Intercom* (February):8–11.

Mossavar-Rahmani, Y. 1983. Family planning in post-revolutionary Iran. In *Women and revolution in Iran,* ed. G. Nashat. Boulder, Colo.: Westview Press.

Obermeyer, C.M. 1992. Islam, women, and politics: The demography of Arab countries. *Population and Development Review* 18(1):33–57.

Obermeyer, C.M., and F. Mostashari. 1991. The reversal of Iran's population policy. Paper presented at the Center for Population and Development Studies, Harvard University.

Omran, A. 1992. *Family planning in Islam.* London and New York: Routledge.

Rahman, F. 1980. A survey of modernization of Muslim family law. *International Journal of Middle East Studies* 11:451–465.

Rassam, A. 1984. Arab women: The status of research in the social sciences and the status of women. In *Social science research and women in the Arab world*, ed. F. Pinter. London: UNCESCO.

Stowasser, B.F. 1987a. Liberated equal or protected dependent? Contemporary religious paradigms on women's status in Islam. *Arab Studies Quarterly* 9(3):260–283.

——. 1987b. *The Islamic impulse.* London: Croom Helm.

Tabandeh, S. 1970. *A Muslim commentary on the universal declaration of human rights.* Iran: Goulding and Co., Ltd.

Tekce, B., and F. Shorter. 1984. Determinants of child mortality: A study of squatter settlements in Jordan. *Population and Development Review* (Supplement no. 10).

UNICEF. 1990a and 1992. *The state of the world's children.* New York: Oxford University Press.

——. 1990b. *Sex differences in child survival and development.* Regional Office for the Middle East and North Africa, Evaluation series no. 6.

United Nations. 1989. *Levels and trends of contraceptive use as assessed in 1988.* Department of International, Economic and Social Affairs. Population Studies no. 110. New York.

——. 1991. *World population prospects 1990.* Department of International, Economic and Social Affairs. New York.

——. 1992. *Demographic yearbook 1990.* New York.

World Bank. 1989, 1991b, and 1992. *World development report.* New York: Oxford University Press.

——. 1991a. *Social indicators of development 1990.* Washington, D.C.

Zurayk, H., H. Khattab, N. Younis, M. El-Mouelhy, and M. Fadle. 1993. Concepts and measures of reproductive morbidity. *Health Transition Review* 3(1):17–40.

5

The Weathering Hypothesis and the Health of African-American Women and Infants: Implications for Reproductive Strategies and Policy Analysis

by Arline Geronimus

When policy analysts confront the issue of reducing excessive infant mortality rates among the socioeconomically disadvantaged, they have generally considered maternal age an important determinant of birth outcome. Specifically, in the United States, the relatively high rate of teen childbearing among African-Americans is thought to contribute to their high rates of infant mortality; and a common assumption is that policies aimed narrowly at the reduction of teen childbearing will also result in important declines in infant death rates. In fact, infant mortality figures, when stratified by racial identification, show that African-American infants with teen mothers experience a survival *advantage* relative to infants whose mothers are older. This finding casts doubt on pervasive interpretations of the relationship of maternal age to birth outcome and on the presumptive benefits to infant health of efforts to alter women's fertility timing behavior.

In this paper, I will discuss a different conceptual model for understanding the relationship of maternal age to birth outcome which I call the "weathering hypothesis." This model suggests that high rates of teenage childbearing among identifiable populations within a highly industrialized country such as the United States is an adaptive social response to disadvantage. In particular, I will focus on the possible implications for healthy reproduction at different maternal ages of the impact of social inequality on the health of young through middle aged adults. While absolute differences in health status between populations are well documented, I will also consider the implications of population differences in the *rate* of deteriorating health in young adulthood. In addition, I will consider the constraints that severe health uncertainty may place on disadvantaged populations, if they are to maximize the chances of healthy reproduction, especially in a circumstance where rapidly deteriorating adult health may affect infant health both directly (through maternal health during pregnancy), and indirectly through its impact on the health of other members of the informal social networks on which poor mothers and children often must rely for care and support.

This model has broad implications for research and policy making. If pervasive health uncertainty is more important than inherent biological factors in explaining the relationship of maternal age to birth outcome in socioeconomically disadvantaged populations, then programs which aim to reduce teen births in these populations without addressing the social factors that produce health uncertainty may not reduce infant mortality rates; they might, in fact, result in an increase in infant mortality rates for African-Americans. Such a proposition is clearly a call to consider a reorienting and broadening of the policy agenda to include more than programs aimed at altering women's fertility timing behavior. It may also serve to make more understandable why, in light of the reproductive constraints placed on poor African-American women by their diminishing prospects for continuing health and social support, teen childbearing has been, and continues to be, a persistent fertility timing pattern in this group (despite active efforts to discourage it). However, it would be a misreading to interpret this perspective to suggest that the proper policy approach would be to advocate early childbearing. Rather, considering the factors accounted for in the "weathering hypothesis" may suggest new avenues of research and policy making that address more directly and efficiently the salient factors resulting in higher infant mortality rates among disadvantaged populations.

Background

The logic of the view that high rates of black teen childbearing may contribute to excess black infant mortality is based, in part, on a common presumption that maternal age variables measure a universal developmental process — biological or psychosocial. In this model, the developmental status of teenagers may impede healthy childbearing either because it imposes biological constraints or because it results in unhealthy maternal behaviors or social circumstances. According to this developmental paradigm, mothers in their twenties are assumed to have achieved reproductive and psychosocial maturity and, as a consequence, are "low risk." In research, mothers in their twenties, or some portion of them, are defined as the reference group to gauge the degree to which younger mothers are at increased risk of unhealthy childbearing for reasons related to their adolescent developmental status. However, a variety of studies have found that when potential confounders are controlled, young maternal age ceases to exert an independent effect on birth outcomes (for reviews see Geronimus 1987; Makinson 1985; Strobino 1987; Kline, Stein and Susser 1989), or that the effect may even be in the opposite direction from the one predicted based on the aforementioned developmental model (Geronimus and Korenman 1993; Rosenzweig and Wolpin 1991). Even so, there is still a tendency to rely on a developmental concept of age when interpreting study findings (or making policy recommendations) because of a lack of theoretical consideration of what else maternal age variables may reflect. The failure to consider what maternal age variables measure, other than "development" (or its behavioral manifestations), may represent lost opportunities to move infant mortality research in fruitful directions.

A simple reconsideration of population variation in fertility timing distributions suggests that maternal age variables may measure factors that provide promising clues about the social processes that result in infant mortality differentials. Fertility timing norms vary considerably between populations, with births among more disadvantaged groups concentrated at younger ages than those among more advantaged groups. Similarly, the vast majority of teen births occur to members of disadvantaged populations, leading one to suspect that the higher rate of poor birth outcome among infants of teen mothers may reflect this prior disadvantage, rather than the effects of maternal age, *per se* (Geronimus 1986 and 1987; Geronimus and Korenman 1993). Maternal age variables may well be proxies for social disadvantage. The many studies showing no significant difference in infant outcomes by maternal age when indicators of socioeconomic status are controlled would seem to support this view.

To probe further, one might begin to consider interactive theoretical models. The potential confounding of maternal age and social class raises an important question that would be overlooked by those accustomed to believing that maternal age measures a universal and inherent process, the view implied by the developmental paradigm. The question is, within disadvantaged populations, what are the maternal age patterns of poor birth outcome? Indeed, when one stratifies maternal age patterns of neonatal mortality by race/ethnicity, variation between groups is evident. This variation suggests that different "aging" processes may be occurring among women from different populations who become mothers. For example, in Table 5-1, using the 1983 nationally linked birth and infant death certificate files, the maternal age patterns of neonatal mortality among first births in the United States to 15- to 34-year-old whites, blacks, Mexican-Americans, and Puerto Ricans are shown.[1]

Several points are apparent from Table 5-1: 1) among first births, blacks and Puerto Ricans experience much higher neonatal mortality rates than whites or Mexican-Americans; 2) the maternal age patterns of neonatal mortality vary by race/ethnicity; 3) the white maternal age pattern approximates a "reverse-J" shape, with the highest risks in the teens and the lowest risks in the mid to late twenties; 4) the black and Puerto Rican maternal age patterns are upward sloping, with the late teens having lower risks than the twenties and beyond (although the age-gradient increase appears flatter for Puerto Ricans than for blacks); 5) the maternal age pattern for Mexican-Americans is curvilinear, but it is "J-shaped" rather than "reverse-J," i.e., the thirties are higher risk than the teens. As a function of these patterns, the black/white and Puerto Rican/white neonatal mortality gap increases with maternal age, while the Mexican-American/white ratio hovers close to 1, with Mexicans faring relatively better in the teens and worse in the thirties than whites. By implication, for all three minority groups (unlike for whites) teens' neonatal mortality rates do not raise the overall (or averaged) rate, while for two of the three they *lower* it. Similarly, the minority/white ratios are lower among the teens than for the comparison overall. This diversity of

Table 5-1 Neonatal Mortality Rates and Rate Ratios by Maternal Age: First Births, United States, 1983

Age	Neonatal Mortality Rates				Rate Ratios		
	White	Black	Mexican	Puerto Rican	Black/ White	Mexican/ White	Puerto Rican/ White
15 to 19	7.2	9.8	5.3	8.5	1.4	0.7	1.2
20 to 29	4.6	10.4	4.7	9.2	2.3	1.0	2.0
30 to 34	5.6	15.0	7.9	11.9	2.7	1.4	2.1
Total	5.4	10.6	5.2	9.0	1.9	0.9	1.7

maternal age patterns of risk defies simple biological or psycho-social developmental explanations.

Furthermore, the rates presented in Table 5-1 are not stratified by any indicators of social class within race/ethnicity, and, thus, may understate the rates of poor infant outcomes for older relative to younger mothers in poverty populations (where neonatal mortality rates are excessive compared to those experienced by more affluent populations). That is, since mothers who have postponed their first births until their mid-twenties are, on average, more advantaged than teen mothers, these estimates may understate the degree to which infants of older poor African-American mothers face diminished prospects for survival compared to those with teen mothers. Suggestive empirical support for this interpretation has been reported (Geronimus 1993; Geronimus and Korenman 1993; Rosenzweig and Wolpin 1991; Collins and David 1990).

These descriptive statistics also beg several questions: Why is the black maternal age pattern of neonatal mortality upward-sloping? Why are black/white differences in neonatal mortality *larger* at older ages than at younger ones? What clues or information might these descriptions offer us towards understanding the true causes of the persistent black/white infant mortality differential? And, even more speculatively, what clues might they offer toward understanding the social forces underpinning the equally persistent early first-birth timing distributions among blacks compared to whites (Evans 1986). (Although they will not be discussed explicitly here, the Puerto Rican data raise similar questions).

The Weathering Hypothesis

I will pursue one possible explanation that follows the analytic lead of Mosley and Chen (1984). They argued for the importance of connecting disease processes to socially-defined populations when studying infant mortality. The variant of this general approach I have developed is the hypothesis that observing racial disparities in neonatal mortality that widen with maternal age may be consistent with a theoretical view of aging as a "weathering" process (Kline, Stein and Susser 1989; Susser 1968) reflective of how life circumstances promote or undermine women's health on a population level in ways that can affect reproduction (Geronimus 1987; Geronimus and Bound 1990). The "weathering" hypothesis encapsulates how social inequality may affect the health of population groups differentially and how these differences may be compounded with age. Between populations, infant health is unequal; during childhood and adolescence the healthy growth and development among the disadvantaged can be impeded (Baird 1964); while in young and middle adulthood gaps in health status between populations may intensify (U.S. Department of Health and Human Services 1985). The effects of poverty on child health can be lasting, leaving even those who escape poverty in adulthood at a reproductive disadvantage compared to those who have enjoyed life-long advantages (Emanuel 1986; Emanuel, Hale and Berg 1989; Forsdahl 1977). For all social classes, members of minority groups are subject to racial or ethnic discrimination that can be costly to health. This can take concrete or observable forms, such as diminished access to health services and health education or residence in segregated neighborhoods with excessive exposure to environmental hazards. It may also be the product of evolving concepts of psycho-social risk. For example, there are empirical indications that prolonged, effortful, active coping with social injustice may, itself, exact a physical price (James 1987). Thus, the weathering hypothesis predicts that crude estimates of the black/white infant mortality differential should be reduced, but not eliminated, by including measures of current maternal socioeconomic status in empirical models.

Weathering, therefore, goes beyond the view that maternal age variables are proxies for social disadvantage to suggest that they be seen as reflections of how, on a population level, socioeconomic inequality, racial discrimination, or race bias in exposures to environmental hazards may affect differentially the health of women who will become mothers, not only in absolute terms, but also interactively with each other and increasingly as women age. The weathering hypothesis suggests that socioeconomically disadvantaged women may be subjected to many sets of health risks, the consequences of which may accumulate with age, whether or not they become mothers. It implies that, for mothers, interactions between the health consequences of these exposures and age will result in sets of maternal health and behavioral characteristics prior to (or during) pregnancy that vary among and within populations; and that social inequities in the distribution of health services and technologies will interact with maternal health status to exacerbate infant mortality differentials. This theoretical approach emphasizes variation, context, and the social epidemiology of disease processes. It implies that, for a given population group, the direction or functional form of the trajectory of infant risk by maternal age should not be taken as universal or axiomatic, but as an empirical question. In contrast to the developmental paradigm where the twenties are included in research protocols as a low-risk reference group, the weathering hypothesis suggests the twenties should be a focus of research and policy in their own right.

Specifically, I hypothesize that the health status of black women may begin to deteriorate in young adulthood. According to this hypothesis, and the general analytic framework seeking to connect disease processes to populations, such deterioration would be a manifestation of social processes. Black women, as a result of their social inequality, may experience with age an increasingly greater number of insults to health, and may also have relatively decreased opportunities to utilize health service interventions that may remediate the impact of poor maternal health on infant outcome. The concept of "insults to health" could include a broad range of factors that may affect health status negatively, among them the development and untreated progression of chronic conditions and diseases; increased stress, as poor women's obligations to dependents, kin, and work activities may multiply with age; an increased likelihood with age of engaging in behaviors that are both ways of coping with stress and adversarial to women's and fetal health (such as smoking, drinking or other drug use); and the accumulation of exposure to environmental hazards as a product of continued residence in geographic areas or "selection" into jobs where such exposures are concentrated. Each of these "insults" would have negative implications for women's health, generally, and for infant outcome among women who become pregnant.

In this regard, it is noteworthy that in the 1983 national linked data, while the lowest risk maternal age groups were found to differ between blacks (15 to 19) and whites (the twenties), within each racial identification, the maternal age group with the lowest risk of neonatal mortality was also the age group at which first births occurred with the greatest frequency. Among blacks, 48 percent of first births occurred to 15- to 19-year-olds and 82 percent had occurred by age 25. For whites, 68 percent took place at the lowest risk ages. This observation raises the related questions of whether peak maternal health and access to social support for childbearing might converge at different ages for African-Americans compared to (non-Hispanic) white Americans, and whether population variation in fertility timing distributions may reflect culturally patterned responses to this situation.

Empirical Evidence for the Weathering Hypothesis

While the weathering hypothesis is, in broad strokes, a heuristic model, it does imply a set of testable hypotheses.[2] One line of inquiry has been to address the following question that is implied by the weathering hypothesis: within race, are women's age patterns of the prevalence of health characteristics that can adversely affect reproduction similar to the maternal age patterns of poor birth outcome? Those health characteristics we have studied to date suggest that they may well be. Our findings, some of which are summarized below,[3] are consistent with the hypothesis that, over the reproductive age-span, black women's health may deteriorate more rapidly than white women's.

As an initial approach to gauging the plausibility of the weathering hypothesis, we analyzed all cause mortality among young adult women as well as mortality due to causes that are also pregnancy risk factors (for example, hypertensive disease) (Geronimus and Bound 1990). Mortality among young women due to specific causes is an indicator of disease prevalence or, because death at such young ages is an unlikely (often avertable) event, of medical under-service. Over the predominant childbearing ages (15 to 29), mortality increases for blacks exceeded those for whites for every death classification we studied. For all cause mortality and for eight out of 10 specific causes of death, the point estimates showed increases in the odds of dying for black women exceeding those for white by more than 50 percent, nine of them by at least 25 percent. The magnitude of the differences was sufficiently large that, despite the fact that the actual numbers of deaths for some specific causes were small, for most causes, we could reject the null hypothesis that the growth in the black rate was no greater than that in the white rate at a 95 percent level.[4]

Of theoretical interest, the trends in odds ratios by age and race followed similar patterns for an array of causes that are often conceptualized as very different, such as "biomedical" causes (e.g., deaths due to hypertensive disease), "bio-behavioral" causes (e.g., deaths due to cirrhosis), and "external" causes (e.g., deaths due to accidents, suicide, homicide or legal intervention). The parallel age/race patterns for these diverse health indicators is consistent with the notion implied by weathering that there may be important bio-social elements to the "medical" or "behavioral" causes. Similarly, the two causes that followed the "weathering" trends the most weakly — chronic obstructive pulmonary disease (COPD) and diabetes — were those with relatively weak links to social factors among youth.[5] Forms of these diseases in which social components have been clearly implicated (non-insulin-dependent diabetes and chronic bronchitis/emphysema) are more likely to be reflected in mortality statistics for older ages. In sum, the causes of death that most clearly followed an age/race pattern consistent with the weathering hypothesis were those that have been consistently linked to social class, racial identification, or other social or behavioral factors.

In subsequent research, we have looked directly at the prevalences of specific health characteristics in women that are risk factors for poor birth outcomes. Using data from the second wave of the National Health and Nutrition Examination Survey (NHANES II), we estimated racial differences in hypertension prevalence over the childbearing ages (Geronimus, Andersen and Bound 1991). As summarized in Figure 5-1, racial differences in hypertension emerged among young women and sharpened over the childbearing ages. Although at age 15 there was essentially no black/white difference in the predicted odds of being hypertensive, black women aged 25 had twice the odds of being hypertensive, and at the end of the childbearing years, black women had

---

Figure 5-1　Estimated Odds of Being Hypertensive Among U.S. Reproductive-Age Women by Age and Race

Figure 5-2　Estimated Odds of Having a Blood Lead Level >15μg/dL Among U.S. Reproductive-Age Women by Age and Race

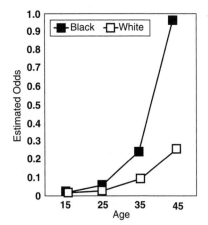

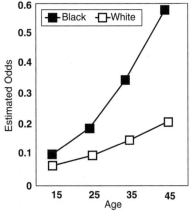

Estimates based on logit analyses of data from NHANES II, 1976-80.
Source: Geronimus, Andersen and Bound 1991

Estimates based on logit analyses of data from NHANES II, 1976-80.
Source: Geronimus and Hillemeier 1992.

almost four times the odds of suffering from clinically documented chronic hypertensive disease as whites.

A larger proportion of black than white women had circulating blood lead levels that were greater than 15 µg/dL, a level thought to place a fetus at risk (Agency for Toxic Substances and Disease Registry 1988). This was true throughout the childbearing years, but the magnitude of the disparity was greater for older compared to younger age groups.[6] As shown in Figure 5-2, at age 15, the black/white differences were small compared to age 25, when black women were estimated to have roughly twice the odds of having a circulating blood lead level above the risk threshold, or compared to the end of the reproductive age-span when the black odds were almost three times the white.

Using data from the National Health Interview Survey's 1987 Cancer Supplement, we have estimated smoking prevalence during the reproductive ages (Geronimus, Neidert and Bound 1993). Retrospective questions on smoking history in these data allowed us to take account of the potential confounding of cohort and age, an important issue in smoking research given the substantial historical changes in levels of smoking among women. Both within cohorts, and in our summary analyses (where we accounted for cohort membership by estimating Cox proportional hazard models), we found similar age patterns of current smoking. An example of the general patterns is provided in Figure 5-3 which shows the predicted age patterns of smoking by racial identification for the cohort of women ages 40 to 44 in 1987. We found that among white women, the odds of currently smoking peaked by age 25, five years younger than for blacks. During their twenties, white women showed only small increases in the odds of smoking, while for blacks the odds of smoking increased by almost 80 percent. White teenage girls were more likely to smoke than their black counterparts; by the late twenties the odds of smoking converged between blacks and whites. At older ages, the findings were suggestive of a cross-over, i.e., that the odds of smoking were greater for black women than for white women. Among pregnant women, we have reported similar age patterns of smoking by race (Geronimus 1993; Geronimus and Korenman 1993). Similar age patterns of other drug use during pregnancy among black women (with older mothers, not teen mothers, more likely to be users) have been reported in studies of alcohol, cocaine, heroin, and methadone use (Geronimus and Korenman 1993; Holtzman and Paneth, *in press*).

Figure 5-3 Estimated Odds of Currently Smoking at Selected Ages by Race, U.S. Women Aged 40 to 44

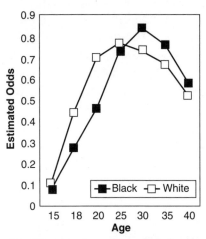

Calculations based on analyses of data from the NHIS, 1987: Cancer Supplement.
Source: Geronimus, Neidert and Bound 1993

Figure 5-4 Estimated Odds Ratios (Black/White) of Health Characteristics Among U.S. Women by Age and Race

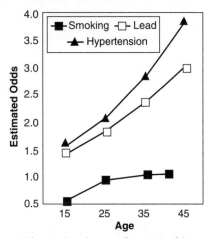

Odds ratios based on transformations of the data presented in Geronimus, Andersen and Bound 1991; Geronimus and Hillemeier 1992; Geronimus, Neidert and Bound 1993

The odds ratios (black/white) by age of women exhibiting the specific adverse health characteristics we have studied (hypertension, blood lead levels thought to place women at reproductive risk, and current smoking status) are shown in Figure 5-4. As with the maternal age patterns of neonatal mortality, in all cases the size of the black/white disparity is lowest in the teens and *increases* over the childbearing ages. Again, a typical typology of health status indicators would place these indicators into different groups. However, the similarity in the age patterns of race-associated differences for all of these health characteristics suggests the possibility of an important commonality which may be social in origin. That the pattern is evident in the variation by age and racial identification of blood lead levels — a health characteristic that is the product of environmental exposure — would seem to challenge the view that the primary explanation for these age/race patterns can be reduced to prominent explanations that privilege either genetic differences between blacks and whites or lifestyle choices of African-Americans thought to be the product of a pathological subculture.

Taken together, our research findings suggest that the health of African-American women may deteriorate more rapidly than that of white women and, more speculatively, that the context for childbearing among African-Americans may be qualitatively distinct from that experienced by more advantaged populations. While most Americans take for granted their good health during their young and middle adulthood — indeed, these ages are referred to as the "prime" of life and the twenties as the "prime childbearing ages" — our findings suggest that among African-American women in low socioeconomic groups, health deterioration may begin on an accelerated course in the mid-twenties and reproductive disadvantage may intensify. Other researchers have noted the extreme shortening of life expectancy among residents of extremely disadvantaged, highly segregated (predominantly black) geographic areas. For example, McCord and Freeman (1990) estimated that the chances that black men in Harlem would survive to age 65 were lower than those for men in Bangladesh. Both women and men in Harlem experienced the largest excess deaths relative to the U.S. white population during what are typically thought of as prime years, ages 25 to 44.

All of these descriptive statistics suggest that the social forces that threaten the well-being of African-American infants may be more insidious than is often recognized, posing increasingly severe threats to women, children, and families as women or mothers age from adolescence through young and middle adulthood. The age patterns of women's tobacco and other drug use may also be suggestive here. One question they raise is whether the black age patterns indicate that the lives of black women in their twenties and thirties may be more stressful compared either to those of their white counterparts or those of black adolescents. The attempt to cope with such stress might be one reason why young adult black women are more likely to smoke than whites or black teens. The sources of this stress, the stress itself, or the physical price of actively coping with chronic stress may contribute to the excess disease, disability, and death of young and middle-aged adult black women. Investigating the psychosocial factors that may precipitate black women's later initiation or persistent use of tobacco or other drugs compared to whites, may deserve further study, perhaps providing insight into weathering more broadly. Overall, while specific details and mechanisms are yet to be described, the findings on weathering suggest a social circumstance with health implications that differ from those suggested by the more conventional view of the relationship of maternal age to birth outcome. The developmental paradigm implies that the primary factors that contribute to the reproductive disadvantage associated with black teenage childbearing are ones that would be outgrown if black women would postpone their first births beyond their twentieth birthdays. The results on weathering suggest they are not, or that they are superseded at older ages by even greater risks.

Interpretations and Speculations

How is one to interpret the evidence to date on weathering and, broadly speaking, what further research is needed? My intent is not to be exhaustive on this point, or even to suggest specific studies to be done. Instead, I will highlight two major working hypotheses that follow from the theoretical and empirical work to date on the weathering hypothesis, while encouraging the formulation of others. These working hypotheses are 1) that the black/white infant mortality differential is, in part, due to the health status differences and age patterns of health status differences between black and white mothers; and 2) that (anticipated) weathering on the population level may lead to collective adaptive responses to reduce its threat to mothers and infants.

The first working hypothesis would suggest that, to some extent, the specific physical manifestations of weathering such as hypertension, cigarette smoking, and high blood lead levels are the proximate causes of excess black infant mortality; that is, that they are the bio-behavioral pathways through which the weathering of mothers is translated into the death of children. According to this hypothesis, one would expect that in further investigations, the black/white infant mortality differential would be reduced by adjustment for specific adverse maternal health characteristics (as would the excess between black older versus younger mothers, especially within the most socioeconomically disadvantaged groups). Measurement problems alone would lead one to expect that such adjustment would be unlikely to eliminate these differentials. However, the extent to which they might diminish would suggest the degree of promise that focusing narrowly on changes or renewed efforts in the medical management of pregnancies (of older black mothers, in particular) might hold for reducing black infant mortality rates.

However, it is also possible that while specific health characteristics of mothers that are symptomatic of inequality may influence fetal and infant health adversely, the "whole" of the impact of racial discrimination or other socioeconomic disadvantages on infant outcome may be importantly larger than the sum of its identifiable maternal-health-related "parts." If this were the case, one might still expect statistical adjustment for specific maternal health characteristics to result in a net, if modest, dampening of the black/white infant mortality differential. However, significant, lasting reductions in black infant mortality rates would not be achieved through an exclusive focus on changes in the content or distribution of prenatal care, except, perhaps, inasmuch as these changes resulted in more equitable access of high-risk newborns to costly tertiary care (Gortmaker et al. 1985). Important additions to a preventive medical approach would be those aimed at improving girls' and women's health before they become mothers. Most importantly, such a finding would call for addressing the larger structural relationships that produce inequality.

The second working hypothesis is more speculative and evolving. As with the general weathering model, it may be appropriately viewed as a suggested analytic framework to generate testable hypotheses. It highlights the possibility that, in order to maximize the well-being of children, African-American communities may have developed collectively patterned responses to the institutional and environmental constraints they face (Geronimus 1987, 1991, 1992a, 1992b). It raises the question of whether such responses might include the adjustment of fertility timing norms and expectations to emphasize childbearing at the ages when women are the healthiest or may have the greatest social support available. In this perspective, the shared and historical experience of community members (including past and present "elders") may be distilled into a pervasive logical structure (e.g., "common sense") that shapes decisions made by community members, the realm of possibilities they perceive as open to them, and the potential strategies for pursuit of available goals. In this case, the uncertain prospects for continuing health or social support suggested by weathering would be incorporated as one set of institutional constraints inhibiting healthy childbearing. For example, the perception of deteriorating health of older relatives may provide (conscious or unconscious) motivation for early childbearing to augment the chances that infants will be born healthy and their caretakers survive until they are grown. In this scenario, African-American children would tend to be born before their mothers were likely to develop the adverse health characteristics described in the weathering research or, at least, before these problems were likely to have become progressive or multiple.[7]

The issues related to social support may be not only those that surround pregnancy, but may also speak to the need for social support at other ages. This working hypothesis builds on the recognition that members of poor communities often have few alternatives but to rely on informal (kin) networks if they are to maximize their ability to find sources of practical support either to solve immediate conflicts or to serve as social "insurance" against the longer-term risks associated with poverty (e.g., risks of severe shortfalls in income; the risk of death or disability; the risk of being widowed or orphaned; the risk of hunger or homelessness) (Jones 1985; Morgan et al. 1990; Stack 1974; Stack and Burton 1993). Early fertility timing distributions may reflect the possibility that, within such systems, it may be, on balance, beneficial to the well-being of community members for women to bear children while older kin members are themselves relatively healthy, able to be more of a resource to new mothers than a drain. In the context of weathering, such benefits may not only accrue to infants, children, and their mothers, but to older networks members, as well. For example, early fertility may be, on balance, beneficial for older network members if it implies any of the following possibilities: 1) that they can meet community expectations to help out with (grand)childrearing at ages where the costs to them may be lower than at older (potentially less healthy) ages, when they might anticipate it to be more difficult; 2) that they will be less likely to have to compete with infant or very young members of descending generations (e.g., grandchildren) for support from their adult children, when they age and face increased risk of becoming dependent again themselves; or 3) that they will have a larger set of descendants to whom they can turn for support as their risk of disability increases.

If such cultural motivation exists, it remains an open question to what extent its influence on fertility timing distributions is direct or conscious, and to what extent it might operate indirectly through other behaviors and pressures that are powerfully structured by economic realities and culture. Furthermore, in the context of extreme socioeconomic disadvantage, it is important to stress that the concept of "benefits" is not meant to paint a rosy picture of early fertility among the poor, nor to suggest that poor women have babies in order to acquire benefits at their children's expense. Indeed, recent evidence from studies controlling for maternal family background suggests not only that children of teen mothers from low socioeconomic groups fare as well as or better than those with older mothers on infant health indicators, but they may also fare as well or better than those with older mothers on indicators of early childhood cognitive and socioemotional development (Geronimus and Korenman 1993; Geronimus et al., forthcoming). Furthermore, social arrangements that are, on balance, "beneficial" can also have substantial "costs." For example, kin network based systems may offer hedges against the worst consequences of weathering, yet they may also contribute to weathering, inasmuch as networks can be sources of stress, as well as support, or network obligations may conflict with other opportunities. Indeed, the general argument I have outlined emphasizes the possibility that network obligations may impose substantial stresses, particularly on young adult members, and substantial burdens on members of all generations. If members continue to accept these burdens — burdens which might be seen as costs of poverty or discrimination — it may suggest the highly constrained nature of their options. It may be worth exploring whether, given constraints, this is a price network members pay to insure against the worst threats they face to their health and well-being or that of their children; that is, whether it may be a cost of engaging life in the face of extreme adversity.

According to the second working hypothesis, weathering may help explain excess black infant mortality, but it might also influence fertility timing and family structure, to the extent that severely compromised health and health uncertainties in African-American communities may permeate their social organization. These health considerations may have profound influences on the modes of family or community organization that are institutionalized, or on the collective wisdom that generates norms, sanctions, and social expectations that regulate fertility timing. This hypothesis also implies that the black/white gap in infant mortality might be even greater in the absence of these social and behavioral responses.

These working hypotheses cast a wide and interdisciplinary research agenda. They highlight the need for ethnographic investigation, as well as more quantitative social scientific and epidemiological approaches. Ethnographic investigation may be an important addition to research in this area, because it is uniquely suited to making accessible unconscious or unstated cultural rationales that may underpin population-specific fertility patterns (LeVine and Scrimshaw 1983). Ethnography, along with other qualitative methods and survey approaches, may also provide insights into the psychosocial dimensions of young adulthood among African-American women (see Geronimus 1987, 1991, 1992a and b;

Geronimus and Bound 1991 for greater discussion of research implications).

The working hypotheses also emphasize the importance of not remaining complacent about the interpretations of the meaning of demographic variables that are statistically implicated in the infant mortality process, if research on the black/white infant mortality differential is to prosper. Arguably, common constructions of such variables may be ethnocentric or based more on researchers' experience and intuition than empirical foundation. In infant mortality research, the most prominent example of this tendency is, of course, the interpretation of the meaning of race variables, themselves, as others have discussed (Cooper and David 1986; Wilkinson and King 1987; David and Collins 1991). Here, I have argued that interpretations of documented association between maternal age and infant outcome have relied heavily on narrow constructs of age. The meaning of other demographic correlates of infant mortality, such as marital status or household structure more broadly, also may deserve such critical examination. In investigations focusing on family or household structure, for example, common tendencies to selectively perceive either costs or benefits of specific family structures should be avoided. And, given the earlier-noted possibility that family structure and the risk of poor birth outcome are jointly determined, including family structure as an explanatory variable in birth outcome equations should be done only cautiously. If the same processes (related to social inequality) contribute to the selection into family structure and the risk of poor birth outcome, it would be inappropriate to interpret variation in birth outcome according to family structure as causal, i.e., as if variation in family structure were random or externally imposed. Thus, when interpreting the coefficients on socio-demographic variables in birth outcome equations, it may be necessary to consider the possibility that part of any estimated effect of the socio-demographic variable may be due to unobserved factors associated with socioeconomic disadvantage and birth outcome, rather than to the measured factor. This may be true, even if typical measures of socioeconomic status (such as income, education, or occupation) have been controlled.[8]

Re-opening the questions of what socio-demographic variables measure and what their associations with social problems may mean can point to new clues in existing data. For example, as noted, the numbers presented in Table 5-1 would appear to contradict the popular view that reducing early fertility among African-Americans alone will importantly reduce the excess black infant mortality rate. They also raise questions about the justification for the common procedure (in research, policy, or obstetrical practice) of uniformly classifying mothers in their twenties and early thirties into "low risk" groups. The higher neonatal mortality rate among older compared to younger black mothers has been discussed above. Another striking aspect of the neonatal mortality rates presented is that those African-American women who postponed their first-births to ages deemed "acceptable" (or "low-risk") by the larger society experienced neonatal mortality rates in excess of white teenagers. Although the teen neonatal mortality rate of 7.2 was the largest among whites, it was exceeded by that for black 20- to 29-year-old mothers, which was 10.4. Those African-American women who postponed motherhood until their early thirties experienced a neonatal mortality rate that was more than twice the rate experienced by white teenagers. Given observed population variation in fertility timing distributions, this comparison illustrates a need to re-think both the conceptualization of the meaning of maternal age and how to socially construe the direction of causality between the poor health of members of socioeconomically disadvantaged populations and their social organization more broadly.

There may be merit to taking as a general approach the view that, until it has been shown otherwise, behavior patterns that appear unfamiliar or perplexing to members of advantaged populations, but are the statistical norm in disadvantaged populations, may represent collectively patterned coping strategies, not necessarily individual deviance or community pathology. If it is true that the infant health consequences of teenage childbearing among African-Americans have been exaggerated, as the findings discussed here and elsewhere imply, it would only be because the severity of the adverse effects of social inequality on the health of African-American women and children may not have been fully acknowledged or absorbed. The weathering hypothesis suggests a cumulative pattern of racism. It raises the question of whether variation from "mainstream" values on the aggregate level may signify resourcefulness, in the face of extreme hardship and constrained options, to be understood. Through attempting to develop such understanding, the research agenda is opened: causal processes and mechanisms may be identified, the nature or magnitude of true hardships clarified, and new points for effective action may emerge.

Our failure to take into account that variations in population parameters may reflect adaptive cultural responses to socioeconomic and environmental exigencies may have constrained policy development such that current programs do not act on conditions which fundamentally affect infant mortality rates. Such a situation has broad implications for policy making, both internal to the United States and through its international aid programs. While the preceding discussion is specific to the African-American case, general implications for impoverished populations in less developed countries can be drawn, while needing to be tailored to the specific environmental exigencies and cultural traditions of those populations (Geronimus 1987). The weathering perspective suggests that a reconsideration of the data to account for the effects of social inequality on health — and then the effects of health uncertainty on fertility timing and social organization — may reveal new points for effective policy action.

Acknowledgements

Support for this work was provided by Grant HD24122 from the National Institute of Child Health and Development. The author is grateful to John Bound, Sherman James, and Sanders Korenman for comments. Parts of this paper are reprinted with permission from *Ethnicity and Disease*.

Notes

1   Beyond this table, I will not be discussing birth outcome among Mexican-Americans or Puerto Ricans. I include these groups here to underscore that variation exists between socially defined populations in maternal age patterns of poor birth outcome. In addition, the discussion is limited to 15- to 34-year-olds for several reasons related to the infrequency with which first births occur at younger or older ages. Indeed, in 1983, only 2.8 percent of first births occurred to women outside the ages of 15 through 34. First-time mothers younger than 15 or older than 34 represent very highly selected groups of women or mothers, yet the ways in which they are so select are not fully understood. How that selection may affect their neonatal mortality rates is unclear, implying that their inclusion would exacerbate problems of interpretation produced by selection into age at first birth more generally (see Geronimus 1986, 1987, 1991 for related discussions). It also seems theoretically appropriate to focus on ages to which one might reasonably consider altering fertility timing, if it were determined that by so doing infant health risks could be decreased. For example, those who would advocate delaying childbearing beyond the teens as a measure to reduce infant mortality risk would be unlikely to suggest postponement until the late thirties or beyond.

2   Elsewhere, we have discussed the practical fact that existing data sets leave us highly constrained in our efforts to test the full range of these hypotheses. We

also discuss some of the ways in which we are currently attempting to combine information across data sets to overcome these limitations, although this approach raises its own set of problems. Before we began these more ambitious undertakings, we focused our attention on more modest and indirect approaches to shedding empirical light on the plausibility of the weathering hypothesis (Geronimus and Bound 1991).

3   See Geronimus and Bound 1990; Geronimus, Andersen and Bound 1991; Gernonimus and Hillemeier 1992; and Geronimus, Neidert and Bound 1993 for greater detail.

4   As noted, the excess mortality we observed among black women may be a marker not only for excess disease prevalence, but also for medical underservice (or the synergy between excess disease prevalence and medical underservice that itself may contribute to weathering). That is, among young African-American women, curable or manageable diseases may have gone undetected or untreated and allowed to progress to life-threatening proportions, while this may have been less likely to happen among whites.

5   The prevalence of the form of diabetes that is common at young adult ages — insulin dependent diabetes (IDDM) — has not been demonstrated to be related to socioeconomic status (See Evans et al. 1987; Higgins et al. 1977; and McWhorter et al. 1989), and the data relating socioeconomic status to asthma (the common form of COPD at young ages) are conflicting (See LaPorte, Cruikshank 1985; and Waggenkneci et al. 1989).

6   This was true even though members of the younger cohorts in the study sample may have experienced higher levels of lead exposure than members of the older cohorts, both throughout their lives and during childhood when the level of lead retention is greatest.

7   Paradoxically, if this were the case, specific adverse health characteristics common among blacks might not have large explanatory power in studies of the black-white infant mortality differential. This might lead investigators to understate their importance in the "bigger picture," for example, their potential impact on infant mortality if the black fertility timing distribution were shifted to older ages, without also addresssing weathering (or the specific health characteristics in question), per se. For a discussion of this issue in relation to cigarette smoking, for example, see Geronimus, Neidert and Bound 1993.

8   Commonly used measures of socioeconomic status may suffer from substantial measurement error and, even if reliably measured, are unlikely to capture fully many unobservable aspects of socioeconomic disadvantage that may also influence birth outcome. The coefficient on the socio-demographic variable, therefore, may capture some of the effect of socioeconomic status, as well as any true effect of its own (Geronimus and Korenman 1988, 1993).

References

Agency for Toxic Substances and Disease Registry. 1988. *The nature and extent of lead poisoning in children in the United States: A report to Congress.* Atlanta, Ga.: U.S. Department of Health and Human Services.

Baird, D. 1964. The epidemiology of prematurity. *American Journal of Obstetrics and Gynecology* 65:909–924.

Collins, J.W., and R.J. David. 1990. The differential effect of traditional risk factors on infant birthweight among blacks and whites in Chicago. *American Journal of Public Health* 80:679–681.

Cooper, R., and R. David. 1986. The biological concept of race and its application to public health and epidemiology. *Journal of Health Policy Law* 11:97–116.

David, R.J., and J.W. Collins. 1991. Bad outcomes in black babies: Race or racism? *Ethnicity and Disease* 1:236–244.

Emanuel, I. 1986. Maternal health during childhood and later reproductive performance. *N.Y. Acadamy of Science* 477:27–39.

Emanuel, I., C.B. Hale, and C.J. Berg. 1989. Poor birth outcomes of American black women: An alternative explanation. *Journal of Public Health Policy* 10:299–308.

Evans, M.D.R. 1986. American fertility patterns: A comparison of white and nonwhite cohorts born 1903–56. *Population and Development Review* 12:267–293.

Evans, R., D.I. Mullally, R.W. Wilson, et al. 1987. National trends in morbidity and mortality of asthma over two decades: 1965–1984. *Chest* 91 (6, Supplement):65s–74s.

Forsdahl, A. 1977. Are poor living conditions in childhood and adolescence an important risk factor for arteriosclerotic heart disease? *Br J Prev Soc Med* 31:91–95.

Geronimus, A.T. 1986. The effects of race, residence, and prenatal care on the relationship of maternal age to neonatal mortality. *American Journal of Public Health* 76:1416–1421.

———. 1987. On teenage childbearing and neonatal mortality in the United States. *Population and Development Review* 13:245–279.

———. 1991. Teenage childbearing and social and reproductive disadvantage: The evolution of complex questions and the demise of simple answers. *Family Relations* 40:463–471.

———. 1992a. Teenage childbearing and social disadvantage: Unprotected discourse. *Family Relations* 41:244–248.

————. 1992b. Clashes of common sense: On the previous childcare experience of teenage mothers-to-be. *Human Organization* 51(4):318–329.

————. 1993. The translation of social into reproductive disadvantage: A population-based test of the weathering hypothesis. Paper presented at the Workshop on Preterm Delivery and Other Pregnancy Outcomes Among Black Women, Centers for Disease Control and Prevention, May, in Atlanta, Ga.

Geronimus, A.T., H.F. Andersen, and J. Bound. 1991. Differences in hypertension prevalence among U.S. black and white women of childbearing age. *Public Health Reports* 106:393–399.

Geronimus, A.T., and J. Bound. 1990. Black/white differences in women's reproductive-related health status: Evidence from vital statistics. *Demography* 27:457–466.

————. 1991. Black/white infant mortality differentials in the United States: Towards a more theory-based research. Proceedings of the annual meeting of the American Statistical Association, in Atlanta, Ga.

Geronimus, A.T., and M.M. Hillemeier. 1992. Patterns of blood lead levels in U.S. black and white women of childbearing age. *Ethnicity and Disease* 2:222–231.

Geronimus, A.T., and S. Korenman. 1988. Comment on Pampel and Pillai's "Patterns and determinants of infant mortality in developed nations, 1950–1975." *Demography* 25:155–158.

————. 1993. Maternal youth or poverty? On the health disadvantages of infants with teenage mothers. *American Journal of Epidemiology* 137(2):213–225.

Geronimus, A.T., S. Korenman, and M.M. Hillemeier. Forthcoming. Does young maternal age adversely affect children's development? Evidence from cousin comparisons. *Population and Development Review.*

Geronimus, A.T., L.J. Neidert, and J. Bound. 1993. Age patterns of smoking in U.S. black and white women of childbearing age. *American Journal of Public Health* 83(9).

Gortmaker, S.L., A.M. Sobol, C.G. Clark, D.K. Walker, and A.T. Geronimus. 1985. The survival of very low birth weight infants by level of hospital of birth: A population study of perinatal systems in four states. *American Journal of Obstetrics and Gynecology* 152:517–524.

Higgins, M.W., J.B. Keller, and H.L. Metzner. 1977. Smoking, socioeconomic status, and chronic respiratory disease. *American Review of Respiratory Disease* 116:403–410.

Holtzman, C., and N. Paneth. Forthcoming. Illicit drug use during pregnancy: Perinatal outcomes. In *Effects of drug exposure in utero*, ed. J. Mills and L. Robbins.

James, S.A. 1987. Psychosocial precursors of hypertension: A review of the epidemiologic evidence. *Circulation* 76 (Supplement I):I60–I66.

Jones, J. 1985. *Labor of love, labor of sorrow: Black women, work, and the family from slavery to the present.* New York: Basic Books.

Kline, J., Z. Stein, and M. Susser. 1989. *Conception to birth: Epidemiology of prenatal development.* New York: Oxford University Press.

La Porte, R.E., and J.K. Cruickshank. 1985. Incidence and risk factors for insulin-dependent diabetes. In *Diabetes in America*, ed. M.I. Harris and R.F. Hamman. Washington D.C.: U.S. Department of Health and Human Services.

LeVine, R.A., and S.C.M. Scrimshaw. 1983. Effects of culture on fertility: Anthropological contributions. In *Determinants of fertility in developing countries*, ed. R.A. Bulatao and R.D. Lee. New York: Academic Press.

Makinson, C. 1985. The health consequences of teenage fertility. *Family Planning Perspectives* 17:132–139.

McCord, C., and H.P. Freeman. 1990. Excess mortality in Harlem. *New England Journal of Medicine* 322:173–177.

McWhorter, W.P., M.A. Polis, and R.A. Kaslow. 1989. Occurrence, predictors, and consequences of adult asthma in NHANES I and Follow-up Survey. *American Review of Respiratory Disease* 139:721–724.

Morgan, S.P., A. McDaniel, A.T. Miller, and S.H. Preston. 1990. Racial differences in household and family structure at the turn of the century. Paper presented at The Albany Conference, Demographic Perspectives on the American Family: Patterns and Prospects.

Mosley, W.H., and L.C. Chen. 1984. An analytic framework for the study of child survival in developing countries. *Child Survival: Strategies for Research, Supplement to Population and Development Review* 10:25–45.

Rosenzweig, M., and K. Wolpin. 1991. *Sisters, siblings and mothers: The effects of teen-age childbearing on birth outcomes.* Unpublished manuscript.

Stack, C. 1974. *All our kin.* New York: Harper & Row.

Stack, C., and L.M. Burton. 1993. Kinscripts. *Journal of Comparative Family Studies* 24:157–170.

Strobino, D. 1987. The health and medical consequences of adolescent sexuality and pregnancy: A review of the literature. In *Risking the future: Adolescent sexuality, pregnancy, and childbearing*, vol. II, ed. S.L. Hofferth and C.D. Hayes. Washington, D.C.: National Academy Press.

Susser, M. 1968. *Community psychiatry: Epidemiologic and social themes.* New York: Random House.

U.S. Department of Health and Human Services. 1985. *Report of the Secretary's Task Force on Black and Minority Health: Executive summary.* Washington D.C.: U.S. Government Printing Office.

Wagenkneci, L.E., J.M. Roseman, and W.J. Alexander. 1989. Epidemiology of IDDM in black and white children in Jefferson County, Alabama, 1979–1985. *Diabetes* 38:629–633.

Wilkinson, D.Y., and G. King. 1987. Conceptual and methodological issues in the use of race as a variable: Policy implications. *Milbank Quarterly* 65 (Supplement 1):56–71.

6

Feminist Politics and Reproductive Rights: The Case of Brazil

by Jacqueline Pitanguy

In this text I discuss the role that feminism, as a new actor in Brazilian politics, has played in the enhancement of women's rights as citizens and, more specifically, in the assertion of their reproductive rights. My purpose is to point out the limits and possibilities that the feminist movement has faced as it attempted to reshape the political arena by raising new questions, positioning them as relevant issues, including them in the discourse of those to whom society ascribes legitimacy as speakers, and transmuting women's demands, especially those related to reproductive health, into public policies. Although various actors, including the Catholic Church, have contributed nationally and internationally to advances and backlashes in the configuration of women's reproductive rights, I will focus mainly on the interaction between feminism and the state.

From a methodological point of view, the text combines both description and political analysis. It is neither neutral nor objective. It is a story told by someone whose search for the underlying logic of the events is deeply marked by having been a protagonist in this struggle. This perspective naturally influences my understanding of Brazil's women's movement both as an autonomous political actor and in its interaction with the state.

This chapter is organized in three sections. The first deals with the appearance of feminism as a social force in Brazil, the second discusses the relationship between feminists and other actors, and the third focuses more specifically on reproductive health and rights. The text does not consider the feminist struggles which took place in the first decades of this century because at that time women's movements prioritized the conquest of "formal" political rights such as the right to vote (1932). Health was not a central issue, and reproductive rights had not emerged as part of the struggle for women's citizenship.

Although Brazilian women as a group have been historically excluded from power and social justice, race and poverty color the experience of this exclusion. In multi-racial societies with significant income disparities, social movements do not "speak for" homogeneous constituencies. Nonetheless, in this text, I will present my perception of the main trends in feminist political action which have united women in spite of differences in class or color.

Feminism as a Political Actor

The Emergence of a Feminist Agenda

In considering the rise of the feminist movement in Brazil, some background on Brazilian politics and economics is essential.[1] The history of twentieth century Brazil is marked by two long periods of authoritarian rule. The first, installed in 1930 by a populist civilian leader, lasted until 1946. The second, installed by the military in 1964, lasted for 21 years, with fluctuations over time in the degree of state violence and repression of democratic institutions. Today, Brazil has a multi-party, presidential system and civil society includes a number of associations, non-governmental organizations (NGOs) and social movements. Each state has its own legislative, executive and judiciary body and national decisions are taken at the federal level.

According to the International Monetary Fund's (IMF) figures for 1991, Brazil is the ninth-largest economy in the world in terms of Gross Domestic Product (GDP), but the growth of GDP has never implied greater social justice. Income is highly concentrated; 53 percent of the GDP goes to the richest 10 percent of the population. The social consequences of this situation were aggravated in the 1980s, when the crisis of the external debt interrupted investments, and rigid programs for structural adjustment were adopted. The adjustment policies led to a decrease in the well-being of the population as a result of high inflation rates, increases in the public deficit and decreases in salaries and social investments. Brazil has also seen a rise in urbanization since the 1970s; more than 70 percent of the population now lives in urban areas due to an acceleration in internal migration.

As of the late 1980s, Brazilian women have one of the highest levels of labor force participation in Latin America (40 percent), but median income for women is only 54 percent of men's, and women are highly concentrated in the tertiary sector and in less prestigious occupations. Despite the general context of a deficient and exclusionary educational system, there has been significant improvement in women's access to education over the last decades. Women's participation rates in education are similar to or even higher than men's at all levels of education.

Politically, few women have attained formal power in the legislature, executive and judiciary, although women participate heavily in social movements and civic associations. In 1991, the National Congress had a predominantly male profile; women represented only 5.4 percent of members of the chamber of deputies and 2.5 percent of members of the Senate. Women's movements are, however, considered a strong political force in Brazil and more than 2500 organized groups and associations are estimated to be operating throughout the country. In the last decade, important advances have been made in improving women's legal status and in creating institutional spaces inside the executive body to attend to women's demands.

In Brazil, as in most Latin American countries, women have not been part of the political arena until recently. Exclusion — whether based on sex, class, race, ethnicity or other variables — has characterized the structural arrangements of most Latin American societies, even the so-called democratic ones. In fact, in our societies, the question of exclusion is inherent to any analysis of social and political participation and leads immediately to the following question: who are the citizens? And, consequently, what issues and themes are part of the public debate?

Although repressive governments prevalent in Latin America during the last decades have provided a difficult context for women's struggle for full citizenship, the recent history of this continent also shows that social movements, along with other democratic forces, can overthrow dictatorships and reshape the political sphere. Latin America is still a continent of social injustice and exclusion but new actors, including women's organizations, now play a role in shaping the political debate. How women have resisted political exclusion in Latin America has varied with cultural and historical characteristics as well as with the general political context of each country, but it is possible to identify some trends. Generally, feminism emerged in Latin America's public arena in times of authoritarianism and military dictatorship. With the re-democratization process, which in some countries started in the late 1970s, feminism faced the challenge of expanding the concept of democracy to include gender equity. Beyond this general framework, however, each country varies considerably. In Brazil, it is generally agreed that feminism has been visible and strong, one of the first women's movements to gain access to government power. The success of its collective action is related to the capability of these new protagonists to gain space, visibility and weight in the balance of power.

In 1964 a military regime took power in Brazil, and the late 1960s and 1970s were marked by the consolidation of that regime through the militarization of political power and the diversification and modernization of the State's repressive apparatus. The most repressive phase of authoritarian rule between 1969 and 1973 paralleled the so-called economic miracle, when the growth rate of the Gross Domestic Product reached as high as 13.6% per year and industrialization and urbanization accelerated. However, most Brazilians, as is now widely recognized, benefitted little from this growth.

From 1964 to 1974, the institutions of civil society organized to resist the military regime, to struggle against it and to survive that struggle. There was little room for the individuation of political actors; "the people united against dictatorship" was the slogan used by the opposition. These people, in political terms, had no sex and no race. Political mobilization took the form of mobilizing and strengthening opposition to the government. Civic rights, political freedom, and criticism of the economic model were the predominant and "legitimate" questions of public debate.

In 1974 the military allowed parliamentary elections, confident their candidates would win. Trusting in the substantial economic growth, they expected that an electoral victory would bring legitimacy to the authoritarian system. However, the elections — a clear referendum on the government — resulted in a significant defeat for ARENA, the government party. After 1974, the government began a gradual transition to democracy, relying on a strong ARENA and the maintenance of coercive methods to control the speed and intensity of the transition. During this time, Gross Domestic Product growth rates declined, becoming negative in 1981 and 1983.

In 1978, when the government was defeated in the main urban centers, the process of legislative renewal and transition to democracy speeded up. The opposition party was able to pass a law that ended the two-party system imposed by the military. Other parties, formerly clandestine or recently-founded, emerged. Although the military was not fully displaced until 1985, it is generally agreed that from 1978 forward, the government lost its hegemony (Guilherme dos Santos 1982; Reis and O'Donnel 1988; Diniz 1985).

In 1982 there were elections for state governors, in which the opposition won in most important states and the government party obtained only 36 percent of parliamentary votes. Central power remained, however, in the hands of the military and during 1983-1984, Brazilian society mobilized its largest mass movement, DIRETAS JA, calling for presidential elections. This mass movement had the support of the various political parties, civic and professional associations, unions, and social movements, expressing the diversity of the opposition and the emergence of a new political culture in the country.

The political transition took place, as mentioned earlier, against a backdrop of economic difficulty; there occurred as well significant differentiation among the protagonists previously united in the struggle for democracy. In the late 1970s, the country experienced intense political mobilization with the resurgence of labor unions, which had until then been persecuted and placed under the control of the government, and the appearance of other forms of political activism. The strengthening of social movements such as the black movement, the women's movement, and movements for demarcation of Indian lands and protection of the environment marked the end of a homogeneous concept of "the people." Issues of class, sex and race began to enter the political arena to qualify the opposition and to reshape the concept of democracy.[2]

These new voices joined in with the claims from many different groups and organizations that, acting outside the political parties, already represented a strong voice in the opposition. Movements for amnesty, press associations, human rights groups, and ecclesiastic communities based on Liberation Theology highlighted the violence of the state, individual freedom and political rights. Among the social movements that built collective action on the basis of projecting their individuality politically, women's movements, where feminism was the ideological base, became some of the most expressive.

Although feminist ideas were known to a few women in the 1960s, feminism was largely perceived at the time as a movement more suited to affluent societies. Only in 1975 did feminism appear as an organized social movement, following a seminar organized by a group of women under the auspices of the United Nations. The seminar was held after the government defeat in the parliamentary elections, when the rhetoric of transition was combined with a recrudescence of political violence. The seminar provided the catalyst that brought forward and organized a number of issues that were already percolating in the minds of individuals and small groups.

To many Brazilian feminists, that seminar is a watershed in the sense that it introduced and gave visibility to a number of issues, bringing new controversies and more complexity to the public debate. Women's demands — for control of their bodies, the right to regulate their fertility, sexuality not necessarily attached to procreation, efforts to combat domestic violence and non-discriminatory legislation — had until then been perceived by many progressive forces dedicated to the "major" questions of political freedom as irrelevant and divisive, even ridiculous.

The period from 1975 to 1979 can be characterized as the period in which the feminist agenda was established in the country. The feminist agenda included, basically, two connected proposals: first, to bring women's issues into other large organizations like labor unions, political parties, neighbors' associations, and professional associations; and second, to expand throughout the country the number of groups that explicitly assumed a feminist identity.

It is important to note, however, that the feminist identity itself is not a given, essentialist or ahistorical concept, but the result of a process of alliances, disputes and networking whose configuration developed from the internal dynamics of the feminist movement and from its relations with the other actors in the political arena. Nor did feminists act as a monolithic group. There were differences among the various feminist groups, which were reflected in the issues raised and in the strategic alliances established with other social forces. This trait is not peculiar to feminism, but a general characteristic of social movements; they build solidarity based on the political definition of a common identity. Most of them incorporate, in their dynamics, the discussion of the elements which would define such identity and the ways in which this identity should be projected in the public space (Boschi 1987; Calderon and Santos 1987).

Democratization: Feminists Face Other Actors

During the 1970s, there was no dialogue with the state or federal executive power, which was still dominated by the military and their civilian representatives. The executive branch expressed toward the women's movement the same general attitude expressed toward civil society in general: a deep mistrust and perception as a menace to order. After the government's electoral defeat of 1974 and the strengthening of the opposition party, feminists tried to interact with the legislative branch by proposing changes to the family code, under which men were considered heads of households. Although communication channels with the Congress were more open than those with the executive, they were still frail and no lasting relationships resulted from that attempt.

From 1975 to 1979, feminists engaged in debates and alliances with the political left, although resistance to issues seen as taboo or problematic was present in large sections of the opposition which did not want to break their alliances with the progressive Church. Marxist parties and organizations, which considered class struggle the key motor of historical change, tended to perceive certain issues raised by feminists, especially in relation to sexuality, as superfluous or as secondary "superstructural" contradictions. Since many feminists also defined themselves as leftists, and were involved in various forms of opposition to dictatorship and struggles for social justice, the accusation that they were dividing and weakening the opposition was particularly painful and hard to resolve.

For some feminists, especially those with a Marxist background, the inclusion of questions not "directly" related to socioeconomic conditions represented therefore a difficult challenge. The need to define the movement's agenda, establishing priorities in the face of scarce resources, regional disparities, and unfair distribution of wealth, social benefits and education, led many activists to ask if there was any sense in talking about ownership of the body, about pleasure and sexuality, when women needed food and sanitation. These questions point to the challenge of combining universals and specifics, of drafting agendas that match significant variations in the concrete socioeconomic conditions under which gender relations are experienced, and of building collective identities out of diversity.

Differences among feminists on these questions tended to be not so much a matter of principle as of priorities, alliances and timing for political actions; it was generally agreed that issues concerning sexuality and reproduction were core organizing principles for the movement. The divergence rested on the pertinence of raising such issues at particular political conjunctures. In the end, the double identity of many feminists as leftists and as members of the growing women's movement was responsible for the fact that, by the end of the decade, the "left" was more receptive to the feminist agenda and had begun incorporating some women's issues into its own agenda.

This process was catalyzed by the fact that in 1979, Congress enacted a law that gave amnesty to political refugees. Thousands of Brazilians who fled the country in the 1960s and 1970s returned, including a significant number of women who had participated in the struggle against dictatorship. These men and women brought back to the country new ideas about gender and power. Many had gone to Europe, where they were exposed to feminist ideas, as well as to environmentalist and "green" platforms. On their return to Brazil, they became important activists in social movements. The rebirth of the labor unions also brought a very important new interlocutor for feminists in the early 1980s. Many meetings and conferences were organized jointly by feminist organizations and union leaders, and special attention was given to the social rights of the female worker.

From 1979 to 1982, feminists in many urban centers decided to work inside the more progressive political parties, trying to bring feminist issues to party platforms and discourses. Although in general the parties have a strong male profile, a bureaucratic structure and a traditional perception of power and politics, they could not ignore the new questions raised by women. Many of them began to include some feminist demands in their programs, especially those related to labor and education.

The most progressive sector of the Catholic Church — which had been important allies in the denunciation of the state's violence — was also an important point of reference for feminists, who tried to network with civic Church organizations *(comunidades eclesiasticas de base)* which had an outspoken female membership. From the beginning, the interaction with the Church proved difficult, bringing out important divisions among feminists as to the tactics and strategies that the movement should follow. While the Church accepted the struggle against sexual and domestic violence and incorporated demands for day-care centers and protection of maternity rights, it strongly rejected any discussion of sexuality, contraception, or abortion, thus excluding key elements of reproductive rights from the dialogue. For some feminist groups, the importance of networking with the Church was so significant that they preferred to postpone the discussion of issues that would bring conflict, and to emphasize the questions perceived as legitimate by the Church. For others, it was more important to build a clear feminist identity, in which sexuality and reproduction were central, than to expand alliances at such a cost.

In the 1980s, with the strengthening of political parties, labor unions and other social movements, the Church lost its relevance as a strategic ally and the feminist movement, as a whole, no longer accepted the exclusion of sexuality and reproductive rights from the national debate. In fact, in cities like Rio de Janeiro and Sao Paulo, the decriminalization of abortion became a major issue, bringing public attention to the consequences of illegal abortion in a country where approximately 1.7 million abortions are performed yearly.

This period also brought an expansion in centers for women's studies in the universities, as well as an increase in gender-oriented theses and research. Although still in a ghetto—where, even today, it largely remains — the feminist discourse gained academic legitimacy, expanding the voices that make it visible, and indirectly increasing its weight in the balance of power. Even during the 1970s the universities had been an important site for the development of feminist ideas. During the military period, students and some faculty represented an important force in the opposition to the military and, even though they were heavily controlled by police and most of their forums and organizations were outlawed, the universities provided an important space for conferences, seminars, debates, and activities in which feminist issues were raised with little restraint, and sexuality was not considered an illegitimate theme.

Feminism reached the general public though the visibility given to feminist issues in the media, even if media attention was still permeated by stereotypes and false premises. A feminist alternative press emerged and played an important role in facilitating communication among the various groups and in raising issues not dealt with by the media.

It is generally agreed that, by the end of the 1970s, feminism had gained space in Brazilian society as a political movement, even if not all women's issues had the same visibility or weight in the political debate. Using an analogy from the Christian faith, I would say that some women's issues, like sexual and domestic violence and social rights concerning maternity and labor leave, had gained sufficient legitimacy and were on their way to "heaven." Most others, including those concerning sexuality and contraception, were still in political "limbo," where society places the issues that are kept waiting until a change in the balance of power brings them forward. Others, like abortion, remained in political "hell," where questions which are seen as too dangerous or controversial are kept. By the early 1980s, although women's citizenship rights were still neither a central issue nor one supported by consensus among the dominant political forces, the feminist debate had opened important doors to bring women's issues into public discourse. With the movement for decriminalization, even abortion moved from "hell" to "limbo," where it remains until today.

The road that leads from the critique of power to the exercise of power is a very difficult one. Its contours are framed by the general political processes of the country and involve reshaping of the crucial relationship between state and civil society, between social movements and institutional power.

In 1982, during the first direct elections for state governments and parliaments, women from different groups and political affiliations wrote a common agenda, called the Feminist Alert for the Elections, and presented it to the various parties. This agenda contained their main demands, including a state program to ensure access to contraception, and to safe abortion in circumstances (rape and risk of life) already guaranteed by the law, as well as a proposal to decriminalize abortion. Although abortion still remained taboo, some parties included issues concerning reproductive health in their programs.

Some of the less controversial feminist demands were included in the campaigns of the opposition parties. Even though they were not key elements, the presence of these issues on party platforms indicated an important advance into the institutional channels of power, which had been hitherto indifferent to women's demands. The victory of the opposition in states where the women's movement was quite strong, like Rio de Janeiro, Sao Paulo and Minas Gerais, the presence of feminists in the winning parties, the support that the opposition candidates had received from women's movements, and the visibility and weight of women's demands were all advantages for women in negotiations with the newly-elected state-level executive powers.

This new political juncture challenged feminists to step inside government. There was fear of being co-opted and a lack of consensus among the various women's groups as to the strategies to adopt. Part of the movement considered that it was necessary to participate in the democratization of the country, using state power to bring a gender perspective to public policies and struggling for the creation of state-level councils to improve women's legal and social condition. Another element of the movement approved of the idea of opening such spaces but was not willing to step into them. They offered to work from the outside with those who took government positions. A smaller part of the movement decided to remain autonomous and free to criticize. All three positions proved to be beneficial for the expansion of women's citizenship rights in Brazil. During the 1980s, most feminist groups had some kind of interaction with the government and the relationships were not antagonistic, but respectful and supportive.

The creation of the State Council for Women's Rights (*Conselho Estadual da Condicao Feminina*) in Sao Paulo in 1983 marked the beginning of the transformation of feminist discourses and demands into public policy. Almost a decade had elapsed since feminism emerged as a political actor. By 1985, when the democratization process reached the federal executive level and the first civilian was elected president, there were already two such state councils for women's rights in operation, and the first Special Police Station to Attend Women Victims of Sexual or Domestic Violence (DEAM) had been inaugurated.

Although the dominant forces in government at the time involved an alliance between a conservative and a liberal party, the change of power was welcomed by all progressive sectors. The prospect of democratizing the state and building bridges with civil society marked a moment of hope and belief in government. The idea of creating an organization, operating at the highest national level, that would be responsible for drawing up and implementing public policies with a gender perspective mobilized many feminists who considered Sao Paulo's experience with the State Council for Women's Rights (*Conselho Estadual da Condicao Feminina*) a positive one, in terms of implementing gender sensitive public policies.

The networking, alliances, and disputes involved in creating this body took approximately six months. In this period, the country's elected president died and his vice president, a more conservative man, assumed the presidency. The National Council for Women's Rights (CNDM) was installed by Congressional Law No. 7,353 in August 1985. At that time, the new government needed to expand its base of support to increase its legitimacy and, therefore, the executive branch did not have a very clear ideological profile. It was a government of compromises and alliances. The state's machinery, however, was still heavy and corporate, as it had been adapted to serve the previous military regime. Despite this CNDM could act speedily in its early phase.

Although CNDM was administratively under the jurisdiction of the Ministry of Justice, the President of the Council reported directly to the President of the Republic, and the board had the autonomy to make decisions about the lines of action and allocation of resources. In five years, CNDM developed programs addressing reproductive health, violence, labor and rural women, black women, education, culture and legislation. It also compiled information and documentation and set up a communications department, since the media was widely used in national campaigns.

From 1985 to 1990, the number of state offices dedicated to improving women's situation multiplied. By 1989 there were 34 Councils of Women's Rights operating at the state and municipal level and over 100 DEAM police stations. Operating within a federal system, these organizations were linked to local authorities, but also maintained a direct relationship with CNDM. The latter coordinated a forum of Councils of Women and networked with the DEAMs in order to maintain the national focus so necessary in a country as large as Brazil.

From 1986 to 1988, CNDM devoted special attention to the new Constitution which was being prepared by a newly elected Congress. In 1986 it organized a meeting in the National Congress, attended by more than 2,000 women from very different backgrounds (in terms of class, occupation, color) from all regions of the country. The major result of this meeting was the approval of the "Letter of Brazilian Women to the Constituents," which has largely influenced the work that developed, in partnership with other women's organizations, to ensure women constitutional rights. Approximately 80 percent of their demands were included, partially or totally, in the Constitution.

Public Policies and Reproductive Rights

The story of feminism in Brazil is deeply connected with the struggle against population control programs oriented toward demographic goals, and for the implementation of a comprehensive women's public health program. Feminists have always placed contraception in the framework of a woman's life cycle and have fought for integrated delivery of information, contraception, and reproductive and sexual health services. This philosophy has guided the participation of women's health advocates in ministerial commissions and in campaigns against abuses of women's integrity, whether they come from family planning services or from the doctors and scientists responsible for new contraceptive technologies.

Feminist commitment to reproductive rights has grown even as a dramatic demographic transition is underway in the country, with a large drop in fertility rates, despite a tripling of population size between 1940 and 1991. Demographers recognize two trends operating in this period. A general decrease in mortality rates led to population growth rates of over 3 percent annually in the 1950s and 1960s. The second trend combines the decrease in mortality rates with a sharp fall in fertility rates. As a result, the rate of population growth has fallen from 2.9 percent in the 1960s to 1.8 percent in 1985-1990, even without an explicit governmental anti-natalist policy.

Until the 1960s, overpopulation was not an issue in Brazil; population growth was perceived as a positive factor both for economic development and geo-political security. The power of the Catholic Church, which is influential in government and institutional hierarchies though exerting less influence on people's daily life decisions, also contributed to a passive pro-natalist policy. Despite this policy, and the existence of legislation outlawing all contraceptive devices and abortifacient, family planning was introduced "unofficially" in Brazil on a large scale by private international organizations in the 1960s. By the 1980s, 71 percent of women between the ages of 15 and 54 who were married or with a partner used contraception, a percentage similar to that of European countries or the United States. In certain states, especially in the northeast, the sterilization rate is as high as 70 percent, and in certain socioeconomic groups — where the proportion of black women is highest — 50 percent of the women sterilized are under 29 years old. Sterilization is generally performed during the birth process, and Brazil has one of the highest — 60 percent — rates for cesarean sections in the world.[3]

Until the 1970s the state did little to control population, and the shift from pro-natalist policy to the "official" acceptance of family planning was quite slow. In fact, the government's first two programs in this area, the Prevention Plan for High Risk Pregnancy (PPGAR, 1977) and Prev-Saude (1980), were scrapped for budgetary and political reasons. In 1979, however, the government changed the legislation which prevented the promotion of contraceptive methods. In the late 1970s and early 1980s, the neo-Malthusian perspective, predominant in the countries of the North, gained credence among civil and military "elites" as the preoccupation with territorial occupation lost ground to urban poverty and violence. Family planning also met the needs of increasing numbers of women working and living in urban areas, who had to guarantee family survival in the slum-like conditions of the cities without the support of an extended family network. The 1970s also correspond to the expansion of the media, especially television, which started to operate on a national basis and bring to remote areas, by means of soap operas, the values of the "modern" urban middle class, among them the idea of small nuclear families.

In 1983, an important program resulted from dialogue among the Ministry of Health, a group of feminist women's health advocates and the university. Federal power was still in the hands of the military but the democratic transition was on course and inside the state's machinery there were public officers willing to work with members of civil society. This program was called Program of Integral Assistance to Woman's Health (PAISM). Its introduction made official the involvement of the state in reproductive health and framed this involvement within the feminist perspective of respect for women's integrity. Today, PAISM's philosophy and proposed actions are considered by many as an example of a feminist approach to public policy. Its main goals were to increase the coverage and quality of prenatal assistance and of childbirth assistance, to implement and expand activities for the control of breast and cervical cancer, to prevent and treat STD's, to develop fertility regulation activities through the implementation of family planning methods and techniques, and to diagnose and treat infertility. Although PAISM does not mention abortion, not even to regulate its delivery in circumstances of rape or risk of life, it represented a step forward.[4]

In 1986, health professionals inaugurated the National Health Conference, the first under democracy. At their initial meeting, they set up the principles of public health and the norms to decentralize the delivery of services. For the first time in these annual reunions, women's representatives were given a space to bring the issue of reproductive health to that forum.

The Letter of Brazilian Women to the Constituents which, as stated earlier, was initiated by CNDM, was delivered to the National Congress in March of 1987. This letter had two basic premises: that health is a right of all and a duty of the state, and that women have the right to health care delivered under a comprehensive and integral perspective, independent of her role as child-bearer. These principles clearly indicate the shaping of a new concept of reproductive rights, claiming simultaneously a woman's authority over her body, and a redefinition of the state's duty to that body. Under these general principles, the letter also asked for the prohibition of any coercive measure, from the state or from national or international organizations, to impose or deny contraception. Special attention was given to the issue of contraceptive testing and its effects on women's health. The supervision of the production of chemicals and hormonal methods of contraception and the prohibition of commercialization of drugs still in the stage of testing were also demanded.

The issue of contraceptive testing had mobilized feminists in Brazil since 1984, when doctors at the University of Campinas began to test Norplant under the aegis of the Population Council. Women questioned the testing of subjects without their full knowledge and acceptance, and denounced unethical experimental practices, largely contributing to the fact that in April 1986 the Ministry of Health cancelled the authorization for the tests. While the Norplant episode demonstrated the power of feminists in winning a battle against a very powerful section of physicians, it also indicated the need to look for some common ground with such groups, an effort that was initiated in the late 1980s and early 1990s (Barroso and Correa 1991; Dacach and Israel 1993).

By the time the National Council for Women's Rights (CNDM) was founded in 1985, much had already been done by women's movements to introduce the question of reproductive health and rights into the public debate and government discourse. However, the new government had not taken any further initiative in this matter. One of the first initiatives by CNDM on this issue was to offer to collaborate with the Ministry of Health to produce educational booklets, slides and videotapes, and to ask that large numbers of a booklet planned under PAISM be produced. After negotiations with the Ministry of Social Security, the health minister agreed to print five million copies and distribute them through the public health network, as well as to mothers who took their children to public day-care centers. This agreement was given high visibility in the press.

The booklet talked about women's right to information and contraception, and asserted that it was important for women to join organized movements to preserve and exercise these rights. The booklet also described various contraceptive methods, including the IUD. The reaction of the Catholic Church to the booklet was immediate. The President of the National Confederation of Bishops pressed the Minister of Social Security not to print the booklet, claiming that the IUD was an abortive method and could not be supported by the government. The Church's campaign against the IUD led the Ministry of Health to withdraw this contraceptive device from the range of methods offered by PAISM until it could be evaluated by a body internal to the ministry. CNDM confronted the Church, arguing separation of church and state, and claiming that the IUD should be evaluated for possible side effects rather than on the question of whether it was abortive. The minister came to a compromise, agreeing to alter only 200,000 copies of the booklet.[5]

This episode is important because, for the first time, women, speaking from inside the government, were part of the negotiations. They could not beat the Church, but neither could they be ignored. They were an uncomfortable new actor in a scenario where, traditionally, decisions concerning a woman's body have been made without consulting her. While this episode once again made clear the impossibility of aligning with the Church in matters concerning sexual behavior and contraception, it must also be remembered that this same Confederation of Bishops had asked for CNDM's advice in a national campaign to improve the status of women.

In 1987 CNDM organized, along with the Ministry of Health, the National Women's Conference on Health and Rights, where general principles of the Letter of Brazilian Women to the Constituents and of PAISM were reaffirmed and abortion was declared to be a matter of public health. The more than 3,000 women who attended the meeting were mostly health professionals and women's health advocates. They called for the legalization of abortion and focused attention on abuses of private family planning programs, which were distributing oral contraceptives without considering a woman's physical health, and performing sterilizations on a large scale.

Women's lobbying and strategies were partially successful. Article 226, paragraph 7 of the country's new Constitution defines the protection of reproductive rights as a duty of the state and a right of all citizens.

> ...based on principles of human dignity and responsible paternity, family planning is considered the free choice of the couple. The state is responsible for providing educational and scientific resources necessary for the exercise of this right. Any coercive action on the part of public or private institutions is strictly forbidden. (Brazilian Constitution, 1988)

When the text was originally presented to the Congress by CNDM, it did not include the words "responsible paternity" or "couple." These words were introduced as part of the political bargain with conservative sectors. But, in general, women agreed that an important step had been taken in the redefinition of citizenship rights and the reconfiguration of the relationship between the individual and the state.

Another initiative of CNDM was to address the ministers of health and social security, asking them to "obey the law" by providing abortion services in public hospitals in the circumstance of rape or life-threatening illness. Although, as expected, this initiative received no support, it brought public attention to the discrepancy between laws and actions, the resulting damage to women's health, and to the government's refusal to face the question of abortion, in a country where, in 1991, abortion was the fifth leading cause for hospitalization in the country (DATASUS, Ministry of Health). It is well known that often a woman will induce an abortion and come bleeding to the hospital, complaining that she had a spontaneous "loss."

The struggle over abortion against the Catholics and Evangelists, allied with national and international groups to protect the fetus was one of most difficult battles CNDM has fought. CNDM understood from the beginning that they were up against the strength and commitment of the religious groups and the general indifference of the Congress, who, with very few exceptions, regarded abortion as taboo. Along with women's groups, a common strategy was developed in order to neutralize the arguments of the Church and pro-life groups. Since petitions could be considered by Congress provided they included 30,000 signatures, CNDM argued that abortion was not a constitutional matter and women's groups presented a petition to legalize abortion in order to counteract the pro-life petitions. The strategy was to impede a backlash, and on those terms, the strategy was successful. Both positions were argued on the floor of the Congress, and Congress decided that abortion was not a constitutional issue. Given the strength of the opposition forces in this issue, this result was considered a victory.

A new president was elected in November 1989 and assumed office in March 1990. During the election, the conservative forces in the government gained power. The Board of Directors of CNDM understood that the opposition's power was mounting and that they had only a brief window of opportunity to shape the political dialogue and influence the candidates' platforms on the abortion issue. In July 1989, CNDM organized an unprecedented nationally televised debate where the candidates answered questions related only to women's issues. The questions were compiled by women's groups and state councils, and telephoned to each candidate. All candidates were asked to clarify their position regarding abortion. Only one candidate declared ideological support for abortion, and only one declared that abortion violated his principles; all other candidates gave waffling answers based on political expediency. Their answers reflected the fact that women were too strong to be ignored completely on this issue, but that the Church continued to have a strong and powerful voice. The candidates compromised by saying that they were personally against abortion, but would entertain a plebiscite on the issue. Feminists, as a political force, had succeeded in putting "women's issues" on the political agenda.

In 1989, CNDM organized another meeting where the Letter of Women in Defense of Their Health was prepared and approved. Based on the same principles as the 1986 letter, this document asked for immediate state action in the implementation of PAISM and denounced the high rates of maternal mortality (150 per 100,000), lack of attention to birth delivery and the need for a reduction in caesareans (one of the highest rates in the world, closely associated with sterilization), decriminalization of voluntary abortion, emphasis on reversible contraceptive methods to decrease the use of sterilization, and the reaffirmation that family planning should aim at improving women's health, not demographic goals. This was the last important event organized by CNDM.

After the promulgation of the Constitution, CNDM started to suffer from pressure and criticism from various conservative sectors. Industrialists and owners of commercial enterprises protested against the cost of extended labor rights and social benefits, including four months of paid maternity leave and five days of paternal leave (for birth or adoption), a policy which was ridiculed. Rural proprietors protested against the extension of labor rights to rural women. Changes in the family code — such as the abolition of the male prerogatives as head of the family and requiring a marriage certificate in order to be recognized as a family, the affirmation of the state's duty to impede domestic violence and to provide family planning, among others — were considered too advanced by some conservative sectors. The Church was deeply dissatisfied with women's advances on the reproductive front, and was still smarting from the success of the feminist movement and CNDM in impeding the inclusion of a provision to protect the life of the unborn in the Constitution.

By that time, the government, facing one of the largest external debts in the world, extremely high rates of inflation and acute public deficits, was searching for support among the most conservative parties and sectors of society. The years of ideological flexibility were over. The Ministry of Land Reform, which represented excluded and exploited rural workers, was dismantled. Although the government was not a monolithic block, and certain sectors supported CNDM's initiatives, women as a political category were not strong enough to withstand all these pressures, and simultaneously to struggle against a new and conservative Minister of Justice.

The last large event promoted by CNDM was the launching, in the National Congress, of the campaign, "Women's Health, a Right to be Conquered," in 1989. Soon afterward, the board and the president of CNDM resigned. They realized that their weight in the balance of governmental power was not enough to allow them to pursue critical lines of policy action, and that to remain would have meant being co-opted. As of today, the feminist movement has no direct representation in the federal executive. In spite of the fact that CNDM was not abolished, it lost its political and budgetary autonomy, and is currently occupied by women with no ties to feminism. National articulation of women's issues is now done by the forum of state-level councils, in difficult circumstances.

Conclusion

Given the general picture of women's health in Brazil, and the fact that PAISM is not still fully implemented, that abortion is still illegal, and that sterilization is still the most widely used contraceptive method, one might argue that feminists have had very little impact. That is not, however, my understanding. In some states, largely influenced by the Women's Councils, there are initiatives for the implementation of PAISM and of the responsibility of the state for this program. Feminists constantly challenge Health Ministers and state authorities. Sterilization abuses have been widely discussed throughout the country, the Senate has installed an Investigatory Commission and a new law project is being discussed, with the participation of feminists, so as to impede abuses. Abortion, which was in political limbo for almost a decade, is emerging as a visible and important issue. As a consequence of this political development, civil organizations have grown stronger, and women's groups are a large constituent of the recently formed NGO's. Currently there are two measures, proposed by feminists before both houses of Congress, which would decriminalize abortion. Women are also organizing themselves to influence the government positions for the 1994 World Conference on Population and Development in Cairo.

A feminist health network was created in 1991, which incorporates more than 50 regional groups. The network is called the National Feminist Network on Health and Reproductive Rights, and was recently invited to send a representative to the National Health Council, a board advising the President.

And yet, this is just the beginning of progress after centuries of gender exclusion and discrimination. Much remains to be done in this particular field where political strategies and alliances are allied to sex and sexuality, to values and emotions, and to the taboos and dangers that impregnate the field of reproductive health. In a country with a long history of political authoritarianism, the road to women's reproductive health is constantly being interrupted and rebuilt.

Notes

1   For more detailed information on Brazilian women's social, demographic, political and economic situation see " Latin American Women in Data: Brazil." The study was done by CEPIA, under the general coordination of J. Pitanguy and edited and published by T. Valdez. FLASCO, Santiago, Chile.

2   This political mobilization raises questions that cut vertically and, thus, challenge the horizontal class divisions among groups acting to create a new political culture (Boschi 1984).

3   For more information on contraception and fertility rate decline in Brazil, see Berquo 1989.

4   Abortion is still a taboo for government. PAISM was enacted only in 1987, and today it is not really implemented throughout the country. This distance between discourse and practice characterizes the difficulty of exercising reproductive rights already guaranteed by laws and programs.

5   There is no written account of this episode, of which I give testimony as a protagonist.

References

Alvarez, S. 1990. *Engendering democracy in Brazil.* Princeton, N.J.: Princeton University Press.

Alvez, B., and J. Pitanguy. 1981. *O que e feminismo.* Sao Paulo: Brasiliense.

Alvez, M.H. 1988. Grassroots organizations, trade unions and the church: A challenge to controlled *abertura* in Brazil. *Latin American Perspectives* 11(1):73–102.

Barroso, C., et al. 1987. *Homem-mulher: Crises e conquistas.* Sao Paulo: Melhoramentos.

Barroso, C., and S. Correa. 1991. Servidores publicos versus profesionales laborales, la política de investigacion sobre anticonceptivos. *Estúdios Sociológicos* 9(25):7–104.

Berquo, E. 1989. A esterilização feminina no Brasil hoje. In *Quando a paciente e mulher. See* CNDM 1989.

Blay, E. 1979. The political participation of women in Brazil: Female mayors. *Signs: A Journal of Women in Culture and Society* 1:42–59.

Boschi, R.P. 1983. *Movimentos coletivos no Brasil urbano.* Rio de Janeiro: Zahar Editores.

———. 1984. *The art of association: Social movements, the middle class and grass roots politics in Brasil.* Post-doctoral report. Stanford University.

———. 1987. *A arte de associação: Política de base e democracia no Brasil.* Rio de Janeiro: Vertice.

Brazil. 1988. Federal Constitution.

Brazil, Ministry of Health. 1990. DATASUS, a database of the Ministry of Health.

Brito, A. 1986. Brazilian women in exile: The quest for identity. *Latin American Perspectives* 13(2):58–80.

Bruschini, M.C.A., and F. Rosemberg, eds. 1982. *Trabalhadoras do Brasil.* Sao Paulo: Brasiliense.

Calderon, F., and M. Santos. 1987. Movimentos sociales y gestacion de cultura politica. In *Cultura politica y democratizacion,* comp. N. Lechner, et al. Buenos Aires: CLACSO/FLASCO and ICI.

Conselho Nacional dos Direitos da Mulher (CNDM). 1986. *Carta das mulheres aos constituintes.* Brasilia.

———. 1987. *Para viver o amor.* Brasilia.

———. 1989a. *Carta das mulheres pelos seus direitos reprodutivos.* Brasilia.

———. 1989b. *Quando a paciente e mulher.* Brasilia.

Costa, A. 1992. *O Paism, uma politica de assistência integral a saúde da mulher a ser resgatada.* Sao Paulo: Comisao cidadania e reprodução.

Dacach, S., and G. Israel. 1993. *As rotas do Norplant®.* Rio de Janeiro: CBAG.

Diniz, E. 1985. A transição politica no Brasil. *Dados* 28(3):329–46.

FLASCO and CEPIA. 1993. *Mulheres Latino-Americanas em Dados: o Brasil.* Santiago, Chile.

Goldberg, A. 1982. Feminism in authoritarian regime. Paper presented at the 22d International Political Science Association (IPSA) World Congress, in Rio de Janeiro.

Pitanguy, J. 1985. The women's movement and political parties in Brazil: A discussion on power and representivity. Paper presented at the 23d IPSA World Congress, in Paris.

———. 1990. Políticas publicas y ciudadania. *Transiciones* 13:13–23.

Reis, F.W., and G. O'Donnel, eds. 1988. *A democracia no Brasil: Dilemas e perspectivas.* Sao Paulo: Vertice.

Santos, W.G. 1982. Autoritarismo e Após: Convergências e Divergências entre Brasil e Chile. *Dados* 25(2):151–163.

Sen, G., and C. Grown. 1987. *Development, crises and alternative visions: Third world women's perspectives.* New York: Monthly Review Press.

7

Health versus Rights: Comparative Perspectives on Abortion Policy in Canada and the United States

by Janine Brodie

In the late 1980s, the Canadian and American Supreme Courts rendered key decisions which effectively eliminated each country's national abortion policy and the associated regulatory regimes. In Canada, the 1988 *Morgentaler* decision was celebrated as a victory for women because it struck down the regulation of abortion through the Criminal Code and appeared to recognize women's right to reproductive choice. By contrast, the 1989 American Supreme Court's *Webster* decision was widely acknowledged as a threat to the reproductive freedoms women won in the 1973 decision, *Roe v. Wade*. Although these decisions were fundamentally different both in tone and intent, both effectively decentralized the regulation and politics of abortion. This chapter analyzes this decentralization process and suggests that the current period may provide a strategic opening for pro-choice groups to engage in broad-based coalition-building around the issue of women's right to health.

Both the Canadian and American cases demonstrate an increasing fragility and inaccessibility of reproductive choice for women. They also reveal the complexity of the politics of abortion and, in particular, expose the role played by different institutions and discourses in setting the limits and possibilities of these politics. The politics and status of abortion in each country are quite distinct. This is due, in large part, to different social constructions of abortion and to different delivery systems. In the United States, abortion was initially constructed as part of women's right to privacy, while in Canada it was defined as part of a women's right to health care. This fundamental difference placed abortion politics on distinct trajectories and, until recently, promoted distinct outcomes. Paradoxically, these paths may now be converging, requiring new strategic thinking about both the politics of abortion and issues of accessibility.

Despite these differences, the story of abortion politics in each country is very similar. Both countries, consistent with international trends, liberalized access to legal abortions in the early 1970s. In both cases, the drive for liberalization initially came from professional groups, largely doctors and lawyers. It was only later that each country witnessed the polarization of the issue around opposing assertions of women's and fetal rights. Moreover, the main actors in this struggle — pro-life and pro-choice groups — are strikingly similar in both countries in terms of origins, discourse, and strategies. The politics of abortion has been increasingly characterized by pro-life groups' harassment of and violence toward abortion providers and clinics. Finally, both countries recently have seen the collapse of their national abortion policies and the decentralization of regulatory practices.

The story of abortion politics has many strands which weave through social hierarchies as well as across different cultural representations. This paper will focus on the legislative and judicial strand, in which recent events increasingly threaten women's access to abortion services in North America. These "official" moments, however, rest on and are imbued with broader struggles over representation which challenge women's autonomy and moral agency, attempt to reconstruct the private sphere and the patriarchal family, and intensify the classism and racism of the new world (dis)order. They co-exist with "unofficial" abortion politics, the terrorist attacks on abortion clinics and providers, and the incessant harassment of women struggling to exert some control in their lives. These official and unofficial sides of abortion politics together constitute the site for renewed struggles about the very meaning of choice itself.

Health versus Rights: Competing Official Constructions

Canada, like most other Western countries, relaxed its abortion legislation approximately two decades ago (Glendon 1987). For most of Canada's history, abortion was banned and criminalized under the Offences Against the Person provisions of the Criminal Code. These provisions, inherited from Britain when Canada was a colony, made abortion an indictable offence carrying penalties of up to life imprisonment for abortionists and up to seven years for women attempting to obtain abortions. The permitted exception was an abortion to save the life of the woman.

Although Canada officially maintained a ban on all abortions until the regulatory regime was liberalized in 1969, the government opened some discretionary space for doctors under British common law in the 1939 *Bourne* case. A doctor, charged with performing an abortion on a young gang-rape victim, was acquitted on the grounds that the procedure was necessary to preserve her physical and mental health. Thereafter, British and Canadian doctors could and did perform abortions for health reasons. By the early 1960s, many Canadian hospitals had formalized procedures, such as approval committees, for the termination of pregnancy. Abortion, however, remained a "grey area" in the law which doctors wanted clarified, especially in the face of increasing demand for the procedure (Jenson 1992).

The case for reform of Canada's abortion law was largely cast within liberal and medical discourses. Liberals argued that sexual norms had changed and that the state had no business, as then-Prime Minister Trudeau put it during the 1968 debate, "in the bedrooms of the nation." The movement for reform, however, was spearheaded by the medical profession and its lawyers who wanted established practices legalized to eliminate the threat of criminal prosecution. Women were largely absent from the debate; they appeared mainly as the "victims" of back street abortionists who were in need of protection. The idea that women had the right to reproductive choice and that this choice was integral to women's equality was voiced infrequently and only at the margins of the debate (Jenson 1992).

After a series of consultations, the federal government moved to change the regulation of abortion in 1969. The new provisions were embedded in an omnibus bill which also legalized birth control and homosexuality among consenting adults. The new abortion law, Section 251 of the Criminal Code, maintained a general ban on abortions, but allowed for a "therapeutic exception." An abortion was legal only if it was performed in an accredited hospital and only after the hospital's Therapeutic Abortion Committee (TAC) had certified that the continuation of the pregnancy "would or would be likely to" endanger the life or health of the woman. In effect, the reform replaced judicial control after the fact with medical control before the fact (Dunsmuir 1989).

It is important to emphasize here that the 1969 reform did little more than codify what was already standard practice in some urban hospitals

(Pelrine 1975). It did not grant women any new rights, only the opportunity to receive a medical treatment deemed appropriate by a committee of doctors. As such, abortion became the only medical procedure governed by the Criminal Code of Canada. Moreover, the law did not recognize non-medical indications for terminating a pregnancy. All legal abortions were by definition, therapeutic, a medical intervention necessary to protect the health — however broadly conceived — of the woman. The candidate for an abortion was an exception, an "unhealthy" woman, and thus eligible for medical treatment under Canada's universal health care system provided that a "neutral" third party (the TAC) approved (Kellough 1992). Even after the reform, then, access to legal abortions in Canada was tightly controlled by the medical profession and delivered through the existing health care system. The legislation did nothing to guarantee women's access to abortion; hospitals were not required to establish a TAC, a necessary precondition for providing this exceptional medical service. In a sense, then, the procedure was cast as optional and ancillary to the health care delivery system.

Feminists were immediately critical of the 1969 reform, arguing that the new law did not go far enough; that it put too much control in the hands of doctors and; that it was inappropriate to regulate a medical procedure through the Criminal Code. In the succeeding years, the emerging feminist movement staged a national protest to extend the reforms. They formed pro-choice organizations, and called for decriminalization, women's reproductive rights and "abortion on demand." The Canadian pro-choice movement's resolve intensified when their American sisters appeared to win these rights in 1973.

Although a new national abortion policy came later to the United States than Canada, the momentum for reform had been established in many states during the late 1960s. Between 1967 and 1973, 19 American states liberalized their abortion laws and four of these states (Alaska, Hawaii, New York and Washington) repealed all criminal penalties for abortions performed in early pregnancy (Glendon 1987). Of these four, however, only New York's 1970 legislation allowed out-of-state residents to obtain an abortion. Thus, only American women with the financial means to travel could obtain a legal, "non-therapeutic" abortion before the *Roe* decision. And, indeed, women appear to have taken full advantage of this opportunity: out-of-state residents accounted for 60% of the abortions performed in New York state between 1970 and 1972 (NARAL 1992).

The American Supreme Court decision in *Roe v. Wade* (1973) was significant because it struck down all but one state's (New York) existing abortion regulations and set the guidelines for a new national regulatory regime. More importantly, the Court constructed pregnancy and abortion as a matter of rights, at least in the early stages of pregnancy, unlike Canada and most western European countries. According to *Roe*, pregnancy was a three-stage process with different interests and rights taking precedence at each stage. Extending the logic of previous cases relating to birth control, the Court indicated that during the first trimester the woman's wishes were paramount; the government could not interfere with her decision whether or not to terminate a pregnancy other than to insist that the abortion be performed by a licensed physician. During the second trimester, the state could take a more active regulatory role, but only in ways designed to protect a woman's health. During the third trimester, at the point of potential fetal viability, the balance of rights shifted to the state and its interests in protecting potential human life (Tribe 1990). The state could "regulate and even proscribe" abortion at this stage except when the life or health of the mother was at risk (Frug 1992).

The *Roe* judgement granted women the right to choose during the early stages of pregnancy on the basis that the decision was a profoundly private one, as Justice Powell put it, "grounded in the concept of personal liberty guaranteed by the Constitution" (Tribe 1990). The privacy doctrine recognized the right to decide certain issues arising from marriage and procreation without state intervention (Olsen 1991). Initially, however, the Supreme Court saw the abortion decision as bearing more on the privacy of the doctor-patient relationship than on a woman's right to autonomy and self-determination (Copelon 1990). Indeed, the *Roe* decision, as Justice Blackmun argued, pivoted on the right of doctors "to administer medical treatment according to his professional judgement" (Tribe 1990). Explicit judicial acknowledgement of a woman's right to choose actually did not emerge until 1977 in *Whalen v. Roe*. The Supreme Court's most forceful articulation of this right came as late as 1986 in *Thornburgh v. American College of Obstetricians and Gynecologists,* when Justice Blackmun wrote that "a woman's right" to choose to terminate a pregnancy "freely is fundamental" (Copelon 1990).

The reproductive rights ascribed to American women by the Supreme Court through *Roe* and later decisions were a source of envy in the Canadian pro-choice movement. Even so, the American Supreme Court's construction of abortion as a matter of civil rights and individual privacy actually contradicted aspects of feminist discourse and politics. The notion of privacy applied by the Supreme Court was compatible with the liberal tradition of separating the personal from the political. It enforced the long-standing boundary between the public and private which is fundamental to patriarchal domination within the family, recognizing that there were private spaces upon which the state should not tread either in the form of regulation or the provision of services (Copelon 1990). American women could make a private decision about abortion but the equally critical issue of access to abortion services was also privatized. The state did not have the right to interfere with a private decision but it was not obliged to act affirmatively to allow women to exercise that right. As the Supreme Court reiterated as recently as 1991, "The government has no constitutional duty to subsidize an activity merely because [it] is constitutionally protected" (Henshaw and Van Vort 1992). The provision of abortion services was thus largely left to the marketplace.

Although Canada and the United States liberalized and standardized the regulation of abortion at approximately the same time, each country had a unique definition of the procedure with different assignments of both control and availability. In Canada, all legal abortions were necessary for the health of the woman. Thus, doctors were given the choice, hospitals provided the service, and, because of Canada's universal health care system, the state was responsible for paying for the procedure. In the United States, by contrast, all women were given the choice to obtain an abortion in the early stages of pregnancy, if they wanted one. The issues of location and access, however, were also deemed a matter of private initiative and resources. Put differently, the liberalization of abortion regulation during the early 1970s had quite distinct implications for Canadian and American women. For Canadian women abortion was a question of health needs; for American women it was a question of individual choice. Through these discursive constructions, Canadian women "won a symbolic right to access but without the corresponding right to choose" while American women won "the symbolic right to choice without the corresponding right of access" (Kellough 1992).

Access and the Politics of Health

In both Canada and the United States, the liberalization of abortion was followed by a sustained struggle between pro-choice and pro-life groups over women's access to abortion services. In the United States, with the battle over choice seemingly won, the pro-choice movement focused its efforts on increasing access through the establishment of abortion clinics, while their Canadian counterparts continued to fight for the decriminalization of abortion and the legal recognition of women's right to choose. The pro-life movement in both countries has devised numerous strategies to ban abortion completely or limit access to life-threatening situations only. The strategies and successes of the pro-choice and pro-life movements, however, have been shaped by the distinct forms of definition and regulation in each country.

The medicalization of abortion in Canada served both to depoliticize and localize political struggles around the issue of access. By defining a legal abortion as a technical-medical solution to a health problem, the 1969 abortion law initially insulated politicians from political pressure from both pro-choice and pro-life forces. The pro-choice movement continued to criticize the legislation for denying Canadian women the right to choose while the growing incidence of abortion was taken as evidence by pro-life groups that the new regime was too permissive.[1] The politics of abortion, then, took place outside of the official political arena and, during the early period, was primarily concerned with the issue of access.

The new law required that abortions be performed in an accredited hospital, but hospitals were not required to establish a Therapeutic Abortion Committee (TAC). Moreover, without a clear definition of health, TAC's were free to exercise their religious and political biases to deny women the procedure. Women with the same "health" indications could be passed by one TAC and turned down by another. In addition, the pro-life movement began to intervene in hospital politics to gain majorities on hospital boards and close down the TAC, thus making the procedure unavailable to women in the community. By 1975, less than 25 percent of accredited hospitals had a TAC and, by 1982, 17 hospitals accounted for three-quarters of the therapeutic abortions performed in Canada (McDaniel 1985).

The combined problems of arbitrary and inconsistent treatment of women by hospital TAC's, the requirement that abortions be provided only in accredited hospitals and the domination of local hospital boards by pro-life forces meant that access to legal abortions was increasingly confined to a few urban centers. As early as 1977, a government study concluded that "the procedure provided in the Criminal Code for obtaining therapeutic abortions is in practice illusory for many Canadian women" (Canada 1977).

It is impossible to determine how many women were unable to obtain an abortion as a result of these impediments, although the same government study suggested that 60 percent of Canadian women did not have access to the procedure. Comparative data from the mid-1980s also suggest that problems of access were significant (See Table 7-1). The rate for abortion in Canada was less than half that of the United States. Moreover, in Canada, the vast majority of abortions were provided by hospitals while, in the United States, clinics disproportionately provided the service.

The issue of access and the crucial gatekeeping role of the hospital TAC's led to the Supreme Court's historic 1988 *Morgentaler* decision and the subsequent dismantling of a national abortion policy in Canada. Dr. Morgentaler, one of the few voices calling for abortion on demand during the 1960s reform process, openly defied the restrictive conditions of the new regulatory regime by opening an abortion clinic in Montreal in the early 1970s. Morgentaler claimed that he was acting out of necessity

Table 7-1 **Comparative Abortion Statistics — Canada and the U.S.**

	Canada (1987)	United States (1985)
1) Rate of abortion per 1,000 women aged 15-44	12.1	28.0
2) Abortion ratios per 100 known* pregancies	16.6	29.7
3) Total** abortion rates	299	797
4) Abortion Facilities		
Non-hospital	14.5***	85.5
Hospital	86.9***	13.1

*   Known pregnancies are defined as sum of legal abortions and live births.

**   Total rates defined as number of abortions that would be experienced by 1,000 women during their reproductive lifetimes.

*** These figures are for 1985.

Source: Henshaw and Van Vort 1992.

because the regulatory regime was preventing women from getting the medical care which he, as their doctor, deemed was necessary and appropriate.[2] Throughout the 1970s and early 1980s Morgentaler was repeatedly charged and subsequently acquitted by a jury. He was jailed for over a year after the Supreme Court rejected his "defence of necessity" in 1975. Thereafter, however, the new Quebec nationalist government, strongly supported by the women's movement, decided not to pursue further charges, arguing that the Criminal Code restrictions on abortion were no longer enforceable in the province. The federal government decided to ignore these developments, thus paving the way for the establishment of more free-standing abortion clinics in that province (Morton 1992).

Morgentaler's case reached the Supreme Court a second time in 1987-88 and the Court decided in his favor, declaring the 1969 reforms unconstitutional. The decision did not, however, provide women with constitutional recognition of their reproductive rights. Instead, the majority of the judges decided that Section 251 of the Criminal Code, and the TAC requirement in particular, violated Canadian women's constitutional right to security of the person. Although the language of the Court appeared to support the idea of choice, the decision itself was grounded on the "manifest unfairness" of the procedures, such as the arbitrary decisions of TACs and the delays inherent in the process. These factors prevented women from getting appropriate, timely medical care and thus violated the "security of the person" provision of the charter.

Contrary to popular perceptions that the *Morgentaler* decision had granted women reproductive rights, only one judge cast abortion as a question of women's reproductive rights. Moreover, all judges recognized that the state may have a legitimate interest in protecting the fetus. Women did have rights but these were rights to health care free from potentially harmful regulations and third-party interference. Only within a universal health care system could these rights be read as a code for reproductive freedom, and the pro-choice movement certainly interpreted the decision in this way. Like the *Roe* decision, the *Morgentaler* decision guaranteed nothing. From a strictly legal perspective, the Court simply struck down the 1969 regulatory regime without providing guidelines for a new national policy. In fact, the Court explicitly argued that a new regulatory regime, one which balanced the interests of the woman and the fetus, would have to be negotiated in the political sphere. After three years of political battles, however, the federal government was unable to achieve a new compromise between pro-choice and pro-life forces. As a result, Canada has been without a national abortion policy since January 1988, resulting in uneven distribution of and diminishing access to abortion services (Brodie 1992).

Access to abortion services in Canada has become a matter of geography and resources. Where a woman lives and whether she can afford to pay for travel and/or clinic costs determines whether she obtains the procedure. As Table 7-2 shows, distinct abortion regimes have evolved in the provinces in the five-year period of deregulation.[3] The most liberal regime is in Quebec, which has allowed abortion clinics since 1976. Nineteen of Canada's thirty abortion clinics are in Quebec, and 15 of these are part of the provincial health care system. Thus, these abortions are fully funded by provincial health insurance. Although access remains concentrated in the large urban centers of the province, Quebec appears to have avoided much of the abortion politics and violence that characterizes the rest of Canada and the United States. As the director of one Montreal abortion clinic remarked, abortion is "such a non-issue that we don't even keep statistics on it anymore" (Laughlin 1989).[4]

Women and abortion providers in the remaining provinces have been plagued by violence and harassment from pro-life forces and by restrictive provincial regulations. Pro-life harassment has largely been confined to British Columbia and Ontario, where the recently elected social democratic governments have been most willing to provide and pay for abortion services. In the face of pro-life attempts to close hospital facilities, British Columbia's government has introduced regulations within the Hospital Act mandating that certain hospitals within each region of the province provide abortion services. Ontario's social democratic government has also been actively pro-choice, especially since the 1992 bombing of the Morgentaler clinic in Toronto. Ontario is the only provincial government that provides full funding for abortions either by hospitals or free-standing clinics.

In the remaining provinces, the issue of access is more problematic, if not moot. In the prairie provinces, access is largely confined to one clinic and a handful of urban hospitals, some of which enforce local residency requirements. In the Atlantic provinces, provincial governments have taken an active role in regulating abortion. In New Brunswick, for example, there are no free-standing clinics and the government is against their introduction. Prince Edward Island has passed legislation opposing

Table 7-2 Access to Abortion in Canada: 1993

British Columbia
- two free-standing clinics
- 33 designated public hospitals
- provincial funding of clinic abortions

Alberta
- one free-standing clinic
- three hospital providers, one with local residency requirements
- partial funding (25%) of clinic abortions

Saskatchewan
- one hospital clinic; no free-standing clinics
- limited access to hospitals, most with local residency requirements

Manitoba
- one free-standing clinic
- limited hospital access in one urban center (Winnipeg)
- province forced by court to pay for clinic abortions (currently under appeal)

Ontario
- three free-standing clinics, all in Toronto
- hospital access largely in Toronto: many large urban centers have no hospitals providing service
- full funding of clinic abortions

Quebec
- 19 clinics
- access concentrated in Montreal
- full funding for abortions performed in hospitals, women's health centers and community health centers
- partial funding of clinic abortions

New Brunswick
- no free-standing clinics
- access restricted to three hospitals, all in south of province
- funded abortions must be approved by two doctors and performed by a gynecologist in a hospital

Nova Scotia
- one free-standing clinic
- hospital access concentrated in Halifax
- partial funding of clinic abortions

Prince Edward Island
- provincial legislation opposing abortion in province except in a life-threatening situation
- will pay for out-of-province abortions only if approved by a five-doctor panel and performed in a hospital

Newfoundland
- one free-standing clinic
- only one doctor, in one hospital, provides abortions
- hospital abortions require approval by a gynecologist, a psychiatrist, and a social worker, and counselling by a registered nurse

Northwest Territories
- access restricted to major centers
- funding of travel costs

Source: Childbirth by Choice Trust 1993.

the procedure and only funds out-of-province abortions when they are performed in a hospital and are first approved by a five-doctor panel. Similar restrictions apply in Newfoundland, where access is limited to one hospital and approval from a gynecologist, a psychiatrist and a social worker is required.

The issue of access in the Canadian system is still very much in flux after five years of deregulation. The pro-choice movement celebrated the 1988 *Morgentaler* decision because it appeared to grant women choice without state interference. The intervening years, however, have demonstrated that the struggle for reproductive freedom continues and that court victories, even within the context of a universal health care system, often can be fragile and contradictory (Gavigan 1992). If anything, the decision shifted abortion politics to new terrains — to the provinces, the hospitals and to minute regulatory spaces. The Canadian experience demonstrates that the right to choose means very little without access and that a medical definition of abortion does not ensure access even though, in a public health care system, services are theoretically available to all. Defeat in the courts has induced pro-life forces to concentrate on the micro-level of service delivery, effectively banning the procedure in many community hospitals and discouraging all but the most committed providers from performing the procedure. These factors, coupled with hostile provincial governments, have made abortion services virtually unavailable for many women (especially in rural areas, the North, and throughout much of the Prairie and Atlantic provinces). Increasingly, only those who have the financial means to travel to large urban centers are ensured the procedure and then, often, at the cost of harassment. As a result, subtle class biases have been written into an eroding delivery system. In addition, women able to access fully-funded hospital abortions are subject to the biases and politics of the community hospital. For example, a recent CARAL report (1992) noted that the only hospital providing abortion services in the Northwest Territories had performed as many as 972 abortions, mainly for aboriginal women, without anesthetics because "the anesthesiologist does not believe in abortions." The emerging regulatory regime increasingly resembles the pre-1988 status quo and belies the notion of choice.

Perhaps most disconcerting is the potential for provincial governments, whether because of pro-life sentiments or cost-cutting initiatives, to remove abortions from national health insurance, or attempt to carve a regulatory distinction between "non-therapeutic" and "therapeutic" abortions — the "wanted" and the "needed." Poor and young women are already disadvantaged in provinces where the government refuses to cover (or pays only a portion of) the cost of a clinic abortion. The Saskatchewan government, for instance, has won a non-binding plebiscite in which the majority of voters rejected the idea of government funding for abortion. The government has not acted on this plebiscite and, indeed, recognizes that such an action would lead to litigation. The decision of the Manitoba Court of Appeal in *Lexogest Inc.* (1993), however, may encourage this province and others to further restrict access through funding regulations.[5] Immediately after this decision, a spokesperson for Canadian Physicians For Life suggested that the Manitoba government should use the ruling as an opportunity to ensure only medically necessary abortions. At this point, the distinction between therapeutic and non-therapeutic abortions is largely moot in Canada. But, as the American experience demonstrates, this distinction has acted as the thin edge of the wedge which first denied poor women reproductive choice and now threatens women's reproductive freedoms in a growing number of American states.

Access and the Politics of Rights

Abortion politics in the United States has taken a different trajectory because of the initial judicial construction of abortion rights as a matter of choice and the configuration of the regulatory regime. In particular, the courts have been the site of numerous battles aimed at curtailing the reproductive rights granted to women in *Roe v. Wade*. The pro-life movement has attempted, unsuccessfully, to amend the Constitution to ban abortions; to enact restrictions on choice and access at the state level; and to elect politicians committed to changing the composition of the Supreme Court and, thereby, reverse the 1973 decision. Until recently, the Supreme Court has consistently protected a woman's right to choose, but decisions relating to funding and access have made this right illusory for many American women.

The steady attrition of reproductive rights in the United States is tied to the withdrawal of public funds for the provision of abortion services. Beginning in 1973, the pro-life movement successfully lobbied for bills prohibiting foreign aid for funding or assisting in the procurement of an abortion. By the mid-1970s this prohibition was also applied to public funding of domestic abortion services. In 1977, for example, the Supreme Court upheld a Connecticut regulation that prohibited state funding of "non-therapeutic" abortions (*Maher v. Roe*) and granted that a public hospital was not constitutionally compelled to provide them (*Poelker v. Doe*). More significantly, during the same period, Congress approved the Hyde Amendments which banned the use of Medicaid funding for almost all abortions, even some deemed medically necessary. This federal ban was upheld by the Supreme Court in 1980 in *Harris v. McRae* (Tribe 1990). The United States thus gained the dubious distinction of being the only developed country which does not publicly fund abortions indicated for health reasons unless the situation is life-threatening (Henshaw 1992).

Unlike the Canadian case, the American privacy definition proved vulnerable to pro-life attacks on at least two counts. First, the idea of personal choice carried with it an implicit message that "non-therapeutic" abortions were consumer items, something one chose according to personal preference. While the state might be responsible for providing funding for a poor woman whose life was at risk, it was not obliged to fund a consumer preference. Second, pro-choice advocates were unable to show that the withdrawal of state funding was a threat to women's right to privacy (Tribe 1990). This right no more required the state to fund abortions than the right to bear arms obliged it to make guns freely available. The Court recognized in *Harris*, however, that the denial of state funding would make it "difficult if not impossible" for poor women to exercise their choice (Copelon 1990). In other words, the Court made it clear that abortion was a right for women with the necessary financial resources (Olsen 1991).

The effect of the Hyde Amendments were immediate and highly discriminatory. Before 1976, fully 33 percent of all legal abortions in the United States were funded by Medicaid, a funding program designed to provide medical care to the poor and "indigent" (Tribe 1990). In 1977, the federal government funded 294,600 abortions, but by 1990, this number had fallen to 165. In 1990, there were 162,418 state-funded abortions, although these were available largely only in 13 states (Gold and Duley 1992).

The pro-life movement grasped, perhaps better than its pro-choice counterpart, the fragility and limits of a guaranteed "right." Although pro-life forces in both Canada and the United States have been unsuccessful in gaining constitutional recognition of fetal right to life, they have worked through the political system both to influence judicial process and to devise legislation which tests the judicial boundaries of women's reproductive rights. In the United States, pro-life forces have consistently tested the boundaries of *Roe*, with little success until 1989. More importantly, they helped elect Presidents Reagan and Bush, largely on the candidates' promise that the composition of the Supreme Court would be changed and *Roe v. Wade* reversed.

Both the Reagan and Bush administrations petitioned the Supreme Court to reverse its 1973 *Roe* decision, but the pro-life plurality on the bench was not able to begin to reverse the long string of decisions which upheld women's reproductive choice until 1989. In *Webster v. Reproductive Health Services,* the Supreme Court struck down the national abortion regulatory regime, which had evolved since *Roe,* by granting states the constitutional right to legislate restrictions on women's choice. These regulations have attempted to limit access to abortion services, particularly for young women, poor women and women of color.

The *Webster* case concerned 1986 amendments to abortion regulations in Missouri. The new law had twenty provisions, five of which became the object of scrutiny before the Supreme Court. The act contained a preamble stating that "the life of each human being begins at conception" and that "unborn children have protectable interests in life, health, and well-being." This unmistakably pro-life rhetoric was coupled with provisions requiring that physicians perform fetal viability tests on women believed to be 20 or more weeks pregnant to determine "the gestational age, weight, and lung maturity of the unborn child." Further, the new regulations prohibited both the use of public facilities or employees to perform abortions and the use of public funds, employees or facilities for the purpose of "encouraging or counselling" a woman to have an abortion (Frug 1992).

In a decision which appalled but did not surprise pro-choice activists, the Court voted to uphold the Missouri legislation, arguing that neither the preamble nor the other restrictions affected a woman's decision to have an abortion. Extending the logic of *Harris* and other funding cases, the Court argued that Missouri's refusal to allow public employees to perform abortions in public hospitals "leaves a pregnant woman with the same choices as if the State had not chosen to operate any public hospitals at all." Moreover, it argued that "nothing in the Constitution requires States to enter or remain in the business of abortions." Finally, it suggested that the trimester formula advanced by *Roe* had little constitutional or practical legitimacy and that the state had a compelling interest in "protecting potential human life throughout pregnancy" (Frug 1992).

The Supreme Court did not overturn *Roe* but instead, as Justice Blackmun put it, "with winks, and nods, and knowing glances," invited "every state legislature to enact more and more restrictive abortion legislation" and thus systemically erode women's reproductive choice (Frug 1992). The decision stretched the logic of earlier Medicaid decisions to illogical limits. Previously the Court had decided that, under the privacy doctrine, the state had no obligation to fund abortions. Women were free to exercise their rights if they could pay. In *Webster*, however, the Court allowed that the state could prevent an otherwise "private" hospital from providing abortion services to paying customers simply because the facility was on land leased from the state. Considering that the private-public distinction in the American health care system is nearly moot, the decision effectively freed states to ban hospital abortions. The effect would be to deny access for women who rely most heavily on hospital abortion facilities — poorer women, women of color, rural women, and women requiring later-term abortions, many of whom tend to be young (Copelon 1990). Moreover, the prohibition on counseling willfully prevented women from making an informed decision about the health risks involved in continuing a pregnancy. Again, this lack of counseling is more relevant for some groups than others. Women of color, for example, are more likely to suffer from health conditions — such as high blood pressure, hypertension, and diabetes — commonly recognized as more dangerous during pregnancy (Ross, Hill, and Jenkins 1992). As in the funding cases, then, *Webster* was a direct assault on the reproductive rights of poor women and, disproportionately women of color (Fried 1990b).

By abandoning the trimester framework, the new plurality on the Supreme Court invited state governments to invade and restrict the "private" space granted to women in *Roe*. The conservative-minded judges also intruded on the patient-doctor relationship which had been so central to invoking the privacy doctrine in the first place. The demand for tests for fetal viability — weeks before existing techniques are accurate — served both to delay an abortion, thus adding to the woman's health risk, and potentially to triple the cost of the procedure. Justice O'Connor argued, in what was later to become a key phrase, that the fetal testing requirement did not impose an "undue burden on a woman's abortion decision" (Frug 1992).

Following the decision, the National Right to Life Committee indicated that it would push for new state regulations which, through the fine print and using the letter of the law, would further limit women's choice and access. Since then, a number of significant cases have already been decided by the Supreme Court, each of which progressively expanded the terrain and justification for new state restrictions on women's access to abortion. The first two, *Hodgson v. Minnesota* and *Ohio v. Akron Center for Reproductive Health,* were decided in 1990 and tested state regulatory capacity on the issue of parental notification and consent. In 1976, the Court had upheld parental consent requirements so long as the legislation also allowed for a judicial bypass or, as one lawyer put it, "a judicial shaming process," whereby a judge could provide consent for a minor when a parent refused (Copelon 1990). The Minnesota law under review in *Hodgson* required that young women under the age of 18 obtain the consent of both parents and endure a 48-hour waiting period. No exceptions were made for children of divorced, sole-custody or single-parent families. Indeed, the law required that the minor make a "reasonably diligent" effort to find an absent parent even if she did not know the parent. A minor willing to declare before the courts that she was a victim of parental sexual or physical abuse was exempt from the parental consent requirement. The Akron, Ohio regulations required the youth to provide "clear and compelling" evidence of such abuse before an exemption was granted (Tribe 1990). The Supreme Court upheld both pieces of legislation.

Parental consent laws are obviously consistent with the neo-conservative vision of the patriarchal family as the bedrock of moral order. These requirements put some minors at risk of parental violence and undermine the authority of single parents, the vast majority of whom are women. They do appear successful in preventing teenagers from terminating pregnancies. Soon after the law came into effect in Minnesota, for example, the birthrate among 15- to 17-year-olds rose by 38.4 percent; the birthrate among 18- to 19-year-olds not covered by the requirement rose only .03 percent (Salholz et al. 1989). The legislation did not necessarily reinforce the decision-making structure of the patriarchal family. A survey of four abortion clinics in the state showed that as many as 43 percent of women under the age of 18 obtained a judicial bypass and that this percentage increased with age and lower socioeconomic status. The survey also indicated that minors were more likely to discuss the procedure with their mothers and that those with a religious background were less likely to tell either parent about their pregnancy (Blum, Resnick, and Stark 1992). By 1992, 41 states had enacted laws addressing parental involvement, 17 of which are enforced (Greenberger and Connor 1992).

The Supreme Court dealt another blow to women's choice in 1991 when it upheld the "Title X gag rule" in *Rust v. Sullivan*. The gag rule prohibited family planning clinics supported by Title X funds from providing any information about abortion, even if this information was neutral or specifically requested by the client. Moreover, the law required that, if a clinic receiving Title X funds used private funds to provide abortion-related services, it had to keep these services physically and financially separate. Title X funds over 4000 family planning clinics, most of which tend to serve poor women and women of color.[6] The city and state of New York challenged the gag rule, primarily by arguing that the rule discriminated against poor women (Henshaw and Van Vort 1992). Drawing on *McRae*, the Court explicitly rejected this line of argument. It indicated instead that the "financial constraints that restrict an indigent woman's ability to enjoy the full range of constitutionally protected freedoms are the product not of government restrictions on access to abortion, but rather of her indigency" (Frug 1992). Even if a woman's health was put at risk because of lack of information, her indigency — not government restrictions on what her doctor could tell her — was the cause (Rutherford 1992). The Court made it clear that abortion rights were for those with means and that the brunt of the new restrictions would be borne by poor women and women of color.

After *Webster*, Utah, Louisiana, and Guam effectively banned abortions and enacted tough criminal penalties for doctors breaking the law. Other states such as Kansas, Mississippi, Ohio and Pennsylvania instituted complicated regulatory regimes which created an obstacle course for women seeking a legal abortion. All of these state initiatives came under the Supreme Court's gaze in *Planned Parenthood of Southeastern Pennsylvania v. Casey* in 1992. The case arose from amendments to Pennsylvania's Abortion Control Act, which required a mandatory 24-hour waiting period, a mandatory anti-abortion lecture by an attending physician, spousal consent, informed parental consent for minors, and restrictive emergency exceptions. The case explicitly asked the Court to review the validity of *Roe*.

In five separate opinions, the Supreme Court upheld all of the Pennsylvania restrictions save spousal consent. In doing so, it pushed abortion further away from the 1973 guidelines than any other decision. The Court reaffirmed women's right to abortion before fetal viability by arguing that a complete ban on abortions would be unconstitutional. At the same time, it rejected the trimester framework and argued that the state has an interest in potential life throughout pregnancy. Most importantly, the Court introduced a new standard for judging abortion regulations. The concept of "undue burden" would not invalidate a state-legislated restriction on abortion unless it placed "a substantial obstacle in the path of a woman seeking an abortion before the fetus attains viability." According to the Court, mandatory waiting periods, an anti-abortion lecture, and informed parental consent did not constitute an "undue burden." The decision opened the door for pro-life forces to attempt to determine the limits of the "undue." *Casey* thus marked the end of *Roe* insomuch as the privacy right guaranteed women in the first trimester had been invaded by the state. *Roe*, as Chief Justice Rehnquist explained in his dissenting opinion, "continues to exist but only in the way a storefront on a western movie set exists — a mere facade to give the illusion of reality" (Center for Reproductive Law and Policy 1992). The Supreme Court will probably resist overturning *Roe* explicitly, but to protect the integrity of the Court rather than for any commitment to women's reproductive rights.

The new state regulatory practices, coupled with the escalating harassment of abortion providers and clinics, have diminished access to abortion services. Even before *Webster*, 83 percent of all U.S. counties did not have a single abortion provider (Rossi and Sitaraman 1992). Moreover, one in five urban centers in the United States do not have a single provider. Currently, entire states such as North and South Dakota have only one provider (NARAL 1992). In the United States, as in Canada, where a woman lives, how much she earns and how much she knows increasingly determine whether she can obtain a safe abortion.

Conclusion

The election of the Clinton administration as well as other openly pro-choice politicians in the United States has led many to suggest that the hegemony of the pro-life movement has passed. And, after only three days in office, President Clinton made a number of announcements designed to acknowledge, symbolically at least, this fact. He announced a repeal of the Title X "gag rule," a review of RU-486 (the so-called abortion pill), and allowed for abortions to be performed in military hospitals (for paying patients). He cast these reversals, interestingly, not in the name of women's rights but in terms of health. The death of the "gag rule" would, in Clinton's words, "go a long way toward protecting vital medical and health decisions from ideological and political debate"

(Toner 1993). He seemed to hearken back to the privacy of the patient-doctor relationship recognized and protected by *Roe*. Nevertheless, as this paper shows, the terrain of abortion politics in the United States and Canada has shifted over the last two decades. Although the two countries have been characterized by different discursive constructions of abortion and delivery systems, their situations may indeed be converging: choice in both countries is an elusive concept for increasing numbers of women. If anything, their shared experience underlines the obvious: rights without access mean very little (Fried 1990b).

In the United States, the election of a pro-choice administration will not restore the earlier *Roe* regulatory regime. The Supreme Court's decisions in recent years have opened the regulation of abortion to the political intervention of state governments and determined single-issue groups. The right to choose has shifted from the woman and the private to the state and the public. This decentralization and politicization at the very least requires moving the struggle for reproductive rights to the state level to prevent further constraints on women's choices and autonomy. At the same time, the current debate in the United States about national health care provides other strategic possibilities. Indeed, the pro-choice movement might begin to reconceptualize abortion as a health care need for *all* women, rather than continuing to fight for abstract rights effectively available only to those rich enough to afford them.

At the same time, the U.S. pro-choice movement can draw some lessons from the Canadian experience. Even in the context of a national health care system, reproductive rights can be eroded, especially when abortion is treated as an ancillary service rather than one integral to women's reproductive health needs. Lacking an affirmative national abortion policy, the politics of abortion in Canada is shifting from debates about abstract rights to the fine print of provincial health regulations. These regulations can be used to expand or contract access to abortion and thus are important sites for local political struggles about the health needs of all women, especially those in rural and remote regions. Yet, as in the United States, this constant scrutiny of regulations, while always necessary, concedes too much. Perhaps it is time to shift the terms of the debate.

The decentralization of abortion regulation in both Canada and the United States invites the pro-choice movement to engage in new strategic thinking and to establish new political alliances with broad-based movements concerned with equity and inclusiveness, particularly with respect to health and well-being. For some time now, the politics of abortion has been caught at a discursive impasse which pits the reproductive rights of women against the alleged "right to life" of the fetus. This opposition has been used to deny women access to a basic health need — fertility control. The idea that we shift our thinking about abortion from a rights to a health discourse may be resisted by some because it evokes images of medicalized (and male) control over women's bodies and choices. This is one but not the only possible result of thinking about abortion in the context of women's overall health needs. In Quebec, for example, abortion services have been integrated into an inclusive community health care delivery system. As a result, women have access to safe abortions and, as important, the procedure has not been politicized.

Contrary to the fabrications of the pro-life movement, the central issue has never been whether or not there will be abortions; there always have been. Instead, the central issue, which has been reopened in both Canada and the United States, is what kind of abortions we will have (Miller 1992). In this current round of abortion politics, it is incumbent on the pro-choice movement to struggle for a definition of abortion which integrates it into an inclusive conception of women's health needs and, at the same time, ensures choice for all women.

Acknowledgements

This research was supported by a grant from the Social Sciences and Humanities Research Council of Canada. I would like to thank Catherine Kellogg for her research assistance on this project.

Notes

1   The apparent increase in the number of abortions performed in Canada after the 1969 reform was in fact because the new law made reporting the procedure a requirement (McDaniel 1985).

2   The so-called "defence of necessity" was used successfully in the 1939 *Bourne* case in Britain. It is a rarely used defence which excuses otherwise unlawful behavior if the behavior was intended to prevent a more serious crime or evil. In the early 1980s, the Supreme Court narrowed the grounds for this defence and thereby invalidated the kinds of arguments employed earlier by *Morgentaler*. By the early 1980s, however, the Charter of Rights and Freedoms, the constitutional entrenchment of a bill of rights, provided all Canadians with a right to "security of the person," thus providing grounds on which to challenge the 1969 reforms (Morton 1992).

3   In Canada, the federal government has jurisdiction over the Criminal Code while the provincial governments have jurisdiction over health care. Maintaining abortion within the Criminal Code provided a national regulatory regime. When Section 251 was struck down, it opened the door for provincial governments to regulate abortion through their jurisdiction over health.

4   There are numerous reasons why abortion politics in Quebec differ from those of the rest of the country, but perhaps most importantly, abortion clinics have existed in the province since the 1970s. The French-speaking province also has been isolated from the influence of English-speaking Canadian and American pro-life groups.

5   In 1988, British Columbia's Supreme Court ruled that the provincial government did not have the power to designate whether a procedure was "medically-required" or not but it did have the right not to fund certain medical procedures. In 1987, in fact, the Alberta government "de-insured" sterilization, birth control counselling, and the provision of birth control devices (Brodie, Gavigan and Jenson 1992).

6   1988 statistics show that African-American women comprise 13 percent of women of reproductive age in the United States and 28 percent of those using Title X clinics (Rutherford 1992).

References

Blum, R., M. Resnick, and T. Stark. 1992. Factors associated with the use of court bypass by minors to obtain abortions. In *Abortion factbook: 1992 edition*, ed. S. Henshaw and J. Van Vort. New York: Allan Guttmacher Institute.

Brodie, J. 1992. Choice and no choice in the house. In *The politics of abortion*, ed. J. Brodie, S.A.M. Gavigan, and J. Jenson. Toronto: Oxford University Press.

Brodie, J., S.A.M. Gavigan, and J. Jenson. 1992. *The politics of abortion*. Toronto: Oxford University Press.

Canada. 1977. *Report of the committee on the operation of the abortion law*. Ottawa: Supply and Services.

CARAL. 1992. *Update*. Toronto: Canadian Abortion Rights Action League, April.

Center for Reproductive Law and Policy. 1992. News Release.

Copelon, R. 1990. From privacy to autonomy: The conditions for sexual and reproductive freedom. In *From abortion to reproductive freedom*, ed. M.G. Fried. Boston: South End Press.

Dunsmuir, M. 1989. *Abortion: Constitutional and legal developments*. Ottawa: Library of Parliament.

Fried, M. G., ed. 1990a. *From abortion to reproductive freedom: Transforming a movement*. Boston: South End Press.

————. 1990b. Transforming the reproductive rights movement: The post-*Webster* agenda. In *From abortion to reproductive freedom,* ed. M.G. Fried. Boston: South End Press.

Frug, M. J. 1992. *Women and the law.* Westbury, N.Y.: The Foundation Press.

Gavigan, S.A.M. 1992. *Morgentaler* and beyond. In *The politics of abortion,* ed. J. Brodie, S.A.M. Gavigan, and J. Jenson. Toronto: Oxford University Press.

Glendon, M.A. 1987. *Abortion and divorce in western law.* Cambridge: Harvard University Press.

Gold, R., and D. Duley. 1992. Public funding of contraceptive, sterilization and abortion services. In *Abortion factbook: 1992 edition,* ed. S. Henshaw and J. VanVort. New York: Allan Guttmacher Institute.

Greenberger, M., and K. Connor. 1992. Parental notice and consent for abortion: Out of step with family law principles and policies. In *Abortion factbook: 1992 edition,* ed. S. Henshaw and J. VanVort. New York: Allan Guttmacher Institute.

Henshaw, S., and J. Van Vort, eds. 1992. *Abortion factbook: 1992 edition.* New York: Allan Guttmacher Institute.

Henshaw, S. 1992. Induced abortion: A world overview. In *Abortion factbook: 1992 edition,* ed. S. Henshaw and J. VanVort. New York: Allan Guttmacher Institute.

Jenson, J. 1992. Getting to *Morgentaler.* From one representation to another. In *The politics of abortion,* ed. J. Brodie, S.A.M. Gavigan, and J. Jenson. Toronto: Oxford University Press.

Kellough, G.G. 1992. Pro-choice politics and postmodern theory. In *Organizing dissent: Contemporary social movements in theory and practice,* ed. W. Carroll. Toronto: Garamond.

Laughlin, A. 1989. Court ruling didn't spur demand for abortions, officials say. *Montreal Gazette,* January 12.

McDaniel, S. 1985. Implementation of abortion policy in Canada as a women's issue. *Atlantis* 10:2.

Miller, P. 1992. *The worst of times.* New York: Aaron Asher Books.

Morton, F.L. 1992. *Morgentaler v. Borowski: Abortion, the charter and the courts.* Toronto: McClelland and Stewart.

National Committee on America Without *Roe.* 1992. *Facing a future without Roe.* Washington: NARAL Publications Office.

Olsen, F. 1991. A finger to the devil. *Dissent* (Summer).

Pelrine, E. W. 1975. *Morgentaler: The doctor who wouldn't turn away.* Toronto: Gage.

Ross, L., S. Hill, and S. Jenkins. 1992. Emergency memorandum to women of color. In *From abortion to reproductive freedom,* ed. M.G. Fried. Boston: South End Press.

Rossi, A., and B. Sitaraman. 1992. Abortion in context: Historical trends and future changes. In *Abortion factbook: 1992 edition,* ed. S. Henshaw and J. VanVort. New York: Allan Guttmacher Institute.

Rutherford, C. 1992. Reproductive freedoms and African American women. *Yale Journal of Law and Feminism* 4.

Salholz, E., et al. 1989. Voting in curbs and confusion. *Newsweek,* July 17.

Toner, R. 1993. Clinton orders reversal of abortion restrictions left by Reagan and Bush. *New York Times,* January 23.

Tribe, L. 1990. *Abortion: The clash of absolutes.* New York: W.W. Norton and Company.

Section II

Reproductive Technologies: For Whom, and to What End?

by Rachel Snow

The new reproductive technologies have brought strange new powers to the human race. We now have new technological means for controlling human conception, gestation, and birth. These technologies are being developed and incorporated into the medical mainstream at a rapid pace, and transforming reproductive health care in unprecedented ways. After several thousand years in which contraception consisted of pessaries, douches or sheaths, the last thirty years have witnessed the development of hormonal, intra-uterine and immunologic options. Comparably rapid advances have taken place in infertility care, prenatal diagnostics and birthing technologies.

The chapters in this book address the political and policy dimensions of several new reproductive technologies, including in-vitro fertilization (IVF), contraceptive vaccines, Norplant®, diagnostic technologies for pregnant women and birth technologies. While most of these technologies have been designed in the richest nations, they are tested and promoted throughout the world. Selected papers in this volume provide regional case studies that illustrate the variety of social and political circumstances in which these technologies are now promoted, e.g., in India, Indonesia, Brazil, Australia, the United Kingdom, and the United States.

These technologies have given rise to a wealth of feminist commentary and debate, much of which has been characterized by foreboding: that these technologies are inevitably associated with undesirable health and social consequences for women, for their fetuses, and for society at large. This rejection of high technology reproductive care has been a hallmark of the women's movements in many of the advanced economies for almost three decades. A history of health crises involving reproductive technologies (e.g., the DES crisis, the Dalkon Shield malpractice suits, etc.) may have contributed to this reaction among women, but it was also part of a larger movement by Western feminists to re-claim their bodies and reassert the legitimacy of "natural" self-care, including gynecologic self-exam, natural family planning, natural and home birth, and a return to breastfeeding. The most recent extension of such sentiments is widespread feminist objections to surrogate motherhood, and a re-assertion of the integrity of the maternal-fetal bond, the primary rights of birth mothers, and the abuse potential of shifting fetal care between women.

In many developing countries, feminist objections to reproductive technologies have been characterized by a different set of concerns: namely, frustrations over the predominance of contraceptive technologies, when basic health services are lacking. Unlike their Western sisters for whom high-tech care is the norm, women in poor countries are too often without clinical care, without any attendant birth services, and at high risk of suffering significant morbidity from maternity, or even death. In such circumstances, the advent of coercive or abusive contraceptive care, promoted as less risky than a pregnancy, is particularly galling, and contributes to the distrust of technologies promoted as furthering women's health and well-being.

Common to women's experience on all of the continents, are the long and daunting tales of women's abuse by technologic means in the name of reproductive care. While the nature of abuse may differ in Indonesia and Atlanta, and vary by race and class, the stories of such abuse are uniformly sobering. History warrants reflection in any debate over how best to manage such technologies in an unequal society. But the illustration of such abuse is not a central objective of this volume. Rather, the papers in this volume are addressing, in different ways, the political and policy dimensions of selected reproductive technologies. How can these technologies be used by women and their families, by the health professions, by communities and societies to promote humane values? How can the new technologies be prevented from doing harm to those who they were intended to help? Two main threads connect the responses offered here. The first of these is the thesis that the technologies themselves are not neutral tools being used or abused by society. Rather, they are chosen, designed, evaluated and promoted by select (and often different) political communities, and they manifest the values and interests of those communities. While self-evident to some, this point deserves emphasis, because it provides an organizing principle for addressing many of the feminist concerns about these technologies: who is accountable for problems of abuse? How can abuse potential be avoided in future? And how can the abuse potential of existing technologies be managed?

Judith Wajcman, in *Delivered into Men's Hands? The Social Construction of Reproductive Technology*, the opening paper to this section, investigates the political and economic factors which led to widespread use of numerous technologies: the refrigerator, the stethoscope, forceps, and the contraceptive pill. Drawing on her long experience as a sociologist of workplace and domestic technologies, she introduces the reader to the political dimensions of technology. Applying such an analysis, Judith Richter in *Beyond Control: Anti-Fertility 'Vaccines', Pregnancy Epidemics and Abuse*, gives a detailed account of what motivated the development of the contraceptive vaccine. Reviewing speeches and promotional writings by the developers of this contraceptive, she identifies two overlapping discourses: one drawing on the appeal of using a "vaccine" metaphor for pharmaceutical agents in public health, and a second calling the population problem a social crisis, or "epidemic" of unwanted pregnancies. The confluence of these two discourses, she argues, has led to inflated enthusiasm for the vaccine, and a failure to assess its feasibility with a measured, objective eye. If it were stripped of its metaphorical appeal, she argues, it would be recognized as a pharmaceutical failure, and abandoned. In both these papers, the authors emphasize that reproductive technologies are not neutral products of the laboratory, but subject to political selection and promotion.

Moving beyond product selection, several papers point out that the evaluation of reproductive technologies reflects certain biases of perspective and concern. In my paper *Each to Her Own: Investigating Women's Response to Contraception*, I illustrate how unintended biases in the clinical trial process preclude the availability of data for investigating pharmacologic variability, or the biologic bases of many contraceptive side-effects. Faye Schrater, in her paper *Immunization to Regulate Fertility: Biological Questions*, also points to the problems of variability among women, in this case, in immune response. She argues that the variability among women seems to be discounted by researchers, suggesting an unintended bias in perspective. The reality of this variability, however, will pose a major challenge to any hope of widespread use of this contraception.

Examining a more subtle political dimension of the reproductive technologies, Elizabeth Bartholet in her paper *Adoptive Rights and Reproductive Wrongs*, and Rhadika Balakrishnan in her paper *The Wider Context of Sex Selection and the Politics of Abortion in India*, each identify how selected technologies capitalize on deeply rooted social biases, and further their expression. Bartholet points out how the popularity of in-vitro fertilization (IVF) and other high-tech treatments for infertility in the United States capitalize on and further a biological bias for family formation. Juxtaposing this scenario against the obstacles faced by people wishing to adopt children, she makes a powerful case that the promotion of these technologies is working against another social good: the matching of needy children to people who wish desperately to parent.

In a similar vein, Rhadika Balakrishnan points out that the technical means to identify fetal sex, made possible through amniocentesis and ultrasound, has been used to further the widespread preference for sons in India, providing society a means to exercise such a preference in a new, but devastating manner.

In yet a different approach to the political dimensions of technology, Ruth Hubbard, in her chapter *The Politics of Fetal-Maternal Conflict*, proposes that the opportunity to view the fetus, made possible by ultrasound, has led to an altered social consciousness about fetal and maternal well-being. People can now bond with the "floating fetus," as a distinct entity from the mother; from this, she hypothesizes, has come the myriad of new legislative battles and court cases over fetal rights. As such, the technologies are political instruments because they affect our perceptions of such basic values as biological life, individual integrity, and human welfare.

A second major thread running through the chapters in this volume is the question of what should be done to protect against the abuse potential of the reproductive technologies. Should we legislate against their development and promotion? Should we develop different, and better, social controls? The contributors are not of a single mind on this question, and a meeting of the authors was rife with debate. Judith Richter makes a strong argument for discontinuing research on the contraceptive vaccine; Faye Schrater is cautiously optimistic that, properly used, it may further women's health. Rhadika Balakrishnan does not support laws prohibiting the use of amniocentesis in India, while other contributors supported this action. Sônia Correa, in her paper *Norplant® in the Nineties: Realities, Dilemmas, Missing Pieces*, speaks directly to the failure, in many countries, to develop adequate structures and forces for social mediation between technology and the consumer, raising the possibility that in some societies, prohibition may be the only available course of action.

Even if we agreed that prohibition is an unwise course, and our purpose should be to design better social controls for technology, our job would be extraordinarily difficult. The variety of ways in which women are disempowered through reproductive means makes it difficult to select over-arching ethical principles for "humane" regulation. In China, ultrasound is used to ensure that intra-uterine devices (IUD's) are in place; in other settings, to identify female fetuses for selective abortion; yet in others, for prenatal diagnostics. By what universal rules can the abuse potential of ultrasound be regulated, or rolled back? What is appropriate regulation in one setting may represent the withholding of valuable health care in another.

Despite such difficulties in formulating universal principles for the regulation of these technologies, several authors do recommend specific measures for given technologies. Richter recommends that development of the contraceptive vaccine be halted; in the meantime, she argues that consent forms soliciting women for trials of the "vaccine" should stop using this metaphor; the use of the term "vaccine" leads the public to expect attributes of the contraceptive which this technology does not deliver, and hence consent based on the term is in fact misinformed. Bartholet recommends tax and reimbursement changes to deter the use of IVF technology, and social policies to facilitate the no-tech alternative, adoption.

Reviewing this collection of papers, can one draw conclusions, or over-arching recommendations? Only two persistent unifying themes are evident, echoing perhaps the only unifying themes among feminists worldwide. One is the urgency of education and communication, through every means from formal schooling to informal women's groups, to spread accurate information and promote wise individual and social action. But education is not enough. Broader changes in society, such that more ecumenical interests are brought to bear on the social control of technologies, require more representative governance of scientific education, research and regulatory politics. Given the global transfer of the reproductive technologies, and the myriad institutions through which they pass from design to distribution, we need to increase calls for the leadership of women and minorities in scientific education, biomedical research, regulatory politics, and the international donor community. The papers in this volume are but one small nudge in that direction.

8

Delivered Into Men's Hands? The Social Construction of Reproductive Technology[1]

by Judy Wajcman

We are living in a time when it seems we have unprecedented technological options available to us. We can defy biology altogether and choose to have a child after menopause, we can choose the sex of our child, and (by some accounts) we can choose to have a perfect baby. While it may appear as though technologies are being produced to meet our needs, I argue that women are selecting from a very restricted range of reproductive technologies. These technologies have historical and social relations built into them in such a way that women's choices are in reality highly constrained. Indeed, I would argue that the emphasis placed on women's right to use these technologies for their own ends tends to obscure the way that technologies themselves are shaped by particular political interests.

The Social Shaping of Technology

Before I consider reproductive technology in particular, I would like to address the social shaping of technology more generally because it may be the route to a fuller understanding of our subject today. Too often, technology is seen as the cause of the dramatic positive changes in women's lives that have taken place in the latter half of this century. But the relationship between technology and social change is a complex one and it is important to examine the sources of technologies as well.

For the last decade or so I have been helping to develop an area of study known as the new sociology of technology.[2] Our concern is to challenge the most influential theory of the relationship between technology and society: "technological determinism." According to this theory, technology is neutral, the result of rational technical imperatives.

Technical change is seen as autonomous, outside of society. In its strongest version, technology is seen as having an independent momentum, which not only puts it beyond human control but which also allows it to order all human activity (Ellul 1964). In its milder version, technology is still the driving force of social change but, within the parameters set by technology, we do have a limited range of options. Our human role is to choose the most civilized variant of this technologically determined society. Whilst acknowledging that technological change has political effects, or requires a political response, the theory of technological determinism does not adequately accommodate the fact that technology *itself* is the product of political forces.

Technology is not simply the neutral product of rational technical imperatives; rather, it is the result of a series of specific decisions made by particular groups of people in particular places at particular times for their own purposes. The most recent sociological literature has argued that political choices are embedded in the very design and selection of technology. Through studies of specific artifacts, we can see effects of social relations that range from fostering or inhibiting particular technologies, to influencing the choice between competing paths of technical development, to affecting the precise design characteristics of particular artifacts. Technical innovation is profoundly social; even decisions about whether a device "works" are social. As such, the technical outcomes depend primarily on the distribution of power and resources within society.

Take something you rarely think twice about — the electric refrigerator. We now know from historians of technology that once you could choose between an electric refrigerator and a gas refrigerator, both equally effective (Cowan 1983). General Electric had the financial resources to invest in the development of the electric model, while the manufacturers of gas refrigerators, although they had a product with real advantages from the consumer's point of view, lacked the resources to develop and market their machine. Economic power, not technical superiority, gave the electric refrigerator the edge over its competitor. And that's why we have refrigerators that make an annoying humming noise all night!

If technological innovation is a product of the society which gives rise to it, it follows that technological outcomes of a society structured by gender inequality will reflect this bias. Although gender relations have been absent from mainstream historical and sociological studies of technology, recent feminist research not only explores women's relationship to, and experience of, technology, but looks at the extent to which gender is significant in the making and shaping of technology. Feminist researchers argue that the social relations of technology are gendered relations and that technology itself cannot be fully understood without reference to gender.

This research initially focused on production and paid labor, examining the key role of technology in mediating power relations between women and men and reinforcing sexual divisions at work. It analyzed how women have been actively distanced from technology by men's purposeful monopolization of it, and looked at the currency of popular stereotypes which depict women as technically incompetent. The almost complete exclusion of women from the scientific and technical community until very recently means that the production and use of technology today have been, and continue to be, shaped by male power and interests. Preferences for different artifacts are the result of a set of social arrangements that reflect men's power in the wider society. Patriarchal social relations are thus built into technology.

Feminist Perspectives on Reproductive Technology

Nowhere is this more apparent than in the sphere of human reproduction, but the nature of the relationship between gender and technology here is vigorously contested. The literature on reproductive technology is rife with technological determinist arguments which assume that changes in technology are the most important cause of changes in society. Perhaps here more than elsewhere, major technological advances are seen as having directly transformed women's lives for the better. The technologies of pregnancy and childbirth are said to have ended the dangerous and painful aspects of giving birth. Healthy pregnancies and healthy babies are attributed to the wonders of modern prenatal care, now a highly medicalized and technologized process. The new, sophisticated techniques for monitoring fetal development in the early stages of pregnancy mean that "defective" fetuses can be identified and aborted. Infertile women can now embark on infertility programs that promise the chance of conceiving "naturally." And, most commonly, advances in contraceptive technology are seen as the key to the massive positive changes in women's equality. The widespread availability of reliable contraception and abortion — a right often fought for by women

— has fostered the belief that, for the first time in human history, women are in control of their bodies.

In the early period of the contemporary women's movement, reproductive technology was seen as particularly progressive because it could potentially sever the link between sexuality and reproduction. The much-cited advocate of the use of high technology to liberate women was Shulamith Firestone. In *The Dialectic of Sex* (1970) she emphasized the need to develop effective contraceptive and birth technologies in order to free women from the "tyranny of reproduction" which dictated the nature of women's oppression. She saw patriarchy as fundamentally about the control of women's bodies, especially their sexuality and fertility, by men. A technological fix in the shape of ectogenesis would bring an end to biological motherhood and thus make sexual equality possible.

Genetic research, biotechnology and infertility treatment are now making such dramatic advances that Firestone's ideas no longer seem in the realm of fantasy. The organic unity of fetus and mother can no longer be assumed now that human eggs and embryos can be moved from body to body or out of and back into the same female body. The major proponents of these technologies are the scientists and medical practitioners developing the techniques, and women who have benefited from them. Leading infertility doctors argue that embryo research promises the possibility of eliminating hereditary disease and, most importantly, gives hope to previously childless couples.

In Australia, Britain and North America there is growing debate among feminists over the impact that these novel reproductive and genetic technologies will have on women's lives. Whereas discussions about abortion and contraception challenged the traditional equation of femininity with motherhood, these new technologies are about fulfilling, rather than rejecting, the traditional feminine role. Much of the feminist discussion centers on the notion of choice and whether the right to choose to have an abortion can be equated with the right to choose to have a child. As we shall see shortly, feminist support for techniques such as in-vitro fertilization is founded in the belief that these technologies increase women's choices and that women do indeed have the right to reproduce. First, though, let us look at the arguments of those who vehemently oppose the development of these technologies.

A group of radical feminists, represented here by authors such as Gena Corea (1985), Jalna Hanmer (1985), Renate D. Klein (1985), Maria Mies (1987) and Robyn Rowland (1985), are the most vocal in their opposition to the development and application of genetic and reproductive engineering.[3] These authors see the development of reproductive technologies as a form of patriarchal exploitation. The once celebrated technological potential for the complete separation of reproduction from sexuality is now seen as an attack on women. These techniques are thus an attempt to appropriate the reproductive capacities which have been, in the past, women's unique source of power. The technologies aim to "remove the last woman-centered process from us" (Hanmer 1985).

For this group of feminists, who criticize the ways in which patriarchal society has ignored or sanctioned sexual and domestic violence against women, the new reproductive and genetic technologies are "violence against women in a new and frightening sense" (Klein 1985). Genetic and reproductive engineering is another attempt to end self-determination over our bodies. According to this theory, techniques such as in-vitro fertilization, egg donation, sex predetermination and embryo evaluation will become standard practice and offer a powerful means of social control. Just as other obstetric procedures were first introduced for "high risk" cases and are now used routinely on most birthing women, these authors fear that the new techniques will eventually be used on a large proportion of the female population.

Reproductive technologies are also seen as inextricably linked with genetic engineering and eugenics. Techniques such as in-vitro fertilization provide researchers with the embryos on which to do scientific research. A parallel is drawn between the way in which men experiment on animals to improve their stock and the recent extension of this form of experimentation to human reproduction, or women. The female body is being expropriated, fragmented and dissected as raw material, providing "living laboratories" for the technological production of human beings (Klein 1985).

This approach views science and technology as intrinsically patriarchal. It therefore makes absolutely no difference whether it is women or men who apply and control this technology; this technology is intrinsically an instrument of patriarchal domination. For these writers then, reproductive and genetic technologies are about conquering the "last frontier" of men's domination over women and nature.

Another group of feminist commentators, including Michelle Stanworth (1987), Rosalind Petchesky (1987), and Lynda Birke, Susan Himmelweit and Gail Vines (1990), emphasize the ambivalent effects that reproductive technologies have on the lives of women. A blanket rejection of these innovations is inadequate, they say, because many of them offer women indispensable resources with which to fulfil their maternal desires. These new technologies have the potential to empower, as well as to disempower, women.

These feminists argue that the women's movement has largely ignored the problems of infertility and treated women who participate in high-tech research programs as "blinded by science" and passive victims of prenatal conditioning. They criticize feminists who reject the new reproductive technologies for failing to consider women as active agents who have generated demands for such technologies because of their authentic desire to bear children. Technological intervention may be the only opportunity infertile women have to fulfill this need and, therefore, we should support their "right of reproductive choice".

Defining this "right" is far from straightforward. Within the field of reproductive technologies, we can see that women have different positions in relationship to specific technologies. There is now a much clearer realization that the experience of gender — what it is to be a woman — is mediated by sexual orientation, age, race, class, history, and colonialism. The recognition that new technologies may have very different implications for Third World and First World women, within and between countries, is a strength of much of the literature.

The real dangers for women that accompany medical and scientific advances in the sphere of reproduction are directly related to the different circumstances of women's position in society. Access to the benefits of expensive techniques such as in-vitro fertilization is heavily related to the ability to pay. Women who are poor and vulnerable will not have access to these techniques and furthermore, they will be least able to resist abuses of medical power. For example, urgent ethical issues have arisen over the use of amniocentesis to select female fetuses for abortion in India[4]. In Britain, controversial contraceptives such as Depo-Provera, which were considered unsuitable for the majority of women, have been used extensively on Asian and black women (Rakusen 1981).

There is broad agreement amongst feminists about these dangers but feminists who dispute the radical feminist analysis see these dangers not as inherently patriarchal properties of the technologies themselves, but as a function of their abuse. The technology is described as a double-edged sword.

> On the one hand, they have offered women a greater technical possibility to decide if, when and under what conditions to have children; on the other, the domination of so much reproductive technology by the medical profession and the state has enabled others to have an even greater capacity to exert control over women's lives (Stanworth 1987).

From this perspective, the feminist critique of reproductive technologies goes no further than demanding access to knowledge and resources so that women are able to shape the experience of reproduction according to their own definitions.

This account of the sexual politics of reproductive technology is sophisticated in its understanding of the factors influencing women's use of these techniques. What is less evident is an analysis of how these same sexual politics profoundly affect the direction and pace of technological change. In this area, feminist studies have only recently drawn on the broader field of the social studies of technology. I would argue that the emphasis placed on women's right to use these technologies tends to obscure the way in which historical and social relations are built into the very fabric of technologies. While recognizing the social shaping of women's choices, few participants in the debate acknowledge that the technologies from which women choose are themselves socially shaped.

Women are in fact selecting from a very restricted range of technological options, and the nature of those restrictions are of central importance to feminist interests. Techniques such as in-vitro fertilization, egg donation, artificial insemination, and surrogacy have the potential to place the whole notion of genetic parenthood, and thus conventional nuclear family relationships, in jeopardy. But only those technologies that reinforce the value of having one's "own" child — one that is genetically related to oneself — are being developed. These values determined, for example, the Warnock Committee's[5] assessment of "acceptable" risks to women's health. Despite the dangers, the Committee approved the use of in-vitro fertilization, where egg donation provides an offspring which is genetically related to the husband. Yet the technique of egg donation by uterine lavage (embryo flushing or surrogate embryo transfer) was rejected on the basis of physical risks. The medical risks involved in this procedure are no greater, but it carries the risk of unwanted pregnancy in the donor woman. Both women would then be pregnant from the same genetic parents and the existence of this donor mother-to-be would challenge the usual categories of motherhood. This technology was rejected, not on the grounds that it endangers women's health, but because of its *socially disruptive character* to the identification of blood ties with the family.

The social restrictions that are shaping the availability of technologies is often glossed over by those who are more accepting of the new technologies. In adopting, implicitly or explicitly, the use/abuse model of technology, they limit our role to choosing between the limited range of technologies. Some technologies have more "abuse potential" than others, such as sex-predetermination techniques, and a politics to increase women's involvement in the control and regulation of technologies is crucial. However, Stanworth et al. fail to appreciate the extent to which technologies are not neutral but themselves have political qualities. This is where the strength of the radical feminist analysis lies. In my view, it is right to argue that gender relations have profoundly structured the kind of reproductive technologies that have become available.

To make this claim, though, one does not need to conceptualize this political process in terms of a monolithic male conspiracy. Nor does it imply that men are a homogenous group. While all the stages in the career of a medical technology, from its inception and development, to its consolidation into part of routine practice, are a series of interlocking male activities, the male interests involved are *specifically* those of white middle-class medical experts. The division of labor that produces and deploys the reproductive technologies is both sexual and professional: women are the patients, while the obstetricians, gynecologists, molecular biologists and embryologists are primarily men.[6]

The process whereby certain research paths are taken and some technologies are developed is extremely complex and contradictory. It is hard to generalize about which powerful groups will have the decisive shaping role, even within the area of reproductive technologies. In emphasizing the determining role of patriarchal relations, radical feminist writers tend to gloss over the conflicts of values and interests between different groups of men, and sometimes women, which combine to produce an artefact. This micro-politics of innovation is itself subsumed within a set of wider political forces. The evolution of a technology is thus a function of an interwoven set of technical, social, economic, and political factors.

To make sense of the reproductive technologies we have, we need to examine the social and economic forces that drive research forward or that inhibit more alternative developments. Certain kinds of technology are inextricably linked to particular institutionalized patterns of power and authority. The appropriation of reproductive technology by the male medical establishment has been decisive in attempts to create and maintain control over women. I can demonstrate this best by looking at the emergence of specific technologies and how they figure in the historical establishment of male hegemony in Western medicine. It is striking how crucial was the role of technology in the medicalization of childbirth and its takeover by men. In the final section I will further illustrate the social construction of technology by examining the case of contraceptive technology.

The Medicalization and Mechanization of Childbirth

The growth of the medical profession took place in the context of industrialization, notably in Western Europe, and later North America. Childbirth was the province of women healers and midwives, as it remains today in much of the developing world. Midwives attended women in labor and assisted women in the process of giving birth. Throughout the eighteenth century a bitter and well-documented contest took place between female midwives and the emerging, male-dominated, medical profession, over who would have control over intervention in the birth process (Ehrenreich and English 1979; Donnison 1977). From these accounts, we learn that a particular technology played a crucial role in determining the outcome.

In England from the 1720s onwards an increasing number of men were entering midwifery in direct competition with women. Before that time, surgeons (an exclusively male occupation) had only been called in for difficult cases where natural delivery was not possible. The surgeons had carved out this work in the thirteenth century by forming guilds with the exclusive right to use surgical instruments. Before the invention of forceps, however, surgeons could do there was little to aid the birth process but remove the infant piecemeal with hooks and perforators, or perform a Caesarian section on the corpse of the mother after her death (Donnison 1977).

Obstetric forceps, which were introduced by the 1730s, made possible the delivery of live infants in cases where previously either child or mother would have died, and shortened protracted labor. According to custom, midwives were not allowed to use instruments as an accepted part of their practice. The use of forceps thus became the exclusive domain of physicians and surgeons, and was associated with the emerging profession of medicine. The introduction of forceps gave these men the edge over female midwives who were adept at the manual delivery of babies and who had great practical knowledge about birth and birthing. As soon as this technology was introduced physicians seized upon it and used it far too often, even in the contemporary opinion of the inventor himself. The outcome of the struggle that ensued was that the midwives lost their monopoly on birthing intervention, which became the province of the profession of medicine. For the first time in history, childbirth, which had always been "women's business," was captured by men.

The ascendancy of male obstetrics was the result of several factors, a critical element being the movement of childbirth from home into the newly established lying-in hospitals. At the same time, the invention of one of the first technological aids to birthing, forceps, provided a crucial resource for male medical practitioners. The public debate precipitated by the entry of men into midwifery pivoted around the use of instruments such as obstetric forceps: "The doctors' practice of midwifery was becoming distinguishable by its very technical aspect" (Faulkner 1985). Young male midwives were often incompetent and frequently used instruments unnecessarily to hasten the birth, often injuring the mother and killing the child. The misuse of instruments was common enough to attract criticism from a leading medical practitioner, who wrote in 1834 that some men seemed to suffer from "a sort of instinctive impulse to put the level and the forceps into the vagina" (Donnison 1977). Technical intervention rapidly became the hallmark of male obstetric practice.

Nowadays, in Western societies, childbirth is generally experienced in hospitals and is associated with increased and routine technological intervention. Under the aegis of the predominantly male medical profession, the trend has been towards the routine use of anesthesia, the common use of forceps, the standard practice of episiotomy, and the increase in artificially induced births as well as caesarian sections.[7] Perhaps the most vivid image of women's treatment is "the rack-like delivery bed on which a mother is strapped, flat on her back with her legs in stirrups, in a position which might have been deliberately designed to make her own efforts to bear a child as ineffectual as possible" (Donnison 1977). This medical "management" of pregnancy and childbirth by a powerful professional male elite has arguably reduced women to the status of reproductive objects, engendering adverse emotional experiences for childbearing women. Feminists have been particularly critical of the extent to which birth has been transformed from a physiological process into a pathological one.

Maternal and neonatal deaths have been dramatically reduced in the last century in large part as a result of the increased application of technology during labor and birth, most notably, the use of transfusions. This fact may explain women's apparent tolerance for a system that in some ways has transformed birth into a passive and alienating experience. Along with the technologies that have been of direct medical benefit to women in childbirth has come a host of obstetric technologies that are of questionable value to women or infants. In many, if not most cases, technological intervention in childbirth is unnecessary. But the lingering, legitimate fear of childbirth may have hampered women's objections to the routine use of invasive technologies which shift the basis of obstetric decision-making from prospective clinical observation to the printout on a fetal monitor. The widespread use of these technologies, and their acceptance by women, reflects the structure of power and decision-making within obstetrics.

For most women in the world, the problem is still lack of access to any medical technology rather than routine subjection to technological intervention. Recent sociological and medical literature has also reevaluated the contribution of medical technology to the health of mothers and babies, in comparison with social factors such as the standard of nutrition and sanitation. It concludes that "the single most significant contribution to a cut in the death and handicap rate among newborn babies would be a comprehensive anti-poverty program" (Rakusen and Davidson 1982). Indeed, the women whose welfare might be most enhanced by these medical technologies often have least access to them due to their disadvantaged socio-economic position.

Feminist literature has underemphasized this point, instead equating as increase in technological intervention with a corresponding loss of women's power and control over the birth process. The history of reproductive technology is thus seen in terms of the oppression of women by science and medicine. Modern practices are compared unfavorably with explicit or implicit notions of what childbirth was like in earlier periods or in primitive societies. It is presumed or asserted that until the advent of male medical control, childbirth was a safe, non-alienating and purely "natural" physiological process that women midwives and relatives attended in a sympathetic and supportive role.

Childbirth is socially controlled in all societies. Far from women themselves being individually in control, childbirth is invariably surrounded by rules, customs, prescriptions and sanctions. Indeed, historically and cross-culturally, it is evident that women commonly police the process themselves, not simply deferring to the expectant mother's own wishes (Macintyre 1977). To counterpoise masculine technologized childbirth to women's "natural" ways begs the question. The issue is not what childbirth was or would be like for women without the controls imposed by modern technology, but why the technologies we have take the form they do. Thus we need to look at the social context in which the new reproductive technologies developed. It is one which involves the powerful professional and institutional interests of the medical establishment.

In all professions, claiming expert technical knowledge has been favored as a way of legitimating specialization. The unequal power relations between medical practitioners and their female patients are based on a combination of factors, predominantly those of professional qualification and gender. The technological imperative within reproductive medicine is intrinsic to the defense of doctors' claims of professionalism.[8] "Indeed, retention of absolute control over technical procedures is clearly an absolute necessity for the survival of modern medical power" (Oakley 1987).

Several interlocking socioeconomic factors generate the development and use of medical technologies before their appropriateness and efficiency are determined, even before the grounds for their increased use are established (McKinlay 1981). What are the dynamics of this process in accounting for the massive expansion of medical machinery? Technology is central to claims of professionalism on two levels: having power in the doctor/patient relationship and having power within the profession. Let us turn to the doctor/patient relationship first.

Doctors are regarded as experts who possess technical knowledge and skill that lay people do not have. The doctor/patient relationship is also often a class one, especially in a meeting between a middle-class, highly educated professional and a working-class patient. In addition to being gendered, the relationship is often characterized by racial inequalities. Technology plays a major role in consolidating the distancing of the doctor from a necessarily passive patient, leading to the dehumanization of health care. The growing supremacy of technology in contemporary medical practice is not by any means confined to obstetrics, and patients male and female can find it an alienating experience.

In modern Western medicine, technological advances have transformed the methods of diagnosing illness, and these new methods have in turn altered the relationship between physician and patient. The ubiquitous stethoscope has its origins in the doctor's wish to keep the patient at a distance, overlaid with the requirements of modesty between men and women. According to the apocryphal story, the stethoscope was invented in 1816 by Laennec during an examination of a young woman who had a baffling heart disorder. Restrained by the patient's youth and sex from placing his ear to her heart, he recalled that sound travelled through solid bodies. From rolling some sheets of paper into a cylinder on this occasion he went on to construct the first wooden stethoscope. Thus the human ear was supplanted by the stethoscope not only because of its technical benefits but also because of prevailing social mores (Reiser 1978).

During the course of the twentieth century, doctors have increasingly come to rely on technologically-generated evidence at the expense of physical examination and history-taking. Machines inexorably direct the attention of both the doctor and the patient away from experiential or "subjective" factors and toward the measurable aspects of illness. And this, despite instances where the modern diagnostic machines that have supplanted the more traditional manual methods offer no apparent increased value. That they are so commonly used is not an indication of the reliability of the "objective" evidence they produce but rather a result of doctors' dependence on them. So for example, a great deal of store is set on blood pressure, blood glucose or blood lipid changes as important side effects of contraceptives, because they are measurable by instrument. By contrast, symptoms which are not measurable, such as headaches, are taken less seriously (Chen and Snow 1992).

Obstetrics is a special case because the patients are uniformly women, they are generally not ill, and it is clearly an area where male doctors can have no personal experience of the "condition" being treated. So their claims to expertise might appear tenuous to women. Technology is particularly attractive to obstetricians because techniques such as ultrasound and fetal monitoring enable doctors to claim to know more about the welfare of the developing fetus than the women themselves.

Admittedly, once a technology is available, women as patients may well want and expect high-technology treatment. This desire does not make women the passive victims of reproductive technologies and the doctors who wield them. Many women find technologies like ultrasound exciting and informative. Within limits, women who are already advantaged in the social structure may even experience "a sense of greater control and self-empowerment than they would have if left to traditional methods or nature" (Petchesky 1987). Although some women can take advantage of technologies offered, the promise of enhanced "choices" may indeed disguise restrictions. The imperative to submit oneself to the increasing range of available technologies is strong and these tests are changing the experience of pregnancy for many women. Rather than assuming a healthy baby barring evidence to the contrary, the new procedures are shifting attitudes toward a suspicion that the baby may not be all right — a doubt which, once sown, can only be satisfactorily removed by undergoing a series of tests. As a result, pregnancy itself has become a less enjoyable, carefree state, even as the chances of bearing a perfectly healthy baby are increasing.

Within Western medicine, high technology activities are not only key to power at the level of doctor/patient relations, but also to power within the profession. Status, money and professional acclaim are distributed according to the technological sophistication of the medical specialty. Developing and expanding high technology procedures signals success in the competition for scarce resources — between specialists, between hospitals, and between individuals.

> Medical specialization and technological innovation have a special feature: they are parallel and interactive. Medical specialization leads to technological innovation; then, as a given technology is used, physicians and industrial designers collaborate to improve it. As it is defined, that process leads to ever more specialization and associated work and procedures (Fagerhaugh et al. 1987).

The current enthusiasm for the new techniques of in-vitro fertilization and embryo transfer illustrate this process. In-vitro fertilization and embryo transfer have proceeded without much further work on establishing causes of infertility or improving other treatments. Given the low success rate of these two techniques[9], the level of physical discomfort and health risk, and psychological distress that accompany them, why the current concentration on in-vitro fertilization amongst infertility specialists? How does it happen that resources are allocated to this "unsuccessful" technology?

While new technologies generally have a high failure rate until perfected, it is also the case that "many roads" are not taken in science. There is as yet no detailed description of the stages in the origination of these procedures and techniques. We might ask what set of career choices led Edwards and Steptoe into their collaboration, or why their interpretation of the risk studies in animals was much less cautious than anyone else's, or why there are so few data on the effects of the drugs and invasive procedures used in in-vitro fertilization, or why there are not more data on the causes of infertility (Yoxen, 1985). Questions of inventive success and failure can be understood only with reference to the goals of the people involved.

Without doubt, professional interests explain a great deal about the development of these techniques (Pfeffer 1987). Before the introduction of in-vitro fertilization and embryo transfer, the investigation and treatment of infertility had long been afforded low status in the medical hierarchy. Many of the procedures were carried out by general practitioners, as they required little special knowledge. In-vitro fertilization provides gynecologists with an exciting, high-status area of research as well as a technically complex practice. Status and substantial financial reward are to be had, as well as job satisfaction.

Equally important, but hidden from view, are wider economic forces. The commercial interests of the vast biotechnology industry are particularly influential. Much has been written about the "new medical-industrial complex" and the way in which resources are systematically channelled into profitable areas that often have no connection with satisfying human needs (Yoxen 1986). As yet, little detailed information is available about the financial interests of medical biotechnology corporations in the development of the new reproductive technologies. Furthermore, the potential commercial applications of the products are still unclear, at least to the general public. Some commentators have likened the scope of the biotechnology revolution to that of the microelectronic revolution, seeing it as the next technology-based phase of capitalist development. Is the economic imperative of profit making, rather than the needs of infertile women, the major driving force behind the research agenda?

The Sexual Relations of Contraceptive Technology

Turning from infertility treatments to contraception, we find another set of technologies which have been shaped by gender relations. The written histories of fertility control are redolent of technological determinism. Historians and demographers share the view that in pre-industrial societies, women were the victims of their own fecundity. It is assumed that earlier generations were prevented from practicing birth control because they lacked the necessary technology. Many accounts of the history of birth control begin with the invention of the condom, arguing that it was only in the nineteenth century, with the manufacture of rubber devices, that effective contraception was made possible (McLaren 1984).

Closer analysis reveals that the extent to which birth control is practiced, and the form it takes, is as dependent on a society's attitude to sex, children and the status of women, as it is on effective technology. "For the use of birth control requires a morality that permits the separation of sexual intercourse from procreation, and is related to the extent to which women are valued for roles other than wife and mother" (Greenwood and King 1981). Birth control has always been a matter of social and political acceptability rather than of medicine and technology. Like childbirth, contraception has always been subject to elaborate regulation and ritual.

In her book on birth control in America, Linda Gordon (1977) argues that social institutions and cultural values, rather than medical or technical considerations, have shaped modern contraceptive technology. Like most feminists, Gordon began with the premise that birth control represented the single most important contribution to the material basis of women's emancipation in the last century. She was quickly led to ask however, why the technology of contraception developed when it did, and why, in our generation, the invention of the Pill is seen as the key to liberation. For her, birth control was as much a symptom as a cause of the larger social changes in relations between the sexes and the economic organization of society.

The ability to transcend biology was present in the earliest known societies. In fact, most of our present methods have precursors in societies far less technologically sophisticated than ours. Evidence from old medical texts and from anthropological studies indicates that women have almost universally sought to control their fertility. Far from being invented by scientists or doctors, effective forms of birth control were devised and administered by women in nearly all ancient societies (Greenwood and King 1981; McLaren 1984).

Reproductive knowledge and practice has always been part of women's folklore and culture. The relatively recent establishment of the male hegemony in medicine may have obscured the existence of earlier methods that were more under women's control. Traditionally, knowledge about techniques for birth control, like remedies for other complaints, was developed and practiced by wisewomen and midwives and handed down from generation to generation. An array of birth control techniques were practiced in the ancient world and in modern preindustrial societies. Methods included magic, herbal potions, infanticide, abortion, coitus interruptus, vaginal sponges, douches, and pessaries.

Not only did these techniques vary in their effectiveness, but they had very different implications for sexual relations. Some techniques are more amenable than others to independent and even secret use by women; some give full control to men; others are more likely to be used cooperatively. Women and men may have conflicting concerns and goals in mind when contemplating fertility control and these are reflected in the different techniques available. I will return to this point later.

Gordon argues that it is only by looking at this heritage of birth control customs that we can comprehend the emergence of the birth control movement, for that movement gained strength from women's understanding that traditional methods of fertility control were being suppressed. In particular, while abortion had hitherto been the subject of moral controversy, it was not until the nineteenth century that it was actually criminalized. Abortion laws were intended to eliminate doctors' rivals, such as midwives, and to undermine traditional forms of reproductive control. The result of the medical and legal intervention in this crucial form of birth control was a decline in women's ability to limit their pregnancies. What was new in the nineteenth century, then, was not the technology to control fertility but the emergence of a political movement that campaigned for the right to use contraception.

However, reproductive self-determination for women was not the primary catalyst for the birth control movement. Equally important was the population control movement with its claim that population control (especially among the poor) could cure poverty.

During the twentieth century, contraception and, to a lesser extent, abortion have become respectable, and are largely regulated by the medical profession. However, the influence of population-control ideology is still central to modern birth control programs. Since the 1950s, birth prevention has become a major international industry linked with the politics of state intervention in population planning. Populationist ideology, not scientific discovery, was the catalyst for the major financial investment in research on birth-prevention methods and influenced the specific techniques which have become available. The technological prerequisites for the development of an oral hormonal contraceptive had existed by 1938 but popular morality and pro-natalist policies delayed its development until the late 1950s (Newman 1985). The sudden and popular fear of a world population explosion legitimated work on the Pill and resulted in family planning services becoming a major part of aid packages to the Third World.

Such an analysis may explain the emphasis on hormonal contraceptives and the neglect of barrier methods. "Considering how much time, money and energy is spent on birth-control research, we might expect to be able to choose from among, say, ten different kinds of barrier methods or perhaps a range of morning-after methods. Instead, our options are confined to essentially two barrier methods, the various hormonal methods, a few IUDs and abortion techniques, and a small but increasing number of sterilization techniques" (Newman 1985). Hormonal methods offer effectiveness, a valuable feature for a technology driven by an ideology of "population control."

Although the Pill is one of the most reliable and popular methods of contraception, it has been associated with health risks and side effects for women. Nevertheless its effectiveness reduces the ethical dilemma and health risks of unwanted pregnancy and abortion. From the doctor's point of view, the fact that this method does not require many visits to the clinic, and does not need to be explained at great length to the patient, are additional advantages. The Pill is also profitable: it is economical to produce and market and needs to be taken daily, thus generating vast profits for the pharmaceutical industry that supplies it.

Apart from the corporate interests involved, most of the research into medical contraceptive methods is done by men on techniques for use by women (see Snow, Chapter 11). Given that women and men have different patterns of sexual behavior, might not these differences be reflected in the design of contraceptive technologies? Indeed, Pollack (1985) argues that "male sexual pleasure is the most significant factor taken into account in the methods which become available, and in the ways in which contraceptives are used".

Certainly men prefer methods that "interfere" least with their experience of sex, even at the expense of women's health and enjoyment. The reluctance of heterosexual men to wear condoms (even in the AIDS era) indicates the primacy of their sexual feelings over the medical risks women are taking. While some medical techniques for men have been developed, the dangerous effects tend to be played up more than is the case with female methods. Indeed, the first trials on the Pill involved equal numbers of men and women, but the trials on men were abandoned when one case of shrunken testicles was found (BBC 1993). The paramountcy of men's health is also reflected in the fact that the incentive for the development of the condom was not birth control but rather men's need for protection from venereal disease.

The Pill is also a technology favored by women. As women still have the primary responsibility for pregnancy, the Pill is chosen for its high degree of protection and for the control that women can exercise over its use. This method does not involve touching one's genitals, does not require male cooperation or even knowledge, and it allows for "spontaneous" sex. The Pill has the additional psychological advantage of separating contraception from sexual activity, both in time and anatomically. It does not interfere with what is considered to be "normal" romantic heterosexual sex; that is, for men to be lustful and assertive and for women to surrender. By comparison, the fitting of caps or diaphragms requires some skill, and to use these methods one has to admit to a man and to oneself that one has anticipated sex. The definition of sexual activity as heterosexual intercourse involving penetration thus provides the context in which contraceptives are researched, developed, distributed and used.

The purpose of this section has been to suggest that sexual relations in combination with population policies and market forces have shaped contraceptive technology. And, in turn, the design or form of the technology has been crucial to its use. Having said that, I would assert that the relationship between technological and social change is fundamentally indeterminate. The designers and promoters of a technology cannot completely predict or control its final uses. There are always unintended consequences and unanticipated possibilities, and women have shown themselves well able to derail the original purposes of a technology.

The Pill provides a good illustration of this process. Although the Pill has meant more effective birth control, and in turn more possibilities of sexual pleasure for women, it was not developed for this purpose. As we have just seen, the Pill's inventors thought they were solving the "population explosion" of the underclass. As it turned out, the Pill was mainly taken up by Western women who saw in it a means to free their sexuality from the constraints of reproduction. The inventors had no idea that they were loosing on the market something that would have such profound repercussions for women's lives. It is important not to underestimate women's capacity to subvert the intended purposes of technology and turn it to their collective advantage.

Such contradictions and the space they create for change are instructive if we are to avoid political pessimism about technology. But if women are not passive in the face of male-designed reproductive technologies, we are still largely positioned as consumers. We are confined to choosing between products on the market. And, as I have argued, the range of technologies available to women has been designed more to advance the sectional interests of socially empowered men than to meet women's needs. Identifying the gendered character of reproductive technology need not lead to a wholesale rejection of existing technology. Rather, I suggest is that if technologies were being developed by women, for women, in a different institutional setting, we might have a radically different set of choices.

Notes

1 This article draws on Chapter 3 of my book, *Feminism Confronts Technology* (1991, Pennsylvania, Penn State University Press).

2 For an introduction to this literature, see MacKenzie and Wajcman (1985); Bijker, Hughes and Pinch (1987); Bijker and Law (1992).In *From abortion to reproductive freedom,* ed. M.G. Fried. Boston: South End Press.

3 Some of these views are most commonly associated with FINRRAGE (Feminist International Network of Resistance to Reproductive and Genetic Engineering).

4 See Balakrishnan, Radhika in this volume.

5 Spallone, 1987, p. 173-4. The Warnock Committee, which was established in 1982 and reported in 1984, was set up by the British government to advise on the appropriate regulation policies for reproductive technologies. It recommended restricting such techniques as IVF, egg donation, embryo donation and artificial insemination to stable, cohabiting heterosexual couples. Provisos about which women have access to these technologies are preconditions of current administration practices in this field of medicine.

6 Even in countries where the ratio of female to male obstetricians is approaching equity, women remain underrepresented among the medical leadership.

7 Feminists have also been concerned to expose the increase in hysterectomy, particularly for black and Third World women, as a form of involuntary sterilization or as "a simple solution to everything from backaches to contraception"(Homans 1985, p.5).

8 The term "technological imperative" was coined to suggest that the addition of any new technology generates an increase in further use by its very existence, and this in turn generates still more technology (Fuchs 1968).

9 The most successful clinics in Britain now boast a "take-home baby rate" of around 20 percent, while the success rate remains under 5 percent for some clinics in the United States (Midland Fertility Services IVF Unit 1991).

References

Bijker, W., T. Hughes, and T. Pinch, eds. 1987. *The social construction of technological systems: New directions in the sociology and history of technology*. Cambridge, Mass.: MIT Press.

Bijker, W., and J. Law. 1992. *Shaping technology/Building society*. Cambridge: MIT Press.

Birke, L., S. Himmelweit, and G. Vines. 1990. *Tomorrow's child: Reproductive technology in the 90s*. London: Virago.

British Broadcasting Corporation (BBC). 1993. The Pill. *Time Watch*, March 10.

Chen, L., and R. Snow. 1992. Benefits and risks of the Pill: Perceptions and reality. *Advances in contraception* 7(2):19–34.

Corea, G., R. Duelli, R. Klein, et al. 1985. *Man-made women: How new reproductive technologies affect women. Explorations in Feminism: 10*. London: Hutchinson.

Cowan, R.S. 1983. *More work for mother: The ironies of household technology from the open hearth to the microwave*. New York: Basic Books.

Donnison, J. 1977. *Midwives and medical men: A history of inter-professional rivalries and women's rights*. London: Heinemann.

Ehrenreich, B., and D. English. 1979. *For her own good: 150 years of the experts' advice to women*. London: Pluto Press.

Ellul, J. 1964. *The technological society*. New York: Vintage.

Fagerhaugh, S., A. Strauss, B. Suczek, and C. Wiener, eds. 1987. *Hazards in hospital care: Ensuring patient safety*. San Francisco, Calif.: Jossey-Bass.

Faulker, W. 1985. Medical technology and the right to heal. In *Smothered by invention: Technology in women's lives*, ed. W. Faulkner and E. Arnold. London: Pluto Press.

Firestone, S. 1970. *The dialectic of sex: The case for feminist revolution.* New York: William Morrow & Co.

Fuchs, V. 1968. The growing demand for medical care. *New England Journal of Medicine* 279(4):190–95.

Gordon, L. 1977. *Woman's body, woman's right: A social history of birth control in America.* Harmondsworth: Penguin.

Greenwood, K., and L. King. 1981. Contraception and abortion. In *Women in society*, ed. Cambridge Women's Studies Group. London: Virago.

Hanmer, J. 1985. Transforming consciousness: Women and the new reproductive technologies. In *Man-made women: How new reproductive technologies affect women*, ed. G. Corea, et al. London: Hutchinson.

Homans, H., ed. 1985. *The sexual politics of reproduction.* Aldershot, Hants: Gower.

Klein, R. 1985. What's "new" about the "new" reproductive technologies? In *Man-made women: How new reproductive technologies affect women*, ed. G. Corea, et al. London: Hutchinson.

Macintyre, S. 1977. Childbirth: The myth of the golden age. *World Medicine* (June 15):17–22.

MacKenzie, D., and J. Wajcman, eds. 1985. *The social shaping of technology: How the refrigerator got its hum.* Milton Keynes: Open University Press.

McKinlay, J.B. 1981. From "promising report" to "standard procedure" — seven stages in the career of a medical innovation. *Milbank Memorial Fund Quarterly* 59(3):374–411.

McLaren, A. 1984. *Reproductive rituals: The perception of fertility from the sixteenth century to the nineteenth century.* London: Methuen.

Martin, E. 1987. *The woman in the body: A cultural analysis of reproduction.* Boston: Beacon Press.

Midland Fertility Services IVF Unit. 1991. *Annual report for 1990 from Midland Fertility Services.* Sutton Coldfield.

Mies, M. 1987. Why do we need all this? A call against genetic engineering and reproductive technology. In *Made to order: The myth of reproductive and genetic progress*, ed. P. Spallone and D. Steinberg. Oxford: Pergamon.

Newman, E. 1985. Who controls birth control? In *Smothered by invention: Technology in women's lives*, ed. W. Faulkner and E. Arnold. London: Pluto Press.

Oakley, A. 1976. Wisewoman and medicine man: Changes in the management of childbirth. In *The rights and wrongs of women*, ed. J. Mitchell and A. Oakley. Harmondsworth: Penguin.

———. 1987. From walking wombs to test-tube babies. In *Reproductive technologies: Gender, motherhood and medicine*, ed. M. Stanworth. Cambridge: Policy Press in association with B. Blackwell.

Petchesky, R. 1987. Foetal images: The power of visual culture in the politics of reproduction. In *Reproductive technologies: Gender, motherhood and medicine*, ed. M. Stanworth. Cambridge: Policy Press in association with B. Blackwell.

Pfeffer, N. 1985. The hidden pathology of the male reproductive system. In *The sexual politics of reproduction*, ed. H. Homans. Aldershot, Hants: Gower.

———. 1987. Artificial insemination, in-vitro fertilization and the stigma of infertility. In *Reproductive technologies: Gender, motherhood and medicine*, ed. M. Stanworth. Cambridge: Policy Press in association with B. Blackwell.

Pollack, S. 1985. Sex and the contraceptive act. In *The sexual politics of reproduction*, ed. H. Homans. Aldershot, Hants: Gower.

Rakusen, J. 1981. Depo-Provera: The extent of the problem. In *Women, health and reproduction*. ed. H. Roberts. London: Rowtledge and Kegan Paul.

Rakusen, J., and N. Davidson. 1982. *Out of our hands: What technology does to pregnancy*. London: Pan.

Reiser, S. 1978. *Medicine and the reign of technology*. Cambridge: Cambridge University Press.

Rowland, R. 1985. Motherhood, patriarchal power, alienation and the issue of "choice". In *Man-made women: How new reproductive technologies affect women*, ed. G. Corea, et al. London: Hutchinson.

———. 1988. *Woman herself: A transdisciplinary perspective on women's identity*. South Melbourne: Oxford University Press.

Spallone, P. 1987. Reproductive technology and the state: The Warnock Report and its clones. In *Made to order: The myth of reproductive and genetic progress*, ed. P. Spallone and D. Steinberg. Oxford: Pergamon.

Stanworth, M., ed. 1987. *Reproductive technologies: Gender, motherhood and medicine*. Cambridge: Polity Press in association with B. Blackwell.

Yoxen, E. 1985. Licensing reproductive technologies? *Radical Science Journal* 17:138–48.

———. 1986. *The gene business: Who should control biotechnology?* London: Free Association Books.

Wajcman, J. 1991. *Feminism confronts technology*. Philadelphia, Pa.: Pennsylvania State University Press.

9

Adoption Rights and Reproductive Wrongs[1]

by Elizabeth Bartholet

Reproductive rights talk is full of claims about women's rights to choose whether to conceive, and whether to abort the product of conception. I want to talk about the rights of women who cannot or do not choose to conceive, but who do want to raise children. And I want to talk about the rights of women who don't feel able to raise the children they are carrying in pregnancy, but don't want or haven't been allowed to abort. I want to talk about the right to adopt and the right to give a child up for adoption.

Reproductive rights talk tends to focus on adult rights. I want to link women's parenting rights with their responsibilities, and to assert that children as well as adults should be seen as having rights. Women's groups often fear that recognition of children's rights will mean suppression of women's rights. But the category "children" includes females. And if women will not speak up to protect children, both male and female, who will? I want to talk about the child's right to have a nurturing home.

I believe that the concept of reproductive rights should be expanded to include adoption rights — the birth mother's right to give up her child, the infertile woman's right to parent a child who has no parent, and the child's right to a home. The twin stigmas that surround adoption and infertility today shape and constrain choice in ways that promote a traditional understanding of women's roles. We condition the infertile to obsess over treatment options rather than consider adoption, and we condition birth mothers to feel that it would be "unnatural" to surrender their children for others to raise. "True" women are supposed to be fertile, get pregnant, give birth, and raise the resulting children.

But adoption rights are sometimes seen as being in conflict with women's rights to control their reproductive lives. This is, in part, because anti-abortion forces have pushed adoption as the *only* appropriate route for a woman who does not want or feel able to raise the child she is carrying. They have helped create the impression that to be pro-adoption is to be anti-abortion, but there is no necessary inconsistency between abortion rights and adoption rights. We should not let abortion opponents hoodwink us so easily. Women should be free to choose whether to carry a child to term or to abort, and also free to choose whether to raise a child or give it up for others to raise. True reproductive freedom includes all these choices. The anti-abortion forces purport to be adoption's friends but they have not proven true friends. Their adoption advocacy has not extended beyond the abortion decision point. They simply use adoption as a club to wield in their abortion battle. And this is entirely understandable, because a real commitment to adoption rights would help free women from the traditional role anti-abortion forces generally promote.

A more fundamental concern is that adoption rights for the infertile may mean constraint and exploitation for the birth mother. Many feminists and others committed to liberating oppressed groups worry about adoption's potential for exploitation. Adoption does, typically, involve the transfer of children from those who suffer various forms of deprivation to those who are relatively privileged. Poor birth mothers give up their children to well-off adoptive couples; Third World nations give up their children to the industrialized Western nations; black and brown people give up their children to whites. To a significant degree, this is the pattern that adoption takes.

But adoption does not cause the situations of socio-economic disadvantage that result in some people and some groups and some countries producing children for whom they are unable to care. It is a symptom. And while it is of course true that justice requires new efforts to correct the conditions that make it so hard for some women to care for their children, adoption should not be seen as inconsistent with such efforts. Children are often termed "precious resources," but it does not make sense to think of them that way. Giving up children, like deciding to abort, may be the best choice among the options available at a particular point in time. Children deserve to be treated as human beings with their own entitlements, rather than as resources in which adult individuals and communities have a property interest. From the children's perspective, being given up may mean being given the opportunity to grow up in a nurturing home.

Adoption is now stigmatized and regulated in ways that unduly limit women's life opportunities. Birth mothers are conditioned to think it "unnatural" to surrender children for others to raise even when they are not themselves in a good situation to raise these children. The infertile are conditioned to think of adoption as a last-resort parenting option, and of infertility as a form of disfigurement that needs repair. They are encouraged to pursue reproduction at all costs, with the costs for women and society rising ever higher as reproductive technology expands the infertility treatment horizon.

We need to recognize that adoption generally works to expand life opportunities for birth mothers, for the infertile, and for children in need of nurturing homes. It would work even better if we were to eliminate the stigma and reform the restrictive regulation that shapes adoption as we know it today.

One Woman's Journey through Infertility to Adoption

In the fall of 1985 I flew from Boston to Lima, Peru, to adopt a four-month-old child. Some 18 years earlier I had given birth to my first child. During the last 10 of these intervening years I had struggled to give birth again, combating an infertility problem that had resulted, as is often the case, from my use of a contraceptive device.

I had been married when I produced my first child, but divorced when he was just a few years old. Some years later I decided that I wanted more children, regardless of whether I was married. But I found that I was unable to conceive.

I subjected myself to every form of medical treatment that offered any possibility of success. I had operations to diagnose my problem, I took fertility drugs and charted my menstrual cycles and my temperature, and I had sexual intercourse according to the prescribed schedule. I had surgery to remove scar tissue from my Fallopian tubes. And I went through in-vitro fertilization (IVF) on repeated occasions in programs in three different states. As a single person in my early forties, I was officially excluded from every IVF program in the United States that I was able to find out about. Almost all had a maximum age of forty, and all limited their services to married couples. But I was determined. I begged my way into programs that were willing to consider bending their age rules, and I presented myself as married, with the help of a loyal and loving friend who was willing to play the part of husband. Not being used to a life of fraud, I spent much of my IVF existence terrified that I would be discovered.

I wanted to have another child, and I was obsessed with the need to produce it myself. But IVF did not work for me, and I moved on to adopt.

The adoption experience changed me profoundly. It changed my life and my thinking about life. It changed my understanding of parenting and my view of the law, even though I had been a parent and a lawyer all my adult life. And it changed the focus of my professional energies, because I found myself intensely interested in what I had lived through during my struggles to become a parent, and deeply troubled by the way society was shaping parenting options and defining family.

It was, of course, to be expected that adoption would change my day-to-day life. I went back to Peru in 1988 and adopted another infant, and so am now the mother of two young children. My days start with small warm bodies crawling into my bed, my floors are covered with miniature cars and trucks and Lego pieces, my calendar is scrawled with the kids' doctor appointments and play dates. All this is familiar from 20 years ago, as are the middle-of-the-night coughing fits, the trips to an emergency room to stitch a bloody cut, and the sense that there is not enough time to fit it all in.

But I could not have expected these two particular magical children. I could not have predicted the ways in which they would crawl inside my heart and wrap themselves around my soul. I could not have known that I would be so entirely smitten, as a friend described me, so utterly possessed. And I could not have anticipated that this family formed across the continents would seem so clearly the family that was meant to be, that these children thrown together with me and with each other, with no blood ties linking us together or to a common history, would seem so clearly the children meant for me.

The process I went through to form this family affected my understanding of many issues that I had dealt with during my lawyering life. I had, for example, thought of the law largely in terms of its potential for advancing justice and social reform. In the adoption world, I experienced the law as something that functioned primarily to prevent good things from happening. You need only to step through the door of this world and look around to realize that there are vast numbers of children in desperate need of homes and vast numbers of adults anxious to become parents. It seems overwhelmingly clear that efforts to put these groups of children and adults together would create a lot of human happiness.

But the legal systems in the United States and other countries have erected a series of barriers that prevent people who want to parent from connecting with children who need homes. So, for example, the legal system helped push me away from considering adoption during all those years I pursued infertility treatment. And for five months in Peru, the legal system required me to live through the peculiar form of torture reserved for foreign adoptive parents. Having made my way through the adoption barriers to find Christopher and Michael at the end, I can have no personal bitterness. I came out where I feel I belong. I am also glad that I had the opportunity to come to know and love the land in which my children were born. But I am deeply conscious that the huge majority of people who would delight in the opportunity to parent some of the world's children will not be able or willing to make their way through the barriers that the law has set in their path. The myth is that the legal structure surrounding adoption is designed to serve the best interests of the child. Actually experiencing the system as an adoptive parent shattered this myth for me.

Adoption transformed my feelings about infertility and my under-standing of what parental love is all about. For years I had felt that there was only one less-than-tragic outcome of my infertility battle, and that was to reverse the damage that had been done to my body, the damage that stood in the way of pregnancy. I had felt that there was only one really satisfactory route to parenthood, and that was for me to conceive and give birth. I had assumed that the love I felt for my first child had significantly to do with biological connection. The experience of loving him was wrapped up in a package that included pregnancy, childbirth, nursing, and the genetic link that meant I recognized his eyes and face and personality as familial. Adoption posed terrifying questions. Could I love in the same way a child who had not been part of me and was not born from my body? Could I feel that totality of commitment I associated with parental love toward a child who came to me as a baby stranger? Or did the form of attachment I had known with my first child arise out of the biological inevitability felt in the progression from sexual intercourse to pregnancy to childbirth, and out of the genetic link between us?

I discovered that the thing I know as parental love grows out of the experience of nurturing, and that adoptive parenting is in fundamental ways identical to biological parenting. I have come to think of pregnancy and childbirth as experiences that for me were enormously satisfying but that seem of limited relevance to the parenting relationship. I do not see biological links as entirely irrelevant to parenting, but neither do I see an obvious hierarchical system for ranking biological and adoptive parenting. There are special pleasures involved in parenting the child who is genetically familiar, and there are special pleasures involved in parenting the children whose black eyes and Peruvian features and wildly dissimilar personalities proclaim their genetic difference.

I can, of course, be seen as specially privileged by virtue of having experienced both kinds of parenting. It may therefore be hard for those who have never borne a child to identify with me. If, for example, there is some primal need to project oneself into future generations by reproduction, I have had the luxury of satisfying that need. But it does seem to me that not much is gained by leaving a genetic legacy. You do not, in fact, live on just because your egg or sperm has contributed to another life. It is unlikely that the anonymous sperm donor takes significant pleasure in knowing that his genes are carried forward to the next generation in the person of some unknown child wandering the earth. The sense of immortality that many seek in parenting seems to me to have more to do with the kind of identification that comes from our relationship with our children, and with the ways in which that relationship helps shape their being.

This is not to say that *becoming* a parent through adoption is comparable to becoming a parent through giving birth. I found many aspects of the adoption process terrifying or unpleasant or some combination of the two. It was an entirely unknown world to me, as it is to many. In addition, society has conspired to make adoption extraordinarily difficult to accomplish.

Adoption also involves choice on a scale most of us don't generally experience. You can't fall accidentally into adoption, as you can into pregnancy. You exercise choice down to the wire. Choice forces you to think about what you want and to take responsibility for the consequences of your decision. And the choice to go forward with an adoption means a lifelong commitment, which simply isn't true of most other choices that we make. If you make a mistake in choosing a house, a job, or even a spouse, you can get out of it. Few of those who consciously enter an adoptive parenting relationship would feel comfortable opting out of their commitment.

While choice is difficult and uncomfortable for most of us, there are obvious advantages for both children and parents in parenting that results from conscious choice. In the world of biological parenting, all too many children are raised by parents who neither planned for nor wanted them, and the evidence shows that this is problematic for both the parents and the children. As a parent, I found that one of the gratifying aspects of the adoption process was the satisfaction that came from the sense that I was exercising choice and taking control over my life. Although adoption has been made far more difficult and more frightening than it needs to be, adoptive parenting is an achievable goal, at least for those with the time, energy, resources, and will to pursue it. When I wasn't in the depths of despair and depression in Peru, I relished the Wonder Woman role I had cast myself in, and delighted in my ability to overcome seemingly insurmountable obstacles. The contrast with the infertility struggle is compelling. If your goal is to have a biological child, there is no way that you can take control. No matter what you do or how long and hard you try, there is a good likelihood that you will fail. If your goal is to become a parent, you can do it through adoption. There may be a thousand obstacles, but you can triumph over them.

Current policy with respect to parenting options reflects a powerful bias in favor of biological parenting. As a society, we define personhood and parenthood in terms of procreation. We push the infertile toward ever more elaborate forms of high-tech treatment. We are also moving rapidly in the direction of a new child production market, in which sperm, eggs, embryos, and pregnancy services are for sale so that those who want to parent can produce a child to order. At the same time, we drive prospective parents away from children who already exist and who need homes. We do this by stigmatizing adoptive parenting in myriad ways and by turning the adoption process into a regulatory obstacle course. The claim is that no children are available for adoption, but the fact is that millions of children the world over are in desperate need of nurturing homes. The politics of adoption in today's world prevents these children from being placed in adoptive homes. My claim is that current policies make no sense for people interested in parenting, for children in need of homes, or for a world struggling to take care of the existing population.

Adoptive family relationships are often built on a foundation of human misery. Birth parents generally surrender children for adoption or abandon them because they feel forced to do so by poverty, discrimination or the chaos that results from war or some other disaster. Many of those interested in becoming adoptive parents feel forced to undertake this form of parenting by infertility. In an ideal world, we would eliminate the problems that force some to give up the children they bear and that deprive others of their fertility. But in the world in which we live today and will live tomorrow, adoption should be understood as an institution that works well compared to existing alternatives.

Adoption should not, however, be seen *simply* as a response to some of the world's problems. It should be understood as a positive alternative to the blood-based family form. A more positive construction of adoption would be liberating not simply for birth parents, or for the infertile who want to parent, or for the children who need nurturing homes, but more broadly. Adoptive families are different in some interesting ways from families based on a blood link. Understanding the positive features of adoption could open up our minds to rethinking the meaning of parenting, family, and community.

Parenting Options for the Infertile: The Biological Bias
Shaping Women and their Choices

Adoption is the choice of last resort for most infertile men and women who want to parent. If asked why this is true, many would say, "Because it is natural to want your own child."[2] But it is hard to know what is natural, given the fact that society weighs in to make adoption the last resort. And it is not clear that we should characterize parenting decisions as the product of choice. We are all conditioned from early childhood to equate personhood with procreation and procreation with parenting.

The fertile almost never consider adoption, and the infertile are unlikely to consider it until they have reached the end of a long medical road designed to produce a biological child. This road has lengthened as the medical possibilities have expanded. The infertile seem increasingly eager for what the medical experts have to offer. It is the treatment of infertility that has increased in recent years, not its overall incidence. Visits to physicians for infertility services increased almost threefold from the 1960s to the 1980s, while infertility rates remained stable.[3] It is generally only after people have explored the possibilities for infertility treatment and either rejected or exhausted the various medical options that they give adoption serious consideration.

My own story is simply one example of how the biases built into the system help make adoption the last resort for so many. I went to doctors when, in my mid-thirties, I first began to fear that I had a fertility problem. I knew nothing about adoption at the time or rather, I had the same collection of limited and inaccurate information that most people have. I "knew" that there were essentially no children available and that the waiting lists for any children who were available were impossibly long. I did not know whether single people could adopt, nor did I know any easy way to find out. I had heard a lot of horror stories about adoption, many of them involving the agencies that were supposed to arrange adoptions. I had a lot of fears about adoption — fears of what I knew, of what I thought I knew, and most of all of what I didn't know.

I talked about my parenting options to no one except a tiny handful of friends and family members from 1976, when I started seeing fertility specialists, until 1985, when I flew to Lima for my first adoption. The pain and shame of infertility silenced me. It seemed natural to look first to the medical experts for help, since I was already in their waiting rooms and since my initial instinct was to repair my body so that it would again be capable of conceiving a child. Once on that medical track, I found it hard to get off. Repeated failures resulted in renewed determination to succeed. I had achieved other things that were difficult. I could and would achieve pregnancy, even against all odds.

In 1978 I sat in my paper gown on my fertility specialist's examining table for what I thought would be a final visit. Tests had demonstrated that the tubal surgery he had performed some months before had failed to repair my Fallopian tubes. I was at the end of the existing treatment road. There was no such thing as in-vitro fertilization in the United States and would not be for years. Through my tears I said that I had just read that the first IVF baby had been born as a result of an experimental program in Great Britain. I told my doctor that if by any miracle his hospital was able to develop an IVF program before my body had stopped producing eggs, I wanted to be first on the waiting list. He laughed, but I was not joking. He asked me what I would do now, and I said I was thinking about adoption and wondered if he could give me any help or advice. He said adoption really wasn't possible anymore. Massachusetts had outlawed private adoptions, and that was a good thing too, all those young girls being pressured to sell their babies, what a terrible business that had been. He said adoption really didn't work out well anyway, he knew some sad stories. And I was too old to be a mother. No, he really couldn't help me.

I began clipping newspaper articles on adoption, but I didn't find out much, and it didn't seem worth pursuing if I wasn't married. Interestingly, I had never hesitated about pursuing infertility treatment as a single, and none of the many doctors who had dealt with me had raised a question about it.

Against all expectations, IVF did become available in the United States within just a few years. In the spring of 1983, I was on the telephone to programs around the country, in search of one that would admit me and that did not have a prohibitive waiting list. I was almost forty-three and could not afford to wait. I begged my way into a program in Connecticut, and by the time that IVF attempt failed I had found a program in California that would admit me immediately. When I woke from anesthesia in California to discover that that attempt had also failed, I was able to fly home to enroll in a program in my home state of Massachusetts, which had decided to consider applicants from the over-forty age group. I felt lucky, as this was certainly more compatible with my work and other life. I settled into IVF treatment in earnest, and went through several treatment cycles in the course of the next year.

In the nearly 10 years that I struggled with infertility, I spoke to dozens of different doctors, nurses, administrators, and social workers in connection with a number of different treatment programs. I dealt with people who treated their patients like human guinea pigs, and I dealt with people who were humane and supportive. No one ever asked me to think hard about what I was doing and why. No one ever advised me to seek counseling to deal with my feelings about infertility. No one ever suggested that I consider adoption as an alternative to further treatment, or proposed ways to find out more about adoption. All of this was entirely understandable. These were medical programs, and the people involved thought in medical terms. They were working to press beyond the frontiers of knowledge and make it possible for the patients knocking down their programs' doors to achieve what they desperately wanted to achieve: pregnancy.

In the summer of 1984, I finally did take some steps on my own to explore adoption seriously. I called adoption agencies, obtained their brochures, attended their general information sessions, and became involved with a support group called SPACE — Single Parents for the Adoption of Children Everywhere. I took an adult education course called "Building Your Family through Adoption." I sought out people who had adopted. And I broke the rules by starting the home study process, the process by which adoption agencies determine whether applicants satisfy their criteria for parental fitness. A cardinal requirement is that applicants demonstrate that they have "resolved" their feelings about infertility. By definition, you haven't resolved your feelings about infertility if you are still involved in treatment to reverse the condition.

But I didn't see how I was going to sort through my feelings about infertility and parenting, or understand whether I wanted to be an adoptive parent, without taking some more steps to understand what adoption might mean for me. The logical steps to take included working with the agencies that were in the business of putting together adoptive families. Therefore I was prepared to tell the agencies what I had to in order to start the home study process. As a result of these exploratory steps, I developed for the first time some sense of what adoption was about.

And then I got lucky. I ran out of money. IVF treatment was excluded from health insurance coverage during this period, and I had cursed my fate and timing, as it seemed likely that the exclusion would eventually be eliminated. I had been paying the going price, $5,000 for a full treatment cycle. I had about run through what savings I had.

I woke one morning in March 1985. I learned later that it was the month, and perhaps the very day, my future son was born, and lay in bed thinking that I didn't want to use up my remaining funds on IVF. I would need them if I was to adopt. And I didn't want to use up any more time and energy or any more of my life on the fertility pursuit. I wanted a child, and I wanted to move on. I called my IVF program that day and said that I was not going to go forward with another treatment cycle.

I was one of the lucky infertility patients, because I did move on to adoption and to parenting. Treatment enables only a limited number of the infertile to conceive and bear children, and it helps prevent many from ever considering adoption as a form of parenting. By the time people exhaust their treatment options, many who might once have been interested in adoption do not have the will, the energy, or the resources to get through the many barriers that society puts in the way of becoming an adoptive parent.

I now look back in amazement at the person I was, traversing the country from one IVF program to another in search of an infertility fix. I am bemused at my shifting notions of the "natural" and of "choice." It had seemed to me natural to pursue biological parenting, even when the pursuit led me into the high-tech world of IVF where the doctors and lab technicians largely took over the business of conception, "harvesting" the eggs that they had cultivated in the woman patient's body and inseminating them in glass dishes. It had seemed also that I was choosing when I made the decisions to move on to new stages of treatment. Indeed, I had felt thrilled with the sense that I was pushing against the social and biological constraints that prevented a single woman with damaged Fallopian tubes from giving birth. Now I look back and see a woman driven by the forces that had told her since birth that she should go forth and multiply, that her ability to bear a child was central to her meaning as a human being, and that "real" parenting involved raising that biologically linked child.

The Infertility Problem

A staggering number of people suffer from infertility. Surveys indicate that in the United States, close to five million women (or their partners) have "impaired fecundity," meaning that it is difficult, impossible, or dangerous for them to achieve pregnancy and childbirth. Roughly one in seven of all couples trying to conceive are unable to do so.[4] Many say that these surveys underestimate the problem. The pain the infertile suffer has been documented in numerous studies and anecdotal accounts.[5] For many the discovery of infertility cuts to the very core of being, destroying their sense of self-worth, and indeed of self. Although men and women share almost equally in the responsibility for couples' inability to conceive, it is the women, overwhelmingly, who have given voice to their suffering. In a better world, women would not experience infertility as devastating disfigurement and the destruction of sexual identity, but in this world, many do. It is women who bear the brunt of infertility treatment efforts. There is still not much that the doctors can do for male infertility problems. It may also be that men would not subject themselves to the burdensome and intrusive forms of treatment that women endure in the interest of conceiving and bearing children.

The infertile are potentially a significant resource for children in need of homes, but at present only a limited number of them adopt.[6] Society drives the infertile away from adoption and toward efforts to reproduce with a wide array of conditioning mechanisms and regulatory structures.

Making Adoption the Last Resort

The medical profession has a near-monopoly on the information given out as people discover their infertility and explore and exercise options. When people who have been trying to have a baby realize that something may be wrong, they usually consult their family doctor or their gynecologist, and then, if they can afford it, a fertility specialist. The specialist educates them about the range of treatment possibilities and, if they are willing and financially able, begins to lead them down the treatment path. A couple may start with temperature charts and scheduled sex and move on to fertility drug treatment. They may then decide on an exploratory laparoscopy, which can reveal pelvic adhesions on the woman's fallopian tubes. Tubal surgery may follow, and then tests to see whether the tubes remain open. If the woman still does not become pregnant, the couple may explore and pursue IVF or related high-tech treatment methods.

This treatment scenario has become a common one, and as people move through it, their chief advisers at every step are likely to be doctors. The advice doctors give is inevitably biased toward the treatment option. Doctors think of it as their job to know and advise about the various medical possibilities. Few see it as equally their job to explore with patients why they are considering medical treatment, whether continued treatment efforts are worthwhile, or when enough is enough. Fewer still see it as their job to help patients work through the advantages and disadvantages of treatment as compared with parenting through adoption. Doctors once played a major role in helping infertile patients connect with pregnant patients interested in surrendering their children for adoption. But the specialized fertility experts in today's treatment world have little interest in or knowledge about adoption.

It is only in the IVF programs that any form of counseling is apt to be provided as part of the treatment process. However, IVF counseling has generally been designed to serve the needs of the IVF programs, with a view toward screening out problem patients. In the better programs, counseling may provide some understanding of the nature of the IVF process and of the chances for success, but it is extremely unlikely to provide any opportunity to explore feelings about infertility or alternatives to treatment.

The adoption world does essentially nothing to reach out to the infertile to educate them about adoption possibilities. Indeed, adoption agency rules operate to push the infertile away and thus to prevent them from obtaining the information they need to consider adoption at an early stage. The accepted ethic among adoption workers is that prospective parents must resolve feelings about infertility before they pursue adoption. The idea behind this makes some sense: people *should* try to understand their feelings about infertility and grieve over any loss that infertility represents before they become adoptive parents. They should not enter into adoption thinking of their adopted child as a second-best substitute for the biological child they still ache to produce. But it may be impossible to know what part of the pain of infertility relates to a desire to parent, and whether this desire will be satisfied by adoption, without knowing what adoption is about. An understanding of adoption may thus be essential to resolving feelings about infertility. Adoption agencies are potentially one of the best sources of that understanding. It is in completing the various steps of the application process that the infertile are likely to get a real comprehension of the specific options available as well as of their own feelings about adoption. However, if they admit to any real doubts about adoption or to any ongoing concerns about infertility, they risk an unfavorable rating at the end of the home study process.

There are some organizations and support groups, such as Resolve, that are designed to provide information and counseling to the infertile. But they have limited resources and influence, and so far appear to be reaching limited numbers.

So the information package that is being handed out to the infertile is biased in the direction of medical treatment. The problem is exacerbated by the fact that those receiving the package have little independent basis for understanding their options. The stigma associated with infertility means that those affected rarely discuss their problems openly. Many talk only to their doctor. Many are reluctant to be seen at public sessions where they might learn about adoption.

Other factors contribute to the medical tracking process. The infertile are bombarded with messages that reinforce the idea that it makes sense to consider adoption, if at all, only as a last resort. They are lured into IVF by aggressive advertising, characteristic of the free market world in which medical treatment takes place. They are simultaneously pushed away from the adoption world by negative messages from myriad sources telling them that adoption is an inherently inferior form of parenting.

The infertile can, of course, obtain meaningful information about adoption if they are sufficiently persistent. But many will not have the time, energy, and determination to find out enough about both the treatment and the adoption possibilities to truly understand at an early stage what their options are.

If the infertile do manage to get accurate information about their various parenting options, they find that our society gives vastly preferential treatment to people seeking to produce children as opposed to those seeking to adopt.

First and foremost, those seeking to reproduce operate in a free market world in which they are able to make their own decisions subject only to financial and physical constraints. Those seeking to adopt operate in a highly regulated world in which the government asserts the right to determine who will be allowed to parent.

As a result, those seeking to reproduce retain the sense that they are normal rights-bearing citizens. No one asks them to prove that they are fit to parent. They are perceived to have a God-given right to reproduce if they are capable of doing so. Those in the business of providing infertility services do not see it as their role to regulate access to parenting. The IVF practitioners who made the initial decision to exclude singles from their programs did so in large part because in an era when IVF treatment was highly controversial, the risk-averse course was to limit services to married couples. But IVF programs never enforced their rules excluding singles with the moral fervor typical of the adoption agencies, as my own experience illustrates. Today, as the IVF treatment industry has become more established, many programs are beginning officially to open their doors to singles.

Those entering the world of adoption agencies and home studies quickly realize that they have no right to become adoptive parents. Parental screening is central to the traditional adoption process, with the government determining through its agents who should be disqualified altogether from the parenting opportunity and then how those who are qualified should be rated for purposes of allocating the available children. There are no privacy rights in this world, either. The entire point of the home study process is to find out whether the most intimate events and relationships of a person's life have produced someone fit to parent. It is true that there are significant differences between the screening process in agency adoptions and that in independent adoptions. Prospective adopters with enough money can buy their way around the traditional agency home study process. But many who would like to adopt do not have this kind of money, and even in independent adoptions, the government demands at least a minimum showing of parental fitness.

The parental screening requirement is a very real deterrent to many who might otherwise consider adoption. People don't like to become helpless supplicants, utterly dependent on the good graces of social workers, with respect to something as basic as their desire to become parents. Screening also adds to the financial costs of adoption. Because it takes time, prospective parents must endure the related delays in forming a family. Screening turns the process of becoming a parent into a bureaucratic nightmare in which documents must be endlessly accumulated and stamped and submitted and copied.

Regulation also sends a powerful message about the essential inferiority of adoption as a form of parenting. By subjecting adoptive but not biological parents to regulation, society suggests that it trusts what goes on when people give birth and raise a birth child but profoundly distrusts what goes on when a child is transferred from a birth to an adoptive parent. The specific nature of adoption regulation constantly reinforces the notion that biological parenting is the ideal and adoption a poor second best. Adoptive families are thus designed in imitation of biological families. Prospective parents are screened because as adoptive parents they are suspect. They must be carefully matched with the right children because of the assumed risk that adoptive parenting won't work out. Ideally, they should be matched with the kinds of children they could have produced. And so forth.

Society also discriminates in financial terms, giving preferred treatment to those who choose child production over child adoption (O'Flaherty 1991). People covered by health insurance are reimbursed for many of the costs involved in infertility treatment, pregnancy, and childbirth. Although insurance plans have so far typically not covered IVF treatment, the trend is in the direction of expanding coverage to include it[7]. Treatment and childbirth expenses that are not covered by insurance are tax deductible if they exceed a certain percentage of income. By contrast, those who adopt are generally on their own in paying for the adoption, and only limited subsidies are available for those who adopt children with special needs (O'Flaherty 1992; Bartholet 1991). There is no equivalent to insurance coverage for the expenses involved in adoption, nor are those expenses generally deductible for income tax purposes. Employment benefit policies also favor child production over adoption. Employers that provide health insurance and childbirth leave usually do not provide equivalent benefits for those who become parents through adoption.

This discussion only begins to touch on some of the many ways in which society demonstrates its support for biological parenting and its suspicion of adoptive parenting. We have been conditioned from birth to believe that we should be fertile and should reproduce. Women are taught from birth that their identities are inextricably linked with their capacity for pregnancy and childbirth and that this capacity is inextricably linked with mothering. We are all bombarded on a daily basis with messages that childbirth is infinitely better than adoption as a route to parenting.

High-Tech Reproduction: A Rough Cost - Benefit Calculation

IVF has obviously given many women suffering from infertility the opportunity to get pregnant and bear children. There are thousands of IVF babies alive today to prove the point. But it has also increased the likelihood that more of the infertile will spend more of their lives in infertility treatment. IVF is generally not a substitute for, but a supplement to, other forms of treatment. Typically, a woman who realizes she is having trouble getting pregnant will start with an infertility workup, proceed with a series of increasingly intrusive treatment methods, and arrive at the IVF door at the end of an already long road.

Any serious attempt at an IVF pregnancy is likely to consume several more years. It takes some time to look into the factors relevant to selecting an appropriate program — track record, quality of staff, waiting list, location. It makes little sense to go through one IVF cycle without being willing to go through several more, since the chances of success in any given cycle are very low. Even if there is no waiting list, patients are usually advised or required to wait a minimum of one or two months after one treatment cycle before starting another. Often the wait is much longer, as the programs with the best success rates are often in heavy demand. Therefore, it can easily take up to several years to complete several treatment cycles.

Although most patients do stop after a few tries, one of the insidious things about IVF is that there is often no logical stopping point. Most failures occur after embryo transfer, and the reason for failure at this stage is almost always a mystery. As IVF practitioners are fond of pointing out, most attempts by fertile couples to conceive fail also.[8] For unknown reasons, most embryos that get as far as the uterus, whether naturally or by the IVF process, are unable to attach successfully so that a pregnancy is maintained beyond the early days or weeks. For the IVF patient, the mystery is dangerous. Failure provides no reason to think that you won't succeed the next time. IVF is a numbers game: It is easy to experience any given failure not as a reason to stop but as a reason to keep going. When you have invested so much, it can seem silly to stop, since the next time could be the time your number comes up. Some IVF practitioners exercise responsibility in helping their patients decide when to stop, but many do not. And even those who do often encourage patients whose prospects for success seem good, based on age and other factors, to continue through four to six cycles, at which point the repeated failures are thought to signal a reduced likelihood that the patient will ever be able to achieve an IVF pregnancy. It is not uncommon for patients to undergo ten cycles, and there are many stories of patients who have kept going beyond that.

A quick assessment of the costs and benefits involved in IVF treatment raises serious questions about whether this new methodology for dealing with infertility should be seen as a net plus for women, for children, or for the larger society. On the cost side of the ledger we must list the immediate burden on women, and to a lesser degree on their male partners — the time, energy and pain, both physical and emotional, for those who seek treatment.

Health risks must be added to this list.[9] Women's bodies are bombarded with hormones throughout the treatment cycle, first to stimulate egg follicle growth and later to encourage implantation. Hormone treatment has proven dangerous in the past, and although IVF patients are assured that hormones are being prescribed in safe dosages, the truth is that we do not yet know what risks may be involved. Knowledgeable critics of IVF treatment have expressed concerns that these hormones may cause cancer, and preliminary investigation has produced some disturbing evidence indicating that these concerns may be justified (Whittemore et al. 1993). Some IVF patients suffer from ovarian hyper-stimulation and other difficulties associated with the drug regimes. The treatment produces a high incidence of ectopic pregnancies, with all their attendant risks. It also produces a high incidence of multiple and of pre-term births, and such births are inherently problematic for the babies involved.[10] There is also evidence of a somewhat higher incidence of chromosomal abnormalities and congenital malformations in IVF babies than in the general population (Kola 1988; American Fertility Society 1992).

Financial resources are an obvious item on the cost list. For individual patients and their families, the cost of $5,000 to $10,000 per cycle must be multiplied by the number of attempts. Health insurance will provide at least partial reimbursement for some, but for the vast majority, huge out-of-pocket costs are involved in any given treatment cycle.[11]

For the society at large, it is irrelevant whether the individual patient or an insurance company pays a particular bill; it is the total cost of IVF that is relevant. Estimates indicate that over $100 million was spent for IVF treatment in the United States in 1990.[12] These resources could be devoted to serving some of the most basic health care needs of women and children, which now go unmet; they could, for example, be allocated to prenatal and preventive health services, enabling poor women to give birth to healthy babies and poor children to grow up healthy.

Another important item on the cost list is the pain involved in prolonging the struggle with infertility. A large body of literature documents the intense suffering associated with the discovery of infertility and with efforts to overcome it.[13] Each failed attempt at pregnancy renews the sense of loss, and it is not possible to get beyond the sense of loss and the suffering if you are still fixated on *undoing* the loss.

Finally, the list of costs includes, for the infertile, lost opportunities to parent, and for children, lost opportunities to receive nurturing homes. A major part of what infertility patients think they want is the opportunity to parent. Despite the related stigmas surrounding adoption and infertility, many infertile people express an interest in adoption. Years spent in the IVF pursuit obviously defer prospects for adoptive parenting, and for many, IVF is likely to eliminate such prospects altogether. Age is one problem. Many women are in their mid- to late thirties when they start IVF treatment. Several years later they will discover, if they look into adoption, that they are considered too old to rate as prime parental material; they will be low on the various priority lists and extremely limited in their adoption choices as a result. Battle fatigue is another problem. After years of struggling to overcome infertility, they may feel too tired and too discouraged to take on the world of adoption.

The benefits list for IVF is limited to one significant item: some of the infertile will experience pregnancy, childbirth, and biologically linked parenting. But *not that many* of those who engage in the process will reap this benefit. IVF practitioners have put out wildly exaggerated claims of success, conveying the impression — one picked up and reinforced by the media — that any given IVF cycle has a 25 to 50 percent chance of success.[14] It is only because of pressure by federal officials and agencies that in the past few years it has been possible to learn something about the *real* IVF success rates, those based on the number of live births per IVF cycle initiated.[15] These ranged from 6 to 9 percent during the 1986-1988 period, and reached 12 percent in more recent years, with somewhat higher success rates reported for ZIFT and GIFT.[16] The success rate for women aged thirty-five to thirty-nine was 10 percent, and for women forty and over was only 3 percent.[17]

It is not clear how much better these success rates will ever look. IVF practitioners claim that they are already doing almost as well as nature, arguing that the main reason for failure has to do with the same phenomenon that results in failure in most natural attempts at conception: a high percentage of embryos fail to implant, for reasons that are as yet unclear. There is no reason to think that we will soon unravel the mystery, or that if we do, we will be able to coerce embryos into implanting and developing into healthy babies. In any event, while success rates rose during the early period of IVF development, they have leveled off in recent years (see Kola 1988; American Fertility Society 1992).

There is also no way of knowing how many of those who become pregnant through the use of IVF would have been able to become pregnant if they had not resorted to IVF. Studies of some IVF program populations demonstrate that patients who dropped out of the programs and pursued less intrusive methods of becoming pregnant achieved comparable success rates to those who remained in the programs.

For the infertile population, the addition of IVF to the arsenal of treatment methods contributes only marginally to opportunities to become pregnant and give birth. This benefit must be weighed against the enormous costs involved both for those who succeed in achieving childbirth and for those who don't, as well as for the larger society.

Correcting the Bias

It makes no sense for a society that thinks of itself as sane and humane to drive people in the direction of child production rather than adoption. It makes no sense for the children who have already been born and who will grow up without homes unless they are adopted. A sane and humane society should encourage people to provide for these existing children before bringing more children into the world. It makes no sense for the adults dealing with infertility either. Of course the infertile are begging for treatment, and of course those who manage to produce a child will say it was all worth it. But they have been conditioned to feel that pregnancy and childbirth are the only solutions to their problem. Those who give birth are not in a position to know what they would have done with the years they spent in doctors' offices or what the experience of parenting an adopted child would have been. And most people who go down the treatment road will not succeed in producing a child.[18] Of those who do not, some will move on to parent through adoption. They will often ask themselves later why they wasted all those years on the treatment treadmill. But most of the unsuccessful infertility patients will never become adoptive parents.

We need to correct the biological bias to give children a better chance and to give adults more genuine choices. Many forces at work today seem designed instead to exacerbate this bias — to push the infertile ever more forcefully away from adoption and toward reproduction. There is, for example, significant hostility to transracial and transnational adoption, the forms of adoption that involve the great mass of children who need adoptive homes. The adoption search movement, involving adopted persons and the birth parents who have relinquished children for adoption, has focused new attention on the alleged problems of the adoptive family. Search movement advocates argue that biological links are of central importance to parenting, and that all parties to adoptive arrangements suffer by virtue of the break in genetic continuity that infertility and adoption represent. This new negativity helps make adoption additionally suspect, both for individuals making life choices and for a society making policy decisions. At the same time, the technological possibilities in infertility treatment have exploded. This means a somewhat greater chance for the infertile to produce a biological child. It also means that they may spend their entire adult lives trying. For most women with damaged Fallopian tubes, the treatment road that used to end with tubal surgery can, with the advent of IVF, go on for many years more. The increasing availability of insurance coverage exacerbates the problem. Having to pay upwards of $5,000 per IVF cycle has, to date, functioned as a significant brake on the IVF industry; the infertile are likely to pour into IVF programs in huge numbers if insurance pays the bills. Once in, many will find it hard to make the decision to get out. The treatment process has its own momentum. The sense of inadequacy that makes the medical route appealing in the first place is reinforced by every failure. The fear that you may have wasted yourself and your life becomes greater as the investment becomes greater, and feeds the compulsion to keep going.

We need to shift directions. The project is daunting, since it involves restructuring our understanding of infertility and of parenting. But some pieces of the project are easy to identify. We need to make counseling available on a widespread basis to those suffering from infertility, so that early in their struggles they can begin to deal with feelings of loss and inadequacy, to unravel what part of their pain, if any, relates to a desire to parent, and to puzzle out what parenting is and should be about. We also need to make meaningful information about various parenting options available early, so that people can gain some real understanding of what it would mean to pursue infertility treatment and what it would mean to pursue adoption. The counseling and the information should come from groups that are not tied to or part of any medical establishment. We need to create new support organizations for the infertile. Adoption agencies and organizations should become much more active in outreach efforts.

We also need radically to reform the regulatory system that structures adoption. When the infertile do get an accurate sense of their options, adoption should not look like such an uphill struggle. We need to change our laws and policies so that they facilitate rather than impede the process of matching people who want to parent with children who need homes. And we need to question current practices that push the infertile to pursue treatment.

The "flight into the unknown" that took me to Lima, Peru, in the summer of 1985 was part of a long journey, one that started much earlier and is still going on. I have arrived at a place where many things seem clear to me. I feel that I have learned a lot from my travels through the infertility treatment and adoption worlds, and I am convinced that if others could take this journey, literally or figuratively, they would also learn a lot. My current vision seems to me so clearly right that I find myself impatient with the society that apparently sees things so differently. Adoption can work, and work well, for birth parents, for adoptive parents, and for children. Why structure it in ways that drive prospective parents away from the existing children in need? Why structure the new worlds of infertility treatment and child production in ways that encourage the infertile and others interested in parenting to produce new children, or to spend their lives trying? There may be some inborn need to procreate, but there are also inborn needs to nurture. Why does organized society seem to want to encourage its members to obsess over the former at the expense of the latter?[19]

We need to deregulate adoption. The current regulatory framework creates obstacles on both a practical and a psychological level; it makes the adoption process costly and unpleasant, and it degrades and demeans this form of family. We need to eliminate this kind of restrictive regulation, and redesign the adoption system so that it facilitates, rather than impedes, the placement of children who need homes with the adults who want to provide them. For example, we need to get rid of burdensome parental screening requirements. These requirements deprive children of adoptive homes by driving up the costs of adoption and driving away prospective parents who do not fit the social worker's orthodox vision of the appropriate parent type. We need to get rid of the special restrictions that stand in the way of transracial and transnational adoption. We need meaningful guarantees that children will receive nurturing homes and will not be held in limbo for longer than absolutely necessary. We need new systems providing financial reimbursement for some of the costs involved in adoption, so that more of those who are interested in this form of parenting are able to pursue it. At present we make adoptive parents pay all adoption expenses, except in the case of certain special needs adoptions. By contrast, we provide significant subsidies to those who pursue procreation. We should revise our state and federal tax systems to provide credits for the costs of all adoptions, and we should revise insurance plans and employer benefit plans so that those who parent through adoption receive at least the same benefits as those who parent through procreation.[20]

At the same time, we need to regulate infertility treatment and the new child production methods. The goal should be not simply to protect the rights of parties engaged in these arrangements but to discourage certain practices, such as egg and embryo sale and commercial surrogacy. We need to rethink the meaning of fertility, parenting, and family.

In my post-adoption state, I find all this so obvious that I am left with a genuine sense of puzzlement as to why it is such an uphill battle to argue the case for adoption. Maybe it is too threatening to think what might happen to the family if it was not defined and confined by biology and marriage. Maybe it is too threatening to think what might happen if people were not understood to belong to their racial, ethnic, national, or other groups of origin, if they were free to merge across group lines, if they were free not to reproduce more of the group's "own."

Living life as an adoptive parent forces a person to think about these issues. It provides no easy answers. It represents freedom from some constraining concepts of family, but it hardly brings instant liberation. Single women and infertile individuals may see adoption as opening up new opportunities for parenting, without partners and free of the ministrations of the high-tech fertility doctors. But this society does not make single parenting, whether adoptive or biological, an easy ride. Until and unless such parenting becomes financially viable, it will be oppressive both for the parents involved and for their children.

Adoptive families can be models for the families of the future or they can be poor imitations of the families of the past. Adoptive parents and children have to figure out whether to break the old molds, and if so, what to salvage.

Notes

1 This chapter is drawn in substantial part from material that appeared in Elizabeth Bartholet, *Family Bonds: Adoption and the Politics of Parenting* (Bartholet, 1993) Introduction, chapters 2, 9 and Afterword. It was written with a United States audience in mind, and specific references to legal systems and social policies should be read in that light. Other chapters in the book deal specifically with the empirical evidence on adoptive arrangements, with international and transracial adoption, with surrogacy and embryo donation and sale in the IVF context, and other forms of what I have termed "technological adoption."

2 Sociobiology teaches us that we are genetically programmed for reproduction. See Dawkins, 1976.

3 U.S. Congress, Office of Technology Assessment, *Infertility: Medical and Social Choices* (Washington, DC; Government Printing Office, May 1988) pp. 4-5. Also William D. Mosher and William F. Pratt, "Fecundity and Infertility in the United States, 1965-1988," Advance Data No. 192. December 4, 1990, National Center for Disease Statistics, Hyattsville, MD. Infertility rates have increased for certain subgroups of the population, such as women who postpone efforts to get pregnant until later in life.

4 U.S. Congress, *Infertility*, 3-5 (one in seven estimate based on a population that excludes the surgically sterile).

5 Patricia Conway and Deborah Valentine, "Reproductive Losses and Grieving," *Journal of Social Work and Human Sexuality* 6 (1987): 46-64. For a review of the literature, Sarah Eaton, *Adoption v. Reproductive Technologies: The Biological Link Reexamined* (unpublished manuscript, Harvard Law School, 1990, pp. 13-16).

6 Only 50,000 nonrelative adoptions take place per year in the United States. A recent survey indicates that only 200,000 women are currently taking steps to pursue adoption, while 2 million have investigated it at some time. See C. Bachrach, K.London, and P. Maza, "On the Path to Adoption: Adoption Seeking in the U.S." In *Journal of Marriage and the Family* 53 (August 1991): 705-18; "New Study Challenges Estimates on Odds of Adopting a Child," *New York Times*, Dec. 10, 1990, p.B-10.

7 U.S. Congress, *Infertility*, 149-52.

8 Among such couples there is a 20 to 25 percent chance of achieving a pregnancy after trying for one month.

9 See generally, U.S. Congress, *Infertility*, 128-32, 303.

10 See American Fertility Society, "In-vitro fertilization-embryo transfer (IVF-ET) in the United States: 1990 results from the IVF-ET Registry," In *Fertility and Sterility* 57(1992) 17. Five percent of all IVF pregnancies were ectopic; 22 percent resulted in live multiple births, with other multiple pregnancies resulting in spontaneous abortions and stillbirths; 13 percent of live deliveries were pre-term.

11 A number of states now mandate insurance coverage, and some insurance companies voluntarily provide it. Many patients and doctors obtain reimbursement for some aspects of the IVF process, such as hormone treatment, simply by submitting the claims without informing the insurance company that the treatment was related to IVF. See U.S. Congress, *Infertility*, 148-55.

12 See U.S. Congress. House. Committee on Energy and Commerce. Subcommittee on Health and the Environment. *Fertility Clinic Success Rate and Certification Act of 1991: Hearing on H.R. 3940*, 102nd Congress, 2nd Sess., Feb. 27, 1992, Richard F. Kelly, written testimony, p.1, note 2. More than $1 billion was spent in 1990 for infertility services as a whole.

13 See review of the literature in Eaton, "Adoption v. Reproductive Technology." See also Charlene E. Miall, "The Stigma of Involuntary Childlessness," *Social Problems* 33 (1986):268.

14 The doctors have measured "success" on the basis of the number of IVF patients out of the group who go through the embryo transfer process who are able to become pregnant. They do not include the many cases in which women who start a cycle of IVF treatment never get as far as embryo transfer, or the many cases of women who manage to become pregnant but lose the fetus after a few days, weeks or months, or give birth to a dead child. Another problem is that the success rates that have been generally touted are often those at the most successful clinics in the country, rather than those at the average clinic, the clinic that is advertising, or the clinic that is promoting its services to a particular patient. See generally U.S. Congress. House Committee on Small Business, Subcommittee on Regulation, Business Opportunities, and Energy. *Consumer Protection Issues Involving In-vitro Fertilization Clinics*, 101st Congress, 1st sess., March 9, 1989, p.1; and Robert Pear, "Fertility Clinics Face Crackdown," *New York Times*, Oct. 26, 1992.

15 See e.g., Committee on Energy and Commerce, Fertility Clinic Success Rate, testimony of Richard F. Kelly: "The success rate formula that is least likely to mislead consumers is one that takes into account all significant negative results. Thus the starting point...should be the rate of live births per stimulation cycles" (p.7).

16 See U.S. Congress, *Infertility*, p. 182; U.S. House of Representatives, *Consumer Protection Issues*, p.2. The 12 percent figure is based on statistics in American Fertility Society, *In-vitro fertilization: 1990 results*, 16-17. This material indi-

cates 2,345 live deliveries out of 19,079 stimulation cycles. Actual success rates may well be lower, since the IVF-ET Registry has data only for clinics that volunteer their results; there is reason to believe that non-reporting clinics are less successful.

17 American Fertility Society, *In-vitro fertilization: 1990 results*, 19, Table 3. Calculated based on live delivery per stimulation cycles.

18 A recent government report estimates that only about one half of those who pursue an extensive series of treatment programs, including tubal surgery and two IVF cycles, will produce a child. See U.S. Congress, *Infertility*, 143.

19 Sociobiologists describe adoption as a "mistake," a "misfiring of a built-in rule." As Dawkins puts it in *The Selfish Gene*: "The generous female is doing her own genes no good by caring for the orphan. She is wasting time and energy which she could be investing in the lives of her own kin, particularly future children of her own." But Dawkins also writes that human beings have the capacity to defy their genetic programming and to deliberately cultivate altruism. 101, 200-01.

20 See O'Flaherty, "Financial Support for Adoption," which describes recently proposed federal legislation that would expand support and makes related recommendations. For information on private sector support, which, although limited, is growing, see National Committee for Adoption, *1989 Factbook*, pp. 213-14; Bureau of National Affairs, *Adoption Assistance: Joining the Family of Employee Benefits* (Washington, D.C.; BNA, 1988); and National Adoption Exchange, *Adoption Benefits Plans: Corporate Response to a Changing Society* (Philadelphia: NAE, 1984).

References

American Fertility Society. 1992. In-vitro fertilization - embryo transfer (IVF-ET) in the United States: 1990 results from the IVF-ET registry. *Fertility and Sterility* 57:17.

Bachrach, C., K. London, and P. Maza. 1991. On the path to adoption: adoption seeking in the U.S. *Journal of Marriage and the Family* 53 (August):705–18.

Bartholet, E. 1991. Where do black children belong? The politics of race matching in adoption. *Pennsylvania Law Review* 139:1163, 1198–99.

——. 1993. *Family bonds: Adoption and the politics of parenting*. Boston: Houghton Mifflin.

Bureau of National Affairs. 1988. *Adoption assistance: Joining the family of employee benefits*. Washington, D.C.: BNA.

Conway, P., and D. Valentine. 1987. Reproductive Losses and Grieving. *Journal of Social Work and Human Sexuality* 6:46–64.

Dawkins, R. 1976. *The selfish gene*. New York: Oxford University Press.

Eaton, S. Adoption v. reproductive technologies: The biological link reexamined. Course paper. Harvard Law School.

Kola, I. 1988. Commentary: Embryo and fetal abnormalities in IVF. *Birth* 15:145–47.

Miall, C.E. 1986. The stigma of involuntary childlessness. *Social Problems* 33:286.

Mosher W.D., and W.F. Pratt. 1990. *Fecundity and infertility in the United States, 1965–1988.* Advance Data no. 192. Hyattsville, Md.: National Center for Disease Statistics.

National Adoption Exchange. 1984. *Adoption benefits plans: Corporate response to a changing society.* Philadelphia, Pa.: NAE.

National Committee for Adoption. 1989. *Adoption factbook: United States data, issues, regulations, and resources.* Washington, D.C.: The Committee.

O'Flaherty, K. 1992. Financial support for adoption: Programs, issues and proposals. Course paper. Harvard Law School.

U.S. Congress. House Committee on Energy and Commerce. Subcommittee on Health and the Environment. *Fertility clinic success rate and certification act of 1991: Hearing on H.R. 3940.* 102nd Cong., 2d sess.

U.S. Congress. Office of Technology Assessment. *Infertility: Medical and social choices.* 1988. Washington, D.C.: GPO.

U.S. Congress. Committee on Small Business, Subcommittee on Regulation, Business Opportunities, and Energy. *Consumer protection issues involving in vitro fertilization clinics.* 101st Congress, 1st sess.

Whittemore, A.S., R. Harris, J. Itnyre, et al. 1993. Characteristics relating to ovarian cancer risk: Collaborative analysis of twelve US-case control studies. Invasive epithelial ovarian cancers in white women. *Am J Epidemiol* 136:1184–1203.

10

Beyond Control:
About Antifertility "Vaccines,"
Pregnancy Epidemics, and Abuse

by Judith Richter

The prospect of regulating fertility by manipulating immune mechanisms has hitherto been a pious hope linking the aspirations of family planners and reproductive immunologists. Now at last the rational and practical application of this exciting yet frustrating tract of science is at hand. (Warren R. Jones 1982)

In the early 1970s, contraceptive researchers set out on a quest for a totally new type of contraceptive. The aim was to develop a long-acting, highly effective and easy to administer birth control method using the immune system: in short, an antifertility "vaccine."

Today, research on immunological contraceptives is gathering momentum. Although clinical trials have not yet gone beyond phase II, "it is now generally accepted that vaccines will come to be used for the control of fertility" (Mitchison 1990). The developers are enthusiastic. "The vaccine may prove to be as important a development in birth control technology as the contraceptive pill," said World Health Organization research coordinator David Griffin (WHO 1986). The Indian immunologist Pran Talwar hopes to apply for registration for his anti-pregnancy hormone "vaccine" within the next three to six years (Barriklow 1993). Members of the media all over the world are speaking in euphoric terms about the benefits which this revolutionary technology will bring to humankind. "If perfected and mass distributed, the vaccine could have enormous implications, especially for women in the developing world," reported the magazine of the United Nations Development Program (Barriklow 1993).

Women's and health action groups are less enthusiastic. They would like to know what risks are dormant in this complex, long-acting birth control technology. They wonder what advantages immunological contraception will offer over current fertility regulating methods.

As a health professional and consumer activist, I have been concerned about the development of immunological birth control methods since 1989, when I was invited to participate in the WHO's Symposium on Antifertility Vaccines (Ada and Griffin 1991). The aim of the symposium was to discuss the further course of development of immunological contraceptives. At that time I was working as a research and information officer with a Thai consumer protection group concerned with raising public awareness regarding the role of medicines in society and the corporate interests involved. This work had sensitized me to the limitations and omissions of public debates about medical technology. I became concerned about the way discussion of socio-political and ethical problems were kept under a lid at the WHO Symposium. I also became concerned when the main researchers recommended declaring antifertility "vaccines" a major method for family planning programs, at a time when none of the methods had passed efficacy trials (for critical reports on the Symposium, see Hardon 1989; Richter 1991).

I have since had the opportunity to learn more about immunological birth control methods, both through my work on a review of such methods for the BUKO Pharma-Kampagne and Health Action International (Richter 1993) and during a second WHO seminar on immunological contraceptives in 1992, which brought together the main researchers and women's rights and health advocates.

The aim of this chapter is not to give a critical review of immunological contraceptives. This has been done elsewhere.[1] (Schrater 1992 and in this volume; Richter 1993) My aim is to examine some of the main forces guiding the research. Like Judy Wajcman (1991), I hold the view that technology development is shaped by many forces in society. I also share her view that technologies, in turn, can shape socio-political and cultural realities.

After a brief review of the action and types of immunological contraceptives, I shall examine the framework underlying their development and forecast some of the implications for users and society. My hope is to stimulate debate and prompt action to prevent immunological contraceptives from becoming a reality.[2]

What are Immunological Contraceptives?

The mode of action of immunological contraceptives is based on the relationship between the immune and the reproductive systems. Most people know the immune system as the "police of our body." The immune system — a complex interplay between cells, molecules and organs is our most powerful defense mechanism against infectious microorganisms, such as viruses, bacteria, parasites and fungi. Few people realize that there is another, equally important function of our immune system, the prevention of "self" attack by the immune system, i.e., *the attack on the body's own components.* The effector mechanisms of our immune system — in particular antibodies and immune cells — are capable of attacking constituents of our body as well as foreign microorganisms. If this occurs, severe autoimmune diseases such as myasthenia gravis, forms of rheumatoid arthritis and diabetes can result.

The capacity of the immune system to protect the body from immune-mediated self-destruction is known as "self-tolerance." As yet, little is known about how self-tolerance actually works. We do know, however, that our immune system starts to build up self-tolerance early in life. By the time we are born, our immune system is already tolerant of most of our cell types, enzymes and hormones.

Immune-mediated contraceptives aim at temporary interference of the "self"-tolerance which allows successful reproduction to occur. Immune-mediated contraceptives interrupt one of three basic reproductive processes:

- production and/or maturation of human gametes, i.e., sperm or egg cells,

- fertilization, or

- implantation and/or development of the early embryo.

To disturb any of these processes, researchers encourage an auto-immune attack on the cells or molecules involved. This is done by tricking the immune system into believing these molecules are "foreign" antigens. An altered version of the reproductive cell or molecule is linked to a "non-self" antigen such as diphtheria toxoid or tetanus toxoid so that the whole complex is recognized as "foreign," and the immune system responds with antibodies to the natural structure. The following reproductive cells or molecules have been identified as targets for immunological intervention.

1) The first class of potential targets are non-pregnancy associated (reproductive) hormones which regulate the monthly ripening and release of egg cells in women and the continuous production of sperm in men. The aim of the auto-immune attack is to disturb maturation of eggs or the production of sperm.

2) The second class of target components are our egg and sperm cells. The aim is to incapacitate them such that they become incapable of fertilization.

3) The third class of targets are either pregnancy-associated hormones or enzymes, or the early embryo itself. This group includes hCG (human chorionic gonadotropin), a hormone produced by the early embryo which facilitates implantation and which is regarded as the most "promising" target antigen. Immune-mediated neutralization of this hormone prevents implantation. Another target is an actual component of the early embryo, called the trophoblast (it is from the trophoblastic cells of the early embryo that the placenta develops); neutralization of this component can also disrupt implantation.

As such there is a variety of potential immunological contraceptives.[3] The profile of action and potential adverse effects of specific types of immunological contraceptives will differ considerably depending on the role and location of the target antigen, and whether the product is developed for women or men.

Guiding Threads Behind Antifertility "Vaccine" Development

History

The general direction of contraceptive development has been determined primarily by the interests of scientists and the population control establishment, and very marginally by the major user group — women (Wajcman 1991). According to sociologist Adele Clarke (1990):

> The driving force behind the development of "scientific" means of contraception was and remains reproductive scientists' desires for professional autonomy as "basic" researchers.

Until the 1960s, most academic scientists did only "basic research," that is, on the physiology of reproduction. They left the explicit exploitation of their research for contraception to clinical practitioners and the pharmaceutical industry. If ever they did participate in explicit contraceptive research, it was almost never in the area of improving simple existing user-controlled technologies such as diaphragms and spermicides, but rather on the development of new "scientific" means of contraception, i.e., technologies "which rely for effectiveness more on biological and medical research and expert control than on users' motivation" (Clarke 1990).

Scientists' involvement in contraceptive development became significant only in the 1960s after a "coalescence of the various birth control movements into a fully legitimate, middle class and professional international population control establishment" (Clarke 1990). Publicity about the threat of the so-called "population explosion" made contraceptive development a socially acceptable, even desirable, endeavor. Funding from public sources and private foundations became significant.

The idea for immune-mediated contraception emerged at the end of last century, when two immunologists, Landsteiner and Metchnikoff, discovered independently that immune reactions against sperm could lead to infertility. The 1920s and 1930s saw the first wave of human trials. Ease of administration and low cost were seen as major advantages of immunological contraception:

> Think, how wonderful it would be if one could immunize a patient by a simple hypodermic injection once every six months, just as we today immunize children against diphtheria. It will indeed be a new and wonderful era in the practice of preventive gynecology (Daniels 1931, quoted in Clarke 1990).

> Devices are all very nice for those who can afford them. The poor people with whom we are really concerned in this [Depression] recovery program cannot afford them... it is quite necessary to be concerned with something that can be applied much more cheaply. Spermatotoxins [as anti-sperm "vaccines" were called at the time]...are one of the methods (McCartney 1934, quoted in Clarke 1990).

There were at least 12 studies in women between 1920 and 1934 (Joel 1971, quoted in Jones 1982). This first wave of research culminated in 1937, when M.J. Baskin was awarded a U.S. patent for an anti-sperm "vaccine" for women. However, a discouraging evaluation report regarding the potential of immunological contraceptives ended this research in the late 1930s. The report concluded:

> When one compares.. the fertility of the injected animals with the controls, it appears that parenteral injection of live sperms reduces slightly the fertility of the recipients, but the reduction is neither of significant degree nor of practical importance. (Eastman, Guttmacher and Stewart 1939, quoted in Clarke 1990)

The lack of efficacy was not the only concern: according to the gynecologist and contraceptive researcher Warren Jones, at least in the U.S., "ethical restrictions[4] also proscribed further attempts at parenteral immunization against semen in man" (1982).

Two decades later, Seymour Katsh undertook a Population Council funded review of these first studies with the hope to "stimulate intensive experimentation and clinical investigation in this broad area of the control of infertility and fertility by immunological means." Katsh saw the availability of an "effective and reliable method... for inducing infertility (temporary or permanent) in both males and females which will meet with the approval of the greatest number of people..." as the "core" of the urgently needed "control of populations" (1959).

The time was not yet ripe. The advent of new immunological techniques and a favorable funding climate allowed immunologists to take up the interrupted endeavor in the early 1970s. The current aspirations of the developers go far beyond the induction of immune reactions in women against the sperm of their partner. As we have seen, today's immunological contraceptives are directed against a variety of reproductive components and are meant for both females and males, although the majority of prospective methods are still for women.

In the 1990s, five major institutions are conducting the bulk of research:

- ■ The National Institute of Immunology, New Delhi, India;

- ■ The Special Program of Research, Development and Research Training in Human Reproduction [HRP] of the World Health Organization, Geneva, Switzerland;

- ■ The Population Council, New York, USA;

- ■ The Contraceptive Research and Development Program (CONRAD), Norfolk, USA; and

■ The National Institute for Child Health and Development (NICHD), Bethesda, USA.

Not all immune contraceptive types are at the same stage of development. As of late 1993, some are being tested in humans, while a large proportion of research is still geared towards identifying appropriate antigenic structures. By far the most advanced research is on anti-hCG methods. Indian researchers are preparing for phase III trials for one anti-hCG immune contraceptive method and HRP is about to start phase II trials for another anti-hCG method in Sweden.

Funding comes from a variety of sources. They include the World Bank, the United Nations Population Fund (UNFPA), The United Nations Development Program (UNDP), The Rockefeller Foundation, The US Agency for International Development (USAID), The International Development and Research Center (IDRC, Canada), and the governments of Germany, Great Britain, India, Norway, Sweden, and the United States (Richter 1993). In the public sector, about one-tenth of current contraceptive research funds is devoted to research on immunological contraceptive methods (Spieler 1992).

Disagreements about the Feasibility of Immunological Contraception

What drives the second wave of research on immunological birth control methods? HRP's Task Force Manager David Griffin suggests the "objective... [is] not to produce replacements for existing birth control technologies but to widen the choice of safe, effective, acceptable and affordable family planning methods" (1992). This explanation raises two questions. First, will antifertility "vaccines" ever be safe, effective, acceptable and affordable? Second, will they positively widen the choice for women? The opinion of the experts invited to the 1989 HRP Seminar on antifertility vaccines was divided. According to chairperson N. Avrion Mitchison (1991):

> Our discussions revealed that an antifertility vaccine can be regarded from sharply contrasting points of view. Some see it as little more than an extension of existing methods of medium-term contraception, such as Norplant; others feel that the potential for ease of administration, coupled with cheapness and long-term effect place it in an entirely new category. Some regard it as tampering with germ cells and the complexities of the immune

system, and therefore extremely dangerous; others see it as safer than steroids [i.e., hormonal contraceptives], because it immediately stops something from happening rather than continually blocking a normal activity. Some hope for a vaccine simply because it will provide women with a worthwhile new birth control option, while others hope that it will provide an unprecedented effective instrument of demographic control.

Doubts about the idea of contraception through manipulation of the immune system are sparsely expressed in scientific literature. The immunologists Deborah J. Anderson and Nancy J. Alexander admonished in 1983 that "however exciting and yielding the new technology may be, the biology of reproduction is complex, and extreme caution must be exercised to ensure that the new methods are both biologically safe and effective."

The major research teams express optimism about the future of immunological contraceptives and promote them for their "lack of pharmacological activity and the often attendant side effects" (WHO 1988). They forget to mention that immunological contraceptives, instead, generate immunological activity that may well result in a range of immune-mediated adverse effects. Criticisms about the concept of immunological contraceptives are quelled by the argument that it is far too early to make any conclusive statements, and that as yet completely untried improvements in product formulation may bring breakthroughs (Griffin, quoted in Hof-Mussler 1993).

Contraceptive researcher David Hamilton, at the University of Minnesota, questions the major argument that problems of autoimmunization could be circumvented with careful selection of the antigen:

> But doesn't the inherent problem remain — that we are immunizing against body constituents and that this may cause autoimmunity? Although you may say we have examples already from human chorionic gonadotropin (hCG) immunization, I think these cases have not been followed properly. What do we know about those women who were immunized? Do you know what sort of delayed autoimmune disease is possible? I am very skeptical that immunization against body constituents would ever work without side effects. (Hamilton, in Alexander et al. 1990)

Agreement over their Demographic Effectiveness

There is little disagreement that, in the words of U.S.-based researcher Vernon Stevens, "the research conducted during the past decade has brought us to the threshold of making available a new method for more effectively meeting the challenge of ever-increasing global population expansion" (1986). His Indian colleague Pran Talwar is also thrilled that "the field of birth control vaccines is no longer just a myth — not a fantasy as it used to be not long back" (Schaz and Schneider 1991).

Explication on the motivations behind research on immunological contraceptives is provided by Talwar:

> Well, you just have to go, for example, to Bombay or to any other metropolis for that reason; at the time that the offices close; see this sea of humanity that flows: trains are overloaded, buses are overloaded — everything is overloaded. The population stress is expressing itself in many walks of life...I would even say that several of our political problems — the uneasiness of the youth, the uncertainties of getting jobs, all the reservation issues — anti- or pro-reservations — are all caused by this problem of too large numbers looking for too few places...(even) the terrorist problem is related in a way to the population problem and the social strain that it is causing — the inability of the structure to cope with the numbers (Schaz and Schneider 1991).

Many researchers seem to agree that "new methods of birth control are necessary to halt, and ultimately reverse, this inexorable trend in population growth" (Henderson, Hulme and Aitken 1987).

What justifies the "hope" that antifertility vaccines will be "unprecedented effective instruments of demographic control"? Why would they be more effective than, for example, hormonal injectables and implants, or intrauterine devices? "Long-action" and "lack of user failure" are two intrinsic characteristics of immunological contraceptives which are mentioned as "theoretical advantages" throughout the scientific literature. The "model" contraceptive vaccine would have an action of one to two years after a single injection (Basten et al. 1991), but the ultimate length of action of immunological contraceptives is as yet unclear. Some immunological contraceptives, such as anti-sperm immune contraceptives for women, may well turn out to have life-long action (Anderson and Alexander 1983; Schrater this volume). As HRP consultant Jones stated in 1982, "the capability of reversal is an attractive but not essential facet of any contraceptive method and its abrogation by a vaccine would at worst only limit the utility of such an approach... the ultimate place of a contraceptive vaccine may indeed evolve as a form of medical sterilization." And for the Population Council, "irreversibility... is not always an adverse effect; some vaccines may be designed to be used as non-surgical means of sterilization" (Thau et al. 1990).

Whatever the duration of action, the problem is that once people are "immunized" there is actually nothing they can do to reverse the action, unless they took immunosuppressive drugs which suppress not only the specific autoimmune reaction against the reproductive target antigen but cause a general suppression of the immune system. Users have to wait until antibody levels drop below the contraceptive threshold.

Population controllers can also hope on an additional predicted advantage of immunological contraceptives, their "ease of administration" (Brache et al. 1992). It is unclear what the final form of delivery of immunological contraceptives will be. Most will probably be injectables; others, such as the anti-sperm vaccine, may be oral preparations. An injectable or oral form of delivery, together with the projected "low cost" of the vaccine (Ada and Griffin 1991), makes it a better vehicle for mass fertility control than the IUD, which has to be inserted through the vagina, or Norplant, which has to be implanted in the arm through minor surgery.

The "Vaccine" Metaphor

Contraceptive developers apparently also agree on another positive feature of immunological contraceptives: they can be positively identified with vaccines, with all of the attendant attributes. The "vaccine" metaphor permeates scientific discussion of the method. At an early meeting, researchers stated:

> Immunization as a prophylactic measure is now so widely accepted that it has been suggested that one method of fertility regulation which would have wide appeal as well as great ease of service delivery would be an anti-fertility vaccine (WHO 1978)

Senior USAID Biomedical Research Advisor Jeff Spieler sees "compelling advantages for service delivery because vaccines would provide long-acting fertility regulation, could be administered by paramedical and nonprofessional personnel, and could be integrated not only with family planning services but with other health care programs as well" (1987). And Population Council's senior advisor Sheldon J. Segal writes:

There is perhaps no health technology with greater programmatic and policy implications than vaccines. Because of the cooperative policies of many governments, for example, the World Health Organization (WHO) was able to lead the vaccination program that eradicated smallpox in the 1970s. Immunization against specific diseases has proven to be the most effective approach available for disease prevention. It may also become a technology for pregnancy prevention (Segal 1991).

Above statements are addressed to either fellow researchers, or funders and policy makers. The vaccine metaphor is slightly different when directed at the general public. Talwar, for example, asserts:

[Birth control vaccines are] more physiological in the sense that it is your own body which is trained now to react selectively against a substance which is important for reproduction. So therefore there are all these advantages — and then historically, as you know, vaccines have been medicine's biggest weapons against diseases (Schaz and Schneider 1991).

Griffin's account of the birth of the antifertility "vaccine" concept at the 1992 meeting between women's health advocates and researchers is similar:

Following detailed review of the options for the development of new methods, immunological intervention was considered a promising area for investigation. The objective being to use the body's own immune system to provide protection against pregnancy in essentially the same way that it provides protection against unwanted diseases. In other words, to develop a fertility regulating vaccine.

Such statements contain the implicit suggestion that vaccines have always been good, therefore antifertility vaccines are also good. The analogy between antifertility "vaccines" and anti-disease vaccines obscures the technical realities of immunological contraceptives. There are profound differences in the aim, action and acceptable benefit risk balance of these two types of immunological technologies.

The major technical similarity between the two is that both rely on an activation of the immune system by administration of an altered antigen. However, there are major differences:

1) Antidisease vaccines mimic the body's specific *immune defense* against harmful micro-organisms. Immunological contraceptives aim to imitate an *immunological disorder*, namely autoimmune infertility.[5]

2) Anti-disease vaccines are targeted at *"foreign" micro-organisms*; immunological contraceptives are targeted at *human cells, hormones or enzymes* which are essential for reproduction. These components are seen as "self" or "self-like" by the immune system (I disagree with the view regarding sperm as "foreign" to the female immune system). Throughout the history of the human species, the immune system has elaborated "safeguards against autoimmune reactions," i.e., "self-tolerance," to these reproductive components. If they did not exist, the human species would have become extinct.

3) The ultimate aim of anti-disease vaccines and immunological contraceptives is profoundly different, and therefore the *risk/benefit assessment* is profoundly different. The analogy, vaccines have been good therefore antifertility "vaccines" must be good, is wrong. An efficacy profile which is acceptable for anti-disease immunization may not be acceptable for immunological contraceptives. Adverse effects which may be acceptable for a method which prevents harmful diseases, and for which there is no alternative, may be unacceptable for a contraceptive which aims at preventing a physiological process, especially given that alternative contraceptives are available. Immunological contraceptives must be evaluated for their usefulness as contraceptives; their benefits and risks must be measured against other contraceptive methods.

For these reasons, I consider it important to use the term *immunological contraceptives* or *birth control methods*, and to question the use of the term "vaccine" when referring to this kind of fertility control technology.

Potential Consequences of Perpetuating the "Vaccine" Metaphor in the Context of Population Control Ideology

I see three major problems with the intersection between the population control framework and the use of the vaccine metaphor. First, it results in a biased risk benefit assessment. Second, there is the danger that participants of clinical trials will be ill- or misinformed. Third, it paves the way for abuse of antifertility "vaccines," particularly as it contributes to the perpetuation of the ideologic framework that women in LACAAP[6] countries are irresponsible "breeders" whose fertility has to be controlled at all costs.

Biased Risk Benefit Assessment

In my view, both the population and immunological frameworks have resulted in the neglect of a significant shortcoming of immunological contraceptives — their problematic efficacy profile.

As already stated, the "model" immunological contraceptive is reversible after one or two years. The researchers' main concern has been whether immunological contraceptives can be effective for this time period and in what percentage of women.

For any immunological contraceptive there will be a lag period (period during which the antibody titres begin to increase) after the first administration, a contraceptive phase (a period during which the antibody titre is above the effective threshold) and a waning phase. This process is an inherent aspect of in the immunological response.

The first problem is the *lag period* of several weeks to two to three months before the antibody titre rises above a contraceptive threshold. A woman must not get pregnant during this time, or the fetus will be exposed to the effects of an ongoing immune reaction.

A second problem — even with the best possible immune contraceptive — may be the relatively high *method failure rate,* i.e., the rate of accidental pregnancies under best possible circumstances. As Spieler points out, "a fertility regulating vaccine... would have to produce and sustain effective immunity in at least 95% of the vaccinated population, a level of protection rarely achieved even with the most successful viral and bacterial vaccines" (1987). In phase II of the Indian trials the rate of "low-responders" (i.e., women not reaching the putative effective threshold) was 20 percent.

The problems to be expected under real usage conditions are infinitely greater. The biggest hurdle of immune contraceptives will be their *inherent unpredictability* for the individual woman. There will be considerable variations in the duration of the lag phase and the contraceptive phase.[7] Women with a predisposition to inappropriate immune responses (allergies or autoimmune diseases) might find themselves unexpectedly infertile for indefinite periods. On the other hand, an unexpected low immune response may occur during times of stress, malnutrition, or with the onset of immuno-suppressive diseases such as malaria, tuberculosis, and HIV infection.

Finally, it will be extremely difficult, if not impossible, to stop ongoing immune reactions. This greatly compounds problems if a women gets pregnant during the period or if she develops adverse effects.

Although some of these problems may be reduced by novel ways of formulating the product, in essence they will remain. The problem is not that of a particular prototype "vaccine," but that the immune system is an interconnected, open, regulatory system and that the magnitude and duration of immune responses varies depending on genetic, environmental and psychological factors.

The population control and immunological frameworks of thought have resulted in an overemphasis on statistical efficacy. The former framework focusing on the reduction of birth rates; the latter on the percentage of women who might become accidentally pregnant within one year of use. Questions about the reliability of the method for any individual woman, about the inherent link between unpredictable gaps in the immune-meditated contraceptive effect and exposure of the fetus, and about the consequences of being unable to "turn off" the immune response in case of adverse reactions or accidental pregnancies, have been relatively neglected.

Kalpana Mehta, from Saheli Women's Resource Center, comments that for researchers working within a demographic mindframe, the reliability of the method for an individual woman is of little concern. For them, any injection that will make at least 85 percent of women infertile for a prolonged — even if lifelong — period, would be counted as a success in contraceptive research (Mehta 1993).

The implicit risk/benefit assessment of the population control framework is best summarized in the words of the immunologist N. Avrion Mitchison (1991). He brushed aside all concerns raised during the 1989 HRP Meeting with the words:

> To the extent that the impact of that [demographic] crisis increases, the need for more effective family planning technologies must increase. At the very least, failure to develop something that may provide a more effective technology would be to take a grave and unnecessary risk.

This framework weighs the risk of "overpopulation" against the human rights and health risks to women and their future children.

I maintain that from a biomedical perspective which centers on the advantages for individual users, the risk/benefit assessment of immunological contraception will remain negative. Potential health risks of immunological contraceptives range from autoimmune diseases to allergies, as well as exacerbation of diseases and the high risk of exposing the fetus to ongoing immune reactions. Even if some of the problems are eliminated in the final products, the efficacy profile of immunological contraceptives is too problematic to justify their continued development.

Misinformed Consent in Clinical Trials

The way in which antifertility "vaccines" are presented to the general public also raises questions about how women and men are solicited for participation in clinical trials. The cornerstone of ethics in clinical trials is that the voluntary, *informed* consent of the trial subjects must be sought. According to David Griffin, the researchers refer to anti-disease vaccines to help people grasp the nature of immunological contraceptives (1993). In fact, the analogy between anti-disease vaccines and immunological contraceptives tends to obscure the novelty of the approach. For example, Talwar's explains:

> Vaccines have been the most effective control of communicable diseases. Vaccines have been developed to prevent diseases, but why not for control of fertility? An antifertility vaccine will make women produce an immune response to the pregnancy hormone. The concept of vaccination is very well accepted by now. It is totally organic (Dhanraij 1991).

This conflicts profoundly with Spieler's (1987) statement:

> Immunocontraception is a radical departure. No method of regulating fertility has ever rested on immunological principles, nor has any vaccine ever been directed towards the inhibition of a "self-like" component or secretion.

The trial subjects should remain aware that the trials are actually meant to determine the unknown efficacy and potential adverse effects of immunological contraceptives. They must be conscious that the acceptable benefits and risk balance is profoundly different between antifertility "vaccines" and anti-disease vaccines.

Abuse

Most women's rights and health activists agree that the technological features which determine the "demographic effectiveness" of immunological contraceptives also predispose them to abuse. As already stated, they are meant to be long-acting, they cannot be stopped by the user at will, and they are easy to mass administer — with or without the knowledge of the "users."

The demographic effectiveness and risk of abuse of immunological birth control technologies will not only be based on technical features. Cultural features also help. The emphasis by developers that antifertility "vaccines" offer the advantage of "administration with a high level of acceptability" should raise concern. The scientists underscore that they are "easy to administer without manipulation of the genitalia" and will enjoy "the general popularity of immunization" (for examples, see Ada and Griffin 1991; Griffin 1992; Spieler 1987).

Most people understand abuse of contraceptives as forcing people to use a contraceptive against their will or without their knowledge. However, there are many, more subtle ways of pushing particular contraceptives. Women can be persuaded to "prefer" certain contraceptives by incentives, or by misinformation about the benefits and risks. By "abuse" I thus mean the *uninformed, misinformed or coercive provision of a birth control technology.* Abuse can happen for a variety of reasons and does not necessarily have to be premeditated. It often arises from the simple assumption that a provider or policymaker knows better what is best for a particular person.[8] In the past, the major targets of contraceptive abuse have been women of lower social classes, "unwanted" ethnic groups, differently-abled women or simply women in developing countries who were thought to be too fertile (and not able to use specific types of contraceptives).

A great deal of abuse resides in the grey area of "misinformed" consent, putting the spotlight on validity of the information provided with particular technologies. *Product positioning* has by now become an integral part of the introduction of new contraceptive technologies. According to The Population Information Program of The John Hopkins University:

> "Positioning" is a marketing term that means presenting a product or service in a way that helps to distinguish it from other, similar products of services, usually by emphasizing one or a few important characteristics. Positioning helps to create a perception of a product or service — which marketers call an image — in the minds of both public and providers (1992).

The aim of product positioning of contraceptives, is presented as "to help clients make informed choices."[9] Pharmaceutical companies tend to maximize sales by presenting a misleading image of a product and distorting information, generally by overstating the therapeutic benefits and understating adverse effects (see Chetley and Mintzes 1992). The Population Information Program admits that "developing a positive image for Norplant and any other method is more difficult, if family planning services in general have a negative image." It omits to point out that the validity of product information depends on the perceptions and intent of those who are responsible for it. For developers and providers of contraceptives who think in a demographic framework, the major aim is to bring birth rates down. From this perspective the image of new contraceptives serves to "attract new users" and ensure "maximum acceptability."

The "vaccine" image cannot be called an image which enhances *informed* choice. The researchers know that "in rural areas, for example, [people] even like injections, partly because they are associated with Western medicine, and also because they are associated with vaccination, which has been very helpful to them to avoid various diseases" (Talwar 1993). The "vaccines" image plugs into the pre-existing popularity of injections and anti-disease vaccines and reinforces them for the purpose of fostering broad-based acceptability of immunological contraceptives.

Biasing women's choices towards long-acting methods is done not only through biased counseling but through selective product availability. In many official family planning programs, the introduction of a new, long-acting contraceptive means the withdrawal or reduced emphasis on shorter acting ones. As the community health researchers Rani and Abhay Bang (1992) reported from India:

> In reality, the choice of contraceptive methods is not made by women. The decision is actually often made by the government health program officials and workers. Any new method is pushed aggressively without bothering to evaluate and learn from the failures of the previously propagated methods. This ultimately brings discredit on all the contraceptive methods of the whole family planning program.

Linking the introduction of immunological contraceptives to the "vaccines" image may have a specific, paradoxical, consequence. Concepcion, Mundigo, and Reeler (1991) warned:

The fact that the vaccine is easy and quick to administer makes misuse of it a potential danger. Abuse of the birth control vaccine would not only harm family planning in general but it could also have negative consequences for public attitudes to other vaccines and to the health care system in general.

This warning only anticipated what is, in fact, already occurring in parts of India. Rumors about the introduction of "sterilizing vaccines" have already led people to refuse vaccination (Bang 1992). This loss of trust is not irrational — it arises from a long, painful collective history of women encountering birth control methods in population control-oriented settings. This raises the question of whether the mere existence of antifertility "vaccines" may ultimately result, not only in a loss of trust of even the best contraceptive services but also in a backlash against decade-long efforts to propagate immunization programs.

Reduction of Women to Wombs Infected by the "Pregnancy Epidemic"

Critical literature on population ideology has long pointed out that the discourse of "overpopulation" and "population explosion" has resulted in a specific view of people, particularly women, in LACAAP countries. There are recurrent images of women as "breeding rabbits," "too dumb to take modern contraceptives," or — in more recent literature — "women who would take a contraceptive if their husbands would let them." Feminist literature has explored how both the medical establishment in the West and the international population control community have reduced pregnancy to a pathological process: women are abstracted to walking wombs infected by pregnancy germs.

The vaccine metaphor exacerbates this image. The pregnancy disease has become a harmful, contagious, fast-spreading epidemic, the reproductive process "a process which left unchecked threatens to swamp the world" (Shearman 1982). Sustained use of the analogy of immunological contraceptives with vaccines which helped "eradicate" smallpox will result in weighing the risk of the "pregnancy epidemics" for society against the risks (or even "benefits?") of antifertility "vaccines" to "the wombs infected with the pregnancies."

The "vaccine" metaphor not only legitimizes the pursuit of the development of immunological contraceptives. It also paves the way for public acceptance of population control through mass vaccinations with this new "antigenic weapon" (Shearman 1982). Press articles mirror the images conveyed by developers.

According to the German liberal weekly, *Die Zeit*, "European ways of birth control cannot function in developing countries" because these methods are supposedly too expensive, too complicated and too risky for people in poor countries. I do not share this view. However, *Die Zeit* is glad that,

> The future has already started: The researchers Talwar and Jones have tried in India and in Australia, to render women "immune" to pregnancies through a preventive vaccination, just as if it were an infectious disease (Bräutigam 1992).

Another journalist reports about the Indian researchers' vision:

> Talwar sees population as an epidemic not unlike the tetanus, diphtheria and smallpox epidemics that once ravaged human-kind. And it can be defeated, he declares, the same way by a vaccine... Pregnancy would be warded off with the same powerful immunological weapons the body uses to fight disease (Kanigel 1987).

And under the headline "New animal vaccines spread like a disease," *The New York Times* reports about a "new family of genetically engineered vaccines [which] will soon be perfected as powerful weapons against... animal pests like rats and rabies" (Browne 1991). The "vaccines" in question consist of sperm antigens which are incorporated into live viruses, then hidden in bait. Once swallowed by an animal, these antifertility viruses spread to other animals of its species, just like any infectious disease.

> Since the vaccines work by immunizing a female against the male's sperm, the same principle should be effective as a contraceptive in humans... American research leaders believe that within the next decade an oral contraceptive vaccine could be available for test on human subjects. A single dose, it is hoped, could confer temporary infertility for years. ...the method could make contra-ception far more accessible to residents of poor countries (Browne 1991).

The image of people and animals as uncontrollable "pests" and the fascination about the novel technology seem to justify the development of whatever antifertility "vaccine." The article gives little room to questions of responsibility if the transmissible immune-sterilizants get out of control. Who can ensure that the sterilizant for rabbits acts only in Australia? What if the antifertility viruses mutate and spread to other than the planned species?

An oral human anti-sperm contraceptive which incorporates the antigen into the DNA of (altered) salmonella bacteria is being developed by John C. Herr of the University of Virginia at Charlottesville in collaboration with Roy Curtis at Washington University in St. Louis. Also, Talwar considers the use of live viruses as "vectors" for his antifertility antigens. Unlike the animal "vaccine," these products are not meant to spread. At the present time, however, the risk of accidental transmission of such "vector-based" vaccines is unknown. Will the benevolent representation of antifertility "vaccines" forestall public debate about the complete loss of user control over a long-term (lifelong) anti-sperm pill whose antifertility effect might be contracted by accident?

How to Redress this Situation

By the time a technology is sufficiently well developed and diffused for its unwanted social consequences to become apparent, it is no longer easily controlled. Control may still be possible, but it has become very difficult, expensive and slow (Collingridge 1980).

In sum, two major frameworks shape the development of immunological contraceptives: the population control framework and the Western scientific framework. The hope that these novel birth control methods will lend themselves to easy mass administration and that their acceptability will be facilitated by the popularity of "vaccines" is expressed throughout the scientific literature. I have argued that the "vaccine" metaphor — which obscures the technical realities of these novel birth control methods — results in a neglect of their problems, ill-informed consent in clinical trials, and prepares for their abuse. I have finally argued that the metaphor reduces women to wombs infected by a harmful, fast spreading "pregnancy epidemic" and puts people on par with "pests" to be eradicated, and that these images further bias the risk/benefit assessment of antifertility "vaccines" and forestall public debate on the need for immunological contraceptives and sterilizants.

Stop the Development of Antifertility "Vaccines"

The first and most straightforward conclusion of this analysis is that the development of immunological contraceptives should be stopped. By fall of 1993, an encouraging number of people share this opinion. On the 8th of November, 230 groups and organizations from 18 countries sent an open letter to the main research and funding institutions. The petition called for "an immediate halt to the development of immunological contraceptives" and a "radical reorientation of contraceptive research":

> Population control ideology should not guide the development of contraceptives…The aim must be to enable people — particularly women — to exert greater control over their fertility without scarifying their integrity, health and well being. Contraceptive development must be oriented to the realities of women's lives. Above all it must consider local health care conditions and the position of women in society. (Call 1993)

Independent scientists have started to raise their voices. Graham Dukes, editor of the International Journal of Risk and Safety in Medicine and former long-term Regional Officer of WHO-Europe, for example, commented: "Years ago, when I was myself working in endocrinological research, vaccination ideas like this were raised and promptly dismissed as unethical and dangerous; I do not think the balance of arguments has changed, except that the threat has come closer, and people are now actually being exposed" (1993).

Dismantling the "Vaccine Metaphor"

Given the importance of the "vaccines" metaphor in fostering acceptability of immunological contraceptives, I feel it is vital that this metaphor be dismantled. Only if people remain aware of the complete novelty of immunological contraceptives, will there be an informed public discussion of their development.

Some people may have a different opinion about my proposal to change the name to immunological contraceptives. For example, the Indian women's rights activists Swatija Paranjape and Chayanika Shah commented:

> We [will] continue to call it the "antifertility vaccine" and not "immunological contraceptives." We feel that the basic assumption behind the development of this contraceptive is an under-

standing of fertility as a disease — a communicable one at that! It is considered to be an epidemic in the context of the poor, marginalized women all over the world. The name that they [the researchers] have given highlights their mentality in producing it and we who are against developing any such method of contraceptive should not be giving them a term under whose garb their real motives can be hidden (1993).

Taking Abuse Seriously

The abuse potential should be included as a criteria in any risk/benefit assessment of a new antifertility technology. Admittedly this is not easy, because the abuse potential is composed of technical and cultural features. However, it is important because the abuse potential harbors risks, such as the loss of client power over fertility, and the administration of the contraceptive without necessary checks for contraindications and pregnancy.

In my view, the abuse potential of the vaccines alone justifies a halt to their development. David Griffin called this position "another form of abuse," because it would deprive women of an alternative contraceptive. He argues that abuse potentials can only be assessed once a method is approved (Griffin quoted in Hof-Mussler). What Griffin calls "abuse" may be seen as the outcome of a prospective technology risk assessment. I believe that even at the design stage one could have recognized that the abuse potential of antifertility "vaccines" is greater than for other long-acting birth control methods. The window of contraceptive effect is longer for the "vaccine," than for hormonal injectables, e.g., Depo-provera. While IUDs and Norplant can be removed by a provider, the action of the "vaccines" cannot be stopped by user or provider. Immunological injectables or pills are easier to administer without informed consent than intrauterine devices or implants. And it is easier to manufacture consent to the use of "vaccines" than to methods which rely on intravaginal or subcutaneous insertion.

Several antifertility "vaccine" researchers have assured me that they are against abuse of their product. They do not seem to see the tension between ensuring voluntary and informed use of antifertility technologies and meeting demographic targets. The question is not one of intent. The question regards social accountability for predictable outcomes of certain types of technologies given specific socio-political climates. All long-acting birth control methods have been abused. Do we have to wait for evidence that antifertility "vaccines" will be beyond control? Who will take responsibility when the fear of sterilizing injections erodes public trust of contraceptive and health care services?

Acknowledgements

I am very grateful to Jane Cottingham, Rachel Snow and Jennifer Poulos for valuable comments and their editorial help. I am also indebted to Loes Keysers for clarifying the difference between risk/benefit assessments from a demographic and from a women's centered perspective. The responsibility for this article, however, is mine. I finally wish to thank Jane Cottingham, Vincent Girardin, Edith and Michaela Richter, Maja Villat, Laura Stewart and Oliver Sunlover for taking care of my physical and emotional well-being while writing this article.

Notes

1   For a detailed review of biomedical concerns regarding immunological contraceptives, see Schrater in this volume.

2   Throughout this chapter I use *immunological contraceptives* interchangeably with *immunological birth control methods* or *immune-mediated contraceptives*. They are also called "antifertility vaccines," "fertility regulating vaccines" or "birth control vaccines" by researchers and others. The fundamental problem with the "vaccine" terminology is elaborated in this chapter.

3   See appendix.

4   Jones does not specify what aspects of the approach were considered unethical: whether there were moral objections to the principle of immunizing women against sperm or concerns about the potential risks.

5   Yet, unlike natural autoimmune infertility, immunological contraceptives aim at a *predictable* infertile period.

6   LACAAP stands for Latin American, Caribbean, African, Asian and Pacific countries.

7   For HRP's hCG formula the lag phase was 5 to 6 weeks; the theoretically effective phase was 2 to over 9 months; for the Indian hCG formula in phase II the lag phase was even longer; the contraceptive phase ranged from 6 months to over two years — for the 80 percent of women who reached the contraceptive threshold.

8   Kaufmann (1992) and Huezo (1990) have shown that the choice of contraceptive method is significantly influenced by the attitude of the provider. Provider attitudes, in turn, are shaped by beliefs, working conditions and the type of information the providers receive.

9   According to the Population Program (1992) another aim of creating a positive image at the very outset is to avoid the situation wherein "negative images spread by groups who oppose family planning and those who distrust new medical technologies may shape the public's perception" — without discussion of arguments and motives of such groups.

References

Ada, G.L., and P.D. Griffin, eds. 1991. *Vaccines for fertility regulation: The assessment of their safety and efficacy.* Cambridge, Mass.: Published on behalf of the World Health Organization by Cambridge University Press.

Alexander, N.J., et al. 1990. *Gamete interaction: Prospects for immunocontraception.* New York: Wiley-Lyss.

Anderson, D.J., and N.J. Alexander. 1983. A new look at antifertility vaccines. *Fertility and Sterility* 40(5):557–571.

Bang, R. (on behalf of Society For Education, Action and Research, Gadchiroli, India). 1992. Statement made at the WHO/HRP Meeting to Review the Development of Antifertility Vaccines, August 17–18, in Geneva.

Bang, R., and A. Bang. 1992. Contraceptive Technologies: Experience of rural Indian women. *Manushi* 70 (May/June):26–31.

Barriklow, D. 1993. An Indian institute's breakthrough vaccines. *Choices — The Human Development Magazine* (June):28–30.

Basten, A., et al. 1991. Assays for relevant immune responses. In *Vaccines for fertility regulation: The assessment of their safety and efficacy*, ed. G.L. Ada and P.D. Griffin. Cambridge, Mass.: Published on behalf of the World Health Organization by Cambridge University Press.

Brache, V., et al. 1992. Whole beta-hCG: Tetanus toxoid vaccine. Paper presented at the Scientific Session on Immunological Aspects of Reproductive Health, on the occasion of the 20th anniversary of the WHO Special Program of Research, Development and Research Training in Reproduction, June 16–18, in Moscow.

Bräutigam, H.H. 1992. Verhütung ist Luxus: In den Entwicklungsländern können europäische Verfahren der Geburtenkontrolle nicht funktionieren. *Die Zeit*, 16–17 April.

Browne, M.W. 1991. New animal vaccines spread like diseases: In the wild, artificial viruses curb both rabies and rabbits. *New York Times*, November 26.

Call for a stop to research on antifertility "vaccines" (immunological contraceptives). 1993. Open letter. November 8.

Chetley, A., and B. Mintzes, eds. 1992. *Promoting health or pushing drugs?* Amsterdam: Health Action International (HAI).

Clarke, A. 1990. *Contraceptive technologies and choices: The realignment of social worlds and generative entrenchment, 1925–1990.* Paper presented at the

Conference on Technological Choices: European and American Experiences, in Bloomington, Indiana. To be published in Clarke, A. Forthcoming. *Disciplining reproduction: Biological, medical and agricultural research.* University of California Press.

Collingridge, D. 1980. Quoted in Hamelink, C. 1988. *The technology gamble.* Norwood: Ablex Publishing Corporation.

Concepcion, M., A. Mundigo, and A.V. Reeler. 1991. Social aspects related to the introduction of a birth control vaccine. In *Vaccines for fertility regulation: The assessment of their safety and efficacy,* ed. G.L. Ada and P.D. Griffin. Cambridge, Mass.: Published on behalf of the World Health Organization by Cambridge University Press.

Dhanraij, D. 1991. *Something like a war.* Documentary Film. Equal Media.

Dukes, M.N.G. 1993. Letter to N. Wieringa, Faculty of Pharmacy, Groningen University, The Netherlands. October 25.

Griffin, P.D. 1992. *Fertility regulating vaccines.* A background paper for discussion at a meeting of women's health advocates, members of the Steering Committee of the Task Force on Vaccines for Fertility Regulation, vaccine developers and representatives of interested agencies, WHO Special Program of Research and Research Training in Human Reproduction, August 17–18, in Geneva.

———. 1993. Personal communication with the author, March 1.

Hamilton, statement in Alexander, N.J., et al. 1990. *Gamete interaction: Prospects for immunocontraception.* New York: Wiley-Lyss.

Hardon, A. 1989. An analysis of research on new contraceptive hCG vaccines. Amsterdam. *WGNRR (Women's Global Network for Reproductive Rights) Newsletter* (April–June):15–16.

Henderson, C.J., M.J. Hulme, and R.J. Aitken. 1987. Contraceptive potential of antibodies to the zona pellucida. *Journal of Reproductive Fertility* 83(1):325–43.

Hof-Mussler, S. 1993. Nachgefragt: Impfung gegen Schwangerschaft. *Deutsche Apothekerzeitung* 133(29):38–39.

Huezo, C. 1990. *Factors affecting method selection and continuation: Preliminary data from a 6-country study.* Paper presented at Steroid Contraceptives and Women's Response: Regional Variability in Side-Effects and Steroid Pharmacokinetics. Workshop sponsored by the Harvard School of Public Health, Department of Population and International Health, October 21–24, in Exeter, New Hampshire.

Jones, W.R. 1982. *Immunological fertility regulation.* Oxford: Blackwell Scientific Publications.

Kanigel, R. 1987. Birth control: the vaccine alternative. *Span* (August):26–29.

Katsh, S. 1959. Immunology, fertility, and infertility: A historical survey. *American Journal of Obstetrics and Gynecology* 77(5):946–956.

Kaufman, J., Z. Zhang, X. Qiao, and Y. Zhang. 1992. The quality of family planning services in rural china. *Studies in Family Planning* 23(2):73–84.

Mehta, K. 1993. *Imagining Indian family planning services offering immune contraceptives.* BUKO Pharma Brief 4–5 (June):1–5.

Mitchison, N.A. 1990. *Lessons learned and future needs.* In Alexander et al., pp 607–614.

———. 1991. Chairman's summary: Present status and future prospects of antifertility vaccines, in G.L. Ada and P.D. Griffin, eds. *Vaccines for fertility regulation: The assessment of their safety and efficacy.* Cambridge, Mass.: Published on behalf of the World Health Organization by Cambridge University Press, pp 247–250.

Paranjape, S. and C. Shah. 1993. Letter to the author, July.

Population Information Program, Center for Communication Programs, The John Hopkins University. 1992. *Population Reports: Decisions For Norplant® Programs.* 20(3) (November):16,17.

Richter, J. 1991. Research on antifertility vaccines: Priority or problem? *VENA Journal* 3(2) (November Special Issue):22–27.

———. 1993. *Vaccination against pregnancy: Miracle or menace?.* Will, A. and B. Mintzes, eds. Bielefeld, Germany: BUKO Pharma-Kampagne; Amsterdam: Health Action International.

Schaz, U. (filmmaker), with the co-operation of I. Schneider. 1991. *Antibodies against pregnancy: The dream of the perfect birth control from the laboratory.* Documentary film (English copy available through U. Schaz, Bleicherstr.2, D-22767 Hamburg 50, Germany).

Schrater, F.A. 1992. Contraceptive vaccines: Promises and problems. In *Issues in reproductive technology I: An anthology,* ed. H. Holmes. New York: Garland Publishing.

Segal, S.J. 1991. The role of technology in population policy. *Populi* 18(4):5–13.

Shearman, R.P. 1982. Foreword. In *Immunological fertility regulation,* ed. W.R. Jones. Oxford: Blackwell Scientific Publications.

Spieler, J. 1987. Development of immunological methods for fertility regulation. *Bulletin of the World Health Organization* 65:779–783.

———. 1992. *An overview of funding of vaccine research.* Paper presented at the HRP Meeting to Review the Development of Antifertility Vaccines, WHO Special Program of Research and Research Traning in Human Reproduction, August 17–18, in Geneva.

Stevens, V. C. 1986. Current status of antifertility vaccines using gonadotropin immunogens. *Immunology Today* 7(12):369–374.

Talwar, G.P. 1993. Interview by J. Gupta, February 4.

Thau, R., et al. 1990. Advances in the development of an antifertilty vaccine. In *Reproductive Immunology*, ed. L. Mettler and W.D. Billington. Amsterdam: Elsevier Science Publishers.

Wajcman, J. 1991. *Feminism confronts technology.* Cambridge: Policy Press.

WHO. 1986. *First human trial of birth control vaccine begins in Australia.* Press release. February 17. Geneva.

WHO Special Program of Research Development and Research Training in Human Reproduction. 1988. *Research in human reproduction: Biennial report 1986–87.* Diczfalusy, E., P.D. Griffin, amd J. Khanna eds. Geneva: World Health Organization.

WHO Special Program of Research Development and Research Training in Human Reproduction, Task Force on Vaccines For Fertility Regulation. In press. *Report of a meeting to review fertility regulating vaccine development.* Geneva, August 17–18, 1992.

WHO Task Force on Immunological Methods for Fertility Regulation. 1978. Evaluating the safety and efficacy of placental antigen vaccines for fertility regulation. *Clinical Experimental Immunology* 33:360–375.

11

Each to Her Own: Investigating Women's Response to Contraception

by Rachel Snow

The grumblings of the weak are called forth by everyday experience, and they certainly begin by being incoherent, directed toward a number of apparently unrelated and superficial annoyances. To the powerful, these seem to have nothing to do with the matter at hand, or else to be so vague...as to defy definition.

'What is your problem?' the powerful ask the weak, once they decide that this dissatisfaction can no longer be ignored or laughed off. 'Tell us what is wrong, and we will try to do something about it.'

But for the weak the only honest answer may well be 'Everything is wrong!'

'Oh well,' say the powerful..., 'if you can't tell us what the trouble is, how can we do anything about it? Besides, if you can't state it clearly, it really can't be so bad.'

— from Powers of the Weak, Elizabeth Janeway 1981

Introduction

What does the public, particularly the female public, want in contraception? The global family planning revolution is almost three decades old. But despite these three decades of research and implementation, data on women's perceptions and preferences for contraceptive technology remains limited, and our understanding of how women's technical needs may vary given different underlying health conditions is sparse.

In the first decade of international family planning assistance there was little incentive to conduct extensive market research or tailor contraceptives to individual women. Women's collective unmet need for *any* means to prevent unwanted pregnancy was great, evidenced by the rapid adoption of modern contraceptives worldwide.

But in the last decade women's health activists have increasingly drawn attention to the problems of contraceptive side effects, episodes of coercive population control measures, and health risks of specific methods (e.g., note the U.S. controversy over depot medroxyprogesterone acetate (DMPA) in the mid-1980s). Recent papers by women's health activists have prompted new debate on the risks and benefits of contraceptive technology from a woman's perspective, and several of these have called for a redistribution of "the relative weights assigned to safety, efficacy, affordability and acceptability" in contraceptive development (WHO/HRP/ITT 1991; Corea 1991; Germain 1993; Norsigian, forthcoming; Barrosso & Orr, forthcoming). There are common concerns expressed in these papers: that there has been insufficient research attention to barrier methods, to viricidal or microbicidal agents, to male methods, and to user controlled methods; and that there has been undue emphasis on effectiveness at the expense of safety or acceptability.

These papers, and the meetings that gave rise to them, have been pivotal in drawing attention to possible dissimilarities between users' and scientists' perspectives on contraceptive technology. But at the moment we are left with more questions than answers; activism has outpaced research. Women's needs and preferences for contraceptive technology are identified by occasional "women's voices," and have not been documented in a systematic or scientific manner.[1] We can infer women's *preferences* from user statistics and KAP tests, but these are hampered by the fact that use and preference are conditioned by availability. What we need are new data on women's preferences for specific attributes of the technologies, and we need it for different populations in different social circumstances. The techniques of market research have largely eluded the population establishment, but hopefully the feminist critiques will now prompt increased documentation of women's perceptions and preferences for contraceptive technology.

With respect to women's *needs* for contraception, I would argue that contraceptive developers have, on the whole, delivered safe and effective methods. The risk of thromboembolic or diabetic crises have been seriously and effectively addressed. Now, however, closer examination of the physiological synergies between contraceptive technology and underlying reproductive health are warranted, such that women can use effective contraception without bleeding irregularities, without an increased risk of genital infections, including HIV, and without psychogenic side effects. Given that underlying risk factors for irregular menstrual bleeding, reproductive infection and osteoporosis vary among women and by population, and that women vary in their metabolic response to contraceptive steroids, the impact of contraceptive steroids on these aspects of women's health cannot necessarily be generalized across regions or ethnic groups.

Further promotion of family planning and contraceptive technology will require improvements in existing technologies, and these will require increased understanding of the interplay between contraceptive technology and women's underlying health. This paper discusses a variety of unmet needs in contraceptive research, focusing on the need for greater attention to the variable social and biological circumstances of women's lives, and the need for data that would allow better matching of available methods to individual women.

Contraceptive Attributes: What Do Women Want?

Barrier Methods and Microbicidal Agents

Given the epidemic of HIV, the feminist call for increased research on barrier methods is unequivocal. And given the widespread problem of reproductive tract infections (RTI's) (Wasserheit 1989), and the positive association between RTI's and HIV infection (Wasserheit 1992; Berkley 1992; Zewdie and Tafari 1992), there is strong incentive to identify microbicidal agents that can be used with, or without, a contraceptive agent (Elias and Heise 1993; Barroso and Orr 1993; Norsigian 1993). Elias and Heise (1993) have provided an eloquent justification for such investment, substantiating the public need for and interest in such a product.

Such recommendations are already being heeded by selected agencies, including the U.S. federal research institute for contraception, the Contraceptive Development Branch of the NICHD. NICHD allocations are difficult to decipher and categorize because a large fraction of their total allocations (71% in 1991) are made as institutional awards[2], but the fraction of the remaining itemized budget that went to barrier research increased from approximately 5 to 6 percent in 1989 and 1990 to nearly 28 percent in 1991 (Office of Science Policy, 1989, 1990, 1991).

According to Elias and Heise (1993), NICHD, USAID and NIAID have all invested resources in microbicidal research, but specific allotments are not mentioned. The World Health Organization (WHO) has recently undertaken plans to develop protocols for clinical evaluation of vaginal microbicides (FDC Reports, 1993), but it remains to be seen whether

efforts will be undertaken to link such agents to contraceptive preparations. To date, the Special Programme for Development, Training and
Research in Human Reproduction at WHO has never devoted significant
resources to barrier methods of contraception[3].

User Control

Aside from the excellent case made for a female-controlled microbicidal
agent (Elias and Heise 1993), feminist recommendations for more "user
controlled" contraception have been difficult to translate into specific
contraceptive attributes. User control is an ambiguous term (and one I
recommend dropping). "Control" is a term alluding to relationships of
power between people, but as an attribute of contraceptive technology,
it defies definition.

For example, if secrecy is an essential feature of control, e.g., as for
many women in the Gambia (Bledsoe et al. in press), then injectable
contraceptives such as depot medroxyprogesterone acetate (DMPA) may
offer the best opportunity for user control. DMPA leaves no detectable
mark on the woman, requires no incriminating paraphernalia in the
house, and allows a woman short, predictable intervals of protection. It
allows the woman to exercise control over her own fertility, while other
methods do not.

In contrast, for many women living in the West, the call for user
controlled contraception implies something quite different — the term is
usually used to infer a class of contraceptive methods that do not require
regular contact with a health professional, i.e., the opposite of provider-
dependent methods, or methods that allow coitus-specific decision-
making about protection. This class of methods usually includes the
sponge, the diaphragm, and the cervical cap (alone or in combination
with natural family planning). If the term "user" can be extended to the
couple, rather than the woman alone, then the condom would also
qualify. Such a definition of "user control" has arisen from Western
feminists' desire to recoup control over their bodies from the overly
technical (often male) health care system.[4]

The call for "user controlled" contraception is ridden with problems
because there has been little unravelling of the different contraceptive
needs of third and first world women, or of rich and poor women in the
same society. Given that good clinics may take advantage of the
consultation for birth control to carry out beneficial health promotion

(screening for cancer, i.e., Pap smears, and counseling), the elimination of clinic contact is not necessarily a good thing for many women, even in the richest countries, who otherwise have little or no health care. In many developing countries women are not fed up with the excess of reproductive health care — they would welcome decent medical services, if they were only clean, affordable, and local. These women may need control *in relation to* the family, the state, and intrusive population policies. The provision of greater "control" to users requires different features for users in different countries, and even for different sectors of society within countries.

Women all over the world probably share concern about the potential for abuse in contraceptive services. In the United States, China, Indonesia, India, and many other countries, family planning services have been abusive and coercive at times, or at least highly directive. The desire to end such abuse, and to reduce the potential for abuse, is central to the activist call for "user controlled" contraceptive technology. But the solutions are far from simple, and it is difficult to typologize specific technologies according to the criteria of user control without examining the cultural context of "control".

More information on women's preferences for control in *specific* dimensions of contraceptive technology would be helpful, and could be acquired through survey data. As one example, scientists lack information about women's preferences for a window of non-reversibility. The once-a-month injectable, norethisterone enanthate (NET-EN), and DMPA cannot be reversed for 1, 2, or 3 months, respectively; the HRP vaccine may be non-reversible for one year. Are these consistent with women's preferences? How long a period of non-reversibility do (which) women want? It has been suggested that clinics should not try to offer too many injectables, so that they will not be inadvertently mixed up, and to ensure that the quality of client information is not compromised. If so, we will need methods for selecting which injectable is most appropriate to which client population, and data on womens' preferences for the length of non-reversibility will be a valuable piece of information. Presumably the new HRP Task Force on Introduction and Transfer of Technology will address this, among other such issues; for that reason this task force may fill a critical research gap in the juncture between contraceptive development and the promotion of women's interests.

Efficacy

The claim that there has been undue emphasis on efficacy at the expense of safety and acceptability is actually several critiques in one: that efficacy is more important to the population establishment than to actual women, that the push for efficacy has compromised safety standards, and that features which affect the ultimate acceptability of a method (other than efficacy) have been largely ignored. The first point will be addressed here, and the third will be addressed in a later section of this paper.

The question is not whether efficacy has been emphasized, but whether such emphasis is beyond the bounds of what women want. Effectiveness has definitely been a dominant feature of at least the HRP research agenda for the last twenty years. The annual task force allocations within HRP from 1972 through 1991 indicate that systemic methods with long-term effectiveness received substantially more financial support than barrier and/or natural methods. Of $64.8 million (U.S.) spent among the research task forces in the 1972-1991 period, the largest percentage (24 percent) was allocated to the Task Force on Long-Acting Systemic Agents; this was followed by 19 percent to the Task Force on Vaccines, 12 percent to the Task Force on Male Methods, and no more than 10 percent to each of the remaining task forces (See Figure 11-1).

In the last three years, the pattern appears somewhat different (Figure 11-2), as the allocation to the Task Force on Natural Methods has risen from about 10 to almost 20 percent, and the combined total for the Vaccine and Long-Acting Task Forces declined from almost 70 percent of the total research budget in 1989, to just more than 40 percent in 1991.[5]

Bruce and Shearer (1979; 1983) pointed out such discrepancies over a decade ago. But what is the evidence that such emphasis is inconsistent with user preferences? How important is efficacy to women? Contraceptive prevalence data collected in the mid-1980s from developed countries where many contraceptive choices were available show a much higher use prevalance of sterilization, Pills and IUDs compared to diaphragms or other less efficacious methods (Mauldin and Segal 1988). Recent data show that among poor, young (over 70 percent <30 yrs), rural women in Tennessee, ever use of the Pill is 10 times more common than ever use of the diaphragm, and there is no difference in client satisfaction between ever-users of the two methods (Rosenfeld et al. 1993). Such data imply that many women prefer more effective methods. Even if women will sometimes trade off efficacy for other features, such as ease of use, acceptability or cost, this does not necessarily imply that at a policy level,

Figure 11-1   The proportion of research funds allocated to individual Task Forces of the Special Programme for Research, Development and Research Training in Human Reproduction (WHO), 1972–1991.

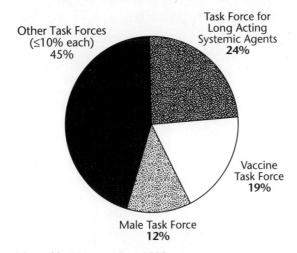

Other Task Forces (≤10% each) 45%

Task Force for Long Acting Systemic Agents 24%

Vaccine Task Force 19%

Male Task Force 12%

Source: World Health Organization, 1993

Figure 11-2   The proportion of research funds allocated to specific contraceptive methods of the Special Programme for Research, Development & Research Training in Human Reproduction (WHO), 1989–1991.

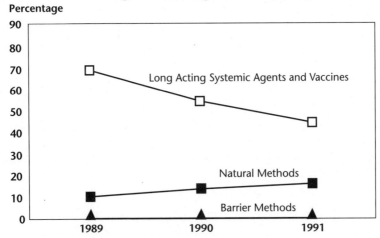

Percentage

Long Acting Systemic Agents and Vaccines

Natural Methods

Barrier Methods

Source: World Health Organization, 1993

efficacy should be less important in the ideal profile of prospective methods.

If a women of average fecundability and exposure used the diaphragm from age 18 until age 48, with no intention to have children, a conservative estimate of method failure (15 percent) would require six safe abortions as backup.[6] In the event that one or two pregnancies were carried to term, the number of abortions ought still to give pause. Given the number of countries where abortion is illegal and unsafe, ignoring the importance of efficacy would be a grave error.

Regrettably, efficacy is not an obvious feature of several methods currently under development. I hope this is not the result of a naive perception that efficacy is *not* important to women, when, in fact, such an implication (intended or not) has never been substantiated. If efficacy standards were the dominant criteria for new methods then Dr. Talwar's prototype hCG vaccine might have been abandoned long ago (Richter 1993, and in this volume). Paradoxically, women's health activists may soon find themselves in a position of arguing that the vaccine or new steroid methods are untenable precisely because they fail to meet efficacy standards of the Pill, DMPA, or Norplant®.

The challenge is to increase the efficacy of safe, convenient methods (Bruce and Shearer 1983; Germain 1993), and the safety and convenience of highly effective methods. Part of that challenge will require improved method design, but it will also require more research on the physiological basis of pharmacological variability among women, and the biological factors that predict individual effectiveness (Garza-Flores et al., in press; Nash, in press).

Biological Variability and Contraceptive Side Effects: Filling the Research Gap

Beyond the need for better documentation of women's perspectives and preferences for contraceptive technology, there is also a need for greater attention to the physiological synergies between contraceptive technologies and underlying health conditions. Our understanding of the interplay between health status and contraceptive technology is reasonably good in some areas: more than two decades of research have identified the important thromboembolic contraindications to oral contraceptive use. This has allowed appropriate screening to dramatically increase the safety of oral contraceptive use.

At the same time, our understanding of pre-disposing risk factors for many less dangerous side effects of contraception is quite limited (Chen and Snow 1992; Barrosso and Orr 1993). For example, recent studies on dysfunctional menstrual bleeding in response to contraceptive steroids (d'Arcangues and Alexander 1992) underscore the complexity of this problem. Despite significant advances in our understanding of the endocrinology of bleeding, explanations of why some women bleed on Norplant®, but not others, remains largely elusive.

Regarding other longer-term reproductive health problems, there is much speculation, but little evidence, of whether contraceptive use constitutes a health risk or not. For example, a recent review on contraceptive use and osteoporosis points out that there has been only one study regarding the impact of DMPA on bone density (Mehta 1993), despite evidence that the blood concentrations of DMPA vary considerably between women (Garza-Flores et al., nd). Finally, research on whether specific contraceptive steroids increase or decrease the risk of reproductive tract infections, including HIV, remains largely inconclusive (Hunter and Mati 1991; Rehle et al. 1992).

Possibile life-threatening side effects of contraceptive use have appropriately garnered the attention of researchers during the last two decades. But expansion of contraceptive markets into poor countries, especially where "good health" is uncommon and fleeting, demands increased understanding of the impact of contraceptives on women with variable health conditions. Risk factors associated with irregular menstrual bleeding, reproductive infection and osteoporosis vary by region, as do the pharmacokinetic profiles of contraceptive steroids. Therefore, physiological analysis of their interactions must be local and comparative. The following section identifies several research questions that may be of importance to contracepting women and their longterm health.

Dysfunctional Menstrual Bleeding. Dysfunctional menstrual bleeding is a common side effect of many contraceptive steroids, and a major cause for discontinuation (d'Arcangues, Odlind and Fraser 1992). As many as 55 percent of Norplant® users experience irregular bleeding in the first year of use, and nearly 10 percent are amenorrheic (Shoupe, Ballagh and Mishell 1992). Use of injectables is also associated with menstrual irregularities: bleeding patterns with DMPA, a three-month injectable, are highly unpredictable, with a general tendency towards amenorrhea with increased use. By one year of use, as many as 50 percent of users are amenorrheic.

The physiological cause for irregular bleeding is different for different contraceptive preparations, but it also varies between women. The state of our understanding of menstrual bleeding, and the causes of contraceptive-induced irregularities in bleeding can be reviewed in the excellent recent volume by Alexander and d'Arcangues (1992). The research summarized in this volume stands out as a singular example of concentrated research attention to contraceptive side effects. More such efforts are warranted, for additional research attention will be required before we can anticipate bleeding response to steroid contraception and counsel accordingly.

One of the characteristic features of female reproductive function is it's variability. Sioban Harlow (1992) has emphasized the paucity of data on population variability in menstrual regularity — this variability is most dramatic between women, but in given cases may be equally significant within a given woman, from month to month, or during her reproductive lifetime. A variety of population factors are associated with menstrual irregularity, such as physical work (Cumming 1987; Snow et al. 1989), caloric restriction (Schweiger et al. 1988), low weight for height (Frisch and MacArthur 1974), dietary fiber (Snow et al. 1990; Wyshak and Snow 1993), and stress (Schweiger et al. 1988). However, with the exception of weight for height (Belsey et al. 1988; Nash in press; Sivin 1988), almost none of these factors have been evaluated in the context of contraceptive-induced menstrual irregularities.

Without more fundamental data on normative menstrual bleeding patterns for different populations it is difficult to evaluate the impact of a given contraceptive method on bleeding (Harlow, forthcoming). Attempts to simplify research protocols by excluding women with idiopathic oligomenorrhea (women with unexplained irregular menstrual bleeding) from clinical studies of contraceptive effects make it impossible to generalize from clinical data to a population at large.

Bone. Caucasian Americans and Northern Europeans have the highest rates of osteoporotic fractures on record. Rates of such fractures are comparatively low throughout the developing world, but progressive increases in life expectancy, coupled with recent data on fractures among Indian women, suggest that osteoporosis may be an emerging health concern among Asian women (Gopalan 1993).

The three-month injectable contraceptive DMPA suppresses ovarian function, leading to low circulating levels of estrogen. Low estrogen levels are important to osteoporosis, because hypo-estrogenicity (for example, among post-menopausal women) is associated with a loss of vertebral bone density. It is in conditions of low circulating estrogen that bone loss is most acute.

Studies of circulating estrogen among DMPA users indicate that estrogens are low, but on average are still above those of a post-menopausal woman. This might imply that estrogens are low, but not dangerously low. However, the only study to date on the impact of DMPA use on bone density indicated that women who had used DMPA for at least five years showed significantly lower bone densities in both the femoral neck and the lumbar spine compared to premenopausal controls (Cundy et al. 1991); compared to post-menopausal controls, DMPA users had significantly higher bone densities in the lumbar spine, and the differences in the femoral neck were not significant. There are problems with this study as noted by Mehta (1993), including the failure to control for smoking or prior oral pill use. Nonetheless, we now recognize that amenorrheic athletes with estrogen levels of between 30-40 pg/ml[7], levels in the same range as those among DMPA users (Cundy et al. 1991; Mishell et al. 1972), have lower bone densities in the lumbar spine than eumenorrheic athletes (Marcus et al. 1985; Snead et al. 1992).

Given that we observe regional variability in blood concentrations of DMPA among women (Garza-Flores et al., in press), is there regional variability in the degree of ovarian suppression (and hence, hypo-estrogenicity) among DMPA users? Would this imply that some populations of women may be at some increased risk of osteoporosis with long-term DMPA use? Would the risk/benefit profile vary for women of different nutritional circumstances, or women using DMPA at different ages? Improved understanding of the underlying dynamics of bone loss would be helpful, but even greater attention to the extent and variability of ovarian suppression among DMPA users would indicate whether there is any, or no, risk of osteoporosis associated with DMPA use. Such information could then be used to inform counseling and method matching to clients.

Infection. A third under-explored question is whether individual methods of steroid contraception increase or decrease the risk of acquiring reproductive tract infections (RTI's), or HIV. A recent meta-analysis of 29 studies on chlamydia risk and oral contraceptive use suggests an almost two-fold increased risk of chlamydia infection for oral contraceptive users

(Cottingham and Hunter 1992), but programmatic integration of such data is not evident.

Regarding steroid contraceptive use and HIV risk, the available data are largely inconclusive and incomplete. Considerable methodological problems hamper such research, including the large number of confounding variables. Hunter and Mati (1992) reviewed much of the available research, and concluded that while the available case-control data show no evidence of an increased risk of HIV transmission with oral contraceptive use, the high relative risk indicated by the only prospective study in their review (RR of 4.5, confidence interval 1.4–13.8), warrants further investigation. A separate prospective study of Kenyan prostitutes (Plummer et al. 1991) found both oral contraceptive use and chlamydia trachomatis to be significant risk factors for HIV-1 seroconversion, and there was no observed confounding between them.

Regarding DMPA use, Hunter and Mati report preliminary results from their own study in Kenya indicating no excess risk of HIV infection (Mati et al. 1990). A subsequent report on HIV infection among Thai prostitutes reports no significant association between oral contraceptive use and HIV infection, but a significant risk of infection associated with the use of DMPA (Rehle et al. 1992); a follow-up study is currently being carried out in this population. Clearly, more and better data are warranted, and the possiblity of population-specific biological risk may be worth considering.

Pharmacokinetic Variability Among Women

Women vary in their underlying risk of bleeding irregularities, the integrity of bone, and the risk of reproductive infection. Some of this risk may be inherited, some the result of social constraints on growth and development, and some attributable to biological conditions. Women bring different and often unique risk profiles to their contraceptive experience. It is such variability between individual women, and populations of women, that has eluded much of the research on contraceptive side effects.

Underlying variability in ovarian function, body composition, liver enzyme activity and steroid excretion may account for the accumulated observations that women vary in their metabolism of contraceptive steroids (Goldzeiher in press; Fotherby in press; Garza-Flores et al., in press). A forthcoming publication reviews documentation of the last two decades regarding the pharmacokinetic variability of contraceptive steroids among women (Snow and Hall, in press). Despite limitations of the available data, several papers point to the apparent regional variability of these pharmacological responses. For example, important population differences have been reported in pharmacokinetic profiles of DMPA among Thai and Mexican women (Garza-Flores et al. in press). Thai women consistently show a greater area under the serum concentration curve, have higher maximum serum concentrations of the drug, a shorter elimination half-life, and reach serum concentrations below the limit of detection significantly earlier than Mexican women. Consistent with their more rapid elimination of the drug, Thai women have an earlier return of ovulation following an injection than Mexican women.

What are the causes of variability in pharmacokinetic profile among women using the same steroids? There is evidence that drug use affects liver metabolism of steroids (Back and Orme, in press), and body weight is weakly correlated with the pharmacokinetic profile of Norplant® (Nash, in press). But beyond these known factors, the state of science is largely speculative — perhaps factors known to affect endogenous steroids are responsible (i.e., the binding proteins (SHBG), body fat, liver metabolism, or entero-hepatic recirculation) (Snow and Hall, in press).

The most common concern prompted by observations of such variability is whether there are implications for the efficacy of the method in specific populations. Indeed, in some cases, it was the regional variability in contraceptive efficacy that prompted pharmacokinetic investigations (Garza-Flores et al., in press). But more subtle questions are relatively under-explored. Do side effects vary with blood concentrations? For example, if blood concentrations of levonorgestrel vary, does the extent of ovarian suppression and the extent of menstrual disruption correlate with blood concentrations? Would variability in the serum concentrations of DMPA have implications for bone density? Many unanswered questions are prompted by these observations; more documentation of the extent and pattern of variability is warranted, either to nullify or justify further research into possible health implications of such regional diversity.

Clinical Trials: Untapped Opportunities for Research

Contraceptive clinical trials offer one opportunity to increase the collection of more and better data on reproductive health and contraceptive acceptability. For example, with limited additional investment, clinical trials might include protocols to investigate whether pharmacokinetic patterns are associated with any aspects of clinical experience. If such associations were significant, there would be stronger motivation to disentangle the factors responsible for differing pharmacokinetic profiles among users.

Pharmacokinetic studies of contraceptive steroids (i.e., those in which blood samples are drawn at regular intervals after administration to measure blood concentrations, and evaluate absorption, metabolism and clearance of the steroid), are conducted on small numbers of clients in early phases of human trials. Studies of side effects are conducted *separately,* and there are specific recommendations that subgroups of side effect studies should not be included in metabolic or pharmacological studies.

> Such studies (specific studies on biochemical or other pharmacological variables) should run concurrently with the study on efficacy and side effects but they must be designed as separate studies. Subgroups of the larger efficacy and side effects study should not be used since the subgroup will immediately become a population subjected to abnormal assessment and, as such, will have different reasons and rates of discontinuation from the remainder of subjects in the main clinical trial. (Michal 1989)

In an effort to avoid potential confounding within the research design, a subtle, but significant limitation has been introduced. The trial process ensures that individuals in studies of side effects will not be the same individuals on whom metabolic or pharmacokinetic data is available. This precludes any subsequent investigation of hypotheses regarding the possible biological basis of those side effects. For example, the extensive data base available from clinical trials, collected over many years, cannot be used to investigate any hypothetical associations between plasma concentrations, pharmacokinetic parameters, and side effects. This large base of valuable data has not been collected in a manner that allows us to ask questions of fundamental clinical interest to women.

Clinical trails present an important untapped opportunity for documenting both the extent (and co-variates) of pharmacokinetic variability among women, and the significance of such variability to women's experience of contraceptive side effects.

Concluding Remarks

The feminist campaign to reform contraceptive research and development has made important inroads to date: it has encouraged the international agencies to recognize the extent of women's dissatisfaction with the available technologies, prompted increasing representation of women at many agencies, provided unprecedented opportunities for women to voice their needs and interests for contraceptive technology, and it may have raised the standards of contraceptive safety. But the handicap of women's historical *lack* of engagement in contraceptive research is evident in the limitations of available data for informing us of women's needs and preferences for these technologies. The next wave of reform needs information, requiring new initiatives for research and documentation. Such undertakings should be at the top of the feminist agenda.

The lack of sound data on women's preferences for contraceptive attributes, on women's variable pharmacological response to contraception, and the bases of contraceptive side effects leaves women in the awkward, but heady position of being asked "what women want," without resources to investigate the question. The pressure on health activists and women scientists to provide a "women's" agenda without the means to investigate and substantiate such an agenda is a political pitfall for women. The information gap is the result of the historical gender imbalance in scientific, academic and political leadership, and recent trends to redress that imbalance provide new opportunities for shifting the direction of contraceptive research.

Acknowledgements

I would like to thank Mercy Bercerra-Valdivia, Ade Lucas, Judith Richter, Gita Sen and Grace Wyshak for their thoughtful comments on earlier drafts of this chapter, and Sarah Hemphill and Patricia Jeannette Snow for their invaluable support throughout the writing process.

Notes

1 Women's *needs* are identified here as those requirements that can be determined objectively, e.g., the need to prevent unwanted pregnancies, to prevent genital infections, etc. Women's *preferences* are identified as those things women want or demand. The two are related but not identical, as preferences convey a perception of needs, but needs includes both perceived and unfelt needs.

2   For example, in fiscal year 1991, three institutions, Eastern Virginia Medical School, the Population Council, and Family Health International, collectively received 71 percent of all allocation.

3   HRP is the only major agency we approached that provided us with data on specific resource allocations to method type. Other programs approached included CONRAD, USAID, FHI and the Population Council, but officers at those agencies explained that they do not maintain budget records by method type. For the NICHD data, we disaggregated the allotments by reviewing documentation of specific awards; even using such a process, as much as ten percent of total funds awarded by NICHD could not be classified.

4   In the spirit of *Our Bodies, Ourselves,* 1973. I thank Gita Sen for clarifying the distinction between the Western "anti-medical" meaning of user control, and the struggle for control against family pressure and population control policies that often characterizes the lives of women in Southern countries.

5   These data are provided to illustrate general trends, but they have numerous caveats: namely that several Task Forces were dissolved or recombined between 1979-1991, and others were only established recently. Also it's possible that male contraceptives have been investigated by other Task Forces, and therefore may have received more funding than indicated by the Male Task Force budget alone.

6   The # of failures over a woman's reproductive life time was estimated using a standard equation for the total fertility rate:

$$\text{(TFR)} = \frac{\# \text{ ovul cycles} \sim \text{ ages 20-40 years}}{\text{mean length of the birth interval}}$$

where:
the # of possible cycles= 260 (13 per year),
and the mean length of the birth interval includes:
— duration of pregnancy (= 9 months)
— post-partum amenorrhea (2/3 duration of breast-feeding)
— waiting time to conception (1/p[1-e])
         p= fecundability
         e= efficacy of contraception (85%)

If any of these pregnancies are aborted, the mean length of the interval between pregnancies would be reduced, increasing exposure time, and the chance of additional unwanted pregnancies.

7   Marcus (1985) reported mean ($\pm$ SEM) estrogen levels of 36.3$\pm$3.5 pg/ml among 11 amenorrheic athletes; Snead (1992) reported levels of 37 $\pm$9.4 pg/ml among 11 amenorrheic runners. Mean ($\pm$ SEM) estrogen concentration among 30 women who had been using DMPA for more than 5 years was 22.1 pg/ml (Cundy 1991); among 90 women who had been using DMPA for 1-2 years mean estrogen level was 36 $\pm$ 2.0 pg/ml (Mishell 1972).

References

Alexander, N.J., and C. d'Arcangues, eds. 1992. *Steroid hormones and uterine bleeding.* Washington D.C.: AAAS Press.

Back, D., and M. Orme. In press. Pharmacokinetic drug interactions with oral contraceptives. In *Steroid contraceptives and women's response: Regional variability in side-effects and pharmacokinetics,* ed. R. Snow and P. Hall. New York: Plenum Publishers.

Bancroft, J., D. Sanders, P. Warner, N. Loudon. 1987. The effects of oral contraceptives on mood and sexuality: a comparison of triphasic and combined preparations. *Journal Psychosomatic Obstetrics and Gynecology* 7:1–8.

Barrosso, C., and B. Orr. 1993. The reality of unmet needs: Women's perspectives on contraceptive research priorities. Paper presented at the International Symposium on Contraceptive Research in Developing Countries for the Year 2000 and Beyond, March 8–10, in Mexico City.

Belsey, E.M., C. d'Arcangues, and N. Carlson. 1988. The determinants of menstrual bleeding patterns among women using natural and hormonal methods of contraception. II. The influence of individual characteristics. *Contraception* 38(2):243–57.

Berkley, S. 1991. The public health significance of sexually transmitted diseases for HIV infection in Africa. In *AIDS and women's reproductive health,* ed. L. Chen, J.S. Amor, and S. Segal. Plenum Press: New York.

Bledsoe, C.H., A.G. Hill, P. D'Alessandro, and U. D'Alessandro. Forthcoming. Local cultural interpretations of western contraceptive technologies in rural Gambia. *Population and Development Review,* March 1994.

Boston Women's Health Book Collective. 1973. *Our Bodies, Ourselves.* New York: Simon and Schuster.

Brandt, A.M. n.d. Behavior, disease, and health in twentieth century America: The moral valence of individual risk. Unpublished manuscript.

Bruce, J., and S.B. Shearer. 1979. *Contraceptives and common sense: Conventional methods reconsidered.* New York: Population Council.

———. 1983. *Contraceptives and developing countries: The role of barrier methods.* New York: International Program Division, The Population Council, and Population Resource Center.

Burfoot, A. 1990. The Normalization of a New Reproductive Technology. In *The new reproductive technologies,* ed. M. McNeil, I. Varcoe, and S. Yearley. New York: St Martin's Press.

Chen, L., and R. Snow. 1992. Benefits and risks of the Pill: Perception and reality. *Advances in Contraception* 7(2):19–34.

Corea, G. 1991. Depo-Provera and the politics of knowledge. In *Reconstructing Babylon: Essays on women and technology*, ed. P. Hynes. Bloomington: Indiana University Press.

Cottingham, J., and D. Hunter. 1992. Chlamydia trachomatis and oral contraceptive use: A quantitative review. *Genitouri Med* 68:209–16.

Cumming, D.C. 1987. The reproductive effects of training and exercise. *Curr Probl Obstet Gynecol Fertil* 10:225.

Cundy, T., et al. 1991. Bone density in women receiving depot medroxyprogesterone acetate for contraception. *British Medical Journal* 303:13–16.

D'Arcangues, C., V. Odlind, and I.S. Fraser. 1992. Dysfunctional uterine bleeding induced by exogenous hormones. In *Steroid hormones and uterine bleeding*, ed. N.J. Alexander and C. d'Arcangues. Washington D.C.: AAAS Press.

Dixon-Mueller, R., and A. Germain. 1993. *Four essays on birth control needs and risks*. New York: International Women's Health Coalition.

Elias, C.J., and L. Heise. 1993. *The development of microbicides: A new method of HIV prevention for women*. Programs Division Working Paper no. 6. New York: Population Council.

European Study Group on Heterosexual Transmission of HIV. 1992. Comparison of female to male and male to female transmission of HIV in 563 stable couples. *British Medical Journal* 304:809–13

FDC Reports. 1993. *The Blue Sheet* 36(47): November 24.

Fotherby, K. In press. A critical evaluation of the pharmacokinetics of contraceptive steroids. In *Steroid contraceptives and women's response: Regional variability in side-effects and pharmacokinetics*, ed. R. Snow and P. Hall. New York: Plenum Publishers.

Frisch, R.W., and J.W. McArthur. 1974. Menstrual cycles: Fatness as a determinant of minimum weight for height necessary for their maintenance or onset. *Science* 185:949.

Garza-Flores, J., P. Hall, and S. Guo-wei. In press. Population and delivery systems: Variability in the pharmacokinetics of long-acting injectable contraceptives. In *Steroid contraceptives and women's response: Regional variability in side-effects and pharmacokinetics*, ed. R. Snow and P. Hall. New York: Plenum Publishers.

Germain, A. 1993. Are we speaking the same language? Women's health advocates and scientists talk about contraceptive technology. In *Four essays on birth control needs and risks*, ed. R. Dixon-Mueller and A. Germain. New York: International Women's Health Coalition.

Goldzeiher, J. In press. Pharmacology of ethinyl estrogens in various countries. In *Steroid contraceptives and women's response: Regional variability in side-effects and pharmacokinetics*, ed. R. Snow and P. Hall. New York: Plenum Publishers.

Gopalan, C. 1993. Osteoporotic fractures: An emerging public health problem in Asia? *Bulletin of the Nutrition Foundation of India* 14(4) (October).

Gordon, L. 1977. *Woman's body, woman's right: A social history of birth control in America.* New York: Penguin Books.

Graham C.A. 1989. Unpublished PhD Dissertation. McGill University: Montreal, Canada.

Greer, G. 1984. *Sex and destiny: The politics of human fertility.* New York: Harper and Row.

Harlow, S. 1992. What we do and do not know about the menstrual cycle or questions scientists could be asking. Paper prepared for the Ebert Program in reproductive health at the Population Council.

———. In press. Variability in menstrual bleeding patterns comparing treated and untreated menstrual cycles. In *Steroid contraceptives and women's response: Regional variability in side-effects and pharmacokinetics*, ed. R. Snow and P. Hall. New York: Plenum Publishers.

Hunter, D., and J.K. Mati. 1991. Contraception, family planning, and HIV. In *AIDS and reproductive health*, ed. L. Chen, J.S. Amor, and S. Segal. New York: Plenum Press.

Janeway, E. 1981. *Powers of the weak.* New York: Morrow Quill Paperbacks.

Klein, R. D. 1987. What's 'new' about the 'new' reproductive technologies? In *Man-made women*, ed. G. Corea, et al. Bloomington: Indiana University Press.

Marcus, R., et al. 1985. Menstrual function and bone mass in elite women distance runners. *Annals of Internal Medicine* 102:158–64.

Mati, J.K.G., A. Maggwa, D. Chewe, et al. 1990. Contraceptive use and HIV infection among women attending family planning clinics in Nairobi, Kenya. Abstract Th.C.99, VI International Conference on AIDS. San Francisco, June.

Mauldin, W.P. and S.J. Segal. 1988. Prevalence of contraceptive use: Trends and issues. *Studies in Family Planning* 19(6):335–53.

Mehta, S. 1993. Bone loss, contraception and lactation. *Acta Obstet Gynecol Scand* 72:148–156.

Michal, F., ed. 1989. *Safety requirements for contraceptive steroids.* Cambridge: Cambridge University Press on behalf of the World Health Organization.

Mishell, D.R., et al. 1972. Estrogenic activity in women receiving an injectable progestogen for contraception. *American Journal of Obstetrics and Gynecology* 113(3):372–6.

Nash, H. In press. Pharmacodynamics of Norplant® implants. In *Steroid contraceptives and women's response: Regional variability in side-effects and pharmacokinetics*, ed. R. Snow and P. Hall. New York: Plenum Publishers.

Norsigian, J. 1992. Women's Perspectives on Contraceptive Development. Paper presented at The 1992 Annual Meeting of the Society for the Advancement of Contraception, November, in Barcelona.

Office of Science Policy and Analysis in cooperation with the Center for Population Research, National Institute of Child Health and Human Development. 1989. *Inventory and analysis of federal population research: Fiscal year 1989.* U.S. Department of Health and Human Services, National Institutes of Health, Public Health Service.

———. 1990. *Inventory and analysis of federal population research: Fiscal year 1990.* U.S. Department of Health and Human Services, National Institutes of Health, Public Health Service.

———. 1991. *Inventory and analysis of federal population research: Fiscal year 1991.* U.S. Department of Health and Human Services, National Institutes of Health, Public Health Service.

Plummer F.A., J.N. Simonsen, D.W. Cameron et al. 1991. Cofactors in male-female sexual transmission of human immunodeficiency virus type-1. *Journal of Infectious Diseases* 163:233–9.

Raymond, J. 1987. Preface. In *Man-made women*, ed. G. Corea, et al. Bloomington: Indiana University Press.

Rehle, T., U. Brinkmann, T. Siraprapasiri, P. Coplan, C. Aiemsukawat, and K. Ungehusak. 1992. Risk factors of HIV-1 infection among female prostitutes in Khon Kaen, Northeast Thailand. *Infection* 20(6):328–331.

Rosenfield, J.A., P.M. Zahorik, W. Saint, G. Murphy. 1993. Women's satisfaction with birth control. Journal of Family Practice 36(2):169–72.

Richter, J. 1993. *Vaccination against pregnancy: Miracle or menace?* Bielefeld, Germany: BUKO Pharma–Kampagne. Amsterdam: Health Action International.

Schrater, F. Forthcoming. Immunization to regulate fertility: Biological and cultural frameworks. *Social Science and Medicine.*

Schweiger, U., R. Laessle, M. Schweiger, F. Hermann, W. Reidel, K-M. Pirke. 1988. Caloric intake, stress, and menstrual function in athletes. *Fertility and Sterility* 49:447.

Shoupe, D., S. Ballagh, and D.R. Mishell, jr. 1992. Bleeding patterns in Norplant contraceptive implant users. In *Steroid hormones and uterine bleeding*, ed. N.J. Alexander and C. d'Arcangues. Washington D.C.: AAAS Press.

Sivin, I. International experience with Norplant and Norplant-2 contraceptives. 1988. *Studies in Family Planning* 19(2):81–94.

Snead, D.B., et al. 1992. Reproductive hormones and bone mineral density in women runners. *Journal of Applied Physiology* 72(6):2149–56.

Snow, R., and P. Hall, eds. In press. *Steroid contraceptives and women's response: Regional variability in side-effects and pharmacokinetics.* New York: Plenum Publishers.

Snow, R., R.L. Barbieri, and R.E. Frisch. 1989. Estrogen 2-hydroxylase oxidation and menstrual function among elite oarswomen. *Journal of Clinical Endocrinology and Metabolism* 69(2):369–376.

Snow R., J.L. Schneider, and R.L. Barbieri. 1990. High dietary fiber and low saturated fat intake among oligomenorrheic undergraduates. *Fertility and Sterility* 54(4):632–7.

Wajcman, J. 1991. *Feminism confronts technology.* University Park, Pa.: The Pennsylvania State University Press.

Wasserheit, J. 1989. The significance and scope of reproductive tract infections among Third World women. *International Journal of Gynecology and Obstetrics* (Supplement 3):145–168.

———. 1991. Epidemiological synergy: Interrelationships between HIV infection and other STDs, In *AIDS and women's reproductive health*, ed. L. Chen, J.S. Amor, and S. Segal. New York: Plenum Press.

Waites, G. 1991. Personal communication with author. June 13.

WHO Special Program of Research, Development, and Research Training in Human Reproduction and The International Women's Health Coalition. 1991. *Creating common ground.* Geneva: World Health Organization.

Wyshak, G., and R. Snow. 1993. Fiber consumption and menstrual regularity in young women. *Journal of Women's Health* 2(3):295–299.

Zeidenstein, G. 1993. Dilemmas. Paper presented at the International Symposium on Recent Advances in Female Reproductive Health Care, June 5, in Helsinki.

Zewdie, D., and N. Tafari. 1991. Human immunodeficiency virus and syphilis infection in women of childbearing age in Addis Ababa, Ethiopia. In *AIDS and women's reproductive health*, ed. L. Chen, J.S. Amor, and S. Segal. New York: Plenum Press.

12

Immunization to Regulate Fertility: Biological Concerns and Questions

by Angeline Faye Schrater

Introduction

Antifertility vaccines are the newest among methods of birth control. They are unique from all other contraceptives in that vaccines utilize an innate physiological process, the immune response, to interfere with normal reproductive processes. Immunization to regulate fertility differs in several significant ways from immunization to control disease.

On a very basic level, the intent of administering traditional vaccines is to prevent infectious disease in the individual, and to reduce morbidity, mortality, and transmission rates in the general population. An important aspect of disease prevention by vaccines is "herd immunity." If the number of immune individuals is sufficiently high, many non-immune individuals will be protected from a highly communicable disease because they will be unlikely to come in contact with an infected person.

One aim of providing fertility-regulating vaccines is to prevent pregnancy in an individual, and the associated morbidity of unwanted pregnancy. Another objective is to decrease the fertility rate of a population (Stevens 1986; Talwar and Raghupathy 1989). However, pregnancy is not a disease, and the concept of herd immunity is irrelevant with immuno-contraception. Further, the widespread use of many different contraceptives is necessary to provide the majority of men and women with adequate and appropriate means of regulating fertility.

Traditional vaccines can be given to children or adults, male and female alike. In many communities parents must provide evidence of vaccination against measles, diphtheria, whooping cough and tetanus prior to enrolling children in school. The elderly in northern climes often seek immunization against the current strain of influenza. Medical personnel are vaccinated for protection against hepatitis; military troops receive vaccines against endemic diseases prevalent in a region of intended operations. In an effort to reduce the mortality and morbidity of preventable diseases, the World Health Organization developed The Expanded Programme on Immunization to vaccinate mothers and children (Kim-Farley et al. 1992).

Relatively few restrictions attend the administration of disease-preventing vaccines. In general, infants are not vaccinated prior to 2 to 3 months of age. Vaccines containing live material, particularly viruses, should not be given to individuals who are genetically unable to generate an immune response, those with Acquired Immune Deficiency Syndrome (AIDS), on chemotherapy, or those who have immunosuppressive disease, e.g., malaria, parasitic infestations, or tuberculosis. Likewise, pregnant women should not be given vaccines containing live virus because of the dangers of viral infections to the developing fetus. Traditional vaccines are given to those at risk of debilitating or life-threatening diseases. They provide long-term immunity that is often boosted (kept active) throughout one's lifetime by intermittent exposure to the disease-causing organism.

In contrast to the near universal acceptability of traditional vaccines, vaccines to regulate fertility would be given only to individuals of reproductive age and ability.[1] Beyond the general exclusion criteria, which would be the same as for traditional vaccines, i.e., subjects with immuno-deficiencies regardless of cause, anti-fertility vaccines would, in all likelihood, require more stringent exclusion criteria, e.g., a personal or family history of allergy; genetic predisposition to autoimmune disease; active autoimmune disorders such as rheumatoid arthritis and diabetes[2]; pregnancy; and breastfeeding (Jones and Beale 1991). These additional exclusion criteria are necessary because of the unique biological mode of action of antifertility vaccines. Health activists, in fact, have questioned the accuracy of applying the term "vaccine" to these immunocontraceptives.[3] Others have written of the importance of discussing the development and use of immunocontraceptives within social and cultural contexts (Concepcion et al. 1991; Hardon 1992; Schrater 1993). The biological targets of antifertility vaccines, their distinct mode of action from traditional vaccines, and the biomedical bases of public health concerns about these new unique contraceptives are the focus of this chapter.

Biological Bases and Immunological Targets

Traditional vaccines are directed at generating an immune response to the harmful organisms which surround every living being. To the immune system, anything chemically unique from one's own cells and molecules is "antigenic" and produces a defensive response from the immune system to destroy the "foreign" substance. The biological bases of traditional vaccines are any materials, or non-self antigens, derived from a micro-organism, and which will induce an immunologically-mediated resistance to disease caused by that particular organism.

Recognition that recovery from infectious disease generally gives life-long immunity ultimately informed the rationale for deliberate immunization, or vaccination, to provide protection against a specific disease. Vaccines prime the immune system for future encounters with an infectious agent by generation of the complex phenomenon termed immunological memory. The effectiveness of traditional vaccines derives from that phenomenon. Because of memory, immunity is seldom reversible, though the response may wane to very low levels.

Vaccines to regulate fertility are designed to prevent pregnancy, not disease. They are directed against the *immunologically* accessible molecules involved in reproduction. These may be molecules on the surface of mature gametes (sperm and ova), or the hormones involved in the reproductive process. Some hormones play a role in maturation of gametes, and others regulate their release. One targeted hormone is necessary to maintain pregnancy once fertilization has occurred. Figure 12-1 presents a diagram of the hormones and cells involved in the early events in human reproduction.

Within the context of fertility-regulating vaccines, the cells and molecules involved in reproduction present *self* antigens to the immune system. (The exception to self would be sperm vaccines designed for use in women.) Along with the ability to respond to non-self antigens, vertebrates also evolved mechanisms to avoid responses to self antigens, lest the body destroy itself with autoimmunity. Therefore, for contraceptive vaccines to be effective, the immune system must be "tricked" into responding. This is usually achieved by chemically bonding self antigens to non-self antigens; the entire complex is then recognized as non-self. Because the intent is to provide *reversible* contraception, the immunological memory characteristic of traditional vaccines must be avoided, lest the immunity lead to permanent sterility. Furthermore, when the response generated by the contraceptive vaccine declines to low levels, the natural

Figure 12-1 Early events in human reproduction and possible sites of immunological intervention.

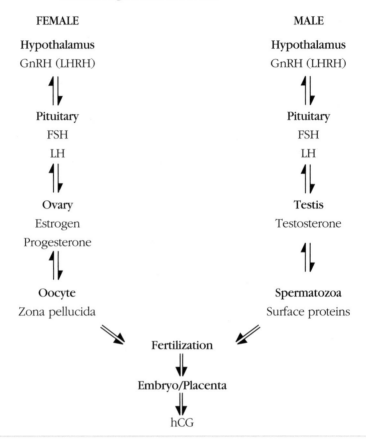

FEMALE		MALE
Hypothalamus		Hypothalamus
GnRH (LHRH)		GnRH (LHRH)
Pituitary		Pituitary
FSH		FSH
LH		LH
Ovary		Testis
Estrogen		Testosterone
Progesterone		
Oocyte		Spermatozoa
Zona pellucida		Surface proteins
	Fertilization	
	Embryo/Placenta	
	hCG	

cells and molecules associated with reproduction must not be able to trigger immunity. Conditions for stimulating memory cells are fairly stringent, however, and usually require the original antigen complex for activation. Developers rely on this stringency to generate a reversible effect with contraceptive vaccines.

Two avenues of research being pursued in anti-fertility vaccine development: *Anti-gamete vaccines* and *anti-hormone vaccines.* The anti-gamete vaccines (reviewed in Jones 1982; Sacco 1987; Naz and Menge 1990) react directly on intact, mature sperm or ova to control fertility by preventing fertilization. Sperm vaccines are potential contraceptive candidates in part because their action would not interfere with endocrine or sexual function, side effects often cited as disadvantages of birth control pills or condoms, for example.

Anti-gamete vaccines were considered to be particularly attractive because they act prior to fertilization rather than afterward. Interestingly, development of anti-gamete vaccines was considered possible because immunity to sperm (Mathur et al. 1987) and to zona pellucida (ZP), the extracellular, glycoprotein matrix of mature ova (Dunbar 1989), was implicated as an agent of clinical infertility. But clinical studies of anti-gamete vaccines and experimental results from animals indicate that more research is needed before any of the anti-gamete vaccines could ethically be tested in clinical trials, much less be useful in family planning programs.

Anti-sperm vaccines appear risky for men because of the high probability of inducing autoimmune orchitis and testicular damage. Whether or not infertility and pathology would be reversible with time is unknown. Similar problems are inherent with anti-ova vaccines for women. Further, although spermatozoa are continuously generated once a man reaches puberty, a woman is born with all the eggs she will ever have (barring some sort of gamete transfer). Thus the use of anti-zona vaccines as a fertility-regulating agent for women engenders the unacceptable possibility of irreversible eradication of the entire complement of a woman's ova.

Although sperm vaccines given to women would not generate the autoimmune pathologies cited above, they bring different unacceptable possibilities to fertility regulation, notably those of permanent sterility or of immunological tolerance. For a woman, sperm have several deficiencies, both as vaccine antigens and as immunological targets. They are foreign, non-self antigens and would likely induce a memory-based immune response. Each act of intercourse would expose the woman to antigen, and could "boost" immunity, leading to permanent sterility. Alternatively, frequent antigen exposure could lead to immunological tolerance to sperm antigens, thus leaving the woman vulnerable to an unwanted pregnancy, were she relying on anti-sperm immuno-contraception. Furthermore, it is unclear whether sufficient quantity of blood-borne antibodies generated by the vaccine will be accessible to sperm deposited during coitus. Likewise, the effectiveness of secretory antibodies present in the mucosal lining of the vagina — and induced by intravaginal vaccine — remains in question. Lastly, I object on philosophi-

Table 12-1   Pituitary and Hypothalamic Hormone Vaccines

Institution	Immunogen	Clinical Trial	No. of Subjects	Sex
Indian National Institute	FSH	Phase I	6	M
of Immunology	GnRH	Phase I	12	F
	GnRH	Proposed	ND	M
Population Council	GnRH	Phase I	4	M

Note: FSH is follicle-stimulating hormone (from anterior pituitary);
GnRH is gonadotropin-releasing hormone (from hypothalamus).

cal as well as biological grounds to burdening women with another contraceptive method with so many and such obvious, inherent pitfalls.

Research on anti-hormone vaccines constitutes the bulk of fertility vaccine research. The prototype vaccines are of two basic types, those against the hormones necessary for maturation and release of gametes, and those against a placental hormone necessary to maintain the early stages of pregnancy. Both types have been tested in clinical trials (see Tables 12-1 and 12-2).

Clinical trials of hormonal vaccines include the following: anti-FSH (follicle stimulating hormone) vaccine for men (Talwar 1992); anti-GnRH (gonadotropin-releasing hormone) vaccine for men (Population Council and National Institute of Immunology of India (NII)) and women (NII).[4] Anti-GnRH would reduce libido as well as sperm counts in men, thus

Table 12-2   Chorionic Gonadotropin Vaccines

Institution	Vaccine		Clinical	No. of
	Immunogen	Carrier	Trial	Subjects
World Health Organization	ß-hCG-CTP	DT	Phase I	30
			Phase II	(Planned 1993)
Indian National Institute	ß-hCG:a-oLH	TT/CHB	Phase I	101
of Immunology		TT/DT	Phase II	59
Population Council	ß-hCG	TT	Phase I	24

Note: CTP is carboxy terminal peptide (amino acid 109-145 of ß-hCG subunit); DT is diphtheria toxoid; TT is tetanus toxoid; CHB is cholera toxoid chain B; TT/CHBT is either carrier used; TT/DT is carriers used alternately with boost.

requiring testosterone replacement for users. In women, the long-term consequences of immunity to hormones that are continually present in the brain and blood, and are necessary for normal sexual functioning, are unknown and remain a source of worry (Rose et al 1991; Schrater 1992b). Further concerns raised over immunizing lactating women, as the NII trial did, are potential side effects including inhibition of gonadal steroid hormones, and adverse effects on bone metabolism and on the developing infant.

The most advanced contraceptive vaccines are those against the hormone human chorionic gonadotropin (hCG) (reviewed in Jones 1982; Stevens 1992; Schrater 1992a), which is necessary for implantation and maintenance of early pregnancy. Three prototype anti-hCG vaccines, utilizing all or part of the beta subunit of the hormone, have been developed: one by Pran Talwar and colleagues at the National Institute of Immunology in New Delhi; one by Rosemarie Thau and colleagues at the Population Council in New York City; and one by Vernon Stevens and colleagues at Ohio State University in Columbus, under the auspices of the World Health Organization. All three prototypes have undergone small-scale clinical trials (Jones et al. 1988; Talwar et al. 1990; Thau et al. 1990).

Scientists working on beta hCG vaccines agree that these are prototype vaccines, in need of improved formulation which would give higher, longer-lasting responses and would require fewer injections. All insist their particular formulations are safe. It must be kept in mind, however, that the early clinical trials are performed with healthy, highly-selected and highly-motivated individuals, and their physiological and psychological welfare is attended to diligently. Those conditions of optimum health and surveillance are unlikely to prevail should contraceptive vaccines become widely available. Given that the general population will manifest variation in quality, quantity, and duration of protective antibody titer, and in predilection to allergic reactions, the initial stages of large-scale immunization programs must be very closely monitored.

Concerns

Generating Adequate Immunity

I have several health concerns about these vaccines due to the nature of the immune response. A lag period of three to six weeks precedes effective immunity, therefore, vaccine recipients will need an additional contraceptive for that period. Because the degree and duration of immunological responses vary among individuals, it will be difficult to predict the time span of protective immunity for each person. (It should be noted that scientists are developing vaccines that would provide 12 to 18 months of protection against pregnancy.) A more troublesome issue arises because immunity is cryptic, thus the body gives no signal that immunity has fallen to non-protective levels. For traditional vaccines, the latter issue is of little concern: immunological memory initiates a rapid, effective response upon exposure to the infectious agent. But because contraceptive vaccines must generate a reversible effect, continued protection cannot be based on immunological memory. Rather, it will be based on human memory and a blood test at the appropriate time to determine whether antibody titer (a measure of immunity) is still above protective levels. Although developers talk of a simple, home-use finger-prick kit to test immunity, those kits are only in the planning stage. Until, or unless, kits become widely available, women worry about their cost, about getting to and from clinics to have blood drawn, the time delay in learning results, and especially about the transfer of HIV (Human Immunodeficiency Virus) and hepatitis viruses from unsterile needles or lancets.

Hypersensitivity and Hyposensitivity

Although the bacterial antigens[5] of the anti-fertility vaccines are strong, effective carriers, they also tend to induce hypersensitivity, or allergy, in some people. To avoid complications from allergic responses, all persons should be tested prior to each injection; results are often not definitive for 48 hours, a delay that most ordinary people would find burdensome. For others, the opposite problem might ensue, wherein repeated immunization with tetanus or diphtheria toxoid could induce hypo-responsiveness to those antigens. Any individual who responded poorly to tetanus toxoid, for example, would respond equally poorly to the linking self antigen, e.g., hCG, and therefore be at risk of unintended or unwanted pregnancy. Moreover, tetanus and diphtheria are serious diseases in any part of the world, and the ability to generate immune protection against them should not be compromised. Aware of these problems, scientists are working on synthetic vaccines that would not require bacterial carrier antigens to trigger immunity to reproductive antigens (Schrater 1992b; Stevens 1992; Talwar 1992).

Autoimmune Pathologies

Additional biological concerns are related to the possibility of inducing autoimmune pathologies as a consequence of long-term cross-reactivity to pituitary hormones, or of inducing autoimmune-mediated destruction of gametes. In spite of the assurances of the scientists from NII in New Delhi and the Population Council in New York City (who developed vaccines deliberately designed to induce cross-reactions to lutenizing hormone), most women — and some scientists — worry about long-term sequelae resulting from cross-reactivity. Only time and the immunization of many women (or men) will tell whether such concerns are warranted. Women's health advocates, and the WHO (whose scientists developed a vaccine free of cross-reactivity), are reluctant to take that chance.

Non-Reversibility

Women's health advocates in general take issue with the long window of non-reversibility that is characteristic of immunocontraception. Although scientists may develop a vaccine that provides some *average* duration of contraception, the length of such a window will be unpredictable for individual women. Health-care settings in many parts of the world are inadequate or non-existent. An immune response is not easily abrogated; should a woman suffer serious side effects, it is unlikely she would find immediate surcease from the consequences, even were it pharmacologically possible. Although scientists say the immune response to beta-hCG can be thwarted by injecting large doses of progesterone or the hCG hormone itself, the method would be prohibitively expensive and would (or should) require hospitalization to monitor and treat any untoward effects of "the cure." Nor would such injections stop the immune response, but merely negate the effects *temporarily.* Reversal by hormone injection is of dubious value for the population at large. The fact that reversal is clinically possible conveys no assurance that such reversal would be available to all women. One has only to recall the refusals to remove Norplant in Bangladesh (UBINIG 1991) and Brazil (Gomes dos Reis 1990) to appreciate the abuse potential of fertility-regulating vaccines.

A related, though different concern is whether the contraceptive effect would be predictably reversible over time, *without intervention,* especially if recipients use immuno-contraception for several years. Thus far, all the preclinical experiments in non-human primates suggest that once the immune response wanes to low levels, fertility returns. Results from clinical trials in women proffer similar optimism.

In spite of the optimism derived from the studies to date with the chorionic gonadotropin vaccines, it should be remembered that results obtained in the wider world of humans, with their diverse genetic, physiological and psychological characteristics, are likely to much more varied than those obtained in clinical trials. Certainly the clinical results cannot be extrapolated to the population excluded from the trials, e.g., adolescents, women who are anemic and malnourished; nor can the effect of immunization be predicted in populations who have access only to sub-optimum health-care infrastructures (Hardon 1992).

Conclusion

By the turn of the century, fertility-regulating vaccines may well provide a safe and effective means of contraception and expand the range of choices for birth control. Yet in their present form, the anti-gamete vaccines are unsafe and unreliable for use in humans. Vaccines against chorionic gonadotropin, however, hold great promises — safety, ease of use, non-invasiveness, and reversibility. To date, they still carry biological problems: inconstant and unpredictable titers, hypo-/hypersensitivity, and possible teratagenicity. These problems will be especially acute among women who lack access to basic health care, and among the poor, because poverty compromises the immune response in variable and unpredictable ways.

I am optimistic that the biological problems can be solved to nearly everyone's satisfaction. Certainly the more money that is spent, the more likely the chances of success. But science is inherently an uncertain endeavor, and the time and expense that will be necessary to perfect fertility-regulating vaccines are unpredictable commodities. The question posed by me and many other women's health advocates is not whether science can solve the problems, but whether the expenditures will yield the optimum results for women and for human welfare in general. Science and its resultant technologies must be examined within the cultural frameworks of both design and destination. Only then can this new contraceptive technology fulfill its great promise.

Notes

1 While neither biology nor logic dictate whether men and women could receive these vaccines, most anti-fertility vaccines are designed for use in women.

2 Women suffer a higher incidence of autoimmune disease than do men (Sinha et al. 1990), an issue of particular importance to safety considerations for contraceptive vaccines.

3 For a thorough discussion of this nomenclature, see Judith Richter in this volume.

4 Population Council and NII have initiated clinical trials of anti-GnRH vaccines for treating prostate cancer; both intend to apply for permission to test the vaccine as a contraceptive in men.

5 These bacterial antigens enable the immune response to the self-antigens.

References

Concepcion, M., A. Mundigo, and A.V. Reeler. 1991. Social aspects related to the introduction of a birth control vaccine. In *Vaccines for fertility regulation: The assessment of their safety and efficacy*, ed. G.L. Ada and P.D. Griffin. Cambridge: Cambridge University Press.

Dunbar, B. 1989. Ovarian antigens and infertility. *Am. J. Reprod. Immunol.* 21:28–31.

Gomes dos Reis, A.R. 1990. Norplant in Brazil: Implantation strategy in the guise of scientific research. *Issues Reprod. Gen. Engin.* 3:111–118.

Hardon, A. 1992. The needs of women versus the interests of family planning personnel, policy makers and researchers: Conflicting views on safety and acceptability of contraceptives. *Soc. Sci. Med.* 35:753–766.

Jones, W.R. 1982. *Immunological Fertility Regulation.* Oxford: Blackwell Scientific Publications.

Jones, W.R., and A.J. Beale. 1991. Clinical parameters in pre- and post-registration assessment of vaccine safety and efficacy. In *Vaccines for fertility regulation: The assessment of their safety and efficacy*, ed. G.L. Ada and P.D. Griffin. Cambridge: Cambridge University Press.

Jones, W.R., S.J. Judd, R.M.Y. Ing, et al. 1988. Phase I clinical trial of the World Health Organization birth control vaccine. *Lancet* 1:1295–1298.

Kim-Farley, R., and the Expanded Programme on Immunization Team. 1992. Global Immunization. *Ann. Rev. Public Health* 13:223–237.

Mathur, S., M.R. Neff, H.O. Williamson, et al. 1987. Sperm antibodies and human leukocyte antigens in couples with early spontaneous abortions. *Int. J. Fertility* 32:59–65.

Naz, R., and A. Menge. 1990. Development of antisperm contraceptive vaccine for humans: Why and how? *Human Reprod.* 5:511–518.

Rose, N.R., G. Wick, P. Berger, et al. 1991. Immunological hazards associated with human immunization with self of self-like antigens. In *Vaccines for fertility regulation: The assessment of their safety and efficacy*, ed. G.L. Ada and P.D. Griffin. Cambridge: Cambridge University Press.

Sacco, A. 1987. Zona pellucida: Current status as a candidate antigen for contraceptive vaccine development. *Am. J. Reprod. Immunol. Microbiol.* 15:122–130.

Schrater, A.F. 1992a. Contraceptive vaccines: Promises and problems. In *Issues in reproductive technology I: An anthology*, ed. H.B. Holmes. New York: Garland Publishing, Inc.

———. 1992b. Personal notes taken at the Meeting to Review the Development of Anti-fertility Vaccines, WHO, Geneva, August 17–18.

———. 1993. Forthcoming. Immunization to regulate fertility: Biological and cultural frameworks. *Soc. Sci. Med.*

Sinha, A., M.T. Lopez, and H.O. McDevitt. 1990. Autoimmune diseases: The failure of self-tolerance. *Science* 248:1380–1388.

Stevens, V.C. 1986. Development of a vaccine against human chorionic gonado-tropin using a synthetic peptide as the immunogen. In *Reproductive immunology 1986*, ed. D.A. Clark and B.A. Croy. Amsterdam: Elsevier Science (Biomedical Division).

———. 1992. Future perspectives for vaccine development. *Scand. J. Immunol.* 36 (Supplement 11):137–143.

Talwar, G.P. 1992. Vaccines for control of fertility. Paper presented at Meeting to Review the Development of Anti-fertility Vaccines, WHO, August 17–18, in Geneva.

Talwar, G.P., V. Hingorani, S. Kumar, et al. 1990. Phase I clinical trials with three formulations of anti-human chorionic gonadotropin vaccine. *Contraception* 41:301–316.

Talwar, G.P., and R. Raghupathy. 1989. Anti-fertility vaccines. *Vaccines* 7:97–101.

Thau, R., H. Croxatto, T. Luukkainen, et al. 1990. Advances in the development of an antifertility vaccine. In *Reproductive Immunology 1989*, ed. L. Mettler and W.D. Billington. Amsterdam: Elsevier.

UBINIG. 1991. "The price of Norplant is TK.2000! You cannot remove it." Clients are refused removal in Norplant trial in Bangladesh. *Issues Reprod. Genet. Engin.* 4:45–46.

13

The Social Context of Sex Selection and the Politics of Abortion in India

by Radhika Balakrishnan

Reviewing third world development strategies with an eye to the status of women adds a new and important perspective. Women's position, relative to men, can be viewed from many vantage points; in this chapter I look at gender relations through the examination of the ratio of women to men in the population. I will argue, as others have before me, that the sex ratio is the manifestation of an interplay between biological and social factors. Identification of some of the key social, particularly socioeconomic, reasons that explain the circumstances of women's excess mortality is crucial to the formulation of development policy. Such an approach can indicate how certain development policies may not only enhance the lives of women but, more important, save their very lives.

In this paper I will focus on the practice of sex-selective abortion within the cultural and material context of India. In India, this practice is only the latest manifestation of a long history of gender bias, evident in the historically low, and declining population ratio of women to men. In order to combat the practice of using technology to abort female fetuses, one needs to look at the wider social and historical context of gender bias on the population. I examine legal activism against amniocentesis by placing the issue of sex-selective abortion against the larger backdrop of socioeconomic, cultural and ideological factors that contribute to the neglect and murder of females beyond the fetal stage. I call for a radical rethinking of our focus on technology, and question the underlying concepts of 'normality' that lie uninterrogated.

Comparative Data

The relationship between economic well-being and population size has long been examined, since the early theoretical work by Thomas

Malthus (*An Essay on Population* was published in 1798). Catherine Gallagher's interpretive research (1986) establishes the longevity of Malthusian ideology, which exhibits a "zest" for checks in the population (death by starvation, infanticide) within the context of an inexorable competition between population growth and economic well-being. Building on this, I use the connection between the ideology behind the analysis of population growth and gender as the basis for exploring the question of sex differentials. This Malthusian ideology, in conjunction with an examination of existing power hierarchies based on gender relations, may shed new light on the discussion of sex differentials in the population.

Comparative data on sex ratios worldwide indicate many differences between countries, as well as between regions within national borders. A cross-national and intra-regional examination of demographic variations in India highlights the impact of economic and cultural differences on the relative number of women in any population.

In 1901, the sex ratio for all of India (female/1000 males) was 972; in 1971 the ratio had declined to 930 and after a small climb in 1981 to 936 the ratio in 1991 was 929. Table 13-1 compares the female death rates of 10 Third World countries, selected because they represent a broad cross-section of the Third World. This data does not control for emigration, or under-counting of females by the census. While there are various problems with using Indian census data, especially when studying questions regarding women, I agree with Sen that the sharp decline in the population cannot be answered by the under-counting of females alone (Sen and Sengupta 1983). The percentage of females to males over the last few decades has shown a marked decline, barring the very small increase in 1981.

The biological sex ratio (rather than a cultural one) is commonly accepted as 105 males per 100 females at birth (Kelly 1975). For example, the sex ratio in the United States is 105.5 males to 100 females (below the age of one) (Miller 1981) Following birth, male infants have a lower chance of survival than females primarily due to respiratory distress syndrome among males. Using a teleological argument, it is hypothesized that the biological sex ratio compensates for the greater vulnerability of male infants, allowing the sex ratio to even out as children grow older (Miller 1981). Therefore, in a perfect world where both sexes are treated equally, and the only reason for differential survival is the sex-linked biological ability to survive in the same environment, the sex ratio will

Table 13-1   Number of girls who die for every 100 boys who die
(Most recent year since 1986)

Country	< 1 Yr Old	1-4 Yr Old
Bangladesh	93	112
Egypt	100	122
Nepal	97	110
Peru	89	102
India	109	300
Pakistan	89	126
S. Korea	86	105
Ecuador	89	105
Malta	52	133

Source: Seager and Olson 1986.

approach unity with the possibility of a slightly higher female survival rate.

Intra regional variations

There have been many studies that have analyzed the connection between social variables and sex ratios. While a thorough analysis of the socio-cultural and gender dynamics as they relate to sex ratios is beyond the scope of this chapter, I will briefly summarize key arguments pertinent to South Asia in order to illuminate the complex nature of the association (see Balakrishnan 1990).

Since India is a country made up of many different cultural groups, the study of sex ratios permits an analysis of the impact of cultural differences and socioeconomic practices on sex differential in the population. Variances among regions are evident in language, food habits, clothing, inheritance patterns, purdah (female seclusion), and female work force participation. Isolating the co-variates of intra-regional variations in the sex ratio may illuminate which cultural practices enhance the ability of women to survive (see Table 13-2).

I will summarize several studies from South Asia, predominantly from different parts of India which, taken together, illustrate the complicated linkage of cultural, economic and social conditions which increase female mortality. This review attempts to tease out the factors that have led a society as complex as India's to practice male preference to such an extent

Table 13-2   Sex ratio in Indian states that show the greatest variation in sex ratios. (Number of females per 1000 males)

Census years

Source	1901	'11	'21	'31	'41	'51	'61	'71	'81
INDIA	972	964	955	950	945	946	941	930	936
Bengal	945	925	905	890	852	865	878	891	911
Bihar	1054	1044	1016	994	996	990	994	954	947
Kerala	1004	1008	1011	1022	1027	1028	1022	1016	1034
Mysore	983	981	969	965	960	966	959	957	963
Punjab	832	780	799	815	836	844	854	865	886

Source: Mitra 1979.

that the relative population of females is significantly decreasing, even today (see Table 13-3). Karkal (1987) emphasizes the need for examining connections between social practices and demographic variables; Caldwell (1982) hypothesizes that increased payment of dowry costs may lead to deterioration in the status of women; Das Gupta (1987) reminds us of the importance of kinship patterns and the economics of the family, and Kumar (1989) calls for more investigation into women's political mobilization. In my own work I suggest the need to explore the relationship between access to property and sex ratios (Balakrishnan 1990). Finally, I review key papers which illustrate the mechanisms through which male and female children are provided differential care.

Karkal (1987) argues that differences in female mortality rates for South Asia, in general, and India in particular, are related to the relative status of women. Karkal disagrees with the widely accepted argument that high female mortality rates are symptomatic of the poor health conditions prevalent in Third World countries, or merely signs of innate biological differences between the sexes. Instead, she attributes these differentials to the subordinate status of women:

> It has been suggested that differentials in mortality of the two sexes reflect the differences in their biological makeup. In societies such as India, high mortality for females is a reflection of the role and status of females, both within the family and in society at large, as much as they represent the health consequences of social, economic and cultural discrimination against them. (Karkal 1987)

Table 13-3   Age-wise grouping of the percentage of females to males
for the census years 1951, 1961, and 1971

Age	1951	1961	1971
0-1	97.4	99.5	92.5
1-4	99.8	97.1	94.3
5-9	96.7	96.6	95.1
10-14	93.8	94.8	90.6
15-19	94.6	94.2	94.4
20-24	97.1	94.8	97.6
25-29	96.0	94.9	97.4
30-34	92.9	92.8	95.0
35-39	89.9	89.0	90.6
40-44	88.4	87.2	87.1
45-49	88.6	86.7	85.2
50-54	90.4	87.0	85.7
55-59	93.8	89.0	88.3
60-64	98.1	93.4	90.2
65+	101.8	106.1	93.5

Source: Mitra 1979.

Caldwell, Caldwell and Reddy (1982), charting demographic changes in Karnataka state, describe changes in marriage customs that may indicate why sex ratios have been declining in Karnataka.

The major change was the coming of dowry. In the early 1950s the first dowries in Bangalore were paid by some Brahmin families. Not until the beginning of the 1960s did the first Brahmin landlord family in the study area provide a dowry, and not until 1965 was this done by the first Vokkaliga (the major peasant caste) family. It is still not paid by Harijans, although in the largest village they ceased paying the Tera five years ago, and the payment is still small among some of the backward castes. Nevertheless, they all anticipate its arrival. In all castes, the bride's family now bears the major portion of the wedding costs, and it is they who seek loans and sell land. (Caldwell, Caldwell and Reddy 1982)

Looking at family life in Punjab, Das Gupta (1987) reports that discrimination against girls is not general, but closely related to individual family building strategies. Using data from 11 villages in Ludhiana district, Das Gupta points out that excess female mortality is seen in girls who are born to a woman who already has one or more surviving daughters. The educational attainment of mothers is an important effect modifier, such that mortality of daughters is 50 percent higher if mothers have no education (relative to mothers with some education). Among women who already have one or more surviving daughters, land holding size makes no difference to female child mortality.

Das Gupta also reports a gender differential in the allocation of food, clothing and medical care to children, especially during the first two years of life;[1] people who owned land seemed to discriminate less in terms of food allocation and health care expenditure than the landless.

Offering an hypothesis of how cultural practices in Punjab contribute to Punjab having one of the lowest sex ratios in the country,[2] Das Gupta emphasizes that patrilineal descent is a key organizing principle of the Jat kinship system.[3] "There is no question of women owning land. If she should insist on her right to inherit land equally under the civil law, she would stand a good chance of being murdered" (Das Gupta 1987). The resource flow is always from the woman's father to the man's family. This occurs even after the initial payment of dowry.

> Son preference is the interest of the lineage, whose continuity depends on sons alone. It is also in the interest of the household, for whom daughters are transitory members....Indeed a woman's position in her husband's home is not consolidated unless she produces at least one son. [Das Gupta 1987:94]

Das Gupta suggests that state policies or propaganda campaigns providing women the right to hold property may be a primary way to redress the high female mortality. The flow of resources is unidirectional from the woman's father to the man; a man inherits property and the wealth acquired from his wife's parents. These practices strongly reinforce son preference.

Das Gupta's study is important because it draws connections between inheritance patterns and sex ratios. Gopalakrishna Kumar (1989) also emphasizes the importance of exploring the influence of women's political and economic power to regional variation in sex ratios. Reporting that excess female mortality in Kerala does not decrease with increases in life expectancy, Kumar emphasizes that sex differentials stem from factors other than overall level of well-being. In particular, Kumar argues that Kerala disturbs some of the convenient North-South topology described by others; existing theories are not easily applicable to the case of Kerala.

Kerala is the only state in India that has historically shown an absence of sex bias. Kumar dismisses arguments that attribute this positive sex ratio to male emigration; Kerala has shown this positive sex ratio consistently over the past century. Relative to other regions of India, Kerala also has other characteristics that suggest better gender equity: it has generally had the lowest fertility rates, the highest level of female literacy, a high age at marriage and fairly good receptivity to contraception. Kumar points to the preponderance of matrilineal inheritance as a possible explanatory reason for both the positive sex ratio and the greater gender equity that set Kerala apart.

Land reform measures in Kerala required the partitioning of large landholding into smaller cultivating units. Kumar suggests that this agrarian transformation pushed women in increasing numbers into the labor market. Because these new wage labor opportunities are increasingly outside the agricultural sector (in rural household industry or urban trade services), over 78 percent of women in Kerala perform non-agricultural work. Kumar argues that, at a general level, there exists a relationship between female participation and reduced discrimination. He suggests that further work that links women's labor force participation and the gender dynamics within the household is vital.

Kumar also points to the manner in which increased social status of women translates into political action. He asserts that the increased level of literacy throughout Kerala has led to many protest movements.

Protest movements focusing on the advancement of low caste women seem to have been particularly successful and the results were manifest from the 1920s onwards, particularly in the expanding wage-earning opportunities and occupational diversification of the Ezhava caste. Indeed, the occupational diversification may reflect the influence of these factors. Grassroots pressures resulted ultimately in demonstrations demanding equal pay for equal work, and educational facilities for girls from destitute families. The impact of the incipient radicalization of this period is difficult to underestimate [sic], and forms an important element in an explanation of the relatively less disadvantaged position of women in more recent times (Kumar 1989).

This approach to understanding women's relative position is indeed new and much needed. The creation of a grass roots movement that empowers women to claim an equal position in society is recommended by many authors as a policy prescription. Though it is difficult to point precisely to such mobilization as the crucial remedy, a more in-depth study of political movements in Kerala that dealt with women's issues is warranted.

A close examination of the history of matrilineal inheritance as affects women's relative position and status is also important to understand the dialectic between cultural practice and material condition (Balakrishnan 1990). I have examined the history of matrilineal inheritance in Kerala to better understand the cultural and material impact of inheritance on sex ratios in Kerala. In my work, by closely examining the history of Kerala, I show that access to property as well as women's labor force participation has a definite impact on the population ratio. Focusing in particular on inheritance, we see that if women inherit property, the burden that parents have toward their daughter is minimized. Daughters have access to whatever the parents can accumulate. The birth of a daughter among the Nayars is awaited, since only through her can the property be passed down. Daughter preference as a cultural phenomenon is guided by real economic factors. Gender relations, examined through inheritance patterns within a community, are therefore a determining factor in sex composition of the population.

Nutritional Allocation

A gender difference in food allocation has been cited by many scholars as a key contributing factor to the higher mortality of girls in South Asia. Chen (1982), D'Souza and Chen (1980) and Chen, Huq and D'Souza (1981) use data from rural Bangladesh to investigate whether a decline in the sex ratio is due to differential mortality rates by sex, and they examine household dynamics for important insights about the value of females and sex ratios.

Chen (1982) shows that the predominance of males over females in Matlab is attributable to both differential migration and mortality between males and females. Migration has accounted for an increased number of women in the rural areas of Matlab, for male out-migration has been much more common than female migration. The mortality patterns indicate that differential survival occurs, and predominantly during childhood.

D'Souza and Chen (1980) indicate that there are higher female mortality rates than males shortly after birth and through childbearing ages. They point out that son preference in parental care, feeding patterns, intra-family food distribution, and treatment of illness favoring males, are possible causes of the differences in child mortality rates.

Chen, Huq and D'Souza (1981) examine the validity of the assumption that sex differentials in mortality are due to son preference in the areas mentioned above. Utilizing extensive field data on dietary patterns demonstrate that some of the disparities in nutritional status between the sexes can be attributed to sex discrimination against females in intra-family allocation of food. They also indicate that male children are brought to the hospital much more frequently than female children. These data provide important evidence of the social mechanisms by which sex preference is manifest in access to health and nutrition.

Chen's research is important in that it highlights several methodological problems with Bangladeshi (and Indian) data. Contradicting the National Bangladesh Nutrition survey, his data indicate that caloric intake for females is less than that of males; for the population cohort ages 0 to 4 years, females received 14 percent fewer calories than males. Chen calls for in-depth regional studies as a basis for improving data collection and quality, and for providing comparable data for India. Indeed, his research provides a solid understanding of the Matlab District. Its micro-perspective strength, however, renders it less useful in understanding the overall dynamics of sex differentials in a country like India.

Overall, this body of research demonstrates quite conclusively that the low sex ratio can be attributed to the son preferential behavior on the part of the parents. Chen, Huq, and D'Souza can only speculate as to the reasons why females are undervalued in this area. A reversal of this trend, they argue, would require an overall structural change in the role, status and economic value of women. Chen (1982) recommends a closer examination of Kerala to be able to find the specific nature of Kerala's society that would explain its consistently high sex ratio. Chen sees that this problem cannot be easily addressed by minor policy revisions (i.e., increased education of females). Long-term solutions rest in fostering an overall change in the position of women.

> Rather, it seems likely that fundamental structural changes in the role, status and economic value of women in society will be required, in addition to the alleviation of economic poverty. (Chen 1982)

The authors conclude with the suggestion that an important social indicator for evaluating the performance of development programs should be the reduction in sex differentials.

The range of factors emphasized by these studies makes it clear that gender preference is articulated at numerous stages in a female life, and that it does not start or stop before birth. The entrenchment of gender preference in social custom, and the number of female deaths is an urgent reminder that, while sex-selective abortion is an important manifestation of son preference, the significant decrease in the female population occurs after birth and before the age of four. From 1978 to 1983, 78,000 female fetuses were reported to have been aborted following using amniocentesis (Kelkar 1992). During the same time period, of the twelve million girls born each year, only 9 million will live to be fifteen (Patel 1991).

Abortion

It is within the context described above that we need to analyze the issue of sex-selective abortion. India has allowed abortion on broad medical and social grounds since the Medical Termination of Pregnancy Act was passed in 1971. Abortion can only be performed in institutions that are government-approved, and by authorized physicians. By the mid-1980s, with over 106 million women of reproductive age, only 4,600 medical facilities and fewer than 15,000 physicians had received official approval. It has been estimated that four to six million illegal abortions are conducted in India every year (Dixon-Muller 1993).

Therefore, access to safe abortion, although legal, is still denied to a majority of women. Technology that allows genetic selection has posed a very complicated challenge to feminists. Son preference, and the introduction of technology that helps in determining the sex of a fetus, leads to a great number of female fetuses being aborted.

The problem of the abortions of female fetuses is one that is being addressed by feminists throughout India. In the face of increasing abuse of amniocentesis, Maharashtra state decided to ban this medical procedure in 1987.

> In one hospital, from June 1976 to June 1977, 700 individuals sought prenatal sex determination. Of these fetuses, 250 were determined to be male and 450 were female. While all of the male fetuses were kept to term, 430 of the 450 female fetuses were aborted. (Miller 1985)

Until recently, the technology was prohibitively expensive. Presently, however, as a result of increased demand, amniocentesis is available on the market for as little as Rs.500 (and some claim that it is as little as Rs. 50). Regardless of the cost, there is still serious concern over the consequences of this technology in a culture saturated with son preference.

The Changing Nature of Gender Relations

In order to convey the complex nature of the crises of sex selection I will describe an incident from a recent visit to India. While visiting a women's reproductive health program in Gujarat, I was in a village with an NGO (nongovernmental organization) representative, who had worked in the region for several years. I asked my colleague the extent of abortions that occurred in this village, and whether, and how, the NGO hospital handled abortions. She explained that the hospital had decided against providing abortion services because of the increasing number of women who came for sex-selective abortions. (Though the hospital itself did not provide the technology for sex determination, there was a "shop" not far away that claimed to provide the test.) Consequently, in the last few years there had been an increase in the number of women and girls going to a traditional birth attendant for abortions. This factor contributed to an increase in female mortality in the village.

Until recently, the community in this village had traditionally accepted sex outside of marriage and premarital sex. Children born to unmarried women were incorporated into the family. A recent censure of unmarried pregnant women, my colleague suggested, had resulted from the introduction of television and through its programs, a new perception that sex outside of marriage was immoral. Consequently, more unmarried women and girls were seeking abortions. Dowry and son preference were also a fairly new phenomena; sex-selective abortion was only the most recent addition. As we walked and talked to people who were busy making clay pots I noticed a satellite dish in one of the mud huts, and many villagers conversing while watching television.

This visit posed a very complicated set of issues for me, as I reconsidered policy solutions to improve reproductive health. There was an increase in the number of women dying from unsafe abortions because the hospital would not provide abortions, but the hospital's policy was a response to the large number of women requesting sex-selective abortions, based on information from an unauthorized clinic.

This case illustrates the many technologies that are operative in changing the character of gender and health relations. Technology was complicit here in enabling sex-selective abortion, and through television, having an impact on the sexual mores of the community to the extent that a premarital pregnancy was now to be terminated. For feminists to be able to respond to the issue of sex-selective abortion in a context where poor women do not have access to basic health care, we need to take account of the multiple dimensions by which technology is affecting women's lives.

Legislative Strategy

Amniocentesis was introduced to India by the All India Institute of Medical Sciences in 1975. It was designed and promoted for detecting abnormalities in the fetus. Yet, couples who used this technology increasingly aborted fetuses that were known to be female.

> Subsequently, through an order of the Indian Council of Medical Research the use of amniocenteses was restricted to suspected cases of genetic diseases. Between 1977 and 1985 three Circulars to government departments at the centre and in the states made use of pre-natal sex determination for the purpose of abortion a penal offence (Menon 1993).

This ban on government institutions led to the commercialization of the technology; private clinics providing sex determination tests through amniocentesis multiplied rapidly and widely. These tests were made available in areas that did not even have potable water, with marginal farmers willing to take loans at 25 percent interest to have the test (Menon 1993). Advertisements began appearing that blatantly encouraged people to abort their female fetuses in order to save the future cost of dowry.

It was in this climate that feminists began to organize against this use of amniocentesis. In 1984 a coalition was formed, the Forum Against Sex Determination and Sex Preselection. With the need to do something fast and bring attention to this problem, one strategy they used was to campaign for legislative action. They were successful in bringing about the Maharastra policy and have publicized the incidence of sex-selective abortion (Menon 1993).

Drawbacks

With hindsight, several drawbacks to the legislative strategy are evident. I would like to explore three points of concern which this strategy, and its outcome, highlight for feminists: notions of normality, our focus on legal remedies, and the complexity of attempting to regulate technology.

The value of female "normality" is protected by the legislative restriction against using amniocentesis for sex selection; but other social concepts of "normality" may be indirectly endorsed by such a policy. Amniocentesis is a technology providing genetic information. Societal norms establish which genetic characteristics are abnormalities and which are normal. As feminists, we need to be very careful in agreeing to the use of technology for one kind of genetic selection and not another. After all, the justifications used to abort female fetuses are often the same as those used by people who want to abort fetuses that have been diagnosed with "medical abnormalities." An "abnormal" fetus and a female fetus are accorded similar drawbacks: expensive to maintain, less productive than "normal" (or male) persons, detrimental to the parents' emotional and financial well-being, and is better off not being born. Arguing for restrictions against one specific application of genetic selection may suggest we are endorsing other applications of the technology, which themselves promote eugenically-prescribed notions of normality and value.

How effective was the legal remedy that was sought? When there was pressure to restrict information regarding the sex of the fetus, the information did not disappear but went underground. The consequences included reduced access to safe, legal and affordable abortion. There is no guarantee that the clinics claiming to provide the illegal information are even conducting the test. Legalizing and criminalizing access to technology impacts primarily on government hospitals. In the case of abortion, although the procedure was legalized in 1971, access to safe abortion is limited to a few women because of logistical constraints (see above). Criminalizing access to information on fetal sex has made the information more expensive and abolished any possibilities for regulation or quality control.

Rapid and frequent developments in medical technology further complicate our reliance on legislative strategy to control the use of amniocentesis. Ultrasound is already used for sex determination; it is only a matter of time before new blood testing techniques will make it possible to determine fetal sex from a simple maternal blood test. These new kinds of information will be harder to police and regulate. The expansion of medical technological in the service of sex selection threatens to concentrate our efforts in the area of advocating for restrictions, diverting political capital from changing the existing social structures and norms that encourage son preference and daughter neglect.

Possible Remedies

We need to approach this very difficult issue by going back to the broader question of the material and ideological conditions that create a world in which women are dying. Bina Agarwal (1988) has emphasized the connection between ideology and its material manifestations. In her critical evaluation of India's post-independence policies and their impact on women, she highlights the economic factors which affect the relative valuation of males and females in the family. While stressing the importance of cultural factors that lead to the high payment of dowry, thereby reinforcing daughter neglect, Agarwal suggests wider interplay between economic position and cultural practice, thereby making the important dialectical connection between ideology and material conditions.

A closer look at dowry and inheritance practices is warranted. Just as position within a class system can determine the number of children born to different groups, so too the relative position within a gender hierarchy can determine the sex of the children who survive. Further, within an economic system, sex differences in the demand for labor and the reward for labor create incentives for the survival of one sex over the other, thereby contributing to the sex ratio in the population. However, demands and rewards for labor are not the only conditions that give incentives to sex-selective behavior. People who are not dependent on the wage labor market may still exhibit sex-selective parenting if there is sufficient economic reward guaranteed when one sex survives over another.

As Krishnaji (1987) points out, land-holding communities are less influenced by labor market conditions. Nevertheless, inheritance patterns, including the connection to the payment of dowry, provide incentives for sex selection.

In India, the character of wage and inheritance practices remains sex-specific. Wages that men and women receive depend on a specific sexual division of labor, as well as the broader ideological constructs that place women's work in a lower position than men's. The origins of particular systems of sexual division of labor are beyond the scope of this study. But accepting the existing set of gender relations that form, and are formed by, the dialectic between ideology and material conditions, I assume that the patterns of inheritance as well are derived from existing sex-specified rules.

In most of India, both the sexual division of labor and the inheritance pattern that predominate establish the male as more valuable, because he can earn higher wages and he inherits property. In general practice, despite some carefully circumscribed legal rights, a woman has no right to her familial property except for the right to be maintained until marriage. Most families that do not allow female inheritance give property to a woman's husband and his family in the form of dowry (Liddle and Joshi 1986). The amount given in dowry is determined by the groom's caste, his earning potential, and the specific demands of his family. Wealth of the bride's family is not a significant determinant of dowry.

Payment of dowry is closely linked to the inheritance system. Das Gupta (1987) shows evidence of the association between patrilineal inheritance patterns and payments of dowry. When women do not inherit property from their parents, a payment of dowry becomes a substitute.

The female child represents a heavy economic drain on her family. As a woman, she will either be excluded entirely from the wage labor market or relegated to its least remunerative position. Her exclusion from family property creates the impetus for large dowry payments at the time of marriage. The male, on the other hand, receives better wages, inherits the wealth that is accumulated by his family, and also gains a dowry.

Policy Implications

In India, dowry has been treated as a paramount social evil and many government programs have been dedicated to education about the social evils of dowry. Women's organizations have actively campaigned over the years to end that practice. Many stories of bride burnings and female infanticide due to dowry have been publicized by the media. Brides have been murdered by their in-laws, so that the groom can marry again and receive more dowry. These incidents cross class boundaries. The payment of dowry is linked to inheritance patterns. When women receive inheritance from their parents, dowry payments are less frequently necessary.

However, while the elimination of dowry as a practice is most certainly an important goal, I feel that looking at dowry alone without examining any other form of access to property is problematic. For example, dowry is often viewed as a form of inheritance.

> Most women see their dowry as the only share they will get of their parental property. In a situation where women do not have effective inheritance rights, dowry is the only wealth to which they can lay claim on. (Kishwar 1988)

If we view the decline in the female population as partially due to lack of access to property, several policy options may be considered. Equal inheritance to family property can be campaigned for, while continuing to work toward a corresponding decline in the practice of dowry. An increase in female work participation and increasing wages for women will decrease the obvious material disadvantages that females are seen to pose to the family.

A grass roots movement that works toward changing the ideology of sexism can be enhanced with evidence that shows that access to property through inheritance and increased wages can impact on the lives of women. Examples from regions in India where there have been, for example, matrilineal groups can illustrate that the relationship between property and gender is not a concept imported from outside of India.

I would argue that the strategy of seeking legislative restriction of sex-selective abortions has not been effective in combatting sex preference, and has decreased women's access to safe medical care. We need, rather, to attempt more broad-reaching strategies that will address the economic and cultural roots of the problem. One such strategy would be to advocate for female inheritance of parental property as an alternative to dowry, as well as sustained efforts to reduce the level of dowry. Such reforms will require more than legislative advocacy, but require changing cultural norms that effect women's position in society.

Although sex-selective abortion is appalling, we must not minimize the tragedy of the millions of girls who *are* born every day, but were never meant to survive.

Acknowledgements

Parts of this paper is taken from the research I conducted for my dissertation (Balakrishnan 1990), and for this portion I would like to thank Temisan Agbeyegbe, Lourdes Beneria, William Milberg, Michele Naples,

Nina Shapiro and Robert Stuart. I would like to thank Arati Rao whose advice, editing and support made finishing this paper possible. I would also like to thank Emanuela Toma and Pearl Harrison for their technical and moral support. I would like to thank Gita Sen and Rachel Snow for inviting me to be a part of this exciting collection, and for their and Jennifer Poulous' editing help. Lastly, I would like to thank David Gillcrist for his support, in this paper and in all that I do.

Notes

1 Clothing expenditure is *significantly higher* for boys than for girls, an important factor in a region that can experience freezing temperatures.

2 Despite high rates of female literacy and a high age of marriage, the sex ratio in Punjab is one of the lowest in the country.

3 The dominant group in this area are the Jats, a land owning caste.

References

Afshar, H. (ed.) 1985. *Women, work and ideology in the Third World.* New York: Tavistock Publications.

Agarwal, B. 1988. Who sows? Who reaps? Women and land rights in India. Paper presented at the Workshop on Women in Agriculture. Centre for Development Studies, in Trivandrum, India.

Balakrishnan, R. 1990. Access to property and its relationship to sex ratios in India. Ph. D. diss. Rutgers University.

Bardhan, P. 1982. Little girls and death in India. *Economic and Political Weekly,* September 4.

——. 1974. On life and death questions. *Economic and Political Weekly* (August):1293–1304.

Caldwell, J., P. Caldwell, and P.H. Reddy. 1982. The causes of demographic change in rural South India: A micro approach. *Population and Development Review* 8(4):689–728.

Chen, L. 1982. Where have the women gone? Insights from Bangladesh on the low sex ratio of India's population. *Economic and Political Weekly,* March 6:364–372.

Chen, L., E. Huq, and S. D'Souza. 1981. Sex bias in the family: Allocation of food and health care in rural Bangladesh. *Population and Development Review* 7(1):54–70.

Clark, A. 1987. Social demography of excess female mortality in India: New directions. *Economic and Political Weekly,* April 25:12–14.

Dandekar, K. 1975. Why has the proportion of women in India's population been declining? *Economic and Political Weekly*, October 18:1663–1667.

Das Gupta, M. 1987. Selective discrimination against female children in rural Punjab, India. *Population and Development Review* 13(1):90–95.

Dixon-Mueller, R. 1990. Abortion policy and women's health in developing countries. *International Journal of Health Services* 20(2):297–314.

D'Souza, S., and L. Chen. 1980. Sex differentials in mortality in rural Bangladesh. *Population and Development Review* 6(2):257–270.

Forum Against Sex Determination and Sex Pre-Selection. 1983. *Campaign against sex determination and sex pre-selection in India: Our experience.* Bombay.

Gallagher, C. 1986. The body versus the social body in the works of Thomas Malthus and Henry Mayhew. *Representations* 14 (Spring).

Govind, K. 1993. Stopping the violence against women: Fifteen years of activism in India. In *Freedom from violence: Women's strategies from around the world*, ed. M. Schuler. New York: UIFEM; WIDBOOKS.

Heyer, J. 1992. The role of dowries and daughters' marriages in the accumulation and distribution of capital in a South Indian community. *Journal of International Development* 4(4):419–436.

ICSSR. 1974. *Toward equality.* Government of India.

India. Office of the Registrar General. *Census of India 1981.* New Delhi.

Jain, D., and N. Banerjee, eds. 1985. *Tyranny of the household: Investigative essays on women's work.* New Delhi: Shakti Books.

Karkal, M. 1987. Differentials in mortality by sex. *Economic and Political Weekly*, August 8:1344–1443.

Kelkar, G. 1992. India stopping the violence against women: Fifteen years of activism. In *Freedom from violence: Women's strategies from around the world*, ed. M. Schuler. New York. UIFEM; WIDBOOKS.

Kelly, N.U. 1975. Some socio–cultural correlates of Indian sex ratios: Case studies of Punjab and Kerala. Ph.D diss. University of Pennsylvania.

Kerala Bureau of Economics and Statistics (KBES). 1978. *Women in Kerala.* Trivandrum.

Kishwar, M. 1988. Rethinking dowry boycott. *Manushi: A Journal About Women in Society* 48.

———. 1989. Toward more just norms for marriage. *Manushi: A Journal About Women in Society* 53.

Koblinsky, M., J. Timyan, and J. Gay. 1993. *The health of women: A global perspective.* Boulder, Colo.: Westview Press.

Krishnaji, N. 1987. Poverty and sex ratio: Some data and speculation. *Economic and Political Weekly* 22(23):892–895.

Kumar, G. 1989. Gender, differential mortality and development: The experience of Kerala. *Cambridge Journal of Economics* 13(4):517–54.

Kynch, J., and A. Sen. 1983. Indian women: well-being and survival. *Cambridge Journal of Economics* 3/4(7):363–380.

Liddle, J., and R. Joshi. 1986. *Daughters of Independence: Gender, caste, and class in India*. New Brunswick, N.J.: Rutgers University Press.

Loudon, I. 1986. Obstetric care, social class, and maternal mortality. *British Medical Journal* 239:606–608.

Malthus, T. 1933. *An essay on population*, vol. 1. London: J.M. Dent.

Mamdani, M. 1972. *The myth of population control: Family caste and class in an Indian village*. New York: Monthly Review Press.

Menon, N. 1993. Abortion and the law: Questions for feminism. *Canadian Journal of Women and Law* 6:103–118.

Miara, M. 1991. The dilemma of sex selection...the issue in India. *Perspectives in Genetic Counseling* 13(2):1–2.

Miller, B. 1981. *The Endangered Sex: The neglect of female children in rural North India*. Ithaca, N.Y.: Cornell University Press.

———. 1983. Son preference, daughter neglect, and juvenile sex ratios: Pakistan and Bangladesh compared. Working paper no. 30, Michigan State University, Lansing, Mich.

———. 1985. Prenatal and postnatal sex-selection in India: The patriarchal context, ethical questions and public policy. Working Paper no. 107, Michigan State University, Lansing, Mich.

Mitra, A. 1979. *Implications of declining sex ratio in India's population*. Indian Council for Social Science Research, Programme of Women's Studies I. Bombay: Allied.

Overall, C. 1987. *Ethics and human reproduction: A feminist analysis*. New York: Allen & Unwin.

Patel, S. 1991. The dilemma of sex selection..the issue in the U.S. *Perspectives in Genetic Counseling* 13(2):1–2.

Seager, J., and A. Olson. 1986. *Women in the world: An international atlas*. New York: Simon and Schuster.

Sen, A. 1993. The economics of life and death. *Scientific American* (May):40–47.

———. 1984. *Resources, values and development*. Cambridge: Harvard University Press.

Sen, A.K., and S. Sengupta. 1983. Malnutrition of rural children and the sex bias. *Economic and Political Weekly* 13 (Annual Number).

Sen, I. 1986. Geography of secular change in sex ratio in 1981: How much room for optimism? *Economic and Political Weekly*, March 22.

Smyke, P. 1991. *Women and health.* London: Zeb Books.

14

Norplant® in the Nineties: Realities, Dilemmas, Missing Pieces

by Sônia Correa

"In 1986 the further enrollment of subjects in the Brazilian Norplant® trial was suspended by the Ministry of Health... Pessimists saw the Brazilian Norplant® episode as a no-win game. However this may prove not to be the case...The quality of communication (between feminists and researchers) was surprising when compared to the usual pattern...The general public was never so well informed about technical procedures, physiological principles..and ethical aspects. Scientific isolation was broken and contraception policitized...This made the Norplant® episode a moment of democratic communication... It is this kind of communication that may result in long-term change, since real change in the role of the state of other forms of social control of scientific activities will not occur by decree" (Barroso and Correa 1990).

Norplant® is a long-acting female contraceptive consisting of six silicone rods containing 30 mg of synthetic progestin.[1] The rods are implanted under the skin in the upper arm. Special equipment and technical proficiency are required to insert and remove the device. The implants protect against pregnancy for five years, by continuously releasing a sustained, low hormonal dose, which simultaneously suppresses ovulation and thickens the cervical mucus. Norplant® is considered by its creators to be an advance over previous methods of steroid contraception (pills and injectables) because it provides for a sustained, relatively constant blood concentration of the delivered steroid; this represents a significant improvement over the diurnal or tri-monthly variability inherent in other delivery systems.

Reproductive rights activists throughout the world have raised critical concerns about Norplant® since the first multi-center clinical trails began in the early 1980s. Through a review of literature, I will explore the feminist concerns and dilemmas within the present "Norplant® realities."

I assess the validity of feminist concerns regarding the gap between written protocols and field operations, the efficacy and safety of the method and its potential for abuse. I also examine the limits of prevailing analytical and political frameworks as they inform the positions taken in the debate. As such, I point out the importance of context-specific mechanisms that mediate women's experiences of contraceptive technology.

Fifty-five countries have Norplant® implant experience[2] and 26 countries have regulatory approval for distribution. The number of users worldwide is estimated to be between 1.5 and 2 million women. These figures indicate that Norplant® has become a global "reality" in fertility regulation. In addition to its widespread, and growing, use Norplant® is an excellent case to examine several critical dimensions of the new reproductive technologies. Multiple funding sectors (public, private and commercial) brought the method into development, and the composition of the investment affects distribution patterns. In developing countries the dissemination is almost exclusively achieved through the so-called public sector, which includes governmental and non-governmental programs. In the United States, a combined model prevails, in which Norplant® is sold at market price to those who can afford it while remaining cheap or free for poor women. This mixed format may emerge in other settings, wherever Norplant® becomes acceptable among high-income women.

Worldwide, the delivery of implants to less privileged, less educated and less informed women is, therefore, dependent on public or "made public" investment. When delivery is cloaked as being in the "public interest," in less-than-democratic situations, women's ability to insist upon adequate services and defend themselves against abuse is necessarily weaker; in such applications, ethical considerations about the method may be raised. Such considerations must necessarily address both the potential for abuse, as well as the ideological priorities in government subsidy.

Norplant® is a subject of controversy among feminists, researchers, and providers, as well as a matter of debate within the international reproductive rights movement itself.[3] In the feminist community, the critique of Norplant® developed within the framework of demographically-oriented population policies. The critique raised questions about the increasing control it was possible to wield over women's lives and bodies with the new technologies. On the opposite side of the fence, others advocated wide dissemination of Norplant® as part of a program of draconian fertility-control measures. Some voices, while recognizing the potential risks, have welcomed the implants as a new contraceptive option that may respond to the increasing preference for long-term methods in various contexts.

The Norplant® debate should not, therefore, be misinterpreted as a mere and occasional disagreement between factions of the feminist community and those involved in contraceptive technological development. The controversy is a manifestation of a deeper tension arising from the conflict ingrained in the *social production of technology*, which Judith Wajcman examines more fully in chapter 12 in this volume. Consequently, if a democratic perspective is to prevail, we cannot avoid or deny the uncomfortable confrontations and interrogations Norplant® demands. In fact, three volumes on Norplant® have been published recently,[4] each of which provides up-to-date information as a basis to evaluate the dilemmas posed by Norplant®.

Norplant® Geography

The development of a hormonal contraceptive implant has been global since its initiation in the early 1970s.[5] In the early 1980s, the Population Council began a global program of multi-center clinical trials and acceptability studies, involving 44 developing and developed countries, including the United States, Finland and Sweden. National programs frequently encompassed more than one research center, as was the case in Brazil, where 20 units were involved. The method is presently registered in more than 50 percent of the countries where trials have been performed. The most widely publicized exceptions are Brazil and India, following feminist action against early research efforts. The Food and Drug Administration (FDA) approved Norplant® for use in the United States in December 1990, which may have legitimated the method worldwide.

Norplant® has received regulatory approval for distribution in 26 countries.[6] A brief evaluation of the present "Norplant® map" demonstrates an enormous heterogeneity of cultural, political and economic conditions. Particularly striking are the discrepancies inherent in the structure and functioning of the existing health-care systems and the capacity of societies to monitor the dissemination of the method. We may consider, for instance, the difference between Sweden and Finland, on one hand, and Haiti or Rwanda on the other.

As global as Norplant® is, it is estimated that approximately 80 percent of users are concentrated in Indonesia and the United States. In 1992, 1.3 million Indonesian women were using the implant, while the Allan Guttmacher Institute (1992) has estimated the number of American women using Norplant® to be between 300,000 and 350,000. After a general review of the characteristics of Norplant®, I will focus mainly on the social context in which Norplant® has been approved and delivered to the public in Indonesia and the United States. The differences between these two countries in relation to dominant political and cultural values as well as social mediation mechanisms will be highlighted. They provide a provocative framework in which to scrutinize the social risks and benefits of Norplant®.

The Norplant® Debates: Agreements

In the ongoing and unresolved Norplant® debate, feminists, on the one side, and researchers and providers, on the other, agree on some major points. The first concerns the large amount of information available about Norplant®. Unlike conditions prevailing during the development and dissemination of earlier modern contraceptive technologies, research has been performed throughout the Norplant® process and the results are easily accessible. This vast literature includes pharmacological and acceptability studies, user's perception surveys and evaluations of insertion and removal procedures. Currently, a joint program of the World Health Organization (WHO), the Population Council (PC) and Family Health International Action (FHIA) is to conduct post-marketing surveillance studies in seven countries, involving an estimated sample of 8,000 subjects. Multi-level reports concerning the operational aspects of Indonesia's program have also recently been published.

Moreover, Norplant's® characteristics were widely debated in the media, although the quality and content of the information circulated is the subject of disagreement. Feminists stress, for instance, that the press tended to praise Norplant's® merits, while downplaying its risks and side effects. All agree, however, that Norplant's® negative aspects, as well as the divergent opinions regarding the benefits and usefulness of the method, have been canvassed in the media and that the general public, in various countries, has been exposed to the controversy.

Common ground also exists regarding the characteristics of the method, common implant side effects and contraindications. Norplant® is highly effective in averting births; it is also systemic and long-acting. Its delivery requires previous and comprehensive health screening; technical expertise to insert and remove the device; and adequate follow-up including effective procedures to locate users by the end of the five-year period.[7] Because it is "a method potentially subject to involutarism because of the difficulty of self removal after insertion" (Petitti 1992), all parties agree that ensuring Norplant® removal on demand is probably the most critical dimension of an ethical delivery process.

The Norplant® Debates: Disagreements

Disagreements run through different and overlapping levels of analysis, but the primary area of controversy is in the area of research protocols and program guidelines. Policy makers tend to consider documents — presented and agreed upon by governments and providers — to be consistent with the realities of delivery system. Feminists, while valuing protocols and norms, identify and address the wide gap existing between written reports and field operations. The feminist critique originally addressed the limits of informed consent in early trials, where women frequently signed the consent form without being entirely aware of its meaning (Barroso and Correa 1990; Dacach and Israel 1993). Later on, the feminist critique expanded to include the drawbacks in screening and follow-up procedures, and most importantly, access to removal on demand in the context of existing delivery programs.

Finally, feminists were, and still are, deeply concerned with the ethical problems that may occur in the context of Norplant® delivery. Since the clinical trials, feminists have identified the potential for abuse, whether from the technical or non-technical characteristics of the method. They have often examined the macro- and micro-level constraints that may restrict women's autonomy in relation to reproductive decisions. As authors such as Freedman and Isaacs (1993) indicate, under the influence of these overlapping constraints, the borders between voluntary choice and coercion may become blurred.

Economic conditions, public sector bureaucracy, and the existence or absence of demographically-driven population policies are particularly relevant in the analysis of programs through which Norplant® is delivered. These factors also determine social pressure on women to regulate their fertility, whether exerted by government officers, village heads, religious leaders, or health providers. At the micro-level, gender, class and race inequalities pervade the circumstances surrounding women's reproductive experiences. In a clinical setting, poor and black women might easily submit to the determinations of doctors and other powerful personalities. In some contexts, women will "accept" a provider-dependent method in order to circumvent difficult sexual negotiations with husbands and partners, and/or cultural resistance to fertility regulation.

The Indonesian Context

Indonesia is a nation composed of some thousand islands in South East Asia; the largest islands are Java, Sumatra, Sulawesi and Kalimantan. Against a background of Javanese dominance, the Indonesian culture is as diverse as the geography. Islamic hegemony differs from other countries in the region, because of a complex integration with pre-existing practices and beliefs.

Since the 1960s, the country has been ruled by a bureaucratic authoritarian regime which has been accused of numerous human rights abuses. The high economic growth rates of the 1970s were followed by adjustment policies in the last decade, the effects of which were income contraction, unemployment, and reduced levels of public expenditures. Despite the economic slowdown, the government has managed to maintain its social development infrastructure. But infant mortality rates remain high in some areas: 77 per 1,000 in urban areas, 123 per 1,000 in rural areas and 141 per 1,000 in West Java (World Bank 1990). As Smith (1990) indicates, maternal mortality rates are much worse than those found in neighbouring South East Asian countries: The lowest estimate for maternal mortality rates in Indonesia is 450 per 100,000 live births (UNICEF 1988), while for young women between the age of fifteen and nineteen, it is as high as 1,100 per 100,000 live births, only lower than that of Ethiopia (Smith 1990).

The Indonesian population, estimated at 174 million, is the fifth largest in the world. The country has pursued strong population policies since the late 1960s, encompassing a central family planning structure with ministerial status, the National Family Planning Coordinating Board (BKKBN) and a transmigration program aimed at the spatial redistribution of the population. In an extremely heterogenous society the fertility control policies are strongly centralized and rather homogenous in design and goals.

Mass campaigns — known as "safaris" — have been used extensively to promote contraceptive use in rural areas. BKKBN has promoted the involvement of village authorities in its activities and considers the program to be a "national family planning movement" (BKKBN 1992).

Through dialogue with Islamic leaders, BKKBN has achieved its desired acceptance levels for contraceptive methods, excluding sterilization and abortion. Indonesian fertility control policies have managed to combine clear, target-oriented models, with flexibility to adapt to prevailing cultural circumstances (Warwick 1988).

The total fertility rate (TFR) declined from 5.4 in 1950 to 3.41 in 1988, and contraceptive prevalence rose from 10 percent of eligible couples in 1960 to 46 percent in 1988. In 1987, contraceptive prevalence rates among married women were as follows: Pill, 31.4 percent; IUD, 30.5 percent; injectables, 21 percent; female sterilization, 6.9 percent; male sterilization, 0.4 percent; Norplant®, 0.8 percent; and other methods, 5.5 percent. Norplant® clinical trials have been performed since 1982 and its use was approved in 1985. A Norplant® Regional Training Center functions at the Raden Saleh Clinic in Jakarta, providing technical assistance to other programs in South and South East Asia.

Both Indonesian family planning and transmigration programs have been subject to long-standing and severe criticism. In November 1990, when the Sixth International Meeting on Women's Health was held in Manila, activists from all over the world drafted and signed a letter to the United States Agency for International Development (USAID) harshly questioning the conditions under which the Indonesians were disseminating Norplant. Environmentalists have also critized the effects of the transmigration program and human rights organizations have denounced circumstances of abuse in the relocation of persons to East Timor and Irian Jaya (formerly West Papua).

Despite these critiques, the World Bank (1990) advocates public subsidies for the Indonesian family planning program, as these expenditures will help to compensate for the necessary increase in economic and social investments. The Bank has expressed concerns about a *potential* stall in the fertility decline and advocates the rapid expansion of programs to the urban poor and to outlying islands, strongly emphasizing the need to increase the prevalence of long-acting methods and to overcome resistance to sterilization.

The American Context

In 1991 the American population was estimated at 252,688 million people and the fertility rate (TFR) established for 1988 was 1.9. The contraceptive prevalence rates are as follows: 29.7 percent of couples of reproductive age were sterilized, and 36.7 percent used non-surgical contraception.[8] A large proportion of internationally-oriented population organizations are based in the United States and the majority of scientific analysis and political discourse concerning global demographic growth originate in the United States. Nonetheless, the United States has no government fertility control policy of the kind implemented in developing countries. However, controversies surrounding reproductive politics have been consistent and intense in the last century. This peculiar history combines conservative reactions to family planning and abortion, as well as furor over eugenic measures aimed at the control of population growth among groups perceived as "inferior." Ferringa, Iden and Rosenfield (1992) point out the paradox: compulsory sterilization laws were common in the majority of states; as many as 45,000 people in the United States were sterilized between 1907 and 1945 and many of them were poor; compulsory sterilization was commonly practiced throughout the first half of this century; however, for all intents and purposes, sterilization as a voluntary contraceptive option did not exist for many women.

Coercion has certainly not disappeared in the recent process of fertility decline in the United States, analysis of it requires that other variables be taken into account. Petchesky (1990) demonstrates that the recent fertility decrease started before the surge in Pill and IUD use in the sixties, and that the decrease is linked to women's access to higher education and employment, as well as to structural changes in female occupational distribution. Marriages were postponed and, even given the rapid increase in the use of modern contraceptive methods, abortion remained a primary form of fertility regulation. As Petchesky notes, the Supreme Court decision legalizing abortion in 1973 must be seen as an "accommodation" of the state and the legal system to a *de facto* social practice.

The struggle for reproductive choice, which has been a recurrent organizing principle for the American women's movement, became a major political issue mobilizing the most diverse actors in American society in the 1980s. Norplant® introduction in 1990 provoked mixed reactions from feminists, but given the prevailing anti-choice atmosphere the method was welcomed because they did not want to fuel conservative positions on contraception. The method was also welcomed by those sectors advocating an increase in contraceptive use to reduce pregnancy and abortion rates, especially among black and low-income teen-agers.[9] On one hand, in a context of aggravated social inequality, access to new technology may be constrained for under-privileged groups. On the other hand, numerous initiatives aimed at disseminating Norplant® to low-income women have been proposed since 1990 and will be analyzed in a subsequent section.

Norplant® *Realities*

I will analyze the data collected concerning the present picture of Norplant® realities in a framework paralleling the feminist critique of Norplant. These criticisms emerged during the early Norplant® trials, and it is interesting to note that recent published literature in some cases reiterates these early suspicions.[10] More important than confirming early problems, however, the new material indicates that the drawbacks and ethical questions remain or have been intensified in the context of Norplant® program delivery.

Written Protocols and Field Operations: The Gap

This section focuses on Indonesia, since the data concerning Norplant® dissemination in the United States applies principally to the other aspects under discussion. Data presented was collected from the following sources: BKKBN (1992), Kasidi and Miller (1992), the Hanhart (1993) Lombok case study, Lubis (1989), Noerprama (1991), Prihastono (1990), The World Bank (1990) and Zimmerman (1990). The information on the United States was drawn from Samuels and Smith (1992).

Reading this material leads one to conclude that, in Indonesia, Norplant® insertions do not adequately follow existing guidelines; in particular, comprehensive health status evaluations of potential users are lacking. The absence of screening is directly related to the delivery system, particularly in the context of "safaris," though screening is not routine in clinical settings either. Providers explain that screening guidelines are not followed because women prefer not to have pelvic examinations (Noerprama 1991). This approach could be interpreted as a commitment to "user's perspective," but for the fact that health and gynecological problems that would contraindicate Norplant® use are not detected and, quite often, pregnant women have had implants inserted.[11]

In addition, health providers are not adequately trained and clinical settings lack written information on Norplant's® side effects. Women themselves are not consistently informed about side effects, removal on request, and the five-year term. Zimmerman's (1990) summary of focal group discussions in the Dominican Republic, Egypt and Indonesia confirms the information gap and asserts that health professionals themselves may feel insecure about the method. Ward (1990) describes a conversation with an Indonesian Norplant® user who was entirely unaware of basic information on the method. Consequently, several reports emphasize the need to overcome the absence or inadequacy of counselling services for users.

Observing that clinical records on users were incomplete in some settings, Kasidi and Miller (1992) and Ward (1990) estimate that clinics lose track of an average of 10 percent of acceptors within the five-year period. Thus, an estimated 130,000 women could be using Norplant® after the expiration date. Users may also be difficult to trace because of migration. No analysis of the nexus between Norplant's® drawbacks and the transmigration program in Indonesia is currently available, but BKKBN data indicates a rapid increase in the numbers of Norplant® acceptors in Irian Jaya and Timor between 1990 and 1991.[12]

Concerning insertion and removal proficiency, Ward (1990) documented inadequate technical preparation of providers, shortage of equipment and hurried delivery. Kasidi and Miller's (1992) conclusions, although not explicit, emphasize the need to ensure aseptic techniques. Concerning removal on request, both Ward and Hanhart (1993) confirm that women requesting the procedure because they resented the side effects have been refused removal, or at least had the procedure delayed. Paradoxically, some women had the implant removed when, instead of referring to side effects, they told the providers they wanted to get pregnant. This calls into question the validity of much discontinuation research.

Despite the low public costs of Norplant®, the method is considered expensive by BKKBN and acceptors are expected, and persuaded, to use the implants until expiration. Lubis (1989) also reported "cost" as a drawback to removal after expiration; 37 percent of women using Norplant® after five years "stated that they did not have enough money to pay for removal fees."[13]

The various critical evaluations of Norplant® delivery in Indonesia have provoked a response from BKKBN. In a comprehensive official document circulated in 1992, BKKBN's program board acknowledged the drawbacks and distortions of its delivery system and the Indonesian government stated its determination to implement measures to correct them. Decisions taken in the top of the highly hierarchical Indonesian state machineries, in general, reach the bottom of the system. Therefore, such provisory comments by BKKBN may lead donor agencies to expect that "quality of care" and "choice" will be implemented in the near future.

Most reproductive rights activists disagree. As their framework of analysis is neither instrumental or strictly operational, they consider the idea of enhancing "choice" to be highly debatable, if the broader context of authoritarian government and gender inequalities is not challenged. Observers of Indonesia also state that the changes, if they ever occur, may take longer than expected, and they point out the long-standing incongruence between BKKBN policy guidelines and field operations.

As if to confirm these concerns, the official literature contains no clear indication that BKKBN plans to reduce the rate of Norplant® distribution. BKKBN projects an increase of 17 percent in the number of acceptors for the 1993-1994 period (from 16 to 17 percent of all contraceptive users). Most importantly, World Bank (1990) recommendations indicate that prevailing trends in Indonesia may tend to the opposite direction: new target groups, rapid increases in the number of acceptors, and emphasis on long-term contraceptive use. Under such circumstances, if "quality of care" and "choice" are to become serious parameters for program evaluation, sharp contradictions will necessarily arise among the diverse agents operating the Indonesia Norplant® program.

Efficacy vs Safety

In her overview of eight Norplant® acceptability studies, Hardon (1993) raises a series of concerns deserving special attention. She contends that the clinical settings where the studies took place might have influenced the responses of subjects. She also underlines the lack of anthropological insights in the methodologies used to investigate user's experiences, particularly regarding women's perceptions of side effects.[14] Hardon also questions the criteria of acceptability, suggesting that continuation and discontinuation rates have prevailed as the guiding references in most studies.

The literature on Indonesia supports her argument. The findings concerning Norplant® acceptability could be better interpreted as an expression of dissatisfaction with previously-used methods, rather than as a sign of clear and definite preference for the implants. In Aripurani (1991), the drop-out rate for contraceptive use because of health concerns is 29 percent for the Pill, 26 percent for IUDs, and 37 percent for injections. Lubis (1989) found that 43 percent of subjects shifted to implants because they did not like (or could not tolerate) side effects from the Pill, IUDs or injectables. The Noerprama final report on a five-year clinical trial (1982-1987) found that, in a sample of 338 subjects, 128 (37.9 percent) decided to insert a second set of rods after the five-year expiration term, but 96 (28.4 percent) opted to use condoms.

The efficacy vs. safety dilemma can also be explored from the standpoint of the relative danger of side effects. Scientists in general assess contraceptive hazards on a strict physiological basis and tend to minimize the importance of biological disturbances that are not life-threatening. In contexts where the maternal mortality rate is high — as it is in Indonesia —contraceptive risks may be downplayed because avoiding births is often simplistically equated with reducing the risks associated with pregnancy and childbirth, including septic abortion. The feminist approach, on the other hand, weighs the side effects from contraceptive use as they affect women's subjective and social experience. Heavy bleeding may imply exclusion from social and religious activities (Hanhart 1993). Amenorrhea may also be experienced as a sign of pregnancy, a circumstance often producing anxiety in users who have opted for a long-acting method. Feminists also consider physiological effects to be detrimental to women's well-being and economic abilities in many circumstances, such as the case of heavy tasks performed by female workers in agriculture and factories, or in the very special case of sex workers.

It must be acknowledged, however, that a significant proportion of post-marketing surveillance studies concentrate their attention on bleeding patterns and evaluate women's perception in regard to these disturbances. Zimmerman (1990) best illustrates this new trend, which is certainly welcomed by reproductive rights activists. But the imbalance between pharmacological studies dedicated to verifying efficacy and studies aiming for a better understanding of the physiology of contraceptive side effects has not been overcome. Feminists as well as other authors believe that more bio-medical research is needed to reach a better understanding of short- and long-term Norplant® effects.[15] In the literature, one preliminary report on a post-marketing surveillance survey on user's perspectives of side effects (Sivin 1990) documents a striking difference in the percentage of complaints related to bleeding patterns in Sri Lankan and Thai women. The authors themselves suggest it could be attributed to differences in body weight between the two populations, but the hypothesis is not fully explored on a strict biomedical basis.[16]

Given the rising incidence of sexually transmitted diseases (STDs), reproductive tract infections (RTIs), HIV and AIDS, contraceptive safety parameters must necessarily address contamination risks implied in related medical procedures, and reflect the urgent need to combine disease protection and fertility regulation. This conceptual revision applies to all existing methods (see Norsigian 1993).

Concerning Norplant, the risk of contamination is present in several situations: insertion and removal procedures, since the data demonstrates that aseptic conditions are not the norm; and the questionable promotion of Norplant® in settings presenting a high incidence of STDs, HIV and AIDs. HIV is epidemic in many of the settings in which Norplant® use is being promoted, including Thailand, Haiti, Rwanda, Mexico and Kenya, as well as in poor, urban sectors of the United States.

Potential for Abuse

It is not only in Indonesia, or other non-democratic societies, where there is potential for abuse. In two court actions in the United States, judges sought to require the use of Norplant® as a condition for probation. The Alan Guttmacher Institute (1992) reports during the 1991-1992 period, approximately twenty bills, amendments and welfare reform proposals involving Norplant® use were proposed in 13 legislatures. Analyses of press materials (Gladwele 1991, Kantrowitz 1993) suggest that, while varying in emphases, all of them advanced measures aimed at the promotion of Norplant® use among black teenagers, poor and welfare women, or subjects prosecuted for child abuse.

To date none of these legislative propositions have been enacted. The American Medical Association's Board of Trustees, in April 1992, expressed its opposition to these types of proposals. The Blacks Women's Health Project (Scott 1992), while welcoming Norplant® as a "broadening of choice," listed concerns regarding the risks of coercion among black, poor and welfare women. The concerns of these and other organizations are substantiated by historical evidence of abuse, particularly concerning sterilization. It is also interesting to observe that, even before the FDA approval, the Population Council expressed its concern for abuse potential. In October 1990, George Zeidenstein, then the president of the organization, said that any abusive use of Norplant® would be an "awful perversion of the method" (Zeidenstein 1990). In December, Wayne Bardin, Director of Biomedical Research at the Population Council, asserted that coercion should not be attributed to the technology itself but would be related to social values (USA Today 1990).

This intense debate indicates that, despite increasing numbers of acceptors, Norplant® remains controversial in light of its potential for abuse. The Indonesian case demonstrates that the potential abuse of Norplant® is not a peculiarly American phenomenon. Hardon, Harnhart and Mintzes (1993) document numerous cases of coercion in diverse political and cultural settings. The Thai National Family Planning Program have phased down Norplant® delivery in urban areas, concentrating its effort to expand its use "among the hill tribes populations." (Kiatboonsri et al. 1993) The Finnish case quotes health providers who state that they do not consider Norplant® a method of first choice, but would recommend it to "asocial women" (Hemminki et al. 1993).

Lubis (1989), Hanhart (1993), and Ward (1990) describe subtle mechanisms of coercion at the microlevel in Indonesia. Relative to the American culture, individual views and decisions are less significant than those of important reference groups and authorities. As this is particularly true in the case of women, concepts of "choice," "autonomy," and "entitlement" can be void of substance. In Lombok some women have shifted from IUDs, with which they were satisfied, as a result of pressure from village authorities. Data collected in urban setting showed 10 percent of subjects have changed method after the explicit recommendation of family planning officers (Lubis 1989). The limits between "persuasion and coercion" in the attitudes of field workers may be very thin in some circumstances (Ward 1990).

The history of contraceptive use in the last century tells us that potential for abuse is not solely the attribute of specific methods. Sterilization certainly remains the primary illustration, but circumstances of abuse have also occured in clinical trials for the Pill, injectables and IUDs and in introductory processes. There may be more abuse potential for Norplant® relative to the IUD because of the possibility of divorcing the method from the genitals, and hence from a bodily link to reproduction and sexuality. If technologies in general distance people from their bodies, not all of them manage to complete this disconnection. IUDs convey a clear link to sexual and reproductive function, since they must be inserted through the vagina into the uterus.[17] We can hypothesize that technologies which most effectively disconnect the body from the reproductive experience are those most prone to abuse.

Mechanisms of Social Mediation

The published literature on Norplant® is striking in its absence of context; the lack of comprehensive information concerning social and political structures, particularly regarding gender equity, is suspicious.

The Indonesian materials provide the best illustration of this gap. The collection of data is predominantly confined to the relation between technology and users, or else between users and providers. As the discussion of "delivery systems" is separated from its social and political context, gaps occur. Zimmerman (1990) found that women complain that not all health professionals — in the areas they live — have adequate information about Norplant® insertion and removal procedures or side effects; this is a typical example of the manner in which the delivery system is evaluated, wherein the social factors leading to adequate information or health-care have not been taken into account.

Most reports fail to capture the relationship between the social context of gender equity and the identified limitations of method delivery. Ward (1990), for example, fails to explore the gender implications that may explain the "avoidance of pelvic examination" in the Indonesian context. From Hanhart's (1993) description, where such aspects are examined, BKKBN's target-oriented models are described as perversely interwoven with a whole set of cultural perceptions concerning body, sexuality and women's role. Furthermore, the social power dimensions wherein women, instead of complaining of side effects, say they want to get pregnant to have the implant removed begs further analysis; the underlying motives that may have informed these attitudes on the part of providers and clients are not thoroughly investigated. Much of the feminist literature emphasizes the implications of international fertility control policies and severely criticizes the role played by the so-called population establishment. But other political determinants and social mediating mechanisms — for example, state-society relations, economic trends and gender systems — are often absent or minimized in such analyses.

A clearer understanding of context is critical to the evaluation of Norplant® risks and benefits. Scientists and providers frequently react to the feminist critique by stating that Norplant's technical characteristics must be isolated from the contextual constraints leading to poor applications. It is extremely difficult to disentangle technical dimensions from delivery drawbacks and, most importantly, from structural class and gender inequalities which impregnate societies and the systems through which the technology is being disseminated. The attitudes of Norplant® providers in Indonesia may have resulted from poor training programs and lack of information, but they may also be related to the authoritarian political system, to BKKBN's "target model" approach, and to women's subordination. In the entirely different conditions of the United States, despite of careful training and intense public debate, Norplant® has mobilized an intense appeal to coercion.

A better focus on context may as well illuminate the conceptual underpinnings of the Norplant® controversies. The major divergences defining the debate can be described as the opposition between those advocating "choice" as the privileged approach to fertility regulation, and those asserting that the powers of technology largely prevail over the ability of women to preserve freedom and autonomy of decision. The first approach suggests the individual women is a consumer, facing the product without any social mediation. Power is attributed to the individual as if she can overcome social constraints and technological pitfalls. The existing "safety net" of mediating mechanisms which permits a first decision, occasional changes of mind and complaint against risk or abuse remains subsumed within the *fetichism of choice.*[18]

Anti-technology perspectives, in turn, fall into a similar trap. The conceptual matrix informing this position is anchored in the antagonism between male constructed science and female identity and body, a rather simplified dichotomy. As a result the production, introduction and use of technology is frequently void of its connections with concrete historical and existing social contexts. As the discourse is somehow construed as being "spoken from nowhere" (Harding 1993), what prevails is the *fetichism of systems.* Techniques and devices are depicted as forces far beyond the reach of human beings and consequently impossible to control.

However, the structure and content of mediating processes are fundamental reference points for the examination of all technology versus individual interactions, being particularly critical in the case of contraceptive technologies. Social and political mediating mechanisms always exist, but they may or may not favor women's empowerment and reproductive autonomy. Whenever the second set of circumstances prevail, technologies become powerful tools of political and social control.

Indonesia is a disheartening illustration of the first case and conveys a convincing argument for the anti-technology position. The cancellation of the Norplant® trial in Brazil may fall into an intermediate category, as it cannot be adequately understood without clear reference to the specific political conditions of the period, with particular attention to the emergence of a vocal and active reproductive rights movement (Barroso and Correa 1990). The United States, where multiple mechanisms *do* exist to back up individual choice for some women and provide for "coercion monitoring," remains at the other extreme.

Norplant® is certainly not the best contraceptive method for American women, but the rapid increase in its use since December 1990 was made possible and relatively "safe" because of a strong safety net of political and social mediation mechanisms. The first mechanism is the stability of democratic procedures, and within it operates an articulate and vocal reproductive rights movement, along with other concerned political actors. The second is the market system and the network of consumer advocacy and protection organizations. As history demonstrates, a Norplant® "accident" in the American context would cost millions of dollars to Wyeth.[19] The intense public debates and the media also play a role in the continuing monitoring of Norplant® use and abuse.

These structures do not exist everywhere, and they are particularly weak in most developing countries. Even in the very special circumstances of the United States, the analyses advanced by black women's organizations assert that existing safety nets may not extend to or be effective in those settings most directly affected by racial, ethnic and class inequality.

Looking Forward

The review of recent literature on Norplant® makes clear that many of the concerns raised ten years ago in reference to abuse potential have not lost their pungency. Collected field information illustrates what George Zeidenstein (1992) — confirming early feminist analyses — has recently pointed out as one of the sharpest dilemmas of the contraceptive research field: What we are faced with for present purposes, what creates our dilemma, is that the most effective reversible contraceptive methods — TCU 380 and Norplant® — are both dependable and very long acting. In that sense they can be seen as the Norplant® system has already been seen by some officials in the United States, as short cuts to solutions of larger social problems.

Given these circumstances, the global monitoring of Norplant® worldwide constitutes a mammoth task, requiring substantial human and financial resources. Considering the comprehensive and often overburdened agenda of national reproductive rights movements, it is debatable whether Norplant® monitoring should become a priority in developing countries where the method is being disseminated.

An important lesson to be learned from the Norplant® debate is that feminist critical perspectives must be effectively heard and taken into account in the earliest stages of contraceptive research and development.[20] This is of special interest in the changing political environment leading up to the Third International Conference on Population and Development (ICPD) in 1994, as the new climate may favor the reframing of scientific premises in the field of reproductive technologies.[21]

Finally, if democratic principles and women's self determination are to be preserved and enhanced, the Norplant® trajectory also demonstrates that substantial changes must occur beyond the scientific and technological domain. Profound reforms are also needed throughout the multiple mediating mechanisms which may constrain the daily experience of human subjects making fertility decisions in concrete social contexts.

Notes

1 A different version, labelled Norplant® II, containing just two rods, is currently under trial in various countries.

2 The Population Council lists in this category countries that have clinical trials, preintroduction studies, small-scale service delivery, or through private sector training.

3 Members of the International Reproductive Rights Movement take a broad spectrum of positions on Norplant®. Some groups — such as the Feminist International Network of Resistance Against Reproductive and Genetic Engineering (FINRRAGE), Rede em Defesa da Espécie Humana (Brazil), and Ubinig (Bangladesh) — propose a ban on the method. The National Organization of Women (NOW, United States) has welcomed it as a contraceptive breakthrough. The National Women's Health Network, the Boston Women's Health Book Collective, and the National Black Women's Health Project (all United States) accepts its approval while remaining concerned with potential for abuse and long-term health effects.

4 The first volume, *Norplant®: Under Her Skin*, published by Wemos and the Women's Health Action Foundation in the Netherlands, contains a general overview of Norplant® characteristics and acceptability research findings. It also presents five country case studies: Brazil, Egypt, Finland, Indonesia and Thailand. The second volume, *As Rotas do Norplant®: Desvios da Contracepcao*, reviews the conditions leading to the cancellation of the Brazilian clinical trials in 1986, and provides up-to-date information on remaining subjects. The Kaiser volume, *Norplant® and Poor Women*, addresses a range of interrelated aspects in the United States context: clinical trials, side effects contraindications, potential for abuse, class and race dimensions, and future perspectives on contraceptive technology.

5   The development of a contraceptive hormonal implant was under the direction of Sheldon Segall, senior biomedical researcher at the Population Council. The first clinical trials started in Brazil and Chile in the early 1970s to determine the most effective combination of rods and hormones. The involvement of a Brazilian researcher, Dr. Elsimar Coutinho, in early implant research remains the object of intense criticism from the Brazilian feminist community, as a result of Coutinho's outspoken misogyny and racism.

6   Bangladesh (1990), Chile (1988), China (1989), Colombia (1986), Czechoslovakia (1989), Ecuador (1985), Finland (1983), Indonesia (1985), Jamaica (1992), Kenya (1989), Malaysia (1990), Mali (1993) Mauritius (1991), Mexico (1991), Peru (1987), Palau (1992), Rwanda (1992), Singapore (1990), Soviet Union (1991), Sri Lanka (1987), Sweden (1985), Thailand (1986), United States (1990), United Kingdom (1993), Venezuela (1987). In addition, family planning programs in three countries — Haiti, Nepal and Tunisia — have been authorized to provide implants. Several other countries have also approved Norplant® for distribution, but they are not included on this list because they accept FDA approval in lieu of their own regulatory organizations. This list is from the Population Council's research department.

7   A comprehensive list of criteria to guide Norplant® delivery is provided by the Sample Norplant® Protocol formulated by the Planned Parenthood of America and published in Samuels and Smith (1992).

8   Statistical Abstract of the United States. 1992 US Department of Commerce. Bureau of Census.

9   See Arline Geronimus, chapter 5, in this volume for a discussion of the social fixation regarding low-income, black teenage fertility during the last decade.

10 For example, see Dacach and Israel (1993) for an analysis of the the Brazilian trials. They state that the clinic has moved from its original location without informing the involved subjects, and refer to one case of infertility and one death. The Population Council's representative, in Brazil, Dr. Anibal Faundes, has circulated a letter contesting the first two accusations.

11 Noerprama (1991) found that "5.96 percent of acceptors were pregnant at the time of insertion because of misdiagnosis." For the 1.3 million Norplant® users in Indonesia, this percentage converts to an estimated 77,000 undetected pregnancies. The desire to avoid a pelvic examination was also detected by Zimmerman (1990) in other country settings.

12 Indonesia is a particularly controversial regarding the link between Norplant® use and population mobility, but migrations are frequent and intense in most of the developing countries where Norplant® is being disseminated.

13 Cost-effectiveness arguments are also used by providers to persuade women not to remove implants in Bangladesh and Thailand as Ubinig (1990) and Zimmerman (1990) indicate.

14 In fact, the literature demonstrates that anthropological approaches have been quite frequently used in Norplant® acceptability studies and remain critical in post-marketing surveillance surveys. They have been, however, mostly used to identify and circumvent cultural resistance to the method, instead of problematizing its characteristics and exploring women's experiences of the method.

15 See Rachel Snow's article in this volume, and consult Petitti's (1992) review of 130 Medline titles on Norplant® for the 1990-1991 period.

16 See forthcoming volume edited by Snow and Hall entitled *Steroid Contraceptives and Women's Response* for an up-to-date discussion on the plausible role of body fat in explaining contraceptive side effects.

17 An analysis of the "disconnecting" effects of technology appears in Judith Wajcman's article in this volume. The idea that "body dimensions" could explain Norplant®'s appeal to coercion was an important contribution gathered from discussion at the authors' workshop in May 1993.

18 This term is borrowed from Marx's analysis of the ideological mechanism (le fetichisme de la marchandise) through which all the chains of natural and human exploitation implied in the process of production remain invisible in the final product.

19 International norms providing for precise information sheets in drug advertising has been fully respected in American Norplant® advertising. The risk of litigation also explains the enormous investment Wyeth has made to ensure the careful training of providers, as well as the caution providers themselves express with regard to the method. As one piece of anecdotal evidence supporting this contention, an informer told me that she was persuaded not to choose Norplant® by a Planned Parenthood doctor. Similar behavior was detected in Finland by Hemminki, Kajesalo and Ollila.

20 This is particularly critical in regards to the contraceptive vaccine research currently underway. See chapters in this volume by Judith Richter and Faye Schrater, for more discussion of these new contraceptive methods. See also Rachel Snow and Elizabeth Bartholet for feminist analyses of research priorities and development for reproductive technologies.

21 In May 1993, the Second Preparatory Committee for the ICPD met in New York. The forward-looking agenda which is emerging for Cairo may reframe the conceptual base of the population field. The principles emphasized in New York were the close linkage between population, environment and development; a strong commitment to human rights; an emphasis on women's empowerment and gender equity; and an acceptance of a reproductive health and rights framework to guide future "fertility management" programs.

References

Alan Guttmacher Institute. 1992. *Norplant®: Opportunities and perils for low-income women.* Washington, D.C.

Aripurnani, S., W. Hajidz, and A. Taslim. 1991. Family planning program in Indonesia: A plight for policy reorientation. Paper presented at the INGI Conference, in Washington, DC.

Barroso, C., and S. Correa. 1990. Public servants v. liberal professionals: The politics of contraceptive research. Presented at the Symposium of Induced Fertility Change, Bellagio.

Dacach, S., and G. Israel. 1993. *As rotas do Norplant®: Desvios da contracepção.* Rio de Janeiro, Brazil: REDEH.

Ferringa, B., S. Iden, and A. Rosenfield. 1992. Norplant®: Potential for coercion. In *Norplant® and poor women: Dimensions of new contraceptives,* ed. S. Samuels and M. Smith. Menlo Park, Calif.: The Kaiser Forums.

Freedman, L., and S. Isaacs. 1993. Reproductive health, reproductive rights: Legal, policy and ethical issues. Prepared for the Ford Foundation Reproductive Health Program Officers Meeting.

Gladwele, M. 1991. Science confronts ethics in contraceptive implant: Long term birth control nears approval. *Washington Post,* April 28.

Hanhart, J. 1993. Women's views on Norplant®: A study from Lombok, Indonesia. In *Norplant®: Under her skin,* ed. B. Mintzes, A. Hardon, and J. Hanhart. Amsterdam: Wemos and Women's Health Action Foundation.

Harding, S. 1993. Reinventing ourselves as other: More new agents of history and knowledge. In *American feminist thought at century's end: A reader,* ed. L. S. Kauffman. Cambridge, Mass.: Blackwell Publishers.

Hardon, A. 1993. Norplant®: Conflicting views on safety and acceptability. In *Norplant®: Under her skin,* ed. B. Mintzes, A. Hardon, and J. Hanhart. Amsterdam: Wemos and Women's Health Action Foundation.

Hemminki, E., K. Kajesalo, and E. Ollila. 1993. Experience of Norplant® by Finnish family planning practitioners. In *Norplant®: Under her skin,* ed. B. Mintzes, A. Hardon, and J. Hanhart. Amsterdam: Wemos and Women's Health Action Foundation.

Kantrowitz, B., and P. Wingert. 1993. The Norplant® debate. *Newsweek* (February):36–39.

Kasidi, H., and P. Miller. 1992. *Norplant® use dynamics diagnostics, 1991. Final Report.* BKKBN and The Population Council.

Keeler, W. 1990. Speaking of gender in Java. *Power and difference,* ed. J. Atkinson and S. Errington. Stanford, Calif.: Stanford University Press.

Kiatboonsri, P., P. Panut-Ampon, and J. Richter. 1993. Inserting Norplant® at all cost? A case study of a Norplant® training session in Thailand. In *Norplant®: Under her skin,* ed. B. Mintzes, A. Hardon, and J. Hanhart. Amsterdam: Wemos and Women's Health Action Foundation.

Lubis, F., I. Sigit Sidi, B. Affandi, et al. 1989. User's attitude about Norplant® contraceptive subdermal implant. Yasasan Kusuma Buana Foundation, Jakarta. Mimeo.

Mintzes, B., A. Hardon, and J. Hanhart, eds. 1993. *Norplant®: Under her skin.* Women and Pharmaceuticals Project. Amsterdam: Wemos and Women's Health Action Foundation.

Noerprama, N.P. 1991. The Norplant® removal training and services at Dr. Kariadi Hospital, Semarang, Indonesia. *Advances in contraception* 7:389–401.

Norsigian, J. 1993. Feminist perspective on barrier use. Paper presented at conference sponsored by CONRAD and WHO, March 22, in Santo Domingo.

Petchesky, R. 1990. *Abortion and woman's choice: The state, sexuality and reproductive freedom,* rev. ed. Boston: Northeastern University Press.

Pettiti, D. 1992. Issues in Evaluating Norplant®. In *Norplant® and poor women,* ed. S. Samuels and M. Smith. 1992. The Kaiser Forums.

Population Council Research Division. 1993. Direct communication from Elizabeth Westley, September 14.

Prihastono, J. 1990. *Norplant® removal study: Factors associated with due and overdue 5 years removal.* Yasasan Kusuma Buana Foundation, Jakarta. Mimeo.

Samuels, S., and M. Smith, eds. 1992. Executive summary. *Norplant® and poor women,* ed. S. Samuels and M. Smith. The Kaiser Forums.

Scott, J. 1992. Norplant® and women of color. In *Norplant® and poor women,* ed. S. Samuels and M. Smith. The Kaiser Forums.

Sivin, I., et al. 1990. Contraceptives and women's complaints: Preliminary results from the post-marketing surveillance of Norplant®. Population Council. Mimeo.

Smith, I. 1990. The Indonesian family planning programme: A success story for women? Boston Women's Health Book Collective Documentation Center. Mimeo.

Snow, R., and P. Hall, eds. In press. *Steroid contraceptives and women's response: Regional variability in side-effects and pharmacokinetics.* New York: Plenum Press.

Statistical Abstract of the United States. 1992. U.S. Department of Commerce, Bureau of the Census.

UBINIG. The price of Norplant® is tk 2,000. You cannot remove it. The clients are refused removal in Norplant® trial in Bangladesh. Boston Women's Health Book Collective Documentation Center. Mimeo.

Ward, S., I. Sigit Sidi, R. Simmons, and G. Simmons. 1990. Service delivery systems and quality of care in implantation of Norplant®. Report prepared for the Population Council.

Warwick, D. 1988. Culture and the management of family planning programs. *Studies in family planning* 19(1):1–18.

World Bank. 1990. Indonesia: Family planning perspectives in the 1990's. World Bank Country Study. Washington, D.C.

Zeidenstein, G. 1990. Unreleased press statement. Population Council, October 31.

———. 1992. Dilemmas of public sector contraceptive development. *International Symposium on Recent Advances in Female Reproductive Health Care: Proceedings.* Helsinki: Finnish Population and Family Welfare Federation.

———. 1993. Conversations with the author, April–May.

Zimmerman, M., J. Haffey, E. Crane, et al. 1990. Assessing the acceptability of Norplant® implants in four countries: Findings from focus group research. *Studies in Family Planning* 21(2):92–103.

15

The Politics of Fetal/Maternal Conflict

by Ruth Hubbard

There are all kinds of ways in which societies interpret women's procreative abilities and use these interpretations to structure and define our participation in society. Hence, women's ability to gestate and birth children is used to control our behavior somewhat differently in the United States from the ways fecundity and procreation are used to control women in some of the other societies discussed in this collection. The new procreative technologies and the anti-abortion movement are partially responsible for what is happening in the United States, but so are other social forces.

One way to begin to explore this situation is to look at the way Americans view pregnancy in this final decade of the 20th century. Here, two trends reinforce each other. First, there is the image of the disembodied embryo or fetus, floating somewhere in space. This is illustrated by *NOVA*, in a television program called "How Babies Get Made." The program opens with a gowned male doctor handing a newborn to a gowned nurse who, of course, is female. The rest of the program is about eggs, sperm, cell nuclei, early and later stages of embryonic development, and the developing fetus. At one point, we get to see a piece of the placenta. That famous visitor from outer space would have no way to gather from this presentation that everything shown in the film happens inside the body of a woman. Women and pregnancy are never mentioned.

Now let us look at the changing image of mothers. In her book, *Recreating Motherhood*, Barbara Katz Rothman (1989) looks at the transformations in the image of the mother in popular culture from the 1950s and 1960s to the 1970s and 1980s. Throughout these decades mothers have always been portrayed as bad for their children, but their ways of being bad have changed. In the 1950s and 1960s, mothers damaged their children by being too self-sacrificing, like Portnoy's mother. But in the 1970s and 1980s, the smothering mother was replaced by the selfish mother, the woman out to fulfill herself at the expense of her child. The new prototype is the mother of the movie *Kramer v. Kramer*(1979), the self-absorbed woman who abandons her child to the tender mercies of its father.

Putting together the disembodied embryo and the selfish mother readily leads to the three practices I want us to think about:

1. criminal prosecutions of women for endangering the fetus within their bodies,

2. court-mandated caesarian sections, and

3. fetal protection as grounds for excluding women from jobs with relatively good pay, and health and retirement benefits, that have previously been held only by men and to which women have recently begun to gain access.

All three of these practices produce media stories that strengthen the cultural image of neglectful women putting their fetuses at risk. Although these particular practices demonize primarily poor or working-class women, the aura they create can be used to control the behavior of middle- and upper-class women as well. After all, different kinds of "experts" are always ready to make middle- and upper-class women feel guilty for putting their own career needs ahead of the needs of their future or present children. Middle- and upper-class American women may be spared accusations of fetal abuse, but they are frequently accused of neglecting their maternal duties when they postpone childbearing or when they delegate the care of their children to others (including the fathers of those children). Meanwhile, in the United States, in contrast to several other industrialized nations, there is no public responsibility either for child care or for adequate nutrition or health care for pregnant women. Women get blamed, but there are few places where they can go for help.

Criminal Prosecutions

Numerous women — most of them poor, many of them battered — have been jailed for drinking alcohol or using drugs while pregnant. How do the authorities find out about them? In one case, because a battered women's shelter brought a pregnant woman to the hospital for treatment of her bruises. A blood test revealed alcohol, and she was promptly charged with "felony child abuse."

A case currently being litigated in Massachusetts involves Josephine Pellegrini of Brockton who in 1989 gave birth in a public hospital. The newborn was healthy, but a routine blood test showed traces of cocaine in its blood. The Commonwealth promptly charged Pellegrini with distributing cocaine to a minor via the umbilical cord and also with possession of an illegal substance (McNamara 1989). The "distributing" charge, which carries a minimum sentence of three years in state prison, was dismissed in 1992, since in Massachusetts a fetus does not have legal standing as a minor. In March 1993, however, the Supreme Judicial Court upheld the "possession" charge. A legal issue that remains to be decided is whether the mandatory reporting statute, under which anyone who suspects child neglect or abuse must report the situation, can be used to prosecute someone for the harm that person may be doing to her/himself when there is no evidence that he or she has, in fact, harmed the child whom this statute is intended to protect.

Another legal issue, raised in a review by Kary Moss (1990), is that administering drug tests to an infant without the parent's consent violates parental rights. As Moss points out, "A positive toxicology [drug test] alone does not provide substantive information about the impairment of mother or child…It does not measure frequency of drug use, but says only that a drug was introduced in the last 24 to 72 hours." In practice, using the mandatory reporting statute in this way is likely to deter pregnant women from consulting drug counselors or other providers of health or social services for fear of criminal prosecution, which could deprive the mother of custody and terminate her parental rights. Linking the health care or social service system with legal prosecutions erodes women's often tenuous trust of service providers and may, in fact, imperil the health of women, fetuses, and newborns.

Eventually, most charges of delivering drugs to fetuses *in utero* have been dismissed, either on technical grounds or because a fetus is not a person. As a result, state prosecutors are formulating ever more ingenious charges, such as, for example, the "possession" charge against Josephine Pellegrini. In another case, Jennifer Johnson, a woman in Florida, was convicted of a felony for passing cocaine, this time not to her fetus but to her newborn in the moments before the umbilical cord was cut (*Florida v. Johnson*, 1989). Johnson's sentence included the proviso that she get drug treatment (which she had tried to get), gainful employment (which she had tried to find), and that she not use drugs or associate with anyone who does, drink any alcohol, or enter a bar as conditions of her parole (though no provisions were made to help her move out of her neighborhood). In other words, although she tried, and was unable, to get the services she needed to stop using drugs, she was punished for not having gotten them.

Let us take a closer look at this issue. I suppose most people would agree that it is not a good thing for pregnant women to drink excessive amounts of alcohol, to smoke, or to use drugs. But if the state wants to protect a fetus, a better strategy might be to make it possible for pregnant women — and women in general — to get proper housing, food, jobs, a decent living environment, and good prenatal care. Since 1980, however, resources available to poor women have been diminishing. Public health and nutrition programs for women and children have been slashed, as have jobs and housing. Though overall infant mortality has declined during this century, infant mortality in this country is now twice as high for African American as for Euro American infants, the same as a hundred years ago (Hogue and Hargraves, 1993).

The so-called war on drugs has produced a situation in which a single blood test on a pregnant woman or a newborn is sufficient to label that woman a drug abuser and call in the state. Courts increasingly are criminalizing poor women for behaving in ways that could endanger their fetus, irrespective of whether their babies can be shown to have been damaged. There need be no symptoms or other indications that the baby has been mistreated in any way. This way of implicating drug abuse often results in misdiagnoses and mislabeling (Moss 1990). For example, on the basis of a blood test on the newborn, in 1990 Cambridge Hospital accused a young, unmarried, African American woman of having used drugs while pregnant. The woman and her mother denied the charge and sought legal help. Further tests indicated that the chemicals which were detected in the baby's bloodstream had been administered to the woman by her medical attendants during labor.

The mandatory reporting policy can wreak havoc with the lives of women and children and the more vulnerable the woman, the more devastating the effects. A poor woman, a woman of color, or an abused woman is usually not in a position to defend herself or her parental rights, whether or not she habitually uses drugs. And even if she does use drugs regularly, the present policy is not likely to benefit her or her child, since what she needs is appropriate help and rehabilitation, not punishment.

Yet, that is not what is happening. In New York City, many babies have been taken away from their mothers for insufficient cause and kept in hospitals with insufficient care. Meanwhile, few drug treatment programs accept women and even fewer of them accept pregnant women or women on Medicaid. In a study of New York state, Wendy Chavkin (1990) found that of the 78 drug treatment programs on the state's list, 87 per cent refused to serve women who were either pregnant, on Medicaid, or addicted to crack cocaine. A recent survey of services in Oregon showed that in 1989, 2140 women were probably using illicit drugs while pregnant; yet, there were only 111 programs with a total of 740 treatment slots for pregnant alcohol or drug users (Slutsker et al. 1993). Even worse, only 21 of these programs had on-site child care facilities and only 134 treatment slots were available for pregnant women with children. The authors of this study estimate that "assuming a 1-year course of therapy, current treatment programs [in Oregon] could accommodate only 13% of the estimated number of recognized [pregnant] users of cocaine, methamphetamine, or heroin."

The National Association of State Alcohol and Drug Abuse Directors has reported that only about 550,000 of the approximately 4 million women needing treatment in 1989 received it. Of those 4 million, 250,000 were pregnant, but only 30,000 received treatment (Bertin 1993). All this adds up to the fact that there are few resources to enable addicted pregnant women to get off alcohol or drugs, and even fewer for addicted pregnant mothers who need to be caring for their children.

Women resort to excessive drinking or drug use often out of an emotional and physical need, sufficient to override wanting to do what is best for their future child. Although this is true irrespective of women's economic status, and although the rates of drug use are comparable among poor and affluent women (Kolata 1990), poor women are more likely to be prosecuted for drug use during pregnancy than affluent women are. The reason is that reporting of drug or alcohol use is done almost entirely by public hospitals, where poor women go for care and not by private physicians.

How damaging the behavior is also appears to be affected by economic status. A recent study of alcohol-addicted women found that whereas the incidence of fetal alcohol syndrome was 70.9 percent among the children of the lower-class mothers, it was only 4.5 percent among the children of the upper-middle-class mothers (Bingol, 1987).

Fetal/Maternal Conflict and Legally Mandated Caesarian Sections

How did embryos or fetuses become separate beings in disregard of the women whose bodies sustain them? And how did pregnant women become criminals against whom the state must protect the fetuses growing within their bodies?

No doubt the anti-abortion movement has played into this, but there are other factors as well. Until the 1960s, there was no way of knowing anything about an embryo or fetus except by examining the pregnant woman. If you wanted to know whether the fetus moved or its heart beat, you had to ask her, touch her, or put your ear or a stethoscope up against her swollen belly.

Then, in the 1960s, medical scientists developed a first direct test of fetal health when they became able to determine the Rh-antigen status of a fetus. It was important to know the Rh-status of a pregnant woman and her fetus because, if the fetus is Rh-positive, an Rh-negative pregnant woman may develop antibodies against its Rh-antigen that can damage the fetus. Thus, the fetal Rh-test enabled physicians to be ready to treat an endangered infant as soon as it was born. Actually, today all pregnant women are given rho-gam, a substance that neutralizes Rh-antibodies, so that the fetus's Rh-status is no longer of special interest, but there is no question that this direct measure of fetal physiology was useful.

Since then, numerous other tests have been developed to assess fetal health directly. But the use of ultrasound imaging has been the most crucial innovation for changing the cultural perception of the fetus. Earlier in the century, obstetricians had used X-rays to visualize fetuses, but that needed to be discontinued when X-rays were shown to increase the incidence of childhood leukemia. (Of course, no one knows for sure that ultrasound is risk-free, but so far no problems have been documented and it has become routine to use ultrasound imaging to visualize fetuses during pregnancy.) Real-life ultrasound imaging has rendered pregnant women transparent and encouraged the culture to bond with "the fetus." Nowadays, fetuses are not only female or male; they swallow, pee, suck their thumbs, and their pictures can be shown to relatives and friends.

Thus, the anti-abortion movement has not been alone in transforming the cultural status of embryos and fetuses. Routine technological interventions in wanted pregnancies have done this as well, and so has the in-vitro fertilization technology. Even more recently, the combination of in-vitro fertilization and contractual pregnancy has turned not only eggs and sperm, but also embryos, fetuses, and gestation into commodities that can be ordered from catalogs. An extreme result of this has been a decision, handed down in a case of contested custody by a California judge, in which he stated that Anna Johnson, a woman who had gestated a fetus derived from another woman's egg, is a "genetic stranger" to that child and comparable to a baby-sitter. The egg donor, he ruled, is the biological mother (Reuters 1993).

Setting a pregnant woman and her fetus up as not only separate but as antagonists is of relatively recent origin. As recently as 1979, two adjoining articles were published in the medical journal *Obstetrics & Gynecology*, one by three physicians, the other by an attorney (Lieberman et al. 1979; Shriner 1979). Both discussed the rare situation in which a physician believes that medical circumstances call for a caesarian section, but the pregnant or birthing woman refuses to undergo this surgical procedure. And both concluded that, while physicians can use their ingenuity to try to persuade the woman, they cannot open her belly against her will. A caesarian section performed without the woman's consent would constitute assault and battery.

A mere two years later, an article in the same journal describes one of the first legally mandated caesarians (Bowes and Selegstad 1981). This situation involved a white woman on welfare who arrived at the University of Colorado Medical Center in labor, without prior prenatal care. As the labor progressed, the physician on duty decided a caesarian was indicated, but the woman was afraid of surgery and refused. A psychiatrist, called in to speak with her, testified that she understood the supposed risk to the baby. Thereupon the hospital obtained an injunction and a hearing was held in the woman's hospital room, presided over by a judge from the Colorado juvenile court, in which the hospital, the woman, and the fetus were each represented by a lawyer. At the conclusion, the judge ruled that a caesarian was in order, and at that point the woman consented, so that she did not need to be cut open against her will.

Like the prosecutions for "fetal abuse," most court-mandated caesarians have been performed on poor women, women of color, or on aliens or recent immigrants who speak little or no English. So, again it has been very much a class and race issue (Cole 1990).

It is important to recognize that court-mandated interventions in pregnancy and birth are supported not only by "pro-lifers," whose principal concern is for the fetus, but also by some legal experts who support a woman's right to terminate her pregnancy. For example, John A. Robertson (1983), a professor of law at the University of Texas, argues that *Roe v. Wade* guarantees a woman the right to abortion, but that if she "waives" that right by continuing her pregnancy, she is obligated to do whatever is deemed best for the fetus.

There is a problem here, for who is to say what is best? Medical fashions change as do popular beliefs about what is, or is not, good for pregnant women and their fetuses. The amount of weight a woman should gain during pregnancy and how athletic she should be are recent examples of this. Of the several pregnant women who have escaped court-mandated caesarians, either by hiding or because they were lucky enough to go into labor and give birth before the court order could be implemented, all have given birth normally and they and their babies have been fine (Kolder et al., 1987). As physician Helene M. Cole (1990) points out: "Courts are ill-equipped to resolve conflicts concerning obstetrical interventions." Neither physicians nor anyone else can foresee birth outcomes with certainty. So, it is wrong to give medical predictions legal status.

Mandated caesarians may have been ended by a lawsuit, instituted by a family with access to the necessary resources. (*In re* A.C. 1990) It involved Angela Carder, a woman who had had cancer during her teens. The cancer went into remission, but years later, after she became pregnant, it was reactivated. When she was 26 weeks pregnant, it became clear that she was not going to survive until the end of her pregnancy. Georgetown Hospital in Washington, D.C., where she was receiving her obstetric care, insisted that she undergo a caesarian section so as to try to save the fetus. Initially, Carder agreed, but then changed her mind. Despite her refusal and the fact that Carder's parents, her husband, and the medical specialist who was treating her cancer supported her decision, attorneys for the hospital obtained a court order and a staff obstetrician performed the caesarian. The baby died within two hours of surgery, Carder herself two days later. Her hospital records state that the surgery probably hastened her death. The Federal Appeals Court in the District of Columbia agreed to review the court order under which the surgery took place and in 1990 handed down a very strong opinion against forcing women to undergo caesarian sections against their will. In addition, the family filed a civil suit and Georgetown Hospital had to pay considerable damages.

This dreadful story may have laid court-mandated caesarians to rest, but it is easy to extrapolate from court-mandated caesarians to court-mandated prenatal tests and therapies. This has not happened yet, but it may once prenatal testing or therapy becomes standard medical practice. And what if courts one day decide that, if no therapy is available and a fetus is predicted to be disabled, the woman must have an abortion?

This suggestion is not altogether far-fetched. Insurance discrimination against families predicted to have a child with a disability has already occurred. Medical geneticist Paul Billings and his colleagues (1992), in their research into genetic discrimination, have come across an instance that is not very different from this hypothetical scenario. In this case, a woman who had borne one child with cystic fibrosis decided to have her fetus tested for this condition during a subsequent pregnancy. When the result indicated that this baby, too, was going to have cystic fibrosis and the woman decided to continue the pregnancy (which is not unusual for families who have experience caring for a child with cystic fibrosis), the HMO that provided the family's health care announced that it was prepared to pay for an abortion, but not for continued prenatal care or the health care of the future baby because that baby now had what insurers call a pre-existing condition. Only after the family threatened to publicize this decision and, if necessary, take it to court, did the decision get reversed. As prenatal tests proliferate, these kinds of situations are going to become more common, unless we get laws passed to prevent such forms of discrimination and coercion.

Fetal Protection and Workplace Discrimination Against Women

As we have seen, the ability to visualize a fetus and test for certain aspects of its health status makes that fetus more real, more of a person. And when that happens, the pregnant woman seems to become more of a fetal container and less of a person.

Further detrimental effects of this skewed view of pregnancy are illustrated by the so-called fetal protection policies by which women of childbearing age, as a class, have been excluded from certain job categories in which they run the risk of being exposed to radiation, lead, or other toxic chemicals. These concerns are not raised because the agents pose dangers to the workers — women and men — but because of the dangers they pose to a "potential" fetus, in case the woman is pregnant. In this construct, all women of childbearing age are deemed potentially pregnant, hence excludable, unless they can show that they have been sterilized. Their life-partner being sterile is not enough; they must be unable to become pregnant.

Similar concerns are not raised to protect women who work at jobs that are more traditional for women, as nurses, hospital or chemical laboratory clean-up personnel, beauticians, pottery painters, or indeed housewives. All such women routinely come in contact with toxic chemicals, biologicals, or radiation that can endanger their fetus when they are pregnant. But the concern is reserved for women employed in jobs, traditionally occupied by men, that pay higher wages and include better benefits than traditional women's jobs do. Attorney Joan E. Bertin (1993) makes the telling point that a woman's employment is often critical to a healthy pregnancy and only she, not her employer, can judge what risks are worth taking to continue in a particular job.

So-called fetal protection policies may have been discouraged by a decision the U.S. Supreme Court rendered in 1991. The court held that it was unlawful for Johnson Controls, Inc., a manufacturer of lead batteries, with plants across the country from Vermont to California, to exclude women from working in its lead battery department. (*International Union, UAW v. Johnson Controls* 1991). Johnson Controls had *enforced this policy irrespective of the women's marital status or their intentions not to have (more) children,* so limiting women's access to more than 20 million jobs (Bertin 1993).

Meanwhile, scientific and news articles have reported research showing that men's exposure to pesticides, radiation, and toxic work-place chemicals, as well as their consumption of alcohol and drugs, can affect the quality of their sperm and provoke death or disabilities of the fetuses or children they father (Blakeslee 1991; Friedler 1993).

It stands to reason that sperm is at least as vulnerable to toxic substances and radiation as eggs are, but this society's warped ideology about childbearing and rearing focuses disproportionately on the procreative functions of women. The usual justifications for what employers refer to as their fetal protection policies are (1) that fetuses may be more vulnerable than adult workers, and (2) that all of a woman's eggs are laid down in her ovaries at the time she is born, whereas men produce sperm continually. Therefore, the argument goes, women's eggs age with them and accumulate potential injuries throughout life, whereas sperm is always new.

Both arguments are flawed. Fetuses may be more vulnerable than adults, but no hazards affect exclusively fetuses. The best way to protect fetuses is to clean up workplaces and so protect the workers. As for aging eggs and fresh sperm, sperm is produced continuously by virtue of the fact that sperm-precursor cells keep on dividing. Men are born with these precursor cells, just as women are with eggs. In fact, the sperm-producing cells may be more vulnerable than eggs to radiation or chemical injuries precisely because they keep dividing, which is when cells are at greatest risk from environmental damage.

The Fetus as Patient and Plaintiff?

Control of women by controlling procreation underlies most of the practices discussed in this collection, but the medical-legal measures I have been describing are peculiar to the United States. Here, as elsewhere, women not only bear children, but also are principally responsible for their children's well-being, and the inequities intrinsic to capitalism fall most heavily on them. Since this country makes few economic, social, and medical provisions for people, it has proportionately more poor women and children than other affluent countries, which offer more adequate social services. In no other industrialized country do so many women give birth without regular, or indeed any, prenatal care. As we saw earlier, this country does not have adequate drug treatment programs for women or men, but especially not for pregnant women. The United States also has a higher proportion of non-unionized workers than other industrialized countries, so that there is less protection for workers' health and safety and for the rights of pregnant workers or workers with children.

The individualistic thinking that prevails in the United States lends itself to blaming women for their low social and economic status and for their own and their children's poor health. This ideology becomes actively punitive when "the fetus" is turned into a patient and plaintiff with its own rights.

To improve this situation will require social measures that deindividualize responsibility. None of the problems I have described can be remedied at the individual level. To solve them requires a commitment, at the societal level, to care for people who need care and to provide the opportunities people need in order to be able to care for themselves.

Pitting the interests of pregnant women against those of the fetuses they are gestating does not benefit children any more than women.

Women whom the state considers neglectful of the health of their fetuses, by definition, must be damaging their own health as well. It would be more productive to concentrate on their health needs and to enable them to live healthfully not only while pregnant, but after their babies are born.

As individuals, we cannot improve women's economic lot; we need to organize for political change. But throughout this work we must insist on women's bodily autonomy. Women must have access to abortions when they do not want to be pregnant, irrespective of their ability to pay. And women must be trusted to make the right decisions, recognizing that they will sometimes err and put their fetuses at risk. Have physicians never put fetuses (or people) at risk, and haven't lawyers and judges?

As far as a fetus's medical and legal rights are concerned, I insist that it does not have any. My criteria rely on simple geography: as long as one cannot get at the fetus without manipulating the woman, she is the only one with the right to make decisions. Once the baby is outside and its well-being no longer impacts her physical autonomy, then others can begin to speak for it, provided they take responsibility for what they say or do.

A society that forces a woman to bear a child when she does not wish to have one, offers her little or no support when she does, and punishes her when it decides she is acting irresponsibly, is itself guilty of fetal abuse. Unfortunately nothing in U.S. law mandates equality in access to health resources or care. In fact, the opposite is likely to happen if current discussions about health priorities lead to laws that make cost-cutting a cornerstone of health policy. In that case, present seemingly haphazard and piecemeal discriminatory practices are likely to be regularized and legalized by rationing access to services for certain sectors of the population.

References

A.C., 573 A.2d 1235 (District of Columbia Court of Appeals 1990)

Bertin, J.E. 1993. Pregnancy and social control. In *Encyclopedia of Childbearing: Critical perspectives*, ed. B.K. Rothman. Phoenix, Ariz.: Oryx Press.

Billings, P., M. Kohn, M. de Cuevas, J. Beckwith, J.S. Alper, and M.R. Natowicz. 1992. Discrimination as a consequence of genetic testing. *American Journal of Human Genetics* 50:476–482.

Bingol, N., C. Schuster, M. Fuchs, S. Iosub, G. Turner, R.K. Stone, and D.S. Gromisch. 1987. The influence of socioeconomic factors on the occurrence of fetal alcohol syndrome. *Advances in Alcohol and Substance Abuse* 6 (Special Issue: Children of Alcoholics):105–118.

Blakeslee, S. 1991. Research on birth defects shifts to flaws in sperm. *New York Times*, January 1.

Bowes, Jr., W.A. Selegstad, and B. Selegstad. 1981. Fetal versus maternal rights: Medical and legal perspectives. *Obstetrics and Gynecology* 58:209–214.

Chavkin, W. 1990. Drug addiction and pregnancy: Policy crossroads. *American Journal of Public Health* 80:483–487.

Cole, H.M. 1990. Legal interventions during pregnancy: Court-ordered medical treatments and legal penalties for potentially harmful behavior by pregnant women. *Journal of the American Medical Association* 264:2663–2670.

Florida v. Johnson. 1989. Case no. E89-890-CFA (Seminole County Circuit Court). July 13.

Friedler, G. 1993. Developmental toxicology: Male-mediated effects. In *Occupational and environmental hazards: A guide for clinicians*, ed. M. Paul. Baltimore: Williams and Wilkins.

Hogue, C.J.R., and M.A. Hargraves. 1993. Class, race, and infant mortality in the United States. *American Journal of Public Health* 83(1):9–12.

International Union, UAW v. Johnson Controls. 1991. U.S. Supreme Court, no. 891215. March 20.

Kolata, G. 1990. Bias seen against pregnant addicts. *New York Times*, July 20.

Kolder, V.E.B., J. Gallagher, and M.T. Parsons. 1987. Court-ordered obstetrical interventions. *New England Journal of Medicine* 316:1192–1196.

Lieberman, J.R., M. Mazor, W. Chaim, and A. Cohen. 1979. The fetal right to live. *Obstetrics and Gynecology* 53:515–517.

McNamara, E. 1989. Fetal endangerment cases on the rise. *Boston Globe*, October 3.

Moss, K.L. 1990. Legal issues: Drug testing of postpartum women and newborns as the basis for civil and criminal proceedings. *Clearinghouse Review* 23(11):1406–1414.

Reuters. 1993. Surrogate mother has no rights as a parent, California court rules. *Boston Globe*, May 21.

Robertson, J.A. 1983. Procreative liberty and the control of conception, pregnancy, and childbirth. *Virginia Law Review* 69(3):405–464.

Rothman, B.K. 1989. *Recreating motherhood: Ideology and technology in a patriarchal society.* New York: Norton.

Shriner, T.L. 1979. Maternal rights versus fetal rights — a clinical dilemma. *Obstetrics and Gynecology* 53:518–519.

Slutsker, L., R. Smith, G. Higginson, and D. Fleming. 1993. Recognizing illicit drug use by pregnant women: Reports from Oregon birth attendants. *American Journal of Public Health* 83(1):61–64.

Appendix

The Biological and Biomedical Foundations of the New Reproductive Technologies

Introduction

The following pages are intended to clarify technical vocabulary and concepts discussed in this volume. We have provided basic explanations of key biological terms. At the end of the section is a list of texts that explore the biological and biomedical foundations of reproduction and reproductive technologies in further detail.

Figure 1: The Brain and Reproductive Anatomy

Hypothalamus and Pituitary Gland

The **hypothalamus** is a portion of the brain that secretes hormones ("chemical messengers"), some of which travel to the nearby **pituitary gland**, and direct it to secrete other hormones, called **gonadotropins**. These hormones, which travel to the reproductive organs (gonads), are named **Luteinizing Hormone (LH)** and **Follicle-Stimulating Hormone (FSH)**. When LH and FSH reach the **ovary**, they initiate growth of egg follicle and stimulate regulated secretion of another set of hormones, **estrogen** and **progesterone**. These hormones promote development of the uterine lining. Estrogen and progesterone also travel back to the brain, completing the circle of communication between the brain and the reproductive organs.

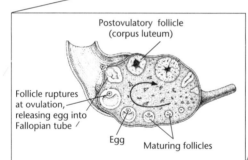

Postovulatory follicle
(corpus luteum)

Follicle ruptures at ovulation, releasing egg into Fallopian tube

Egg   Maturing follicles

After the egg is released into the Fallopian tube, the remaining follicular tissue is called the **corpus luteum**. The corpus luteum secretes hormones that prepare the uterus for implantation, in case conception occurs.

Ovary

The inset shows a cross-section of the ovary, and depicts the development of a single follicle over the course of the menstrual cycle. In a given cycle, a number of follicles begin to mature simultaneously, but only one develops to the point of ovulation (release of the egg into the Fallopian tube).

Uterus

Endometrium (uterine lining)

The lining of the uterus develops and thickens at the same time the follicle is developing in the ovary. When the egg is released, the uterus is prepared to receive a fertilized egg. The development of the uterine lining is controlled by secretion of ovarian hormones.

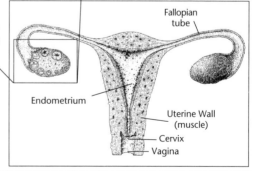

Fallopian tube

Endometrium

Uterine Wall (muscle)

Cervix

Vagina

Figure 2: Norplant®

The Norplant® implant system is a contraceptive device based on the slow continuous release of a synthetic compound similar to progesterone, called levonogestrel. The drug diffuses into the bloodstream from silicone rubber capsules inserted under the skin of the upper arm of the woman. It prevents pregnancy by several mechanisms, and is highly effective.

Mode of action of levonogestrel:
Progesterone-like synthetic hormones like levonogestrel can suppress pituitary function, so follicular development, and thus ovulation, do not occur. Progesterone-like compounds can also cause cervical mucus to thicken, which can block sperm entry into the uterus. They also prevent development of the endometrium, so it remains unable to receive a fertilized egg. 50% of Norplant® users continue to ovulate, and in these cases pregnancy is prevented by levonogestrel's effect on cervical mucus and the endometrium.

The implant:
Six silicone rubber capsules containing levonogestrel are inserted under the skin of the upper arm by trained medical personnel. Initially, about 80 micrograms of the hormone are released per day; this decreases to 34 micrograms per day after a few months. When the level drops below 25 micrograms per day (usually after about five years) the system becomes ineffective and the capsules should be removed. The capsules can theoretically be removed at any time, and fertility returns within a few days.

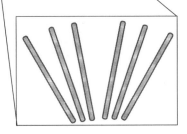

Menstrual cycle effects:
One of the major side effects of Norplant® use is irregular menstrual bleeding. Up to 65% of women experience bleeding pattern changes in the first year of use. This includes the absence of bleeding, irregular bleeding, as well as unusually heavy or prolonged bleeding. Most women have a return to normal menstrual bleeding patterns by the end of the second year of use.

Other Implants:
- A 1-year formulation is available; it includes two capsules.
- A biodegradable form called Capronor is available. It cannot be removed, and is functional for approximately 18 months.

Figure 3: Contraceptive Vaccines

Contraceptive vaccines are based on the body's immune defense system. Molecules important for successful reproduction are "disguised" in vaccine formulations, in order to trick the body into thinking that its own reproductive molecules are foreign. The body then inactivates these molecules, and reproduction is not possible. This technology is still under development, and contraceptive vaccines are not widely available as this book goes to press.

Molecules being studied for potential use in contraceptive vaccines:

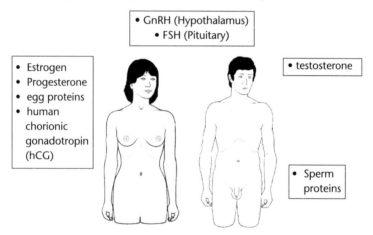

The most promising vaccine candidate is human Chorionic Gonadotropin (hCG). hCG is a hormone produced by the fertilized egg that signals the body that pregnancy has occurred. It is therefore only present in the body when fertilization has occurred. Several vaccines using hCG are being developed.*

How the hCG vaccine works:
This vaccine, which is designed for use in women, stimulates the immune system to attach to and destroy hCG so that the pregnancy is not recognized by the body, and implantation into the uterus does not occur. The uterine lining is therefore not maintained, and menstruation occurs.

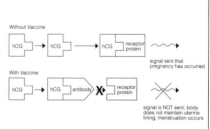

* One serious drawback to the use of the entire hCG molecule as a vaccine is that it is a protein hormone similar to a number of other protein hormones that have many functions in the body. Half of the large hCG molecule is identical to the hormones LH

continued on next page

Figure 3: Contraceptive Vaccines (cont.)

and FSH, which control function of the ovary, as well as TSH (Thyroid Stimulating Hormone), which controls thyroid function. A vaccine that tricks the body into attacking the whole hCG molecule may also attack and destroy LH, FSH and TSH, because they look similar. This problem can potentially be overcome because the end of the hCG molecule (the last 35 amino acid units in the protein chain) is unique to hCG, and so an immune response to this portion of the molecule would be specific to hCG. The World Health Organization has stated that this is the only part of the molecule that should be used for the vaccine, in order to protect against adverse side effects. However, clinical trials are being undertaken in India using parts of the hCG protein that are common to LH and FSH. The type and severity of side effects of this vaccine have not been well documented.

Figure 4: In Vitro Fertilization (Medically Assisted Conception)

A number of procedures make it possible to obtain eggs and sperm from a woman and man who have not been able to conceive through intercourse, allowing fertilization to take place in the laboratory, and a fertilized egg to be placed into the uterus or Fallopian tubes of the woman in an attempt to achieve pregnancy.

In Vitro Fertilization (IVF) is one such procedure, and includes the following steps:

Preparation and harvesting of Eggs:
The woman is given synthetic hormones which mimic those produced by the pituitary to develop follicles. In order to increase the chances of a successful fertilization, hormones sufficient to develop more than one egg follicle are provided. Just prior to ovulation, the eggs are surgically removed and prepared for fertilization in the laboratory.

Preparation and harvesting of Sperm:
Sperm are obtained from the man by masturbation, and are counted and analyzed for their ability to move correctly, as well as for normal appearance. They may be washed and concentrated in preparation for an IVF procedure.

Fertilization:
Sperm and eggs are incubated in a rich nutrient broth under conditions promoting fertilization. This occurs in the laboratory under sterile conditions. The fertilized egg is allowed to undergo the first few cell divisions before it is implanted into the woman.

Implantation:
After fertilization, the fertilized egg (zygote) is placed in the uterus or Fallopian tubes and allowed to implant. This procedure is called ZIFT (Zygote Intra-Fallopian Transfer). Alternatively, eggs and sperm can be mixed and placed in the Fallopian tube, allowing fertilization to occur in the body instead of the test tube. This is referred to as a GIFT (Gamete Intra-Fallopian Transfer) procedure.

Success Rate:
The overall success rate in the United States (per cycle) is 10% to 20%, depending upon both the procedures undertaken and the center where the procedures are performed.

Figure 5: Fetal Diagnostics

Amniocentesis:
The diagnostic procedure which involves removing a sample of the amniotic fluid that surrounds the fetus for laboratory analysis. A needle is inserted through the abdomen of the pregnant woman, and fluid is removed. Cells present in the fluid are examined for genetic abnormalities. This procedure can yield genetic information about the fetus, but can also increase the risk of hemorrhage and miscarriage of the fetus. The risks of amniocentesis depend heavily on the experience of the practitioner.

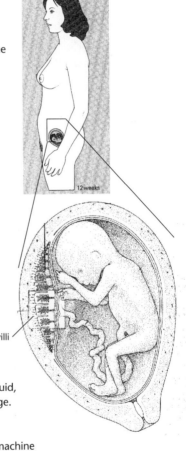

Chorionic Villous Sampling:
A newer procedure that is an alternative to amniocentesis. It involves inserting a catheter through the vagina and cervix, guided by ultrasound, and taking a sample of cells from the early placenta [the chorionic villi (see diagram)]. CVS has the advantage that it can be performed earlier (12 weeks) than amniocentesis (16-18 wks), and doesn't involve puncturing the abdomen. However, it has the disadvantage that fewer tests can be performed because there is no amniotic fluid, and there is a slightly higher risk of miscarriage.

Ultrasound imaging:
Another diagnostic procedure which uses a machine that sends sound waves through the body tissues. The waves change as they interact with objects, and the machine records the "echoes." This information is converted into an image on a screen. Ultrasound is used to visualize the fetus, and to detect physical abnormalities, sex, size and position of the fetus in the uterus.

Recommended Reading

Ammar, C. *The A to Z of women's health: A concise encyclopedia.* New York: Everest House Publishers, 1983.

Damewood, Marian D. *The Johns Hopkins Handbook of In Vitro Fertilization and Assisted Reproductive Technologies.* Boston: Little, Brown & Co., 1990.

Federation of Feminist Women's Health Centers. *A new view of a woman's body.* New York: Simon and Schuster, 1981.

Hatcher, Robert A., et al., eds. *Contraceptive Technology.* New York: Irvington Publishers, 1990.

Jones, Richard E. *Human Reproductive Biology.* New York: Academic Press, 1991.

Mastoianni, Luigi and Christos Coutifaris, eds. *The FIGO Manual of Human Reproduction, vol. 1: Reproductive Physiology.* Park Ridge, NJ: Parthenon Publishing Group, 1990.

The Boston Women's Health Book Collective. *The New Our Bodies, Ourselves.* New York: Simon and Schuster, 1984.

Index

Acronyms

AFDC	Aid to Families with Dependent Children (U.S.)
AIDS	Acquired Immune Deficiency Syndrome
BKKN	National Family Planning Coordinating Board (Indonesia)
BMN	basic minimum needs
CNDM	National Council for Women's Rights. (Brazil)
CONRAD	Contraceptive Research and Development Program (U.S.)
CRDP	Contraceptive Research and Development Program
DEAM	Special Police Station to Attend Women Victims of Sexual or Domestic Violence
DHS	Demographic and Health Survey
DMPA	depot medroxyprogesterone acetate (Depo-Provera)
GDP	gross domestic product
hCG	human chorionic gonadotropin
HIV	human immunodeficiency virus
HRP	Special Program of Research, Development and Research Training in Human Reproduction (WHO)
ICPD	Third International Conference on Population and Development
IDRC	International Development and Research Center (Canada)
IMF	International Money Fund
IUD	intra-uterine device
LNG	levonorgestrel
NET-EN	norethisterone enanthate
NFPP	National Family Planning Program (Thailand)
NGO	nongovernmental organizations

NHANES II	National Health and Nutrition Examination Survey
NIC	newly industrialized country
NICHD	National Institute for Child and Health Development (U.S.)
NII	National Institute of Immunology (India)
NRDP	National Rural Development Program
PAISM	Program of Integral Assistance to Women's Health
PDA	Population and Community Development Association
RTIs	reproductive tract infection
TAC	Therapeutic Abortion Committee (Canada)
TFR	total fertility rate
USAID	U.S. Agency for International Development
WHO	World Health Organization

Notes on Contributors

RADHIKA BALAKRISHNAN works at the Ford Foundation in the Asia regional program in New York. She received a Ph.D in Economics from Rutgers University in 1990 and has taught economics and women's studies at Rutgers. She has also taught economics at Wellesley College. She has been active in promoting HIV/AIDS education in the South Asian communities in New York with South Asian AIDS Action and is a member of the Center for Popular Economics.

ELIZABETH BARTHOLET is Professor of Law at Harvard Law School, and is the author of *Family Bonds: Adoption and the Politics of Parenting* (Houghton Mifflin 1993). She writes, lectures and consults widely on issues involving adoption and reproductive technology. Related publications include "Where Do Black Children Belong? The Politics of Race Matching in Adoption," *139 Penn L. Rev. 1163* (1991); "In Vitro Fertilization: The Construction of Infertility and of Parenting," in *Issues in Reproductive Technology I: An Anthology*, 253-60, Holmes, ed. (Garland Press 1992); and "International Adoption: Current Status and Future Prospects," in *3 The Future of Children No. 1* 89-103 (Center for the Future of Children, Spring 1993). She is the mother of three children; one by birth and two by adoption.

JANINE BRODIE is Professor of Political Science at York University, Toronto, Canada. She is the author of several books on Canadian politics, including *Women and Politics in Canada* and *The Political Economy of Canadian Regionalism* and the co-author of *The Politics of Abortion*. She is a former Director of the York Centre for Feminist Research and is currently holding the Robarts Chair in Canadian Studies.

SÔNIA CORREA, the DAWN Research Coordinator on Population and Reproductive Rights, is a Brazilian researcher and activist from SOS Corpo, of which she is a founding member. In 1991, Sônia was awarded the MacArthur Grant from the Brazilian Fellowship Program to develop conceptual inter-linkages and international networking across the over-lapping fields of gender, development, population and reproductive rights. She is also a member of the Brazilian Commission on Citizenship and Reproduction and the Brazilian Association of NGO's Collective Boards. She holds degrees in Architecture and Anthropology.

ARLINE GERONIMUS is Associate Professor of Public Health Policy and Administration, School of Public Health, and Research Affiliate, the Population Studies Center, the University of Michigan. Her research focuses on the effects of social inequality on health, particularly among women and children, including the role pervasive health uncertainty may play in shaping reproductive strategies for populations facing racism or extreme material hardship. She is the mother of a five-year-old girl.

DIANA HARRIS is a doctoral student in Molecular Biology in the Division of Biological Sciences at the Harvard School of Public Health, and is a Howard Hughes Medical Institute Predoctoral Fellow. She received undergraduate degrees in both biology and international development from Washington University in St. Louis.

JODY HEYMANN is Assistant Professor at Harvard Medical School and at the Kennedy School of Government. She received her M.D. from Harvard Medical School and her Ph.D. in Public Policy from Harvard University. Her clinical training is in pediatrics. Her research in health and social policy focuses on families. She has two children, ages five and one.

RUTH HUBBARD is Professor emerita of biology at Harvard University and the author of The *Politics of Women's Biology* (Rutgers University Press, 1990) and, with Elijah Wald, of *Exploding the Gene Myth* (Beacon Press, 1993).

CARLA MAKHLOUF OBERMEYER is Assistant Professor of Population Sciences at the Harvard School of Public Health. She has carried out research on health and fertility in several countries of the Arab world, and her current projects include an investigation of the cultural context of maternal health care in Morocco, a comparative study of son preference in North Africa, and an examination of breastfeeding patterns in the Middle East. She is the author of *Changing Veils: Women and Modernization in North Yemen* (1979).

JACQUELINE PITANGUY is a sociologist and political scientist. She has been a professor and researcher at Rio de Janeiro's Catholic University and a visiting professor at Rutgers University, where she held the Laurie New Jersey Chair in Women's Studies. She is also an activist in Brazil's women's movement and is the former president of the National Council for Women's Rights. She is now president of CEPIA (Citizenship Studies, Information, and Action) of which she is a founding member, and serves on the Board of Directors of the Brazilian Commission on Citizenship and Reproduction.

HNIN HNIN PYNE received her master's degree in planning from Massachusetts Institute of Technology, concentrating on gender and development. Her thesis research focused on AIDS and prostitution among Burmese women in Thailand. A former MacArthur Fellow at The Harvard Center for Population and Development Studies, she continues to work in the areas of women's reproductive health and rights. She is the mother of an infant son.

JUDITH RICHTER has worked as a retail and hospital pharmacist in Switzerland and Germany, as a lecturer of Community Pharmacy in Thailand, as public health researcher for a Bangkok-based consumer protection group, and as an independent researcher in the Netherlands. Throughout her professional life she has been involved in actions for people-oriented health care. She holds degrees in Pharmacy and in Development Studies.

ANGELINE FAYE SCHRATER is an independent scholar with the Project on Women and Social Change at Smith College, Northampton, Massachusetts, and a current member of the Steering Committee of the Task Force on Vaccines for Fertility Regulation, World Health Organization. After serving with the Peace Corps (Guatemala 1966-68), she earned a Ph.D. in Immunology (University of Pennsylvania), then did basic research on tolerance and response to parasites. She taught at Smith for several years, and resigned from the Biology Faculty to pursue interests in women's roles in science, the impact of reproductive technologies on women's health, and the important but murky interface between development and deployment of such technologies.

GITA SEN is Professor at the Indian Institute of Management in Bangalore, India and a Visiting Professor at the Harvard Center for Population and Development Studies. She received her B.A. in economics from the University of Poona, her M.A. from the Delhi School of Economics, and her Ph. D. from Stanford University. She is a development economist whose research focuses particularly on gender and development. Recently, she has been researching the gender dimensions of population policies, and the linkages between population and the environment. She is coauthor of *Development, Crises and Alternative Visions: Third World Women's Perspectives,* and a founding member of DAWN (Development Alternatives with Women for a New Era), a network of Third World researchers, activists and policy makers committed to alternative development and gender justice. She is currently research coordinator of DAWN's project on alternative economic frameworks. She is the mother of a seven-year-old girl.

RACHEL C. SNOW is Assistant Professor of Reproductive Health at the Harvard School of Public Health, and Faculty Associate at Harvard's Center for Population and Development Studies. A reproductive biologist, her research interests include the effects of nutrition and body composition on hormone dynamics, infertility, and contraceptive pharmacokinetics. A member of the Steering Committee for the WHO/HRP Task Force for Longacting Systemic Agents for Contraception, she is coeditor (with Peter Hall) of *Steroid Contraceptives and Women's Response* (Plenum Press, in press). She has one son, age 18 months.

JUDY WAJCMAN is Professor of Sociology at the University of New South Wales, Sydney, Australia. She is currently a Principal Research Fellow at the Industrial Relations Research Unit, University of Warwick, U.K. She is the author of *Women in Control: Dilemmas of a Worker's Cooperative* (1983), and *Feminism Confronts Technology* (1991), and co-editor (with Donald MacKenzie) of *The Social Shaping of Technology* (1985).